SOVIET SOCIOLOGY

soviet sociology

HISTORICAL ANTECEDENTS AND CURRENT APPRAISALS

edited with an introduction by
ALEX SIMIRENKO

CHICAGO / QUADRANGLE BOOKS / 1966

Library of Congress Catalog Card Number: 66-24161

Grateful acknowledgment is made to the following for permission to reprint copyrighted material:

American Sociological Society for "Russian Sociology in the Twentieth Century" by Pitirim A. Sorokin.

The Russian Review for "Plekhanov and the Origins of Russian Marxism" by Samuel H. Baron.

George Allen and Unwin Ltd. for a selection from *The Spirit of Russia* by Thomas G. Masaryk, and "Between Lenin and Stalin: Nikolai Bukharin" by Sidney Heitman, from *Revisionism* edited by Leopold Labedz.

The University of Chicago Press for "The Sociological Theories of Maksim M. Kovalevsky" by N. S. Timasheff, from *Introduction to the History of Sociology* edited by Harry Elmer Barnes, © 1949 the University of Chicago.

Little, Brown and Co. for a selection from *Politics and Vision* by Sheldon S. Wolin, © 1960 Little, Brown and Co.

Columbia University Press for a selection from *Soviet Marxism* by Herbert Marcuse, © 1958 Columbia University Press.

Oxford University Press for a selection from *The Prophet Outcast* by Isaac Deutscher, © 1963 Oxford University Press.

Foreign Affairs for "Stalin on Revolution" by George Allen Morgan, © 1950 Council on Foreign Relations, Inc.

Survey for "The Soviet Attitude to Sociology" and "Sociology as a Vocation" by Leopold Labedz, and "Meeting the Soviet Philosophers" by Lewis S. Feuer.

Social Research for "Soviet Social Science and Our Own" by Arvid Brodersen.

Center for International Studies, Cornell University, for selections from *Science and Politics: The New Sociology in the Soviet Union* by George Fischer.

American Sociological Review for "Some Principles of Theory, Problems and Methods of Research in Sociology in the USSR" by G. Osipov and M. Yovchuk.

Problems of Communism for "The Dilemmas of Soviet Sociology" by Paul Hollander.

Soviet Sociology for "Soviet Workers' Attitude Toward Work: An Empirical Study" by A. G. Zdravomyslov and V. A. Iadov, and "The Vitality of the Baptismal Ceremony Under Modern Soviet Conditions: An Empirical Study" by D. M. Aptekman.

To my father, V. L. SIMIRENKO,
who sacrificed his life in the cause
of scientific integrity

Preface

One of the striking features of American sociology in the 1960's is the determination of its many practitioners to cut the bonds of parochialism and enter the arena of an international science. This has been partly a culmination of the trend beginning with World War II which dealt a blow to the isolationism of previous decades and brought scholars from abroad to America. The postwar years were a period of rediscovery of European sociological traditions, including translations as well as re-publication in paperback editions of the works of Max Weber, Georg Simmel, Emile Durkheim, Robert Michels, Moisei Ostrogorski, Karl Mannheim, and others. Recently there has been a growing interest in the work of the International Sociological Association, which held its Fifth World Congress in Washington, D.C. in 1962, attended by a large number of American sociologists. At this Congress most of these Americans for the first time came face to face with sociologists from other lands, including the representatives of the Soviet Sociological Association. The 1965 annual meeting of the American Sociological Association was presided over by the Russian-born and -educated Professor Pitirim Alexandrovich Sorokin, and a plenary session was devoted to the new sociology in the Soviet Union.

This anthology provides background material for an understanding of the new Soviet sociology in perspective of its historical antecedents. At the same time we hope that the volume will further a meaningful discourse between the representatives of Eastern and Western counterparts of the European tradition. Contemporary Soviet sociologists still have some way to go before matching the richness and variety of ideas of their predecessors, scholars like Danilevsky, Mikhailovsky, Kovalevsky, Petrazycki, Tugan-Baranovsky, and others. Given favorable circumstances, however, the new sociologists can easily be expected to surpass them. This is, after all, a generation which has experienced at close range the three major European upheavals of the century: the greatest and most far-reaching revolution, the longest and harshest personal dictatorship of modern times, and the most terrifying battles of World War II.

The Soviet Union, the country of my birth which I left as a child, has always held a certain ambivalent attraction for me. Serious interest in its social thought, however, was evoked by my teacher at the University of Minnesota, Professor Don Martindale. Many colleagues have encouraged my work in this direction while I have been teaching at the University of Nevada. My special thanks go to Ned Polsky, Emanuel Geltman, Alex Garber, Carl Backman, Peter Etzkorn, Arturo Biblarz, Dennis Wrong, Bernard Rosenberg, and Jerry and Doris Ginsburg. This volume would not have been possible without the limited funds provided in the course of the past few years by Dean Thomas O'Brien and the Graduate Research Committee, the helpfulness of the library staff, the efficient assistance of Mrs. JoAnn Duncan, and the cheerful support of my wife Marie.

ALEX SIMIRENKO

Reno, Nevada, 1966

Contents

1 INTRODUCTION

An outline history of Soviet sociology with a focus on recent developments

ALEX SIMIRENKO

Sociology of sociology, a specialty that explains the rise, development, and nature of sociology in its historical perspective, is still to be written. The author of such a work will not be able to ignore the development of sociology in the Russian Empire, its subsequent decline shortly after the Revolution, and its revival in the USSR in the past decade. The major historical stages in the development of sociology in the Russian Empire and the Soviet Union are outlined here. (Because of current interest in the new Soviet sociology, most of this introduction is devoted to a discussion of the last stage of development.) Five broad stages can be isolated and portrayed:

STAGES OF DEVELOPMENT OF SOCIOLOGY IN THE
RUSSIAN EMPIRE AND THE SOVIET UNION

	Stages	Most active years
1	Period of proto-sociology	1782-1870
2	Pioneering period	1870-1885
3	Classical period	1885-1924
4	Period of decline	1924-1956
5	Period of revival	1956-

Period of proto-sociology

The date 1782, selected to represent the beginning of sociology in the Russian Empire, refers to the year of publication in Moscow of both the French and Russian versions of Montesquieu's *The Spirit of Laws*. The date also represents the period when the Imperial Academy of Sciences, established by Peter the Great in 1724 and staffed primarily with scholars from abroad, began to produce prominent native scholars who eventually controlled its destiny and the destiny of Russian education in general.

The introduction of western European learning into the Russian Empire, in addition to producing scholars of note, had other important consequences—some of which were anticipated and others not. It was taken as a matter of course that the knowledge of Western practices and ideas might cause men to yearn for changes in the autocratic government of Russia. From the very beginning, therefore, practical learning was stressed in the newly created Academy. Its graduates were immediately placed in the service of the government and received handsome rewards in return for their loyalty.

It was also anticipated that there would be a conflict between the religious authorities and the new scientifically and technologically oriented intelligentsia. The power of tradition, however, was so great that the Tsar feared not the victory of the intelligentsia over religious authorities, but rather the reverse. It was possible that rational solutions to even the most technical problems might be curbed or blocked. Peter the Great did all he could to neutralize and disarm the religious leaders and thus protected the formation of an intellectual opposition which was to emerge at the turn of the nineteenth century.

What seems not to have been anticipated was the degree to which the survival of tsarism was dependent upon the Russian Orthodox Church, whose weak ideological foundations were successfully promulgated largely among the illiterate peasants. Consequently, beginning late in the eighteenth century, a number of scholars and educated men came to the aid of their government by intellectualizing the stale ideology of the Church. The leaders of this group and their supporters came to be known as the Slavophiles. The men who, in the course of a century, waged a bitter and victorious battle against the Slavophiles are known as Westernizers. The beginning history of sociology in the Russian Empire is intertwined with the struggle of Slavophiles and Westernizers for the hearts and minds of the Russian people.

It is not easy to distinguish between the precursors of sociology and the early sociologists of any country. What distinguishes sociologists from proto-sociologists is the degree of their preoccupation with sociological problems in contrast to social problems. Proto-sociologists are intellectuals who are responding to the pressing needs of their society. They were to be found among both the Slavophiles and the Westernizers, although the latter numbered more of them and advanced a greater variety of social ideas.

Among the Slavophiles who posed significant questions about the rise, development, and change of Russian society and the world at large, were A. S. Khomiakov (1804–1860), I. V. Kireevsky (1806–1856), Brothers K. S. Aksakov (1817–1860) and I. S. Aksakov (1823–1886),

Yu. F. Samarin (1819–1876), K. N. Leontyev (1831–1891), and V. S. Solovyev (1853–1900). Although all of these men are important theologians, they are of interest to sociologists because their work was not restricted to theology alone; it spanned the fields of politics, philosophy, literary criticism, and history. They were all familiar with the western European intellectual currents of their day, but they rejected Western social and political ideals as inapplicable to Russian conditions. In their rejection of European solutions they were not necessarily anti-European themselves. Khomiakov, for example, the generally recognized Slavophile founder, was quite fond of many west European practices and especially of the English jury system. Some of the Slavophiles, such as Kireevsky (whom Masaryk considers the founder of the movement), were actually ardent supporters of the so-called "Westernization" of Russia in their early life.

The major theme of the Slavophile proto-sociological discourse is the different historical developments of western Europe and Russia, and the superiority of Russian culture because it was based on spiritual rather than material values which underlay much of European urban and industrial civilization. These arguments remain relevant to sociology because they touch upon significant sociological problems, such as an analysis of west European and Russian social structures, the direction of social change in these countries, and the nature of social bonds in general.

Among the most prominent Westernizers who could also be regarded as proto-sociologists were A. I. Herzen (1812–1870), V. G. Belinsky (1811–1848), T. N. Granovsky (1813–1855), M. A. Bakunin (1814–1876), N. G. Chernyshevsky (1828–1889), and M. P. Drahomanov (1841–1895). The Westernizers cannot be neatly characterized. They were united only in their opposition to the Slavophiles and in the recognition that some form of change nourished by the ideas of science and enlightenment must come to the Russian Empire. Despite their support of the western European intellectual tradition, they were generally opposed to the introduction of capitalism into Russia. While members of the Slavophile group ventured abroad only rarely, Herzen, Bakunin, and Drahomanov spent most of their adult lives in west European countries.

The best sociologist of the period is Alexander Herzen, whose work is compared by Sir Isaiah Berlin to that of Marx and Tocqueville:

> He was one of the most perspicacious observers of the European scene in the nineteenth century—in this respect only Marx and Tocqueville are comparable to him—and the *Letters from France and Italy* . . . contain the best general analyses of the political and social scene of the West just before and during the revolution, anywhere to

be found. He continued to observe, record, and analyze public and private life in France, in England, in Russia, unsystematically, in articles and improvisations, all his life. At once brilliantly entertaining and permanently valuable, these fragments are scattered in the twenty-two volumes of his posthumously published works, and still form a unique account of the life of Europe in the middle years of the last century.[1]

Though brilliant in his insights into the nature of nineteenth-century Europe, Herzen did not explore systematically the sociological problems upon which he touched. In most ways, however, he had a detachment and objectivity characteristic of the best sociologists. Masaryk, who was critical of Herzen's disdain for politics and politicians, remarked that "a brilliant and well-informed article seems to him [Herzen] more valuable and more important than all the tsars." [2] Herzen's aloofness did not represent an unconcern with the state and the future of mankind. Like Karl Marx, Herzen was appalled at the practices of brutality in his time, and like Max Weber, he envisioned a possible spectacle of mass revolts and blood baths which would crush all the traditions of freedom. But unlike Marx, Herzen did not rejoice at the impending doom, and unlike Weber, he did not feel it necessary to oppose the changes which were to come. Herzen did not consider the new world to come any better than the old, but in order to reach "the other shore," or the better world, he was convinced that the old world would have to be destroyed. Writing half a century before Weber, Herzen dedicated his book of reflections on the 1848 European Revolutions to his son with the following sage advice:

> Do not look for solutions in this book—there are none; in general modern man has no solutions. What is solved is finished, and the coming upheaval is only the beginning.
>
> We do not build, we destroy; we do not proclaim a new revelation, we eliminate the old lie. Modern man, that melancholy *Pontifex Maximus,* only builds a bridge—it will be for the unknown man of the future to pass over it. You may be there to see him. . . . But do not, I beg, remain on *this shore.* . . . Better to perish with the revolution than to seek refuge in the almshouse of reaction.[3]

Pioneering period

The death of Herzen in 1870 represents the closing of the period of proto-sociology and the beginning of the pioneering period. The model creative activity of Herzen, Belinsky, Chernyshevsky, and others has been continued into our own time by men like Tolstoy, Dostoevsky, Chernov, and most recently "Abram Tertz."

The turn of the 1870's also represents the rise of a new group of men whose writings were oriented toward sociological problems. They continued to be intensely concerned with the fate of the world, but at the same time they were already narrowing the field of sociology to a set of special problems which was to be of primary interest to the next generation of sociologists. The most outstanding pioneers are N. Ya. Danilevsky (1822–1885), N. K. Mikhailovsky (1842–1904), P. L. Lavrov (1823–1900), G. V. Plekhanov (1856–1918), and P. A. Kropotkin (1842–1921).

In this group Danilevsky is the only scholar of Slavophile sympathies. A natural scientist by training, Danilevsky's fame in sociology rests mainly on one book, *Russia and Europe* (1869), in which he presented a theory of civilizational change later to be advanced in a peculiarly similar but less sophisticated form by Spengler. Pitirim Sorokin, who has presented the best summary and analysis of Danilevsky's work, calls it "a brilliant treatise on the philosophy of history and cultural sociology." [4]

Of the men in this group, Mikhailovsky and Plekhanov had the greatest impact upon the development of sociology in the Russian Empire. Plekhanov is usually referred to as the father of Russian Marxism and Mikhailovsky as the leading non-Marxist scholar identified with the Populist movement. Selections discussing the work of Mikhailovsky and Plekhanov are found in section two of the present volume. The Russian Populists were socialists who continued the Westernizers' traditional opposition to the introduction of capitalism into the Russian Empire. The major task of the early Marxists was to demonstrate that capitalism was already dominant on the Russian scene and that, therefore, Populism was an anachronism.

The most prominent pressing sociological problem in the work of the pioneers is that of social change shaped by the social conditions in the Russian Empire. This contrasts sharply with the work of sociological pioneers in western European countries, whose attention was divided between the problems of structure and change. The most generally agreed-upon definition of sociology by the Russian pioneers was that of a study of social process. In the course of their work on the problem of change, several specific questions came to be routinely inquired into: (1) the relationship of an individual to a group; (2) the formation and destruction of solidarity; (3) the agents of social change; (4) the problem of leadership; and (5) the problem of progress.

Classical period

The work of the pioneers was far from finished when, with Danilevsky's death in 1885, the representatives of the classical period began to emerge. The most creative men of the period include M. M. Kovalevsky (1851–1916), N. I. Kareev (1850–1931), E. DeRoberty (1843–1915), M. I. Tugan-Baranovsky (1865–1919), V. I. Lenin (1870–1924), and L. I. Petrazycki (1867–1931). None of the pioneers had been a university teacher, but the men of the classical period were all professors with the exception of Lenin. They became acceptable to the universities because their work no longer contained an open advocacy of particular value positions as an integral part of their discipline. Lenin alone refused to purge his work of propaganda. He is included in the group not as a model sociologist of the period but because of his brilliant contributions to the theory of organizations. A detailed discussion of Lenin's contributions is provided in the second section of this volume.

Lenin's claim that his university-affiliated colleagues had turned reactionary was far from true. They were all liberals who anticipated and welcomed change. Kovalevsky, the best sociologist of the period, to whom a special selection is devoted in this anthology, was dismissed from his professorship at Moscow University in 1877 for political unreliability. Kareev was an ardent follower of Mikhailovsky; DeRoberty lived and taught most of his adult life in France; Tugan-Baranovsky served as a minister of finance in the Ukrainian Central Rada formed at the time of the Revolution; while Petrazycki was appointed to the Senate of the Provisional Government. Instead of betraying their radical heritage, the sociologists of the classical period succeeded in separating their political views from their scholarly activities.

The second distinguishing feature of the classical period was an emphasis on research studies in addition to theoretical speculations. The maturity of sociology in this period is especially underlined by the fact that these studies were often of countries other than the Russian Empire. Kovalevsky's leading study explores the rise of democracy in western Europe. Kareev's classic study of *The Peasants and the Peasant Question in the French Revolution* was addressed to refute de Tocqueville's thesis of the affluence of the French pre-Revolutionary peasants. Tugan-Baranovsky's first study attempted to explain the industrial crises in England; the work was highly valued by John Maynard Keynes.

The work of the classical period culminated with the establishment of the Russian Sociological Society in 1916. A. S. Lappo-Danilevsky became its president and P. A. Sorokin its secretary. The events of the two

Revolutions of 1917 halted the activities of the society until 1920. In the meantime, Lappo-Danilevsky died and Kareev took over as president.

Period of decline

It did not take long for the new Soviet regime to consolidate its power before it prohibited the teaching of all non-Marxist sociology in 1922. Sociological research and some teaching continued for almost another decade in various covert forms. The greatest monuments of sociological activity in the period of decline remain the publication of the first edition of the *Great Soviet Encyclopedia* and the 1926 Census of Population. With the coming of the 1930's, however, most social science research, including that of the Marxist scholars, became identified with the so-called "vulgar sociologism" and was brought to a halt.

The men who dominate the period of decline have little in common with men of the earlier periods. They are neither Don Quixotes of rebellion nor Hamlets of intellectual indecision. They are successful revolutionaries, concerned with retaining power for themselves as well as for their party. Their writing in the period after the Revolution is chiefly directed either to the masses or to each other and forms an indispensable part of their political strategies.

Three men dominate the scene of Soviet sociology in its period of decline: J. V. Stalin (1879–1953), L. D. Trotsky (1879–1940), and N. I. Bukharin (1888–1938). Section Three of the present volume is devoted to a discussion of the ideas of these men.

Respect for intellectual preoccupation is greatest in the work of Bukharin and smallest in that of Stalin. It is probably for this reason that Stalin considered Trotsky his most formidable opponent who had to be destroyed first. Bukharin is the only one concerned with a systematic analysis of society. His work entitled *Historical Materialism: A System of Sociology* is the best introductory text on Marxist sociology available. The strength of the contributions of all three authors (as well as others) lies in their analysis of revolutionary and counter-revolutionary practices. Even Stalin is intellectually creative when he turns his attention to the problem of revolution.

Period of revival

In view of the strong sociological tradition developed in pre-Revolutionary times, the revival of Soviet sociology was only a matter of time and opportune conditions. Such a revival became possible after the death of Stalin.

In discussing the development of Soviet sociology in the period of revival, it is useful to distinguish between ideological concerns and distinctly sociological contributions. Our evaluation of Soviet sociology is sometimes blurred because of the overlapping of these two spheres of activities. Political possibilities always channel the ways in which the progress of a discipline can be advanced, but they do not necessarily block its development entirely. Since 1956 Soviet sociology has evolved through two major ideological phases, both of which were accompanied by appropriate scholarly contributions: (1) establishing political and social credibility, accompanied by a strategy of "creative debunking"; and (2) a methodological consciousness, accompanied by a cautious empiricism.

A DECADE OF DEVELOPMENT OF SOVIET SOCIOLOGY

Phase	Typical ideological concerns	Typical scholarly contributions
Phase I (February 1956 to October 1963)	Establishing political and social credibility	"Creative debunking"
Phase II (Beginning October 1963)	Methodological consciousness	Cautious empiricism

Phase 1: Establishing credibility. The task of establishing the credibility of sociology as a distinct discipline was divided into three parts: 1) establishing its political reliability; 2) establishing its social usefulness; and 3) reaffirming its uniqueness as a discipline among other social science disciplines.

Establishing political reliability was the single most important task of the new discipline, and it was achieved by tying sociology to the programs and directives of the Communist party of the Soviet Union. This fusion of the new Soviet sociology with politics is well underlined by George Fischer:

> In all of its theory and research, the new sociology in the USSR represents a singular fusion of science with politics. On the level of theory this means the fusion of academic analysis of society with an official doctrine of society. On the level of research the fusion is between scholarship and all-out service to an omnicompetent state.[5]

A commitment to the ideological and theoretical position of Soviet Marxism was the price Soviet scholars had to pay to make sociological research possible. Every Soviet sociologist writing during the first half of the decade could be expected to make solemn declarations of loyalty to the principles of Marxism and support of the decisions of the 20th and 21st Party Congresses. This is not to imply that Soviet sociologists were perhaps disloyal to these ideas, but their behavior did reflect a certain uneasiness on the part of a number of influential party members who viewed the rise of a new discipline with suspicion and distrust. In addition to the declarations of individual sociologists, a series of directives on the conduct of sociological inquiry was also issued. A typical example of such a directive followed a report on the proceedings of the Fourth World Congress of Sociology in Milan:

> Inquiries must be conducted on the theoretical basis of historical materialism, that is, to apply to the particular social fact Marxist understanding of development of socio-economic formations (laws) which determine the relation between the economic structure of society and its superstructures . . . the relationships between classes, etc.[6]

An additional price had to be exacted from those sociologists who wished to participate in an international exchange of ideas, by demands placed upon them to criticize Western theories while defending Soviet Communist positions. An extremely informative directive on this subject is cited by George Fischer:

> The international obligation of Soviet scholars is to intensify the criticism of bourgeois ideology and, first of all, the reactionary conceptions of anti-communism. Criticism of bourgeois and reformist ideology must debunk not only conclusions but also the arguments of anti-communist ideologists fearlessly and on scientific grounds. For this purpose it is essential to study the contemporary economy, politics, culture, and ideology of foreign countries deeply and comprehensively. The direct duty of scholars is to inform the world's public widely about the successes of the Soviet Union in all spheres of life, including the realm of the humanities.[7]

Establishing the social usefulness of Soviet sociology was achieved by defining it as a science, resting on Marxian principles, for the study of social problems and their resolution. Such a definition was advanced and defended by the most vigorous supporter of sociological research in the Soviet Union, Academician V. S. Nemchinov, now deceased. In a speech delivered at the Fourth World Congress of Sociology, Nemchinov formulated the following tasks of Soviet sociologists:

An honored and difficult task arises before the sociological science of the countries of socialism, not only to discover the regularities of planned socialist society, but also to facilitate development and perfection of the organization of social life and the mechanism for execution of societal development, which insures the never-ending, constant, planned, and sufficiently rapid development of the whole society in accordance with the principles of Communism.[8]

The practical approach of Soviet sociologists has been underlined by Merton and Riecken in their report:

> The Soviet orientation toward empirical social research might be described as "practical empiricism": as an effort to obtain just enough systematic information on which to base recommendations for policy and action, with little interest in pursuing, through empirical research, the more theoretical implications of what has been observed. In spirit and outcome, it is most like market-research in the United States: on a low level of abstraction, and largely confined to ferreting out facts that can be taken into account in making practical decisions.[9]

In the initial attempt to make sociological research acceptable to a body of technicians that make up the ruling strata of Soviet party officialdom, Soviet sociologists could do little else but emphasize the "practical empiricism" of the new discipline. Otherwise they would have only invited suspicion and opposition to their plans. There were, however, no special practical or ideological reasons to make so-called basic or pure research impossible. In Leningrad, Merton and Riecken were told that basic research "would be possible but that he [a Soviet sociologist] and his staff would feel acutely dissatisfied if their research were not directed toward visibly useful ends." In theory, too, there are important justifications for the conduct of pure research. These were the tasks outlined for Soviet sociologists by Academician P. N. Fedoseev at the Fourth World Congress of Sociology:

> For our sociologists the problems of the laws of the changes in socio-economic formation in the process of historical development are of foremost importance. On the basis of numerous historical studies, Marxist sociology discovers new proofs of the existence of laws of socio-economic changes in the process of historical development.[10]

It should be noted that Fedoseev is one of the most influential philosophers and social scientists in the Soviet Union, who at the time of his speech served as the director of the Philosophy Institute of the USSR Academy of Sciences and who is a member of the Communist party's

Central Committee. We can safely assume, then, that this "practical empiricism" of Soviet sociology is a manifestation of the first phase of the development of a new discipline and is not intrinsic to Soviet sociology as such.

Every emerging discipline carves out space for itself among other disciplines and invades territories of others. It is not likely to develop without provoking the opposition of those in other disciplines who may have vested interests in maintaining the status quo. Probably the rise of Soviet sociology was facilitated by a particular need for its services, which were enough in demand to overcome the objections of scholars opposing the development of sociology. There is little doubt that such opposition did exist, because of the frequency with which the uniqueness of sociology as an independent discipline among other social sciences was being stressed. A typical argument to this effect was presented by Fedoseev at the Milan Congress:

> The main feature of sociology as a science, in which it differs from other sciences, is that it represents a theoretical synthesis of the social process. Sociology does not deal with separate aspects of social life, but with all social relations, with every aspect of material and spiritual life. Moreover, in revealing the chief laws of social development, Marxist sociology does not claim to supersede economics, law, history, and other social sciences. It is a method of acquiring knowledge and in turn draws from them its general conclusions.[11]

The first major recognition of the new sociology came in the summer of 1958, with the creation of the Soviet Sociological Association which was charged with the following tasks:

> Representation in the International Sociological Association and other organizations of sociologists.
> Strengthening of ties of Soviet scientists working in the area of sociology, and also a cooperation with foreign sociologists working in the interest of developing sociology.
> Spreading of information in foreign countries on the development of sociology in the USSR.
> Facilitate the development of scientific research in the area of sociology in the USSR.
> Facilitate publication of scientific works.
> Facilitate the exchange of books and bibliographical information between Soviet and foreign scientists working in the area of sociology.[12]

Phase 1: "Creative debunking." The major political concerns of Soviet sociologists manifested in the first phase of development did not entirely prevent them from doing scholarly work and contributing to the growth of the discipline. Naturally, such growth had to be accomplished within the bounds of politically acceptable practices, and had to conform to the prevailing standards of the publishers. Given these conditions, American scholars writing on Soviet sociology tended to focus most of their attention on the political manifestations in the works of Soviet sociologists and to ignore many of the constructive contributions of this period.

The contributions of Soviet sociologists in this first phase of their renewal can only be assessed in the perspective of the Stalinist period of Soviet history. It was a period of isolation from the world and, in the case of the social sciences, isolation from their own past. It was a period of seclusion and hibernation for the social sciences as well as for some aspects of the humanities. Aroused from sleep in the post-Stalin period, Soviet citizens have revealed an insatiable hunger for information about their own past and about conditions in the outside world. This curiosity was satisfied in the traditional Soviet manner by criticism of ideas and events, providing information on many areas of knowledge previously unknown to the Soviet reader. The denunciation of Stalin and some of the Stalinist institutions, however, added a new element to the traditional practice of debunking. Scholars were permitted to examine, without having to fear for their lives, the dust-covered books of the past and to become acquainted with foreign literature of the present. Although they had to communicate their knowledge in a critical tone, for the first time they had the privilege of discussing the previously tabooed subjects with their students and the general audience. The ideological debunking turned into a "creative debunking," in which the primary purpose was to impart new information.

It is significant, therefore, that one of the first critical monographs examining the work of pre-Revolutionary social scientists was devoted to Maksim Kovalevsky, the first and most important pioneer of an objective social science in the Russian Empire and the teacher of Pitirim Sorokin.[13] By following the strategy of creative debunking, it was now possible for Soviet scholars to bring Kovalevsky's ideas and his work to the attention of the younger generation who had only heard his name.[14]

Disseminating Kovalevsky's ideas is only one example of many such contributions made by the new Soviet social scientists to the development of their discipline. They also made possible the acquaintance—even if slight—of Soviet readers with the major representatives of functionalism, phenomenology, existentialism, and psychoanalysis.

Thanks to the strategy of creative debunking, Soviet sociologists today reveal an amazingly broad knowledge of Western scholarship, whereas this knowledge was thin only a few years ago. Their best representatives can be spotted by their acquaintance with significant and influential Western scholars, their ability to separate the important scholarly works from the obscure ones, and their general wide range and depth of knowledge of non-Soviet literature.[15] Nevertheless, a Soviet scholar still remains handicapped in many areas where political taboos prevail, and he must continue to depend upon the strategy of creative debunking to overcome his weaknesses.

Phase II: Methodological consciousness. Condemnation of Stalin opened the way for the re-emergence of sociology as a distinct discipline. It did not, however, free sociologists and other scholars from the institutionalized bonds of Stalinism. The problems of rigid dogmatism, falsification and distortion of historical record, the demands placed on scholars to play the role of servile propagandists, and many other problems of the Stalinist period continued to plague Soviet scholars long after Stalin's body was removed from the mausoleum. In the words of Yevgeni Yevtushenko, "we bore him out of the mausoleum, but how, out of Stalin, shall we bear Stalin's heirs!" It was seven and a half year's after Khrushchev's famous denunciation of Stalin before steps could be taken to remove the Stalinist legacy from Soviet science and thus make an objective social science possible.

The new era in the development of Soviet sociology began in October 1963, when the Presidium of the USSR Academy of Sciences directed all its scientific bodies to examine the methodological problems of the natural and social sciences. The section of the Social Sciences of the Presidium of the USSR Academy of Sciences complied with this decision by calling a conference which took place on January 3 and 6, 1964. Thirty-six leading Soviet historians, philosophers, economists, archaeologists, ethnographers, and sociologists took part in the conference, the end result of which was published under the title *History and Sociology*.[16]

Two leading academicians, P. N. Fedoseev [17] and Yu. P. Frantsev, were asked to prepare a paper on the methodological problems of the Soviet social sciences to serve as a focus for the discussions. The paper, entitled "On the Study of Methodological Problems of History," was distributed to all conference participants in advance, and each scholar was thus provided an opportunity to weigh every word carefully while preparing a public statement. Some of the participants welcomed the conference and found relief in recalling the abuses perpetrated by persons in power upon scholars and their work. Other participants preferred to limit themselves to innocuous, non-committal statements on the subject.[18]

While the directives for the conference issued by the Academy are not entirely clear regarding the purposes of such discussions, Fedoseev's and Frantsev's paper makes these aims unequivocally clear: liquidation of old-fashioned Stalinist traditions in the fields of social sciences and a new re-definition of the position of Soviet social scientists. In their words:

> Our task now is to proceed farther and more daringly on the path laid for the historical science by K. Marx, F. Engels, and V. I. Lenin. For this purpose it is necessary to liquidate once and for all the consequences of the cult of personality in the area of social sciences, including the historical science. One of the worst consequences of the cult of personality was the lowering of prestige of the social sciences. This was done by placing the scientists, working in the area of social sciences in those days, into a situation which limited to the extreme their creative activity. Therefore, it became widely believed that Soviet social scientists are capable only of either repeating citations of one and the same man, or restating the contents of these citations and without end commenting upon the directives these contained. The works of social scientists were filled with dogmatism alien to Marxist-Leninism.[19]

Fedoseev and Frantsev acknowledge that the decision to initiate these methodological discussions came from the Central Committee of the party. They underline the fact that a new stage in the development of Soviet social sciences has arrived:

> The Communist party of the Soviet Union and its Central Committee have done everything necessary to overcome the consequences of the cult of personality and to raise high the prestige of the social sciences. The program of the CPSU indicates that the social sciences are the scientific bases for the direction of social life. In fact, a new stage has arrived in the century-long development of the Marxist science of society.[20]

The arrival of the new era did not mean, however, that the party was willing to abandon its claim to the direction of the social sciences. Quite the contrary:

> In this connection, the program of the party has delineated the concrete tasks and the role to be played by the social sciences in the Communist construction and indicated the major direction of research of Soviet social scientists. The party pays great attention to the social sciences and continually guides their development.[21]

Most of this paper discusses the nature of various social science disciplines, especially history, their relationships to each other, and their methodological and conceptual problems. The sub-titles of the paper quite accurately reflect the contents of the discussion:

"The Subject of Historical Science"

"History and Sociology"

"Historical Regularities"

"On the So-called Objectivism and the Actual Objectivity in Historical Investigation"

"Social Formulations and Historical Epoch"

"On the Relationship of Theory with Practice in Historical Investigation"

The *leitmotiv* running through the discussion is the issue of the replacing of dogmatism by the new objectivity:

> In order to facilitate a correct and significant study of the methodological problems of historical knowledge, it is necessary to ask and answer in a novel way the question of the relationship between history and sociology. This problem was badly confused when criticism was directed against the ideas of M. N. Pokrovski. In the conditions of Stalin's cult this criticism turned into the struggle against the so-called sociologism in historical investigations. Broad interpretation and application of the concept of "vulgar sociologism" contributed to the disappearance from historical investigations of sociological generalizations and the fear of historians to ask theoretical questions on the basis of concrete evidence, while it led the philosophers away from studying the methodological problems of history. Obviously, the situation is entirely intolerable when a historian or a philosopher replaces concrete investigation with repetitions of ready-made sociological formulas. It is also intolerable when historical investigation does not search for ways of asking the important questions on the regularities of societal development, without an analysis of which it is impossible to comprehend the march of historical events.[22]

According to Fedoseev and Frantsev, social scientists cannot use facts simply to illustrate well-known laws. The task of social scientists is to explain the operation of these laws under various "concrete conditions," that is, in specific countries and in a specific historical period. Social scientists are charged with investigating not only the economic basis of society, but also its superstructure in all its many manifestations. Fedoseev and Frantsev maintain that scientific investigations should be broadened to study not only those historical forces which triumphed, but also those forces which were "crushed and therefore have not received an opportunity to develop." [23] The most important declaration of all, however, is the insistence by Fedoseev and Frantsev that social scientists concern themselves with theoretical problems of historical development, for illuminating the social processes is a true practical help toward achieving the aims of the party.[24]

There is little doubt that the paper of Fedoseev and Frantsev, which must have received clearance at the very highest levels of the party, initiated a new stage in the activities of Soviet social scientists and opened up many new areas for their investigation. The ideas of the two academicians mitigate the necessity of "practical empiricism" in the works of Soviet social scientists and provide justification for a broad spectrum of theoretically relevant studies.

The conference concluded with the passing of a seven-point resolution concerning the study of methodological problems of history by the Section of the Social Sciences of the USSR Academy of Sciences. The following is a brief summary of this resolution:

1. To undertake a complete study of methodological problems. This includes such studies as the relationship between history and sociology, the relationship between the general laws of world-wide historical process and the unique development of specific countries and categories of countries, scientific periodization of historical process, the role of classes and class struggle in the development of mankind, the role of masses and individuals in history, the relationship between the rational and irrational in a historical process, the regularities in the development of social thought, and criticism of idealistic subjective conceptions in the field of historical methodology.

2. To study the history of scientific Communism and the history of the Lenin period in the development of Marxist theory. To pay particular attention to the study of mankind's movement toward Communism.

3. To study a series of historical processes related to modern history. The suggested topics include the overcoming of contrasts between town and village, between physical and mental labor; the rise of contradictions between nation-states and the resolution of these contradictions; the development of family and culture in general.

4. To coordinate the efforts of all social scientists studying methodological problems of history and to propose to the Academy preparation of a series of works entitled "The Methodological Problems of Social Science."

5. To propose an improvement of history seminars in the Academy of Sciences devoted to the study of methodological problems, and to organize a series of conferences devoted to important methodological problems of history.

6. To recommend to the various journals published in the USSR publication of material discussing methodological problems.

7. To prepare recommendations for the improvement of historical studies in the establishments of secondary and higher education and special seminars and courses devoted to the problems of methodology.[25]

Phase II: Cautious empiricism. It is still too early to determine the result of Soviet sociological research initiated in the period of methodological consciousness. Much of the work published in the new phase is a product of the earlier phase. Nevertheless, even this work has a distinctive quality about it, suggesting that new editorial policies have been introduced. Significant contributions have already been made in this brief period, not only to Soviet sociology but also to a wider international sociology.

A major accomplishment of Soviet sociologists in this new phase consists of a two-volume edition of *Sociology in the USSR,* compiled and edited by G. V. Osipov.[26] Soviet sociologists can rightfully take pride in this thousand-page publication. No work of comparable quality has been published in the USSR since the 1920's.

Sociology in the USSR is a product of the new methodological consciousness of Soviet sociologists. Sixteen of its contributions covering over three hundred pages of text are devoted to theoretical and methodological problems of the social sciences. Significantly, the leading article of the two volumes, entitled "History and Sociology," and written by academicians P. N. Fedoseev and Yu. P. Frantsev, is a revised version of the paper presented at the epoch-making social science conference discussed earlier.[27] Theoretical and methodological discussions are followed by twenty-eight articles that explore various aspects of Soviet life. Although these studies are of extremely uneven quality, most of them are based upon recently collected empirical data. The collection includes studies of Soviet occupational changes, urban growth, family finances, cultural tastes of workers, the uses of leisure time, longevity of men and women, and social values of Soviet men and women.

The collection emphasizes theoretically relevant empirical research and generally pays little attention to contributions of "practical empiricism." Equally important is the fact that the tasks and purposes of sociology are no longer identified with so-called "visibly useful ends." Apparently gone are the days when Soviet sociologists defined sociology as a science for the solution of social problems. The new definition of sociology is undogmatic and remarkably broad, permitting Soviet sociologists to raise their heads in a fellowship of colleagues from other countries.

The following characteristic definition of sociology is given by G. V.

Osipov, editor of the volumes, in his excellent article[28] on the nature and scope of Soviet sociology:

> Marxist sociology *is a science discovering laws on the formation, development, and change of socio-economic structures. These laws appear in the forms of various concrete social (material as well as spiritual) manifestations, processes, and factors.* These factors are not only products of human action which reflect more or less the objective possibilities and necessities of social development of a particular historical epoch, but these are also factors which actively influence the consciousness of people and therefore determine their social behavior and activity.[29]

While scholarly contributions of Soviet sociologists in the first phase of their development were primarily of domestic value, the contributions of the second phase transcend the boundaries of the Soviet Union and enrich international sociology. A large volume of empirical data is provided and interpreted by Soviet sociologists. Although we may not always agree with their interpretation of the data, for the first time we have access to much of the information about an important industrialized socialist society. It is now possible to conduct courses on Soviet society based upon empirical material provided by our Soviet colleagues. This is especially important in light of the fact that information provided by Soviet refugees detailing Soviet life in the late 1930's is rapidly becoming dated.

The phase of methodological consciousness and cautious empiricism has also introduced a new note into the practice of debunking American and generally Western sociological ideas.[30] Such criticisms, when written by the best of Soviet scholars, are generally better informed, more reserved in their tone of attack, and provide more constructive ideas than formerly. One example of the new debunking is represented by Soviet criticism of the concept of industrial society. Soviet sociologists are willing to agree that there exist many similarities between socialist and capitalist industrial societies which distinguish them markedly from non-industrial countries. They contend, however, that we must also look at the crucial differences which separate the industrial countries. In their formulation, the crucial differences between capitalist and socialist countries are determined by the different forms of property and contrasting productive relations.[31] Criticizing the concept of industrial society, Soviet sociologists are also performing a useful service for sociology in general by calling for the development of a more concise typology of industrial societies. This is especially important in view of the fact that the development of such a typology cannot be accomplished without the cooperation of and research by our Soviet colleagues.

Some of the Soviet contributions to sociology are potentially extremely valuable. Such, for example, is a comparative study of a Moldavian village called Kopanka which was initially investigated in 1937 by a Rumanian sociologist, Dmitrie Gusti. The main aim of the research was to study social change undergone by the village in the course of its annexation to the Soviet Union and its transformation into a collective farm in 1950. While the researchers were determined to show the betterment of life brought to the villagers by the Soviet system, they also provided comparative data on the village as of 1937 and 1960. These comparisons cover such topics as the age structure of the village population, the budgets of family expenditures, the length of the workday for men and women, and the availability of social and medical services to the community.[32] Unfortunately, we are offered only glimpses of selected areas of social experience. The forthcoming publication of the full study, should it cover all the major areas of social life, would represent a notable achievement.[33]

A certain skepticism is often advanced about the reliability of Soviet data, especially when it comes to portraying what may be interpreted as the social ills of Soviet society. Without doubt this has been a major problem of Soviet sociology. Lately, however, Soviet sociologists have had considerable success in arguing that certain basic social problems cannot be solved unless one is able to investigate them fully. A rational planning of social life, they argue, requires reliable information on various aspects of Soviet life,[34] even if it may, at times, provide ammunition to the ideologists of hostile countries.

An example of the new level of Soviet objectivity on this issue is a recent study of vocational plans and other related problems of secondary school graduates, accomplished with the acknowledged support of party officials. The study, conducted by a large group of sociologists at Novosibirsk University, was intended to provide a series of factual details on the problems of young people in Soviet society, which would facilitate more effective social planning for the future.[35] It began in 1962 with a pilot study of three hundred secondary school graduates, in the course of which a questionnaire was developed and the methods of the study were outlined. In 1963 almost nine thousand questionnaires were sent to the schools of the Novosibirsk region,[36] encompassing all the secondary schools and 10 percent of those schools that did not offer a complete secondary education. The same mailing was repeated again in 1964 to new graduates to study the reliability of the initial responses, as well as to ascertain the stability of the social processes under study.

Those partial results of the study which have been made available were reported with great candor. The problems revealed by the study were frankly discussed, especially a discovery of disparity between the vocational plans of secondary school graduates and their execution of these plans. Tables I and II illustrate the long road toward objectivity that Soviet sociologists have traveled since their shaky beginnings a decade ago.[37]

TABLE I. PERSONAL PLANS OF GRADUATES AND THEIR REALIZATION *

Plans	Men %	Women %	Both %	Actuality	Men %	Women %	Both %
Planned to work	8	8	8	Went to work	26	35	32
Planned to work and continue part-time studies	7	14	12	Went to work and continued part-time studies	2	3	3
Planned to study	85	78	80	Went to study	48	41	44
Total	100	100	100		100 †	100 †	100 †

* Results of complete 1963 mailing.
† Includes other responses in addition to the three categories.

TABLE II. FAMILY'S SOCIAL POSITION RELATED TO PERSONAL PLANS OF GRADUATES AND THEIR REALIZATION *

Groups to which parents belong		Plans				Actuality	
	Work	Work with study	Study	Work	Work with study	Study
Urban intelligentsia	2%	5%	93%	15%	3%	82%
Village intelligentsia	11	13	76	42	......	58
Workers in industry and construction	11	6	83	36	3	61
Workers in transport and communications	......	18	82	55	......	45
Agricultural workers	10	14	76	90	......	10
Service personnel	9	15	76	38	3	59
Other	12	3	50	63	12	25
Percent of total	7	10	83	37	2	61

* Results of the 10 percent sample selected from the responses of the 1963 secondary school graduates.

In 1966 Soviet sociologists have made themselves indispensable to the party and the state and have wrested for themselves a relative freedom to explore the various problems of their society. Soviet commitment to rational planning, with the realization that it can only be conducted within the framework of reliable information on Soviet society, makes it possible for Soviet sociologists to contribute not only to the development of their own society, but also to the advancement of international sociology.

The future of Soviet sociology

What, then, are the prospects for Soviet sociology? Any projection we undertake at this time will probably tell more about our own hopes than about the actual future. Nevertheless, man's hopes are not always fantasies and are often built upon certain inherent probabilities that under specified conditions may come true. With respect to Soviet sociology we can already observe certain outlines of a new future phase:

PROJECTED NEW PHASE

Phase	*Typical ideological concerns*	*Typical sociological contributions*
Phase III (in 10-20 years)	Ideological tolerance	Comparative empirical research on an international scale

The term ideological tolerance is here best understood in opposition to dogmatism, orthodoxy, or fanaticism. It refers to a certain freedom from narrow restrictions in the sphere of individual action and especially in the sphere of belief or opinion. The best synonym for ideological tolerance is latitudinarianism, which in one excellent definition of the term "does not denote skepticism, laxity, or indifference, but rather a firm adherence to reasonableness and tolerance in matters of belief, taste, and conduct. It is a cultivated attitude of respect for diversity based on belief of human nobility rather than expediency. It denotes reserve and moderation, in contrast to extremism, and an obligation to make an effort to understand and perhaps even learn from others." [38]

Since 1964 a kind of limited ideological tolerance has been evident in Soviet scholarship, and the fight against so-called Stalinist dogmatism has been extended to other more sacred areas of Soviet Marxism. At the April 1965 conference of Soviet biologists with the editorial board of the journal *Problems of Philosophy,* voices were raised not only against the ideas and influence of Lysenko on Soviet biology, but also against the old-fashioned biological theories of Engels. Lysenko's theories were referred to as a brand of idealism, mysticism, and scholasticism. Engels' biological ideas, his explanation of life in particular, have simply been termed as false, despite the fact that all Soviet encyclopedias and textbooks keep repeating Engels' position as an article of faith. Soviet biologists argued that such treatment of the subject "neither paid respect to science nor to Engels." They emphasized that "a position [taken by Engels] was correct for the conditions of science of that day, but that it had become dogma nowdays." [39]

Needless to say, the day is still to come when Soviet scholars will be willing or able to re-examine the social theories of Marx, Engels, or Lenin with similar detachment. Such a fresh look at the ideas of their beloved theorists would not necessarily mean a weakening of belief in their work. Quite the contrary, it might increase the general Soviet respect for these men of genius, for they would be evaluated as men and not as gods.

Introduction of an ideological tolerance would also bring a greater appreciation by Soviet scholars for some of the work of their colleagues in other countries and would permit closer international cooperation among sociologists. It could culminate in large-scale comparative empirical research under the sponsorship of such agencies as, for example, UNESCO. Beginning steps toward such a possible future cooperation are already being made. Sociologists at the Leningrad University are conducting studies similar to those of Frederick Herzberg at Western Reserve University, while Professor Herzberg, on his part, is reported to have agreed to conduct studies similar to those of the Leningrad sociologists.[40]

Prospects for Soviet cultivation of an ideological tolerance in the near future are dim. Tolerance can only be cultivated under a special set of conditions that Soviet scholars themselves can neither create nor control. Time alone can heal the wounds inflicted by the Stalinist past. Only with the passing of the older generation can we expect Soviet sociologists to examine freely the problems of generational conflict, anti-Semitism, the "cult of personality," and others noted by Professor Feuer in his meetings with Soviet philosophers and sociologists.[41]

Time alone, however, will not bring about an ideological tolerance which can only be cultivated in a time of relative international peace.

The requirements of war either transform a scholar into an ideologist or silence him. In the words of Georg Simmel, "in peace, the individual may 'let himself go'—'himself' referring to the various forces and interests of his nature: they may be allowed to develop in various directions and independently of one another. In times of attack and defense, however, this would entail a loss of strength because of the counter-strivings of parts of his nature; and a loss of time because of the continual need for bringing them together and organizing them. The whole individual must therefore take on, as his inner position of conflict and chance of victory, the form of concentration." [42]

We must conclude that although the main foundation for a possible ideological tolerance by Soviet scholars has already been laid, significant changes in Soviet society and the world at large must occur before tolerance can prevail.

Notes

1. Isaiah Berlin, "Introduction," in Alexander Herzen, *From the Other Shore* (London: Weidenfeld and Nicolson, 1956), pp. xiii-xiv.
2. Thomas G. Masaryk, *The Spirit of Russia,* Vol. I (New York: The Macmillan Co., 1919), pp. 426-427.
3. Alexander Herzen, *From the Other Shore* (London: Weidenfeld and Nicolson, 1956), p. 3.
4. Pitirim A. Sorokin, *Social Philosophies of an Age of Crisis* (Boston: Beacon Press, 1951), p. 71.
5. George Fischer, *Science and Politics: The New Sociology in the Soviet Union* (Ithaca, N.Y.: Center for International Studies, Cornell University, 1964), p. 3.
6. A. Okulov and T. Oiserman, "Resultaty chetvertogo mirovogo sotsiologiches-kogo congressa" (Results of the Fourth World Congress of Sociology), *Voprosy filosofii,* XIII, No. 12 (December 1959), 76.
7. See Fischer, *op. cit.,* p. 4. "Zadachi razvitiia obshchestvennykh nauk v uslo-viiakh razvernutogo stroitelstva kommunizma, Postanovlenie obshchego sobraniia Akedemii nauk SSSR" (The Tasks of Developing the Social Sciences in the Course of Actively Building Communism, A Resolution of the General Meeting of the USSR Academy of Sciences), *Vestnik Akademii Nauk SSSR,* XXXII, no. 12 (December 1962), 61-62.
8. V. S. Nemchinov, "Sotsiologicheskii aspekt planirovaniia" (Sociological Aspect of Planning), *Voprosy filosofii,* XIII, No. 10 (October 1959), 19.
9. Robert K. Merton and Henry W. Riecken, "Notes on Sociology in the USSR," in *Current Problems in Social-Behavioral Research,* Symposia Studies No. 10 (Washington, D.C.: National Institute of Social and Behavioral Science, March 1962), pp. 7-14.
10. P. N. Fedoseev, "Sociology in the USSR," *Transactions of the Fourth World Congress of Sociology* (London: International Sociological Association, 1959), p. 179.
11. *Ibid.,* p. 177.
12. "O sozdanii Sovietskoi Sotsiologicheskoi Associaicii" (On the Creation of Soviet Sociological Association), *Voprosy filosofii,* XII, No. 8 (August 1958), 185-186. American sociologists learned of the establishment of the Soviet Sociological Association from Joseph B. Ford, "Sociology in Russia?", *American Sociological Review,* XXIV (April 1959), 255.
13. Boris G. Sofronov, *M. M. Kovalevsky kak sotsiolog* (M. M. Kovalevsky as a Sociologist), (Moscow: Moscow University, 1960).
14. A good summary of Kovalevsky's ideas, including a review of his major work on the rise of democracy, is provided in the volume edited by M. V. Nechkinaia (chief editor) and others, *Ocherki istorii istoricheskoi nauki v SSSR* (Essays on the History of Historical Science in the USSR, (Moscow: Academy of Sciences of the USSR, 1963).
15. It may be noted that one of the difficulties facing American sociologists who write on Soviet sociology is that of distinguishing between significant Soviet works and irrelevant ones.
16. Academy of Sciences of the USSR, *Istoriia i sotsiologiia* (Moscow: "Nauka" Publishing House, 1964), pp. 342.
17. Also vice-president of the USSR Academy of Sciences.
18. A detailed examination of the various positions taken by scholars at the conference is probably inadvisable at this time on political grounds, but it will

certainly remain a remarkable document for the future. The absence from the conference of certain noted Soviet scholars (e.g., academician M. B. Mitin) is also interesting for speculation.

19. *History and Sociology, op. cit.,* pp. 6-7. The "consequences of the cult of personality" which lowered the prestige of the social sciences are detailed by other participants at the conference. Academician F. V. Konstantinov, Director of the Institute of Philosophy at the USSR Academy of Sciences, accused Stalin and Stalinists of falsification and tendentious interpretation of historical truths, subjective use of historical facts, and, most important of all, an open reinterpretation of Marxist and Leninist judgments. Konstantinov mentions such "disorientation of minds, disorientation of views and values," as those in which the Russian Populists of the 1870's have been presented. Among other facts, Konstantinov reveals that Beria used to force Emelianov, the worker who was hiding Lenin in the Razliv, to maintain that Stalin visited Lenin in Razliv on a number of occasions:

> Beria and Beria-men demanded of Emelianov to "remember" this fact. Yet Emelianov kept maintaining that Stalin never visited Lenin in Razliv. It is a known fact that for comrade Emelianov and his family it had a tragic ending. I am saying this in order to recall the atmosphere and the circumstances in the period of the cult of personality which hindered historians to create and write a true history. And everything that was achieved by the party and by our historians which stands as a positive contribution to the Marxist historical science had been achieved despite the cult of Stalin. (pp. 92-93)

20. *Ibid.,* p. 7.
21. *Ibid.*
22. *Ibid.,* p. 13.
23. *Ibid.,* p. 15.
24. *Ibid.,* pp. 33-35.
25. *Ibid.,* pp. 336-339.
26. G. V. Osipov, ed., *Sotsiologiia v SSSR* (Moscow: "Mysl" Publisher, 1965). International Arts and Sciences Press has announced preparation of a condensed, one-volume English edition to be edited by Stephen P. Dunn.
27. The junior author of the revised version is a different academician, which calls attention to the unique custom of scholarly collaboration in the Soviet Union.
28. Osipov's article represents the clearest definition of Soviet sociology made in the past decade and deserves a full translation into English. See "Osnovnye cherty i osobennosti marksistkoi sociologii" (Main Features and Peculiarities of Marxist Sociology), *ibid.,* pp. 41-53.
29. *Ibid.,* p. 42. Osipov's italics.
30. For a larger discussion of the new debunking, see Alex Simirenko, "The Concept of Industrial Society Under Criticism by Soviet Sociologists," in section five of this volume.
31. See M. B. Mitin and V. S. Semenov, "Dvizhenie chelovechestva k kommunizmu i burzhuznaia kontseptsiia 'edinogo industrialnogo obshchestva'" (Movement of Mankind Toward Communism and the Bourgeois Conception of a "Single Industrial Society"), *Voprosy filosofii,* XIX, No. 5 (May 1965), 35-46.
32. *Sociology in the USSR, op. cit.,* pp. 312-331.
33. *Kopanka 25 let spustia* (Kopanka 25 Years Later), Moscow, 1965. Not available at this time.
34. See, for example, "Novaia vekha v sovershenstvovanii sotsialisticheskikh metodov rukovodstva ekonomikoi" (A New Landmark in the Perfection of Socialist Methods in Guiding the Economy), *Voprosy filosofii,* XIX, No. 11 (November 1965), 3-13, an editorial devoted to the Central Committee's decisions during its plenary session in September 1965. The editorial emphasized an urgent need for reliable empirical sociological data to facilitate planning: "Any kind of

serious scientific planning and especially scientific guidance of industrial progress may well become impossible in the near future if we fail to develop empirical investigations of specific problems and make wide theoretical generalizations of the results containing the most varied factual material." (pp. 11-12)

35. See "Molodezh vsupaet v zhizn" (Youth Enters Life), *Voprosy filosofii,* XIX, No. 5 (May 1965), 57-70.

36. According to the 1959 census the region was populated by 2,298,000 persons, among whom 1,274,000 were located in cities and 1,024,000 in villages.

37. *Ibid.,* pp. 62, 65.

38. Jan Hajda, "Latitudinarianism in Religious Organizations," paper read at the Pacific Sociological Association's Annual Meeting in Salt Lake City, April 1965.

39. See "Aktualnye problemy sovremmenoi biologii" (Urgent Problems of Modern Biology), *Problemy filosofii,* XIX, No. 7 (July 1965), 43.

40. Vladimire Yadov, "The Soviet and American Worker: Job Attitudes," *Soviet Life,* No. 1 (January 1966), pp. 36-37.

41. Lewis S. Feuer, "Meeting the Soviet Philosophers," in Section 4 of this volume.

42. Georg Simmel, *Conflict* (New York: Free Press, 1955), pp. 87-88.

2 THE RUSSIAN EMPIRE

Introduction

One sometimes reads that a precondition for the development of sociology is a free society which provides an opportunity to examine objectively all the facets of its social existence.* The development of sociology in the Russian Empire refutes such blanket generalizations. Neither censorship, nor political persecution, nor suspensions from jobs for political unreliability, nor the widespread snooping of the secret police and its intimidations prevented sociology from developing. The political climate of nineteenth-century Russia is well described by the fact that Dostoevsky was condemned to death and later commuted to a Siberian exile for a mere public reading of Belinsky's attack on Gogol, which was widely circulated among the members of the intelligentsia in a hand-written form. The nineteenth-century Russian intelligentsia in general was in agreement with Herzen's characterization of itself as a group of enlightened slaves. The creative ferment of the pre-Revolutionary intelligentsia was in great degree a response to the social conditions of their country. Similar problems of censorship and persecution were also present in nineteenth-century Germany. While some modern totalitarian regimes have been successful in stamping out the activities of its sociologists, not all totalitarian societies have done so. In Yugoslavia and especially in Poland the work of sociologists was never stopped, although there was a time when they were in official disfavor.

The selections in this section are intended to provide a panorama of the creative activity of sociologists in the pre-Revolutionary period. Unfortunately, space does not permit the inclusion of detailed discussions of many more sociologists than we have here. In addition to the general discussion by Pitirim A. Sorokin, included are two representatives of the pioneering period, Mikhailovsky and Plekhanov, and two representatives of the classical period, Kovalevsky and Lenin.

The article by Professor Pitirim A. Sorokin, who is best acquainted with the field, illustrates the variety of sociological orientations of the

* The following quotation represents one recent example of such ideas: "Sociology can thrive only under freedom. . . . A nation cannot have quality in sociology by fiat. . . . Only a nation which provides the conditions for free inquiry may with reason hope for the development of social science knowledge which permits ever deeper understanding of man in society." (Alex Inkeles, *What Is Sociology?* [Englewood Cliffs, N.J.: Prentice-Hall, 1964], p. 117.)

the pre-Revolutionary thinkers. They remain as a forgotten fountain of ideas to be rediscovered by the new Soviet sociologists. Some of the recent writings of Soviet sociologists are peculiarly reminiscent of the pre-Revolutionary works, although the originators of the various ideas remain forgotten. Whatever influence the early sociologists may exert on the future of sociology in the USSR, their work illustrates the inherent possibilities for further development. It was on the basis of the proclivity of earlier generations of sociologists that Pitirim Sorokin was predicting, as early as 1926, the "flaring up" of sociology in the Soviet Union. The contributions of Professor Sorokin himself to the development of an international sociology present the best evidence that the work of the pre-Revolutionary sociologists was not in vain. Sorokin, a student of Kovalevsky, Kareev, Petrazycki, and others, was forced to pursue his career in sociology abroad. He organized and chaired for many years the Department of Sociology at Harvard University and has written more than thirty books which are translated into many languages. In recognition of Professor Sorokin's contributions to sociology, he has been honored with the presidency of the International Sociological Congress and the American Sociological Association.

Samuel H. Baron, author of the article on Plekhanov, is Professor of History at Grinnell College and the author of a definitive biography on Plekhanov published in 1963. Professor Baron presents a vivid description of the development of Plekhanov's Marxist ideas against the background of social conditions in the Russian Empire of his day. Thus it is not only an account of Plekhanov's growth but also of the development of social thought in general and of Marxism in particular. In this beginning period of sociology the two leading giants were Mikhailovsky, spokesman for the Populists, and Plekhanov, spokesman for the Marxists. Their sociological ideas were developed in the struggle with each other and against the state. The support for Marxism grew at the expense of Populist ideas, whose popularity was declining among the intelligentsia.

Plekhanov's writing reared the first generation of Marxists. According to Lenin, Plekhanov's first Marxist work, entitled *Socialism and Political Struggle,* played a role in the Russian Empire similar to that of the *Communist Manifesto* in the West. Lenin himself was reared on Plekhanov's writings. Their paths parted with the split between the Bolsheviks and the Mensheviks. Plekhanov tried first to breach the split but later took the side of the Mensheviks. His continual pursuit of independent thought, however, earned him rebukes from both sides.

The selection by Thomas G. Masaryk is the best available discussion of the sociological ideas of N. K. Mikhailovsky. It is part of a classic two-volume study of Russian philosophy and sociology by a scholar and statesman who became the first President of Czechoslovakia. The study, entitled *The Spirit of Russia* and first published in 1913, remains the single most important reference to nineteenth-century Russian intellectual history available in English. Analysis of Mikhailovsky's work is presented here in an incomplete form touching only upon some of the central ideas of interest to sociologists. Masaryk is especially clear in presenting and defending Mikhailovsky's "subjective method." Mikhailovsky's subjective approach to the study of social reality anticipated later developments in methodology, including that of Max Weber generally known under the name of *Verstehen*. In the context of the language used by the Chicago symbolic interactionists, the subjective method meant "taking the role of others," in addition to the verification of reality through experience. Pitirim Sorokin's integralist conception of reality also draws upon the ideas of the "subjective school" in recognizing three complementary methods for the pursuit of knowledge—the sensory, the rational, and the supersensory-superrational intuition.

The article on Kovalevsky is written by another distinguished Russian immigrant scholar, N. S. Timasheff, a student of Petrazycki and Kovalevsky, who has written some twenty books and hundreds of articles in many languages. He has taught at many famous universities, including the University of St. Petersburg, Prague University, the Sorbonne, and Harvard, and he remains Professor Emeritus at Fordham University. Professor Timasheff provides us with the best available appraisal of the work of the greatest sociologist of the pre-Revolutionary period. Kovalevsky's objectivity as a scientist was so thorough that in his work he refused to mention any of his colleagues, with the exception of De-Roberty, because they were incapable of keeping their personal views entirely separate from their scholarship. Despite the fact that most of Kovalevsky's research—for which he is famous—was centered on countries of western Europe, none of his important works is available in English. Some are available in German, some in French, but the great bulk remains untranslated. With all the thousands of publications pouring out of the Russian and east European institutes, it is a pity that no effort has been made to make the work of Kovalevsky (and that of others) more widely available.

The selection on Lenin by Sheldon S. Wolin, Professor of Political Science at the University of California at Berkeley, provides perspectives on Lenin's organizational theory in the light of contributions made half a century later. It is part of Wolin's large work on Western political thought, entitled *Politics and Vision*. Lenin's creative reformulation of Marx is in large measure due to the sociological heritage of the Russian Empire. His emphasis on the organization of revolutionaries for the transformation of society is in part based on Lavrov's ideas. Although Lenin emerged as an enemy of the remnant forces of the Populists, it is from them and especially from their spokesman Mikhailovsky that Lenin borrowed his ideas on the significant role of the elites in the age of mass society. No greater compliment could have been paid to Lenin than the statement by Professor Wolin that "the measure of Lenin's success is that his lessons have become the common property of the age; the irony is that his prescription for revolution has also been used to preserve giant capitalism."

Russian sociology in the twentieth century

PITIRIM A. SOROKIN

I. Russian sociology in the second half of the nineteenth century

Though up to the beginning of the twentieth century sociology was not offered under its own name in the Russian universities and colleges, nevertheless it was intensively cultivated outside of the Empire's educational institutions, as well as in the universities, under the names of "philosophy of history," "social foundations of economics," "introduction to a general theory of law," "social psychology," and so on. As a result the Russian sociology of that period was scarcely behind that in any other country. This is shown, first of all, by the prominent role played by a series of the Russian sociologists in the development of European sociology. The names of P. Lilienfeld, who published his fundamental work in Russian before H. Spencer's *Principles of Sociology;* of J. Novicow, P. Kropotkin, E. de Roberty, M. Kovalevsky, B. Kistiakovsky, L. Metchnikov conspicuously show this. But these names are only a few among those of the many Russian sociologists whose works are not known outside of Russia, but are as valuable as the works of the foregoing sociologists. It is enough to mention N. K. Mikhailovsky, who, several years before G. Tarde, and probably not less brilliantly than Tarde, developed his theory of suggestion-imitation, mob psychology, and psychology of crowd. Mikhailovsky also was one of the earliest and one of the deepest critics of the organismic theory of society, and of social Darwinism. It is enough further to mention the name of Danilevsky, who, already in 1869 in his *Russia and Europe,* laid down a theory which in all its substantial principles has been recently repeated (possibly without knowing Danilevsky's work) by Oswald Spengler. Engelgard's *Progress as an Evolution of Cruelty* is to be regarded as one of the most original and suggestive books in the field of a "realistic interpretation of social evolution." K. Leontiev's social philosophy set forth in his *Byzantinism and Slavs* can possibly rival the best works of J. de Maistre and Carlyle.

From the *Publications of the American Sociological Society,* II (1926), 57-69.

The works of M. Kovalevsky, N. Kharouzin, Ephymenko, Ziber, Sergee-vitch, and others were some of the best pioneer works in the field of early civilization and evolutionary sociology. The works of P. Lavrov, N. Kareev, Iujakov, and others built what is now known under the name of "psychological school in sociology." M. Tugan-Baranovsky, P. Struve, G. Plekhanov, and in part V. Lenin, produced a series of valuable works in "the economic interpretation of history and social phenomena." V. Kluchevsky, A. Lappo-Danilevsky, N. Korkunov, Chicherin, and other historians and theorizers of law contributed a great deal to juridical sociology or to sociology of law and ethics. These brief remarks are sufficient to show that in the nineteenth century sociology and social sciences generally were intensively and successfully promoted in Russia.[1]

II. Russian sociology in the twentieth century[2]

ITS EXTERIOR SITUATION

Since approximately 1909, sociology, under its own name, began to be taught in a series of Russian colleges. The number of such colleges was progressively growing up to 1917. In 1917 sociology began to be offered in many of the Russian universities. At the beginning of its career the Soviet government assumed a very favorable attitude toward sociology and tried to introduce it even into the secondary schools. The reason for such a policy was the Soviet government's assumption that sociology and Marxian socialism were about the same. Having learned that the assumption was wrong, and that sociology was taught by many of the professors along lines considerably different from Socialism and Communism, the government practically forbade sociology-teaching in the schools, discharged many sociologists, and, instead of sociology, ordered "drill" in so-called "political science," that is, "the Marxian and Lenin's interpretation of history," "Communism," "history of Communism," "history of the Communist revolution," and "the constitution of the U.S.S.R." In this way sociology has been again expelled from the schools—at least formally—and is now in a position rather worse than it was before the revolution of 1917. Its place is now occupied by the foregoing "political science," called in Russia "Communist theology."

An increased interest in sociology on the part of the Russian educated groups since the beginning of the twentieth century called forth, besides many books and papers, a publication of special sociological monographs under the title of *New Ideas in Sociology*. Edited by M. Kovalevsky, E. de Roberty, and by the writer, the monographs were a substitute for a sociological journal. The death of Kovalevsky and de Roberty, and World War I, put an end to the publication. After their death, in their memory, there was founded in 1916 the Russian Sociological Society, with a member of the Russian Academy of Science, A. S. Lappo-Danilevsky, as the president, and with the writer as the secretary of the Society. Many prominent Russian biologists, psychologists, historians, political scientists, and other scholars entered the membership of the Society. Unfortunately, the Revolution, the death of the president, and other factors interrupted the work of the Society at its beginning. In 1920 the work was "illegally" resumed, but imprisonment, banishment, and death of many of the leaders of the Society again interrupted its existence. Similar was the fate of another sociological society, the Society for an Objective Study of Human Behavior. It was started in 1921 with an Academician, Ivan Pavlov, as the honorary president, and with the writer as the chairman. Owing to the conditions mentioned, the Society's work was interrupted at its very beginning. Furthermore, the Soviet's nationalization of almost all printing houses, and the severest censorship introduced by the present government, have made physically impossible a publication of any sociological work which has not been a mere repetition of the "Communist and the Marxian theology." Such a situation continues to exist, in a somewhat milder form, up to the present. This is enough to show that today's exterior situation of Russian sociology is far from being better than it was before the Revolution. In fact, it is much worse. This partly explains why, during the years of the Revolution so few non-Communist sociological works were published in Russia. So much for the exterior position of Russian sociology in the twentieth century.

PRINCIPAL DIFFERENCES OF RUSSIAN SOCIOLOGY OF THE TWENTIETH FROM THAT OF THE NINETEENTH CENTURY

They are as follows: first, the sociological works of the twentieth century as compared with those of the nineteenth century have become less philosophical and less general; second, their methods of study have tended to be less and less speculative; third, the popularity of the sociological schools of "economic interpretation of history" and of "Russian subjective sociology" dominant in the previous period, began to go down; fourth, the various currents of sociological thought have increased in number; fifth, there have appeared new sociological schools, with new leaders who did not play a conspicuous role in the preceding period.

PRINCIPAL SOCIOLOGICAL SCHOOLS OF THE TWENTIETH CENTURY

I. *The Marxian school.*—At the end of the nineteenth century this school produced several valuable works like G. Plekhanov's *A Monistic Interpretation of History,* M. Tugan-Baranovsky's *Periodical Industrial*

Crises, P. Struve's *The Destinies of Capitalism in Russia,* and so on. In the twentieth century the school's creative power went down. Possibly the most serious work of that period is Professor Solntzev's *Social Classes* (1917), a monograph devoted to a survey and analysis of the concept of social class. Since the Communist Revolution there have been published an immense number of various Marxian sociological works; but all these "Communist theologies" amount to nothing from a scientific standpoint. Even N. Bukharin's *A Marxian Sociology,* which is possibly the most valuable work among all the Communist sociological publications, contributes very little new, either to an economic interpretation of history or to sociology generally. Marxian sociology in Russia degenerated into a kind of dogmatic theology and is innerly dead.

2. *Russian subjective sociology.*—Being very near to L. Ward's psychological sociology, this school made many valuable contributions to sociology in the nineteenth century. In the twentieth century it also began to show a decrease of its creativeness. Nevertheless several valuable works have come from it. Among them the most important are J. Delevsky's *Social Antagonisms* and E. Kolosov's *The Principles of a Simple and a Complex Cooperation according to N. Mikhailovsky.* Delevsky's book represents a systematic analysis of the concept, the forms, the causes, and the effects of social antagonisms. As far as I know, it is probably the most complete and systematic monograph in this field in the sociological literature of all countries. Kolosov's work develops Mikhailovsky's theory of "the technical" and "the social division of labor." The author analyzes their forms among various societies, criticizes Simmel's and Durkheim's corresponding theories, studies the effects of both forms of social differentiation, and pleads for a social reconstruction on the basis of "the simple" cooperation. With the exception of the last part of the work it is valuable and suggestive.

3. *Petrazycki's psychological sociology.*—"Psychological sociology" in the sense of Tarde's, L. Ward's, C. H. Cooley's, F. Giddings', or E. A. Ross's and C. A. Ellwood's sociological principles was embodied in the works of E. de Roberty, Mikhailovsky, P. Lavrov, N. Kareev, V. Lesevich, W. Chernov, and of many others in the Russian sociology of the nineteenth century. Quite different from it is "the psychological sociology" founded by L. Petrazycki, formerly (up to 1917) a professor of general theory of law at the University of St. Petersburg, now a professor at the University of Warsaw and a vice-president of the International Institute of Sociology. Having begun his scientific activity with his volume, *Lehre vom Einkommen,* in which, among other things, Petrazycki set forth a theory later on developed by R. Stammler in his *Wirtschaft*

und Recht, Petrazycki, in his later works, *Essays in a Philosophy of Law, Introduction to the Theory of Law and Ethics, A Theory of Law and Ethics* (2 vols.), revised fundamentally the principles of logics, of scientific methodology, and of psychology. It would scarcely be an exaggeration to say that from the standpoint of scientific methodology his mentioned works are among the few important treatises published after J. S. Mill's *Logic.* As a result of such a revision, Petrazycki created his own "emotional psychology," and, on its basis, his own interpretation of social phenomena, of law, of ethics, of social organization, and of social processes. In a few words it is impossible to give an idea of Petrazycki's theory. I can only say that it is quite original, extraordinarily logical, and at the same time quite factual and inductive. And what is more important, it "works" in an analysis of the most complex and concrete social phenomena. Unlike too many psychological sociologists, Petrazycki not only outlined the fundamentals of his theory, but, with its help, has given a real "psychological anatomy" of the phenomena of law, of ethics, of association, of state, and of social organization in its various forms. Further, perhaps more clearly than anybody else, he has shown a psychological mechanism of social processes. The extraordinary value of his works is responsible for the immense influence of his theory upon the Russian social and political scientists, upon philosophers, psychologists, economists, and theorizers of law and ethics. The same value is responsible for an appearance of "Petrazycki's school" in jurisprudence, sociology, political science, and psychology. The Revolution forced Petrazycki to leave Russia; many of his pupils have been dispersed throughout Russia or imprisoned or banished (though Petrazycki himself, as well as his followers, in no way belonged to the old régime); in this way the work of the school has been interrupted. Nevertheless, there are all reasons to expect that in the future the work will be resumed; the theory belongs to the type of the scientific contributions whose influence is long and durable.

4. *Russian behavioristic school.*—As it is known, modern behaviorism in psychology originated in Russia through the works of Ivan Pavlov and, partly, V. Bechterev, and Pavlov's pupils (Boldyrev, Krasnogorsky, Orbelli, Zeleny, Frolov, Lenz, Zavadsky, Anrep, Babkin, Arkhangelsky, Voskresensky, Deriabin, Foursikov, Zytovitch, Krestovnikova, Makovsky, Petrova, and others). Beginning with a study of relatively simple psychological processes, Pavlov and his followers have gradually passed to the experimental study of more and more complex nervous processes among animals, and finally among human beings. As a result they have formulated the basic laws of the "unconditioned" and "conditioned"

responses, and the laws of "inhibition," "stimulation," "extinction," "inculcation," "reconditioning," and "transformation" of the forms of behavior. The most valuable results obtained by the school naturally have stimulated its representatives to apply its methods to the study of social phenomena. As a result we have Dr. Zeleny's sketch of a "social physiology," [3] V. Bechterev's, K. Kornilov's, and M. N. Lapinsky's attempts to interpret social phenomena from the behavioristic viewpoint,[4] Savitch's and Vasiliev's behavioristic sociology of mental phenomena,[5] W. Wagner's "Bio-Psychology," [6] and P. Sorokin's two volumes of *A System of a Behavioristic Sociology, Influence of Food-Factor on Human Behavior, Social Processes, and Social Organization,* and *The Sociology of Revolution,*[7] to mention only some of the works of this school.[8]

In spite of some differences in the severity of an application of the behavioristic principles to the study of social phenomena, all these works have some common characteristics which may be styled the characteristics of the Russian behavioristic school in sociology. They may be summed up as follows: First, a concentration of scientific attention on the study of those social phenomena which are repeating in time and space (sociological "constants"). Second, a thorough objective, and, where it is possible, an experimental and quantitative method of their study. Third, in view of the great flexibility of human speech-reactions (and ideologies), in view of the fact that they are often only a "minor reaction" in human behavior, in view of their unreliability to serve as an adequate basis for a study of real human behavior or of real social process—in view of these and similar reasons, the school intentionally tries to disregard them in a study of social phenomena, at least at the beginning of such a study. Only when other objective data are studied thoroughly they may be taken into consideration. Contrariwise, they may be misleading and in fact are very often misleading. This may explain why, in the opinion of many of the representatives of this school, a great many historical, sociological, political, and other works are quite unsatisfactory. Being based principally on "the speech-reaction material" (of a historical personality, of the writers of the epoch, of various letters, "speech-reaction questionnaires," and so on), such works, as a rule, are fallacious and unscientific. Fourth, a complete expulsion from a scientific study of all evaluative judgments and concepts (of what is good and bad, useful and harmful, moral and unmoral, "progressive" and "reactionary," "just" and "unjust," and so on). Fifth, such an application of the behavioristic principles as would not be a mere terminological alteration of various subjective concepts (which is quite common in a great many "pseudo-behavioristic" works in psychology and sociology, and quite useless scientifically), but would be a real behavioristic analysis of the phenomena studied. Where such an analysis is impossible, it is better not to apply behaviorist methods and terminology; not to deceive the investigator himself and other people. From the foregoing one may see that the school proceeds carefully and systematically in its work. It has already found a vivid response from a series of the young sociologists in Russia. There are all reasons to expect its development in the future, when the conditions of Russia are more normal. This school and Petrazycki's school are probably the most important currents of sociological thought in Russia from a purely scientific standpoint. . . .

5. *Other schools.*—Among them may be mentioned K. M. Takhtarev's *The Science of Social Life* (1920), which combines the principles of Simmel's formal sociology with that of an economic interpretation of social processes. Also akin to Simmel's principles of sociology is S. Frank's sketch of sociology published in his *Philosophy and Life* (1909). A. Gwirzman attempted, in his book, *Sociology of K. Marx and L. Ward in Their Relationship* (1911), to combine synthetically K. Marx's and L. Ward's sociological principles. A. Zvonitzkaya, in her book *Social Bond* (1913), gave a very careful analysis of what F. Giddings would style "likemindedness" (its essence, factors of its origin, growth, and disintegration) from the standpoint of E. de Roberty's "bio-social hypothesis." Voronov, in his *Foundations of Sociology* (1910), has tried to interpret social phenomena from the standpoint of "social mechanics" or "social physics" set forth by the great thinkers of the seventeenth century and more recently outlined by H. Carey, L. Winiarsky, E. Solvey, Haret, Portuendo y Barcelo, and by some others. An outstanding contribution to "mechanistic sociology" is made by E. Spektorsky in his monumental work: *The Problem of Social Physics in the Seventeenth Century,* Vol. I, 1910, Vol. II, 1917.

6. *"Sociologization" of jurisprudence, political science, and economics.* —Besides the foregoing sociological works there have been published many valuable works in the field of economics and political and juridical sciences. Treatment of the problems of these disciplines has been becoming more and more sociological and less and less "formal" in corresponding treatises. As a result the fundamental problems of sociology have been carefully analyzed in them and many of these works may be regarded as valuable courses in sociology. Such, for instance are J. Pokrovsky's *Principal Problems of Civil Law,* B. Kistiakovsky's *Social Sciences and Law,* P. Novgorodtzev's *Contemporary Crisis of Jurisprudence,* and *Theory of Social Ideal,* E. Trubetzkoy's and I. Taranovsky's *Encyclopedias of Law,* N. I. Lazarevsky's *Russian Constitutional Law,* and

so on. Among these works should be mentioned also the *Ethics* of P. Kropotkin, unfinished on account of his death.

The second field of jurisprudence in which there have been made many sociological contributions has been that of criminal law and criminology. The works of M. Gernet, N. Chubinsky, A. Jijilenko, N. Rosin, Drill, Posnyshev, P. Sorokin, and many others have contributed considerably to the science of human conduct, to the problem of factors of criminality, and to the clarification of such forms of social relationship as social prestige and dignity, social shame, social honor, and so forth.

Similar has been the trend within the field of economics. Such fundamental works as Tugan-Baranovsky's *Principles of Political Economy, Theoretical Foundations of Marxism, Social Foundations of Cooperation,* P. Struve's *Economy and Price,* A. Bilimovitch's *Theory of Value,* S. Solntzev's *A Theory of Distribution,* and many other works are essentially sociological in their character and represent valuable contributions.

7. *Sociological methodology.*—In the field of the methodology of social sciences also many important works have been published. Especially valuable among them are A. Lappo-Danilevsky's *Methodology of History* (3 vols.), N. Kareev's *Methodology of History* and *Historical Typology,* A. Shpett's *History as a Science.* The works of A. A. Tchuprov in the field of a statistical study of social phenomena deserve special mentioning. His *Essays in the Theory of Statistics* (1909) and his subsequent works in the field of mathematical statistics and quantitative study of social causation, published during the last few years abroad (he also had to leave Russia), have been so valuable that the Royal Statistical Society of Great Britain and several other societies elected him to honorary membership. Keynes styled his works as an "epoch-making" contribution.

8. *Treatises in general sociology.*—The most important work in this field is M. Kovalevsky's *Sociology* (2 vols., 1910) and his *Contemporary Sociologists* (1905). The first volume of the *Sociology* discusses fundamental problems of sociology; the second one, origin and evolution of principal social institutions (economic organization, religion, law and morals, family and marriage, arts, and so on). *Contemporary Sociologists* is a survey and criticism of principal sociological theories of the present time (G. Tarde, F. Giddings, M. Baldwin, Gumplowicz, Ratzenhofer, B. Kidd, Bouglé, Durkheim, M. Vaccaro, Ammon, Lapouge, Matteuzi, Lévy-Brühl, A. Coste, Simmel, K. Marx, and others). It is somewhat similar to P. Barth's *Die Philosophie der Geschichte als Soziologie,* but much better in its critical part. It possibly is still the most substantial critical analysis of the leading sociological theories in the literature of sociology of all countries. Somewhat similar to Kovalevsky's book is the

Sociology of Professor Khvostov (1917). Its second volume is unfinished on account of the suicide of the author in 1918, caused by the Soviet régime. Later on there were published a series of ignorant Communist sociological textbooks. But, with the exception of the beforementioned book by Bukharin, they have no scientific value.

9. *Social philosophies and philosophies of history.*—During the last few years there has been published by the Russian scholars who are abroad a series of works which may be styled "social philosophies." Some of them are near to what now is styled in Germany "meaning sociology" (Spranger, Th.Litt, partly M. Weber, and others). Some others in their principles remind one partly of J. de Maistre's and De Bonald's theories, partly of the works of Oswald Spengler, Keyzerling, and of this type of thinkers. Almost all these works show an antipositivist attitude. They contain also a deep and thoughtful criticism of the principles of Western civilization. Side by side with this there are many interesting and sweeping generalizations. From a purely scientific viewpoint they have many shortcomings. Several of their conclusions are obviously questionable. On the other hand, they are extraordinarily suggestive, stimulating, and free from that "intellectual chewing-gum" which is so common in various "positivistic" books in sociology. As examples of this category of works I may mention S. Frank's *Downfall of the Idols* (of fundamental values of contemporary Western civilization), N. Berdyaev's *The Logics of History* and *The Philosophy of Inequality,* N. Karasavin's *Philosophy of History,* S. Boulgakov's *Philosophy of Economics,* P. Struve's *Reflections on the Revolution,* and, finally, the publications of the "Eurasians," who try to show that Asiatic culture is not inferior to the culture of the Western World, that Russia is a whole continent in which are synthetically combined the components of the European and of the Asiatic cultures (hence "Eur-Asia"), and that the future history of Russia is to be neither an imitation of the "decaying culture of Europe" nor a return to the culture of Asia, but a synthetic transformation of the valuable components of both cultures.

10. *Conclusion.*—The foregoing gives a very schematic and incomplete picture of Russian sociology in the twentieth century. Nevertheless it may show that sociology there has been progressing and growing. Having always been in closest contact with European and American sociological thought, and having taken from them their valuable contributions, at the same time Russian sociology has been an independent and original product of Russian sociological thought, whose contributions to world-sociology have been very considerable. At the present moment, owing to a lack of freedom of thought and technical means of

publication, sociological work within Soviet Russia is greatly handicapped. Nevertheless, I have no doubt that such a situation is temporary. The country is coming back, and normal conditions are being re-established. Sooner or later the existing unlimited censorship of the government will have to be abolished. As soon as these obstacles are put down, there are serious reasons to expect an extraordinary revival of Russian sociology. Even now there are many valuable works prepared for publication as soon as the mentioned obstacles are removed. The crucificial experience of the Revolution has not passed in vain for those who survived it. It has greatly enriched and stimulated the thought of its observers. Through an extraordinary combination of conditions the Revolution has provided an opportunity to verify many sociological assumptions on the one hand; on the other, to observe human beings and social processes under conditions which do not exist in a normal society. It is not surprising, therefore, that within the present Russia an unseen and most intensive revision of the fundamental principles of social science and a ripening of new sociological theories are going on now. It is probable that in the future they may result in a sudden "flaring up" of Russian sociology. Such a "flaring up" has happened many times after great revolutions; it is likely to happen also in the case of the Russian Revolution.

Notes

1. See J. F. Hecker, *Russian Sociology* (New York: Columbia University, 1915). Hecker's work gives, though inadequate, a more detailed characterization of Russian sociology of the nineteenth century.

2. A somewhat more detailed characterization of Russian sociology in the twentieth century is given in my paper, "Die Russische Soziologie im zwanzigsten Jahrhundert," *Jahrbuch f. Soziologie,* II Band (1926), pp. 462-483, translated into Ukrainian and published in the Ukrainian sociological journal, *Souspilstvo (Society)*, Nos. III-IV (Prague, 1926). *Society* is a publication of the Ukrainian Sociological Institute in Prague, founded by the Ukrainian emigrants from Soviet Russia.

3. Zeleny, "Über die zukunftige Sozio-Physiologie," *Arck. f. Rassen- und Gesellschaftsbiologie* (1912), pp. 405-430.

4. V. Bekhterev, *General Foundations of Reflexology* (Russian), 1918; *Collective Reflexology* (Russian), 1921; K. N. Kornilov, *Theory of Man's Reactions* (Russian), 1922; M. N. Lapinsky, *Development of Personality in a Woman* (Russian), 1915.

5. V. V. Savitch, *An Attempt of a Behavioristic Interpretation of a Process of Mental Creative Activity* (Russian), in *Krasnaia Nov'*, 1922, No. 4; I. Vasillieff, *Studies in Mind's Physiology* (Russian), 1923.

6. W. Wagner, *Biological Foundations of Comparative Psychology* (Russian), 2 vols., 1913.

7. Sorokin, *Systema soziologii* (Russian), 2 vols., 1920-1921. *Influence of Food-Factor,* in Russian, was to be published in 1922, but in the process of printing was destroyed by the Soviet Government. All that the author has left from the book of about 600 pages is 252 pages of its proofs and two chapters published in the *Russian Ekonomist* in 1922, *The Sociology of Revolution,* Phil, 1925.

8. See the bibliography of Pavlov school's experimental studies, in I. Pavlov, *Twenty Years of an Objective Study of the Nervous Activity of Animals (Dvadzati-letniy opyt obiektivnago isouchenia vysshey nervnoy deiatelnosty jivotnykh),* Petrograd, 1923.

Plekhanov and the origins of Russian Marxism

SAMUEL H. BARON

It was in the year of Karl Marx's death that Russian Marxism was born. In 1883 five people in Geneva, Switzerland, joining together as the "Emancipation of Labor" Group, launched the fateful movement that was to lead fifteen years later to the formation of the Russian Social-Democratic Labor party, and was to have such phenomenal consequences in 1917 and thereafter. The outstanding leader of the new revolutionary organization was George Plekhanov, who is rightly called the "father of Russian Marxism."

It was not for lack of acquaintance with Marx's work that the Marxian movement began in Russia at this relatively late date. Literate Russians had had ample opportunity to familiarize themselves with Marxian ideas inasmuch as (1) the works of Marx and Engels were admitted freely into the country at mid-century and for some time thereafter, (2) *Das Kapital* was legally published in Russia in 1872 and sold well, (3) the revolutionary underground published illegally other works of Marx and Engels in the seventies and eighties, and (4) Marxian writings were not infrequently discussed in the periodical press. Leading Russian thinkers, such as Belinsky, Chernyshevsky, Lavrov, Bakunin, Tkachev, and Mikhailovsky, all had knowledge of some of Marx's works, and several of them had high praise for some aspects of Marxian thought.[1] The important revolutionary organization, *Narodnaya Volya* (The People's Will), wrote to Marx in 1880: "The class of advanced intelligentsia in Russia, always attentively following the ideological development of Europe and sensitively reacting to it, has met the appearance of your works with enthusiasm." [2]

But if advanced Russians had had a considerable exposure to Marxism, if various persons had a warm respect for Marx and some of his

From *The Russian Review*, XIII, No. 1 (January 1954), 38-51.

ideas, prior to 1883, Russian thinkers familiar with that system of thought agreed in failing to accept a thoroughgoing Marxism with its economic, political, sociological, and philosophical implications. Radical Russians had not taken Marx's ideas as a basis for their revolutionary activity for, in general, they considered that, while Marx had laid bare the roots and workings of capitalist states, his diagnosis and prognostications were inapplicable to Russia. It was rather the doctrines of populism (*narodnichestvo*) that held almost universal sway in Russian socialist circles. Marxism began to win adherents only when, as a consequence of repeated failures of populist movements to attain their ends, faith in the ideas and methods of those movements weakened. Then there was resumed that quest for "an algebra of revolution" that had engaged advanced Russians for decades. In the course of this renewed quest, Plekhanov, who had been an enthusiastic populist in the first years of his revolutionary career, was drawn to Marxian thought, which appeared to him to offer a more realistic and practicable basis for the Russian revolution. A study of his experience and of the development of his ideas with respect to Russia's social evolution reveals Plekhanov's reasons for abandoning populist views in favor of a Marxian approach. But the lessons that Plekhanov drew from his experience and studies had more than a personal significance; they provided the rationale for defections of other revolutionists from the populist ranks and for the consequent buildup of the Russian Marxian movement.

In 1874 the young nobleman Plekhanov was a brilliant, first-year student at the Mining Institute in Petersburg. In that turbulent decade the universities were hotbeds of revolutionary propaganda. The times were such that a classroom could be used for a revolutionary meeting, while a professor acquiesced in such activity by foregoing a scheduled lecture.[3] Under such conditions, Plekhanov, like so many other youths, was drawn into revolutionary activity and, gradually, he abandoned his studies. The sentiments he felt when, as a neophyte revolutionist, he encountered his first representative of the masses illustrate well both the romantic nature of the populists and the gulf that tragically separated them from those they yearned to help.

When I met Mitrofanov for the first time [he wrote] and recognized that he was a . . . representative of the people, in my soul there stirred a feeling of compassion. . . . I very much wanted to converse with him but did not know how and with what expressions. . . . It seemed to me that the language of . . . [the student] would be incomprehensible to this son of the people . . . and that I would have to use the absurd manner of speech of our revolutionary pamphlets.[4]

By December 1876 Plekhanov, then an agitator for the revolutionary organization "Land and Liberty" (*Zemlya i Volya*), was prepared to burn his bridges behind him. In that month he addressed an illegal demonstration of students and workers on the Kazan Square in Petersburg.[5] The meeting was broken up by the police and, in order to escape arrest, Plekhanov fled abroad. Thereafter he was wanted by the authorities; when in his native land he was obliged to remain incognito.[6]

Some months later, when he returned to Russia, Plekhanov showed unexampled energy for the cause of rebellion. The broad scope of his activity as an agitator can be seen in the series of revolutionary proclamations—the first products of his pen—which he addressed to students, workers, Cossacks, and "educated society." [7] His vigor and talent soon brought him to a position of leadership in the then dominant populist organization, "Land and Liberty"; and, early in 1879, he was made an editor of its periodical publication.

But even in 1879, while Plekhanov was a populist, he was a populist with a difference. His first revolutionary assignment had foreshadowed his future role, for it involved propaganda not among the peasants but among the Petersburg workmen.[8] The aim of the populists in mingling with the workmen was to recruit propagandists for activity among the peasants, those who were expected to provide the mass basis for the revolution. But in order to win the confidence of the workers, the revolutionists had to take part in the workers' struggles. Thus Plekhanov came to participate in strikes, to share the experiences of the workers, and to write propaganda and manifestoes for them. While those who were trying to activate the peasants were having little success, Plekhanov obtained a positive response from the workers among whom he carried on agitation. The significance of this was not lost upon him and, even as a populist, he pointed to the socialist inclinations of the city worker and to the useful role that the latter might play in the social revolution.[9]

Early in 1879 there appeared in the journal, *Land and Liberty,* a long article in which Plekhanov detailed his populist views.[10] He expected that Russia would soon produce a great revolution, a revolution that would establish an anarcho-socialist order. The revolution would be consummated when the intelligentsia, dissatisfied as it was with the political and social order, would, by agitation, succeed in arousing the great mass of discontented peasants and in directing their fury against the existing regime. The revolution would bring the destruction of the state and the distribution of state and noble lands among the peasants. The character of the new society would be determined by the anarcho-collectivist nature of the peasants who were the overwhelming majority of the Russian people. The age-long desire of the peasant for freedom and self-government would lead to the destruction of the coercive, centralized state and its replacement, from the bottom up by a "free federation of free communes." Since the peasants were organized in collectivist-type communes, it was deduced that the future society would be collectivist in nature, with property collectively owned and with production, whether agricultural or industrial, organized on a collectivist basis.[11] Although much was left unsaid, it was clear that, to Plekhanov's way of thinking, Russia would attain socialism through the revolutionary action of the peasantry and without passing through a capitalist stage of development.

The general scheme was by no means peculiar to Plekhanov, the influence of Bakunin is all too clear, and some such outlook was common to most of the revolutionary populists of the period 1876-1879. But what is arresting about Plekhanov's analysis is that in 1879 he already showed concern that his system should be consistent with Marxian principles as he then understood them. Thus he said: "Let us see to what the teaching of Marx obligates us . . . in view of the necessity of establishing the points of departure of our program." [12] Unlike other Russian populists, he argued that Marxian principles were relevant not only to capitalist societies, but to all societies. However, this did not signify that all societies must have identical histories; for, "weaving and combining variously in various societies, they [Marxian principles] give entirely dissimilar results. . . ." [13]

It was significant that the article under consideration was entitled "The Law of the Economic Development of Society and the Tasks of Socialism in Russia." The title suggested, and the contents of the article confirmed, that Plekhanov was at one with Marx in identifying "the economic history of society" as the determining factor in social evolution.[14] He held up to criticism the "utopian" socialists of the thirties and forties who, considering the mind all and life nothing, had supposed that a happily conceived plan for a well-proportioned and smoothly functioning society could, by virtue of skillful use of propaganda, be translated into reality without reference to the stage of economic development existing at a given time and place.[15] Arguing, in effect, that his own populist views could not be described as utopian, Plekhanov insisted that the peasant commune was stable, that its collective ownership of land and the collectivist habits of work and thought that it created among the peasants provided a real and sound basis for socialism in Russia.[16] If Russia differed from the West in this regard, if Russia could attain socialism in a unique way, it was only because the peasant commune had fallen in the West, and with it, the collectivist instincts of the people. When those instincts were replaced by individualism, the possibility of socialism in the West vanished until such time as the growth of large-scale, factory production with its socialization of labor had once again restored the social spirit that had decayed with the decay of the commune.[17] The very cornerstone of Plekhanov's system, then, was the belief that the commune "does not bear within itself the elements of its own doom." [18] In terms of his own theoretical premises, it followed that if the commune should disintegrate, the social conditions essential for the establishment of socialism would no longer obtain in Russia and, in that case, only a utopian could speak of the likelihood of socialism there in the near future.

The early influence of Marx upon him is important in helping to explain Plekhanov's later, definitive, conversion to Marxism; but it is clear that, in 1879, the young revolutionist did not qualify as a Marxist. Plekhanov believed that Marxian principles supported the outlook and program of the populists. But this was, at least in part, an erroneous judgment; for Plekhanov, like most of the populists of that time, considered that the revolution would destroy the state and open the way to an anarcho-federalist order, while Marxists held that a state, and a strongly centralized state, was essential for the transition to socialism. Very shortly before the publication of the article discussed above, he had described all of Russian history not as "the history of class struggle," but, in anarchist terms, as "an unbroken struggle of the state with the commune and the individual." [19] And so poorly oriented was Plekhanov in questions of Western socialism that he grouped Marx and Engels with Rodbertus and Dühring as "the brilliant pleiade" of socialism in 1879,[20] that is, a year after Engels had published his celebrated attack upon Dühring.

Nevertheless, Plekhanov's exposure to some Marxian ideas clearly had produced a strong impression upon him. For the present, he could both be a good populist and be faithful to Marxian precepts, as he then understood them, since there seemed to him to be no contradiction between the two. But in time his faith in the populist creed was shaken, while a more extensive contact with the primary sources of Marxism strengthened his conviction as to the validity of that outlook. Within a very few years he became persuaded of the essential incompatibility of populism with Marxism; and this led to his renunciation of populism.

When within "Land and Liberty" there developed a strong tendency to abandon agitation among the peasants and workmen in favor of a terroristic, political struggle with the government, Plekhanov led the fight against the terrorists. When dissension within "Land and Liberty" led to its dissolution in the fall of 1879, Plekhanov became a leader of the new, anti-terrorist organization, "The General Redivision" (*Chernyi Peredel*), which, in opposition to the terrorist "People's Will," affirmed its adherence to the traditional views and methods of "Land and Liberty." [21] But Plekhanov's faith in the old populist outlook was soon weakened by the failure of "The General Redivision" to compete successfully with the terrorists in attracting fresh forces. When even those who remained loyal to the old populist ideas showed little inclination to carry propaganda to the countryside,[22] doubts arose in Plekhanov's mind as to the correctness of the views of the "redivisionists."

Around the same time, his doubts were compounded by his encounter with Orlov's book, *Communal Property in the Moscow District*. Orlov presented such persuasive data on the decline of the peasant commune that Plekhanov was obliged to revise his opinion concerning its indestructibility. Soon afterward he acknowledged that economic differentiation was proceeding among the commune members, that the commune "is being divided into two parts, each of which is hostile to the other. . . ." [23] Yet, he insisted that the causes of the decline of the commune were external [24] and that they would cease to operate if the socialists should succeed in igniting the revolution, if they should bring the peasants "from a passive expectation of a general redivision" to "an active demand for it." [25] For the moment Plekhanov seemed able to reassure himself, but he reported later that Orlov's work "strongly shook" his populist convictions.[26] By raising serious doubts about the stability of the commune, the book tended to undermine the very foundation of his populist outlook.

As uncertainty came to take the place of conviction, Plekhanov began to deplore the inadequacy of his knowledge and the difficulty of supplementing it under the repressive conditions of Russian life.[27] Hence, he was not entirely displeased when, late in 1879, some of his revolutionary comrades urged that he and other leaders of "The General Redivision" go abroad until such time as the situation was more auspicious for revolutionary work.[28] Plekhanov welcomed the opportunity to secure the information which would quiet his doubts and verify his views. Half in jest, he remarked that he was going abroad "to study and to attain there the scholarly level of a master's or a doctor's degree." [29]

In January 1880 Plekhanov made his way to western Europe and immediately plunged into the study of history, political science, and socialism.[30] The works of Marx fascinated him and, in order to gain more complete access to them, Plekhanov undertook to learn German.[31] Beginning in the fall of 1880, he lived in Paris for almost a year, engaging in intensive study at the *Bibliothèque Nationale* and, in his spare time, making the acquaintance of such leaders of Western socialism as Jules Guesde. His sojourn in the West made a profound impression upon Plekhanov. Experience of Western conditions and increased familiarity with Western socialist political and economic conceptions gave him the perspective for a critique of "Russian socialism." Thus his trip abroad had unexpected results, inasmuch as he did not acquire information that could bolster the populist position; on the contrary, for as Plekhanov recalled many years afterwards, "the more we became acquainted with the theories of scientific socialism, the more doubtful became our populism to us, from the side of both theory and practice." [32] The changes effected in his views were soon evident and, indeed, it is possible to trace, in his writings between 1880 and 1882, Plekhanov's rejection, one after another, of the fundamental theses of populism. In a period of fifteen to eighteen months he renounced the doctrine of a unique social evolution for Russia, abandoned hostility to politics and political struggle, and ceased to identify the peasantry as the mass basis of the Russian socialist revolution.

By September 1880 (nine months after he had gone abroad) Plekhanov was contending that the next stage for Russia would probably be a bourgeois-constitutional regime.[33] This judgment, dropped rather casually in an article, revealed the profound change that had taken place in Plekhanov's outlook in a short time. It signified that Russia would not have a unique social development, involving a leap from her contemporary situation to a socialist order, but instead would experience an intervening capitalist stage. But Plekhanov was not yet prepared to make these affirmations. That for him the situation was not yet entirely crystallized was apparent when he indicated that while the agrarian question was still the chief concern of the socialists, "Russian industry is not standing still." And "along with this, the center of gravity of economic questions is being transferred to the industrial centers." [34] By January 1881 the idea that the next socio-political formation for Russia would be a bourgeois-constitutional regime had passed from probability to certainty for Plekhanov.[35] While the implication was unavoidable that Russia's economic evolution would therefore parallel that of the West, it was only at the end of 1881 that Plekhanov unequivocally stated that Russia was launched on the capitalist phase of development and that "all other routes are closed to her." [36]

The adoption of the point of view described above meant that Plekhanov no longer regarded the peasant commune as a basis for a direct transition to socialism; but nothing was said of this, nor were detailed and reasoned arguments given for his change of front before the publication of his important works of 1883 and 1885 respectively, *Socialism and Political Struggle* and *Our Disagreements*.[37] In those works, and especially in the latter, it became clear that additional study of Russian economic data, on the one hand, and on the other, mastery of Marxian economic theory had led him to formulate his new conception of Russian social evolution.

Plekhanov's new convictions concerning Russian social development led to a revision of his views as to the tactics the socialists must follow. Although they worked for the destruction of the state, the populists, prior to the formation of "The People's Will," did not regard theirs as a political fight. As anarchists, they were opposed to political struggle, since such a struggle signified to them the acceptance of the state principle. Their aim was not to win political rights within the state system, not to reform that system, nor even to capture the state and utilize it for the implementation of their social program. They sought an end to all states, since the latter were considered instruments of coercion and oppression. The members of "Land and Liberty," and of "The General Redivision" after it, believed that their socialist convictions—for they were anarcho-socialists—obliged them to devote all their energies to agitation among the masses, revolving around their *economic* needs. Only in consequence of such activity would there be called into being the popular rising that would destroy the state and permit the development of the anarcho-socialist order. The populists thought that political liberty was intimately associated with, and beneficial mainly to, the bourgeoisie; political freedom and the struggle to attain it had little or no relevance, they thought, to the needs of peasant Russia—needs which were preeminently economic.

Plekhanov had shared these views, but in September 1880 he wrote: "We know the value of political liberty . . . ; we greet every struggle for the rights of man." [38] If this was a notable departure from his earlier views, Plekhanov, as yet, was prepared to accord to political struggle and political liberty only a secondary importance.[39] He still urged that the people everywhere and always were concerned about economic rather than political questions. Therefore, if the socialists were to become a power, and if the people were to register gains at the time of a revolution, the socialists must carry on agitation among the peasants centered around economic demands. This would guarantee that with the coming of a revolutionary crisis, the socialists would not constitute a "staff without an army," but instead would have massed forces behind them sufficient to ensure consideration of the popular needs.[40] If, on the other hand, the socialists should be drawn into a political struggle against absolutism, they would lose contact with the economically minded masses, and the latter, lacking awareness, unity, and leadership, would gain little or nothing from the overthrow of absolutism.[41]

Plekhanov, in common with many other populists, was still inclined to treat politics and economics as mutually exclusive, unrelated spheres;

but for Plekhanov, this situation did not last. In January 1881 advancing another step toward what was to be his life-long position, he articulated, although yet imperfectly, that synthesis of political struggle and socialism which was to be one of his major contributions to Russian revolutionary thought.[42] In the ensuing months, he clarified his thinking further and, in the spring of 1882, in his foreword to the second Russian edition of the *Communist Manifesto,* Plekhanov plainly enunciated a social-democratic strategy.[43] It was indeed appropriate that he should have done so at that time and in that place, for within the *Communist Manifesto* appeared the formula toward which he had been groping. No longer did he place "political struggle" (the fight for political rights and political hegemony) in opposition to socialist activity (agitation among the masses designed immediately to bring the destruction of the state and a socio-economic revolution). Plekhanov had come to believe that "political struggle" and "socialist activity," so far from being mutually exclusive, were intimately interrelated, that neither could be overlooked in favor of the other, that only *by way of* political struggle could socialism be attained. Plekhanov commended the *Manifesto* as a corrective to the one-sidedness of those socialists who, like the members of "Land and Liberty" and "The General Redivision," opposed political activity, and of those, like the partisans of "The People's Will," who became so engulfed in the political struggle against absolutism as to forget about the creation of a mass movement, which alone could ensure the future of the socialist party.[44] Plekhanov's premises were these: Even though the coming upheaval be a bourgeois rather than a socialist revolution, the masses have much at stake. With the fall of absolutism they should win political rights which would greatly increase the possibilities for developing the campaign for economic emancipation, for socialism. The tactic that Plekhanov recommended to the Russian socialists, therefore, was much the same as that which Marx had urged upon the German Communists in 1848. The socialists must fight alongside of the bourgeoisie to the extent that it is revolutionary in its struggle with absolute monarchy, but, at the same time, must not for a moment slacken its drive to develop in the minds of the workers the clearest possible consciousness of the antagonism of the interests of the bourgeoisie and the proletariat.[45] The Russian socialists must draw the workers into the struggle against absolutism as allies of the bourgeoisie, but must make plain to the proletariat that its interests dictated the inauguration of an all-out struggle against the bourgeoisie on the morrow of the overthrow of absolutism.

Finally, it followed that, if capitalism was to dominate the economic life of Russia, the proletariat, that inevitable by-product of capitalist development, rather than the peasantry, would provide the mass basis for the socialist revolution. In September 1880, when he first suggested that Russia stood on the eve of a bourgeois revolution, Plekhanov advised that propaganda for factory workers be published.[46] However, through most of 1881 his uncertainty was reflected in the continued reference to "the toilers" and "the people" as the chief support of the socialists. But at the end of 1881, around the same time that he imparted to the venerable Russian revolutionary leader, Lavrov, his conviction that Russia could not escape capitalist development, he designated the city workers as the only group from which something significant could be expected in the revolutionary movement.[47] Thus, if earlier he had seen socialism coming to Russia by way of a peasant revolution, on the basis of the peasant commune, and without a prior stage of capitalist development, Plekhanov now argued that the socialist revolution was thinkable only after a considerable period of capitalism, which would produce both the productive system requisite for a socialist economy and the proletariat, the class which would overthrow the capitalist system and inaugurate the socialist order.

Plekhanov's evolution had brought him to a position which represented an innovation in Russian revolutionary thought; at the same time it represented a triumph for the Western statement of the socialist problem. He was now convinced that "in Russian history, there is no essential difference from the history of Western Europe." [48] Consequently, he maintained that the problems of the Russian socialists could best be illuminated by the study of west European social development and Western socialist teachings. Plekhanov thus took his place in the tradition of the Russian "Westernizers." As Peter the Great had applied military and administrative techniques to Russia, as the Decembrists and the men of the thirties and forties had hoped to "westernize" Russia in the political sense, now Plekhanov adopted a Western version of socialism and set out to make it the ruling socialist tendency. As Peter had fought the tradition-bound clergy and boyars, as the "Westernizers" of the time of Nicholas I had done battle with the Slavophiles, now Plekhanov undertook to demolish Russian, populist socialism. Now he declared that he was ready to make of Marx's *Capital* "a Procrustean bed" for the leaders of the revolutionary movement.[49]

In early 1881, as a result of an apparent convergence of views of the "redivisionists" and the terrorists, collaboration between the two factions had been suggested by Plekhanov.[50] Some months later, when collaboration had in fact been established, Plekhanov's views once again diverged from those of the terrorists as he moved toward Marxism. Although for two years the factions were in uneasy association, it was apparent that each was trying to use the other. The "redivisionists" (now become Marxists) wished to capitalize on the popularity of "The People's Will," while trying to infuse that organization with a new social-democratic content.[51] The terrorists intended to turn the well-known names and the experience and talents of the former "redivision-ists" to their advantage without, however, allowing the social democrats to gain a predominant voice in the organization.[52] The differences between the two factions were so great that they could not live in connubial bliss; nor did one succeed in assimilatiing the other. Plekhanov and his comrades proved unwilling to sacrifice their principles for the sake of unity, while the terrorists showed themselves unwilling to accommodate themselves to Plekhanov's "Procrustean bed." [53] But if Plekhanov's circle had failed in its attempt to win over the revolutionary movement from within, its members then resolved to create a new revolutionary organization for the propaganda of their ideas. When, in September 1883, they founded the "Emancipation of Labor" Group, it was in order to take over the leadership of the revolutionary movement and thus, in the end, to stamp the imprint of Marx's thinking deep into Russian life.

Notes

1. For a good account of Marxian ideas in Russia prior to the formation of the "Emancipation of Labor" Group, see B. A. Chagin, *Proniknovenie idei Marksizma v Rossiyu,* Leningrad, 1948. With regard to Chernyshevsky's acquaintance with Marxian ideas, V. Shulgin, "K voprosu o proniknovenii Marksizma v Rossiyu v 40-60 godakh XIX veka," *Istorik Marksist,* Nos. 5-6, 1939, pp. 171-173.

2. Ispolnitelnyi Komitet Sotsial-Revolyutsionnoi Partii v Rossii, November 7, 1880, *Perepiska K. Marksa i F. Engelsa s Russkimi politicheskimi-deyateliami,* 1947, p. 206.

3. Such an incident is recounted in an autobiographical article by D. Blagoev, "Kratkie vospominaniya iz moei zhizni," *Proletarskaya Revolyutsiya,* No. 1, 1927, p. 88.

4. G. V. Plekhanov, "Russkii rabochii v revolyutsionnom dvizhenii," *Sochineniya,* Moscow-Leningrad, 2nd ed., 1924, III, 127.

5. Plekhanov's account of this appears in *ibid.,* pp. 62-65.

6. Material relating to Plekhanov's early revolutionary career may be found in the following sources: *ibid.;* numerous memoirs of L. Deutsch, R. M. Plekhanov and others in *Gruppa "Osvobozhdenie Truda,"* Moscow, 1924-1928, 6 vols.; O. Aptekman, *G. V. Plekhanov,* Leningrad, 1925; L. Deutsch, "Kak Plekhanov stal Marksistom," *Proletarskaya Revolyutsiya,* No. 7, 1922; L. Deutsch, "O sblizhenii i razryve s Narodovoltsami," *ibid.,* No. 8, 1923; L. Tikhomirov, *Plekhanov i ego druz'ya,* Leningrad, 1925.

7. A series of these proclamations appear in *Literaturnoe nasledie G. V. Plekhanova,* Moscow, 8 vols., 1938-1940, I.

8. Plekhanov recalls these experiences in "Russkii rabochii v revolyutsionnom dvizhenii," *op. cit.*

9. Plekhanov, "Zakon ekonomicheskogo razvitiya obshchestva i zadachi sotsializma v Rossii," *Sochineniya,* I, 70.

10. The article is cited in the preceding footnote.

11. *Ibid.*, pp. 62-65.

12. *Ibid.*, p. 59.

13. *Ibid.*, p. 62.

14. *Ibid.*, pp. 57-58.

15. *Ibid.*, p. 57.

16. *Ibid.*, pp. 61, 62, 65.

17. *Ibid.*, pp. 59-60.

18. *Ibid.*, p. 61.

19. Plekhanov, "Korrespondentsii," *ibid.*, p. 29.

20. Plekhanov, "Zakon ekonomicheskogo razvitiya obshchestva," *ibid.*, p. 57.

21. Plekhanov, "Stat'i iz 'Chernogo Peredela,' " *ibid.*, p. 108.

22. Plekhanov, "Kak i pochemu my razoshlis s redaktsiei 'Vestnika Narodnoi Voli,' " *ibid.*, XIII, 25.

23. Plekhanov, "Pozemelnaya obshchina i ee veroyatnoe budushchee," *ibid.*, I, 102.

24. *Ibid.*, p. 103.

25. Plekhanov, "Stat'i iz 'Chernogo Peredela,' " *ibid.*, p. 117.

26. Plekhanov, "Russkii rabochii v revolyutsionnom dvizhenii," *ibid.*, III, 197.

27. L. Deutsch, "Kak Plekhanov stal Marksistom," *op. cit.*, p. 117.

28. Marx commented pungently on the appearance in western Europe of the "redivisionists," the majority of whom, he said, had "abandoned Russia voluntarily—in contrast to the terrorists whose heads were at stake—to form a propaganda party. In order to carry on propaganda in Russia, they come to Geneva. How is that for a *quid pro quo?*" The "redivisionists" were accused of a whole catalogue of sins. Yakovlev, *Iz istorii politicheskoi bor'by v 70-kh i 80-kh gg. XIX veka,* Moscow, 1912, p. 470. Thus cordially did Marx, in 1880, welcome those who, a few years later, were to inaugurate the Marxian movement in Russia.

29. P. B. Akselrod, *Perezhitoe i peredumannoe,* Berlin, 1923, p. 347.

30. His notebook for the years 1880-1882 is crammed full of titles which he evidently consulted. "Zapisnaya knizhka G. V. Plekhanova," *Literaturnoe nasledie G. V. Plekhanova,* I.

31. L. Deutsch, "Kak Plekhanov stal Marksistom," *op. cit.*, p. 120.

32. Plekhanov, "Kak i pochemu my razoshlis s redaktsiei 'Vestnika Narodnoi Voli,' " *op. cit.*, p. 26.

33. Plekhanov, "Stat'i iz 'Chernogo Peredela,' " *op. cit.*, pp. 124-125.

34. *Ibid.*, p. 131.

35. *Ibid.*, pp. 134-135.

36. Plekhanov-Lavrov, End of 1881, *Literaturnoe nasledie G. V. Plekhanova,* VIII, 210.

37. These works are reproduced in *Sochineniya,* II.

38. Plekhanov, "Stat'i iz 'Chernogo Peredela,' " *op. cit.*, p. 125.

39. *Ibid.*, p. 127.

40. *Ibid.*, pp. 125-126.

41. *Ibid.*

42. *Ibid.*, pp. 135-136.

43. Plekhanov, "Predislovie k Russkomu izdaniyu 'Manifesta Kommunisticheskoi Partii,' " *ibid.*, pp. 150-151.

44. *Ibid.*

45. K. Marx and F. Engels, *The Communist Manifesto,* New York, International Publishers, p. 43.

46. Plekhanov, "Ob izdanii Russkoi Sotsialno-Revolyutsionnoi Biblioteki," *Sochineniya,* I, 145-146.

47. Plekhanov-Lavrov, November 1881, *Literaturnoe nasledie Plekhanova,* VIII, 208.

48. Plekhanov-Lavrov, Early 1882, *ibid.*, p. 211.
49. Plekhanov-Lavrov (Probably early spring 1882), *Dela i Dni*, 1921, II, 91.
50. Plekhanov, "Stat'i iz 'Chernogo Peredela,'" *op. cit.*, p. 136.
51. Deutsch-Akselrod, June 15, 1883, *Gruppa "Osvobozhdenie Truda,"* I, 165, 168-169.
52. This inference is based on Iochelson's letter in *Gruppa "Osvobozhdenie Truda" v Period 1883-1894 gg.* ed. V. I. Nevsky (Isoriko-revoliutsionnyi sbornik, II, Leningrad, 1924) pp. 402-403; Plekhanov, "Kak i pochemu my razoshlis s redaktsiei 'Vestnika Narodnoi Voli,'" *op. cit.*, p. 33; Tikhomirov-Lavrov, August 6, 1883, *Gruppa "Osvobozhdenie Truda,"* I, 250.
53. Materials relative to the relations between "redivisionists" and terrorists may be found in *Gruppa "Osvobozhdenie Truda,"* I, III; "Pisma G. V. Plekhanova k P. L. Lavrovu," *Dela i Dni*, II, 1921; Deutsch, "O sblizhenii i razryve s Narodovoltsami," *op. cit,;* Plekhanov, "Pochemu i kak my razoshlis s redaktsiei 'Vestnika Narodini Voli,'" *op. cit.;* L. Tikhomirov, *Vospominaniya Lva Tikhomirova,* Moscow-Leningrad, 1927.

The sociology of N. K. Mikhailovsky

THOMAS G. MASARYK

Nicolai Konstantinovich Mikhailovsky [1] is rightly placed beside Lavrov. The two men represent the same philosophical trend, and their writings have considerable resemblance in point of style. Mikhailovsky, a self-taught man thirsting for knowledge, had his attention drawn by Lavrov to the rich sources of European literature. This was his introduction to Comte and to socialism, and he was greatly influenced by the fundamental conceptions of "historical realism." Though he was not pleased by the *Historical Letters* the book had a considerable effect upon his mind.

Mikhailovsky belongs to the younger generation, being younger than Chernyshevsky and Lavrov, and a contemporary of Pisarev and Kropotkin. . . . A good German and French scholar from childhood onwards, Mikhailovsky was not solely dependent upon Russian teachers, but early began to absorb French and German literature, belletristic no less than scientific.

He was chiefly distinguished from his somewhat older contemporaries in that the influence of Hegel upon him was small, whereas the influence of Comte was practically decisive. I might speak of him as a fully conscious Comtist, but I cannot term him a critical Comtist, for he did not sufficiently exercise his faculty of epistemological criticism. Had he done so he would not have remained a positivist. But his outlook on positivism was less naive than that of many of his contemporaries.

In epistemological matters Mikhailovsky was a positivist and an ultra-empiricist. Comte's formula, that while observation cannot take place in the absence of a guiding theory, this theory cannot possibly have been constructed without preliminary observation, is accepted by Mikhailovsky as it was accepted by Mill, the former believing with the latter that this is not to argue in a vicious circle. The observations and generalizations which are at first unnoticed (Mikhailovsky writes that they are "unconscious"), are subsequently developed into clearly formulated gen-

From *The Spirit of Russia*, Vol. 2 (New York: The Macmillan Co., 1961), pp. 136-152.

eral and abstract propositions, which guide the detailed observations. These propositions are generalizations from experience; there is nothing innate or a priori about them.

Mikhailovsky expressly rejects innate ideas, as expounded by the doctrine of idealism. Not merely is he, with Mill, opposed to the notion that there are inborn moral ideas; but further, touching upon the problem of mathematical axioms, he decides with Comte and Mill that these axioms, and axioms in general, are not more than extremely simple and therefore generally recognized truths.

In opposition to Kant, Mikhailovsky borrows here also from Spencer. By empiricism (experience) he understands, in addition to our own experience, the experience of our forefathers. The brain of the newborn is not a tabula rasa. He even believes that hereditary transmission of ancestral experience is manifested physiologically through changes in the descendants' nerves. It is true that Mikhailovsky does not verify the hypothesis, and all that he says under this head amounts in the end to no more than to show that the so-called innate ideas are referable historically to tradition and psychologically to apperception ("apperception preponderates over perception"). It is true that he has certain hesitations, seeing, for example, that tradition may be false as well as true; and seeing that the a priori of idealism, when explained by inheritance, becomes tantamount to "preconceived opinions," i.e., to prejudices. But he is satisfied in the end with the emendations that result from experience and from increasing insight.

In metaphysics, too, Mikhailovsky follows Comte, holding that the nature of things is incognizable, incomprehensible. But the thesis is not precisely formulated in detail; the proposition is reiterated in the terminology of Hume and Comte and sometimes also in that of Kant; on the whole it is Spencer's agnosticism to which Mikhailovsky adheres. Quite in the sense of Comte, he insists upon the idea of the relativity of knowledge. Man cannot get beyond his five senses; there are no absolute truths, but only relative truths, things that are true for men.

It is plain that Mikhailovsky's theory of cognition remains purely positivist. Like his contemporaries, above all like Lavrov, he rejected the Kantian idealism, in so far as this was criticism, in a most uncritical manner; and he reduced the a priori to physiological differences of organization.

Nevertheless Mikhailovsky was not a naturalist, not a materialist like the radical realists; to him psychical phenomena were no less real than physical. Mikhailovsky was here in agreement with Lavrov and with the emphasis the latter laid upon consciousness.

From Comte and Spencer, Mikhailovsky passed to Darwin. Having been trained in the natural sciences, he retained his interest in these branches of knowledge. Darwinism gave him an opportunity to clear up his ideas upon the important question of the social struggle, and evolutionism confirmed for him the positivist doctrine of progress; but, as we shall shortly see, he made a profound, a positively dualistic distinction, between progress and evolution, and he rejected Darwinism.

In ethics, Mikhailovsky was a utilitarian, and he took occasion from time to time to defend this standpoint, all the more since utilitarianism was condemned in official literature. For example, he championed utilitarianism against the theologian Malcev, a Russian writer whose name is not unknown in German theological literature. For Mikhailovsky, utilitarianism was the ethic based on experience. Precisely because based on experience was it preferable to intuitive morality, erroneously preferred as more ideal. Mikhailovsky differed from Lavrov concerning Kant, and Kant's conception of duty, which Mikhailovsky could not accept. Were he a painter, said Mikhailovsky, he would represent the history of mankind in three pictures. The second of these would be named "The Last Criminal." It would show society perishing, but in the very last moment the last criminal would have been executed in the name and in honor of absolute justice. In the main square of the abandoned and ruined city, we should see the crumbling scaffold on which is the skeleton of the last criminal; perched on the skull is a raven; *fiat justita, pereat mundus.*

Despite this rejection of rigorism and its metaphysical foundation (the term metaphysical is used in the Comtist sense). Mikhailovsky laid stress upon the necessity for recognizing the extant contrast between good and evil, which he tended to conceive of as a continuation of the ancient Iranian and Indian dualism. Truth has withdrawn to heaven, and the task of the ethical volunteer corps is to bring it back to earth. For the positivist, truth is merely relative, not absolute; but in practice, says Mikhailovsky, it is after all absolute for man, since man cannot transcend it.

Mikhailovsky was a Comtist, but he apprehended postivism as it was originally conceived by Hume and emended by Mill, for both the English philosophers regarded ethics as an integral portion of philosophy. Spencer, too, showed Mikhailovsky the right path in these matters.

Mikhailovsky was much influenced by the socialists as well as by Comte. Proudhon, Louis Blanc, and Marx, must in especial be recognized as his teachers. Proudhon was commended to him by the authority of Herzen, and exercised a great effect upon his mind in earlier years. In 1867 he translated Proudhon's *De la Capacité politique des Classes ouvrières,* and he learned from its author to prize individuality. He was attracted by Louis Blanc's philosophy of history, was delighted by the principle of the organization of labor, and was an enthusiast on behalf of social workshops; he is said to have spent his inherited property upon the founding of a bookbinders' workshop. Marx's writings, and in especial the first volume of *Capital,* drew Mikhailovsky's attention to the dangers of the division of labor and to the anarchy of the capitalist economic order.

From 1877 onwards, Mikhailovsky was interested in the work of Dühring, the opponent of Marx and Engels, and was interested also in that of F. A. Lange, recommending both Dühring and Lange to the Russian youth. It need hardly be said that Mikhailovsky's thought, like that of his Russian predecessors and contemporaries, was akin to Feuerbach's.

In addition to these influences, we have to consider Mikhailovsky's acquaintanceship with the works of Rousseau, for this led the Russian towards socialism, towards the social collectivity, as contrasted with Proudhonian anarchism.

Russian literature exercised a notable influence upon Mikhailovsky. I have already referred to Lavrov, but Mikhailovsky learned also from Herzen, and still more from Chernyshevsky, whose anthropologism recurs as "humanitism." Mikhailovsky was a consistent opponent of Pisarev and the latter's adherents, and sharply distinguished his own individualism from that of Pisarev. Nor did Mikhailovsky forget Belinsky. It is noteworthy that Mikhailovsky was at an early date intimately associated with Nekrasov and Saltykov, becoming in 1868 a contributor to Nekrasov's periodical. At this time he was on friendly terms with several other Russian authors, amongst whom may be mentioned Eliseev and Shelgunov. Among the Russians who helped to form his mind, Mikhailovsky refers to Nozhin, who died prematurely in the year 1866, being then only twenty-three years old. The two men worked together for several years on the staff of the same journal. Nozhin was involved in the trial of the Karakozovcy. Nozhin was a zoologist. In a European journey he had made the acquaintance of Bakunin. His publicist ideas derived primarily from Proudhon, but he differed from his teacher in his view that the division of labor was injurious to individuality and was the cause of the unequal division of the product of labor. Nozhin denied the reality of the Darwinian struggle for existence among the individuals of the same species, referring expressly to the phenomena of mutual aid. All these ideas recur in the work of Mikhailovsky.

Mikhailovsky was a sociologist, and in sociology was a follower of Comte, but he was distinguished from Comte, and was distinguished no less from Marx and the Marxists, by his insistence upon the "subjective method" in sociology.

In Russian literature, much has been said concerning Mikhailovsky's and Lavrov's "subjective method." The Marxists, in particular, have fiercely attacked it, and one of Plekhanov's principal writings is devoted to Mikhailovsky and to a refutation of the subjective method.

Mikhailovsky, like Lavrov, recognized the existence of psychology, side by side with sociology, as an independent science, differing here from his leader Comte, and accepting the views of Mill and Spencer. The sociologist must employ the subjective method as well as the objective; social and historical facts demand a psychological as well as a material explanation. Consequently Mikhailovsky often speaks of "social psychology."

Mikhailovsky explicitly protested against the idea that the subjective method was not inductive and would conflict with experience. But in sociology, he said, in the explanation of the relationships between human beings, the objective method was not all-sufficing. The historical process, he declared, is teleological, for individual men, groups of men, and humanity as a whole pursue aims. Now an aim implies a desire, the sentiment of what is agreeable, and the consciousness of duty. The sociologist, therefore, in his presention of the historical process and of social organization, must duly take into account this subjective element in man.

Mikhailovsky demands that the observing sociologist shall allow his mind to permeate the observed object, man; the observer, as he puts it, must "merge" with the object, so that the observer may find himself in the place of the observed; he demands that the sociologist shall have the faculty of "impressionability" (imaginative insight).

But this is not to give an exhaustive account of Mikhailovsky's subjective method. Every individual, he says, is a member of a historically given group of human beings, of a class, and shares the opinions and desires of that class. Utterly different are the respective judgments formed by the feudalist and by the socialist concerning historical and social matters. What standpoint should the scientific thinker assume? Mikhailovsky admits that a man's views are invariably suggested by his social position. How, then, is scientific sociology possible? Mikhailovsky adheres to the opinion of Comte. He who desires to devote himself to sociology must attain to a high moral level, that he may be able to do justice to all views and valuations, and that he may be able to overcome preconceived opinions based upon tradition (apperception).

For Mikhailovsky, the objective method in sociology seems no more than a mask, assumed by men without conscience in order to befool their conscientious fellows. Mikhailovsky justifies his departure from Comte's historicism by referring to Comte's own mental development, to the way in which Comte moved on from his objective sociology to the subjective method in politics and the philosophy of religion. He quotes

Balzac's *Le Recherche de l'Absolu,* showing how the brilliant realist had made positivist detachment appear ludicrous and contemptible, by representing a disciple of Lavoisier defining tears in purely chemical terminology as consisting merely of this and that variety of matter. In contrast to such an outlook, Mikhailovsky champions the socio-psychological standpoint, rightly declaring that to do this is not to abandon positivism

Comte had demanded that we should avoid any tincture of enthusiasm or of a spirit of condemnation in our judgement of historical and above all of political facts; we should regard them, he declared, as simple facts of observation, comprehending each fact solely in its setting in relation to coexisting phenomena and in association with the antecedent and subsequent conditions of human development. But Mikhailovsky, while recognizing that this positivist detachment is a demand of "pure rationality," regards it as impossible and unsound. *"Tout comprendre, c'est tout pardonner,"* is a pretty saying, but wrongheaded. *"Tout comprendre"* must not be taken to imply that we are not to insist upon the fundamental opposition between good and evil. *"Tout comprendre"* is impossible; no one can understand everything, and therefore we must not forgive everything. Besides, *"tout comprendre"* is impossible to a decent man; for example, certain meannesses are quite beyond his understanding. In a word, there is no justification for the demand that the historian should display a positivist detachment. Mikhailovsky returns frequently to the exposition of these views, and they are especially to be found in the preface to his *John the Terrible.*

Plekhanov's rejection of Mikhailovsky's subjective method is based on the contention that this method suggests no other criterion than the personal wishes of the individual, that it proposes to replace scientific research by subjective caprice.

Indisputably there are historians and philosophers of history who are guided by caprice, but the objection is none the less fallacious. As a Marxist, Plekhanov adopts the standpoint of purely objective history, the individual consciousness being eliminated by Engels and the other Marxists. Mikhailovsky's views are clearer and more accurate, for he recognizes that the objective interpretation of history is inadequate. Marx believed himself to have proved that the age of communism was approaching by historical necessity; he believed that this proof could be furnished by the use of the Hegelian dialectic. But what would be the result of such a proof for my personal conduct, for yours, for Marx's own, for everyone's? The socialist decides in favor of socialism and communism upon ethical and not upon historical grounds; the Russian socialists are right; Marx's attempt to give socialism a purely objective historical foundation was futile. It is only because men of the present day are deciding in favor of communism, and have reasons and motives for this decision, that historians have been able to point to the beginning of the communistic epoch. Other philosophers of history, differing from Marx, refuse to consider the socialist movement as the opening of a new historical epoch, and look upon it as no more than a morbid episode. Which party is right? Upon whose side, that is to say, is the truth—a truth which, as I see it, can be no more than relative? It is clear that the question with which Mikhailovsky is really concerned when he discusses the subjective method, is whether psychology, and sociology grounded upon psychology, are really possible. Today we may say that the question has been adequately answered, has been answered alike theoretically, epistemologically, and practically, by the advent of a genuinely scientific psychology and sociology, whereby the objections of the Marxists have been rendered simply anachronistic.

But for Mikhailovsky the question has a yet more general significance. If every human being be involuntarily and necessarily guided by the preconceived opinions of his class and of his day, how is science possible? To put the matter in concrete terms, which class can contend that it possesses science, that science is enlisted in its service? Mikhailovsky replies by amending Lassalle and Engels, by saying that science serves the people, that is, the "entirety of the laboring classes of society."

It is necessary to note and to commend the way in which Mikhailovsky invariably pays great attention to the problem of accurate method. When discussing individual scientific and philosophic writers, he never fails to examine their methodology, and to consider how it corresponds to their actual treatment of the topic. As regards sociology, he challenges the validity of analogy as a method capable of giving accurate results, his views in this respect conflicting with those of Spencer and certain Russian sociologists, above all with those of Stronin.

Mikhailovsky contests Spencer's opinion that society is an organism, rejecting at the same time false conceptions of a collective consciousness. For Mikhailovsky, society is an organization of individuals of like kind and of equal value. In his explanation of historical and social facts, the sociologist ought not to set out from the whole, but from the consciousness of the individual. The nature of the individual, says Mikhailovsky, is most conspicuously shown in work; for men, for the human individual, work is what motion is for matter. (It must be observed that Mihailovsky is here drawing an analogy!) Work is the chief attribute of individuality, the chief characteristic of individuality as such. Talent, birth, wealth, beauty—these are non-essentials, to a greater or lesser extent they are chance qualities; talent comes by favor of fortune; a man's wealth is not won solely by himself; and so on. But work is the deliberate use of energy, the expenditure of energy to attain a goal, and work is therefore the manifestation of man's true essence, the manifestation of individuality.

It follows that the essence of sociality is to be found in the collaboration or cooperation of individuals, and that the nature of the cooperation determines the character of succesive epochs.

For this reason, because cooperation socializes men, Mikhailovsky is just as little inclined as Comte and other sociologists to admit the validity of economic materialism. Cooperation is not merely economic in nature but comprises all social work, including intellectual work. In the last resort, culture subserves the purposes of work, and therefore culture cannot be utilized as an explanation of social and historical processes. Of course the cooperation of human beings is explicable by motives and reasons, and is referable above all to inborn egoism and altruism. Here Mikhailovsky follows Adam Smith, for to natural and inborn egoism he counterposes the no less inborn and natural altruism; he appeals to Comte's "altruism," to Feuerbach's "tuism," and to Dühring's "sympathetic natural impulses."

Mikhailovsky was not slow to study Marx. Immediately after the appearance of the first volume of *Capital* he read the book carefully, and was especially interested in the chapters upon cooperation and upon the division of labor, for his attention had already been drawn to these questions by Comte, Adam Smith, and Louis Blanc. In his work on Darwinism, published in 1870, Mikhailovsky stated that in *Capital* he had found the confirmation of his views concerning the disastrous consequences of the division of labor. Mikhailovsky was likewise interested in Marx's philosophy of history, and had frequent controversies with Marx and the Marxists, especially in later years, when the latter had come to regard him as an adversary. Notwithstanding his esteem for Marx, he never accepted the doctrine of historical materialism, but, on the contrary, always energetically combated it.

The way in which Mikhailovsky appealed to psychical energies in explanation of social facts is shown by his studies concerning imitation and suggestive influences, a theme in which he was always greatly interested. From 1882 onwards he penned a series of essays analyzing the way in which human beings influence one another, and why certain men in particular (the "heroes") influence the masses for good or for ill, and compel lesser men to follow their example. Mikhailovsky displayed much industry, here anticipating Tarde, in studying the French writers who have recorded manifestations of imitativeness and have described its pathological forms.

It seems self-evident to Mikhailovsky that history is subject to laws. Man, he says, cannot escape from the domain of natural law. But in the field of politico-moral processes the human will is one factor among many, and within this field therefore freedom of the will has its scope. The formation of ideals and the endeavor to realize these ideals, occur, therefore, likewise in accordance with law. Mikhailovsky understands freedom of the will in the determinist sense, making a sharp distinction between determinism and fatalism.

General laws determine the order of the phases of historic evolution, but individual intervention can retard or accelerate the course of development. Great and vigorous personalities make their appearance upon the frontier between two phases of development.

Mikhailovsky, consequently, takes a critical view of the so-called "great men theory" of recent days. Following Louis Blanc, he shows that great men create, not out of themselves, but out of their environment, and that it is individual circumstances and the circumstances of the day which make these great men representatives and leaders. Precise psychological analysis enabled Mikhailovsky to reduce to reasonable proportions exaggerations à la Carlyle (hero-worship), and to keep close to fact.

Mikhailovsky's social psychology, precise and indefatigable, utterly excludes historical materialism. For Mikhailovsky, as he himself said at times, the stomach question was also a soul question.

The philosophy of history, as Mikhailovsky maintains in opposition to the skeptics in his study of Louis Blanc, ought to expound the meaning of history. Mikhailovsky takes this idea from Comte, the socialists, the evolutionary students of natural science, and above all from Darwin. In practical and political matters it is natural that Mikhailovsky should think as a Russian concerning the meaning of historical development, his outlook being determined by that of his Russian predecessors and contemporaries.

He formulates a scheme of development in three stages, naming them, in conformity with Lavrov, the objective anthropocentric, the eccentric, and the subjective anthropocentric stage.

The objective anthropocentric stage is characterized by the naive belief in accordance with which man holds himself to be the objective, absolute, and real center of nature, determined from without. It is the stage of anthropomorphism and mysticism, the stage of theology and religion, the stage of objective teleology. The second or eccentric stage, pushing dualism of body and soul to an extreme, regards man as under the dominion of abstract ideas. The third or subjective anthropocentric stage is the genuinely human epoch, wherein man, his ethical ideals, a purely human teleology, are realized. It is, at the same time, the era of science and of positivism. Manifestly this scheme is referable to the three stages of

Comte. We are contemplating the theological, the meta-physical, and the positive stage; but whereas Comte maintains as his principle of classification the theoretical relationship of man to the universe, Mikhailovsky is increasingly concerned with the ethical relationship of man to his fellows and to the universe.[2]

We may think also of the three stages of Louis Blanc, which are likewise to some extent a reflex of Comte's ideas; the stage of authority (Catholicism), of individualism (Luther and Protestantism), and of harmony of association. Mikhailovsky himself expounds Louis Blanc's philosophy of history, and does so to clarify his own ideas. He also reproduces Saint-Simon's scheme, in which Saint-Simon distinguished between the organic era and the critical; and he adduces Vico's three stages, the divine, the heroic, and the human. He compares all these schemata with Comte's stages and with his own.

Mikhailovsky devotes much thought to the three stages of development. He moots the question why historians and philosophers of history commonly inclined to speak about three stages, and answers his own question by an analysis of the Hegelian dialectic evolutionary process, which likewise has three stages. He contends that the basis of this conception of three stages is to be found in the natural and obvious contemplation of the future as compared with the present and the past. Since the future is the natural continuation and development of the past, with the idea of the three historical stages there very readily becomes associated the concept of the Hegelian dialectic or that of Vico's *"ricorsi,"* namely that the third stage redevelops itself into the first. But this redevelopment is not a reversion; it is a further evolution upon a higher level. Mikhailovsky therefore distinguishes between the degree of development and the type. When Rousseau, for example, expresses his loathing for civilization and his desire to return to primitive conditions, he is not longing for the savagery and lack of cultivation characteristic of primitive man, but aspires merely to restore primitive simplicity (the type, that is to say) in conjunction with the higher evolution.[3]

The idea of Vico's recurrences (*ricorsi*) is reduced by Mikhailovsky to the simple conviction that the social principles given to man by nature necessarily enter into strife one with another (as we see, in the modern age, in the struggle between authority and criticism), and that ultimately one of these principles secures general validity as the principle of authority has done in science, and so on.

Mikhailovsky likewise applies his three stages in the domain of economics. Society is for him the organization of labor, society is a working and cooperating society.

In the first stage, according to Mikhailovsky, simple cooperation is dominant, a number of individuals working side by side and together for the same practical end. From the very first these individuals are differently endowed and differ in the extent of their training; but even at this stage there are manifest the first and still inconspicuous consequences of cooperation, in the form of the division of labor. Division of labor, however, does not become well marked until the second stage. This "eccentric" stage is not characterized by any aim tending to unite men, by any human aim; theory and practice are severed; the division of labor is perfected; the individual becomes one-sided and a mere organ of society; man ceases to be a complete man and therefore ceases to be man. Not until the coming of the third stage, the subjective anthropocentric stage, does man return to the type of simple cooperation, but does so upon a higher plane of evolution. "Man for mankind, everything for mankind," becomes the saving password.

In the domain of knowledge, the fully developed human being is presented to us as "the profane one." He is the positivist philosopher who has renounced metaphysics and theology, and who endeavors to cognize those things only which are within his mental grasp. He is the positively trained man of culture in contradistinction to men of professional dexterity and the one-sided specialists of earlier days.

Mikhailovsky was compelled to consider Darwin's theory of evolution, for this theory was interwoven with the leading social and political problems, not only by Marx and Engels, but also by the Darwinists and their opponents. History and the philosophy of history were extended to cover biology, zoology, and cosmology; and conversely the theory of evolution in the world of natural science influenced history and the history of philosophy. Mikhailovsky was very keenly aware of this mutual relationship.

Mikhailovsky examined Darwinism and Darwinistic literature to ascertain whether the theory of the struggle for existence must be applied to human society to justify struggle, or at least to show that struggle was inevitable. He admitted that struggle was characteristic of nature, of the animal world, but since he would not admit the applicability of the analogical method to sociology, he considered that biology could not furnish any sociological deductions. He accepted the Darwinian theory in large part, was willing to admit that man is an animal, of animal origin, but did not think that this made it necessary, as he once put it, to regard man as a beast. Experience showed him that the struggle for existence has indeed a place in human society, but it also taught him that man, recognizing the harmfulness of the struggle for existence, endeavors to mitigate it and to put an end to it.

When he speaks of struggle in society, Mikhailovsky thinks not merely of war but also, and still more, of the continuous struggle enduring for entire epochs between the rich and powerful on the one hand and the poor and weakly on the other. In this matter he accepts the view of the socialists, who desire to put an end to the social struggle of the capitalist era with its highly elaborated system of the division of labor.

Like Marx and the other socialists, Mikhailovsky discerns in history a degenerative development of egoism as contrasted with the temporarily weakened altruism of mankind; it is insatiable covetousness which splits society into the two camps of rich and poor, of workers and rulers.

According to Mikhailovsky, Darwinism does not explain the social division of labor. Spencer attempted to identify the physiological differentiation of individuals in the capitalistic epoch. Mikhailovsky considers that such an identification is impossible; the facts with which we have to deal in the two cases are of distinct categories, and analogy is no proof. Moreover, Darwinism affords an explanation of the differentiation of species only, not of individual differentiation.

Mikhailovsky accepts the general law of evolution, in accordance wherewith organized matter becomes ever more complex and the sum of individual energies and capacities continually increases. The increasing complexity consists in this, that the number of the organs increases, that the differences between them become more marked, and that physiological division of labor (i.e., the differentiation of organs for special functions) becomes more effective. Social division of labor, however, as history shows, is not a natural law; it is an empirical law, a social and historical law applicable to a particular epoch, and the division of labor can therefore be replaced by simple cooperation.

Liberalism, with its false doctrine of the necessity for free competition, might endeavor to turn Darwinism to account. But, with Louis Blanc and the other socialists, Mikhailovsky shows that as far as the workers are concerned, liberty and free competition do not entail freedom but slavery. To liberalism, therefore, he counterposes socialism, which demands equality, including economic equality; and he proposes to replace the division of labor, with its differentiation of individuals, by the simple cooperation of fully cultural individuals, of individuals whose cultivation is persistently maintained. Free competition, being in truth anarchy and slavery, must be abolished.

Darwinism is conceived aristocratically and plutocratically, not democratically. Mikhailovsky therefore shows that the boasted democracy of the natural sciences (an idea which appealed to many socialists) has no absolute validity. Sociology, history, and scientific philosophy may be democratic. "All roads lead to Rome," says Mikhailovsky. He admits, too, that the natural sciences, by weakening theology, by establishing the doctrine of the natural equality of men, and by favoring the spread of modern industry and technique, may have exercised a democratizing influence in the era before the great revolution. But he considers Buckle to be wrong in maintaining that natural science is essentially democratic.

Looking at the matter subjectively, Mikhailovsky contends that it is a universalized aspiration of modern man to abolish the division of labor; the modern human being energetically desires to become a complete individuality, to make an end of the partialities and incompletenesses that are entailed by the enforced division of labor. The aspiration is justifiable, and does not conflict with innate altruism; on the contrary, altruism will first become possible in a society of fully developed individuals, of individualities. Mikhailovsky considers that the struggle for individuality comprises the main content of human history and development; this struggle corresponds to the social ideal of the abolition of the division of labor, of the process by which the individual is damaged, restricted, subdivided. The division of labor must yield place to simple cooperation on the part of fully developed human beings.

"Our human ego is not something single and undivided; it is not an 'ego,' it is a 'we.' But the members of this plural have long since, by the process of organic evolution, been reduced to the level of completely subordinated individuals, whose independent significance is merged in the consciousness of the whole." Spencer, the opponent of socialism, might be content with this declaration. Here, as so often, Mikhailovsky's thought is far too biological, so that he himself lapses into the detested objective method. The lack of clearness is connected with the fact that, as regards consciousness, Mikhailovsky adopts the alleged explanation furnished by Haeckel, Maudsley, and others, which assumes man to comprise within himself numerous subjects and consciousnesses which are hierarchically subordinated to the whole; this whole is self-conscious and carries out its will as a unified undivided ego.

In this connection it is necessary to refer to the concept of individuality. Mikhailovsky does not apply this term merely to the isolated human individual, as individuality, seeing that to him the family, the class, the state, the folk, etc., are likewise individualities—"egocentric" individualities fighting for their individuality.

Mikhailovsky's aim is to fuse Proudhon with Louis Blanc, to effect a harmonious combination of individualism and socialism. With this end in view, he gives the following formula of progress. "Progress is the gradational approximation to the totality of individuals, to the maximum possible and most comprehensive division of labor among the organs and to the minimum possible division of labor among men. Immoral, unjust, injurious, and irrational, is everything tending to arrest this movement. Moral, just, rational, and useful, are those things alone which lessen the diversity of society while thereby increasing the diversity of the individual members of society."

Beyond the limits of this formula, says Mikhailovsky, no compromise is possible between the interests of the individual and those of society; beyond the limits of this formula, no end can be secured for the wearisome struggle between these respective interests.

All formulas of this character, precisely because they are so extremely generalized, are liable to divergent interpretations; and this criticism is especially applicable to Mikhailovsky's formula owing to the deliberate vagueness of its terminology (e.g., the use of the expressions "maximum possible" and "minimum possible"). Lavrov contested the validity of the formula, saying that it did not deal with the actual facts of evolution; it was negative; it merely prescribed what history ought not to have been. Later critics, adherents as well as opponents of Mikhailovsky, have refused to accept the formula. Mikhailovsky himself seems to have been aware of its vagueness, for he frequently returns to the subject with elucidations and amplifications. Interesting is Mikhailovsky's relationship to Durkheim, who, following Comte, regards the modern division of labor as the most important factor in recent history and as the foundation of social solidarity. The possibility of this sociological conception and valuation of the division of labor compelled Mikhailovsky to revise and supplement his formula. Durkheim's *De la Division du Travail social* was published in 1893. Criticizing the work in 1897, Mikhailovsky wrote, in definite opposition to Durkheim, that the social division of labor must be conceived as involving class differences and class contrasts. But it is open to question whether the emendation can save the formula or free it from ambiguity.

Notes

1. Mikhailovsky was born in the year 1842, in the administrative district of Kaluga. His parents were of noble birth, but not very well off. After leaving the lower gimnasija he went to the mining academy, from which he was sent down. As early as 1860 he produced an essay on Goncharov. Thenceforward, from his eighteenth year until his death in 1904, Mikhailovsky devoted himself to scientific and philosophical self-culture and to the popularization of science.

2. In a study of Bismarck (1871), Mikhailovsky, quite in Comte's manner, formulates the following aphoristic scheme: I Absolutism, Theology War, Regime of Great Landed Proprietorship; II Constitutional Monarchy, Metaphysics and Professional Dexterity, Stock Exchange, Regime of Capital; III Science, Right to Work and Duty to Work.

3. An example may make the matter clearer. Mikhailovsky holds that economically England is on a higher level than Russia, but that as type Russia is higher than Engand. When Tolstoy said that the melody, "Back to Mother Volga," was loftier than any of Beethoven's symphonies, the assertion was true of the type, not of the stage of development.

The sociological theories
of Maksim M. Kovalevsky

N. S. TIMASHEFF

I. The background of Kovalevsky's sociology

Russian sociology is perhaps the best possible illustration of the fundamental theorem of the sociology of knowledge, according to which scientific thought is looked upon as a function of the total social situation.
During the second half of the nineteenth century the upper level of Russian society was divided into two sectors: (1) the ruling bureaucracy
(supported by the majority of the gentry) and (2) the "intelligentsia,"
a social group consisting mainly of academic teachers and professional
men but also comprising substantial minorities of the groups which supported the opposite camp—there have always been "liberal bureaucrats"
and "social workers" from among the gentry. The first sector developed
a conservative ideology expressed in the well-known triad, "autocracy,
orthodoxy, and nationality," whereas the second adhered to the Western
ideologies of liberalism and socialism. The general structure of Russian
culture demanded that both sectors justify their respective positions on a
high theoretical level. The result was the rise of numerous sociological
systems, all of which had in common the bias of serving political purposes.

The rationalizations used by the conservative sector were derived from
the well-known ideology of the Slavophiles, the basic proposition of
which was that Russia was a special world completely different from that
of the West and therefore not subject to the laws of evolution working
there. The most interesting work of this trend was *Russia and Europe* by
N. Danilevsky, who formulated most of the propositions which received
world-wide attention after they had been repeated by Oswald Spengler.[1]
In our day the theory has been brilliantly revived in the works of the
so-called "Eurasians." [2]

The sociology of the intelligentsia was many-branched. It may be
divided into the following "schools": (1) the subjective school of P. L.
Lavrov (1822–1900) and N. K. Mikhailovsky (1842–1904), which anticipated the modern sociology of knowledge in that it recognized that
"there are truths which cannot be recognized before certain epochs . . . .

From Harry Elmer Barnes, ed., *Introduction to the History of Sociology* (Chicago:
University of Chicago Press, 1949), pp. 441-457.

in consequence of the subjective unpreparedness of society to understand the question in its active setting," anticipated Max Weber in his
attempts to use in sociology the concept of probability, and anticipated
Tarde's doctrine on invention and imitation when studying the role of
personality in the social process, but which made the methodological
error of considering sociology a normative science; (2) the Marxist
school, chiefly represented by the orthodox G. V. Plekhanov and the
heretic V. I. Lenin; (3) the anarchist school of Prince Peter Kropotkin;
and (4) the revolutionary school of V. M. Chernov. All the schools had
in common, first, the acceptance of the idea of unilateral progress and,
second, the idea that sociology should serve as a guide in the struggle for
progress to be carried on against bureaucracy and the conservative
groups supporting it. Outside of these subdivisions but within the general
school of progress was Professor N. I. Kareev (1850–1931), the only
academic person in the movement, who was the first to publish a Russian
text on sociology (1897), which was chiefly an able discussion of the
sociological theories of the time.

The acuteness of the conflict between the bureaucracy and the intelligentsia inhibited the rise in Russia of a purely scientific sociology but
did not make it impossible. The honor of having overcome the political
bias belongs to M. M. Kovalevsky, who was the greatest Russian sociologist of the pre-war period. He completely broke with the Russian
tradition and built up his sociological system not on political considerations but on a thorough study of the history of social, political, legal,
and economic institutions. The breach with the tradition was so radical
that in his works he never mentioned Russian sociologists.[3]

II. Kovalevsky's life and writings

M. M. Kovalevsky was born August 27, 1851, in Kharkov, in the
Ukraine, the son of a rich landowner. After having graduated from one
of the high schools of Kharkov (1863) and from the law faculty of the
University of Kharkov (1873), he spent about three years in western
Europe: in Berlin where he studied with Rudolf Gneist, Heinrich
Brunner, and Adolf Wagner; in Paris; and in London, where he made
the acquaintance of Sir Henry Maine (whom he called his teacher),
Herbert Spencer, and Karl Marx. After having returned to Russia, he
obtained his Master's degree (1877) and was immediately appointed
professor at the University of Moscow; three years later he acquired his
Doctor's degree.[4]

During his years of study outside Russia, Kovalevsky published his
first work. It concerned the *Dissolution of Agrarian Communities in the*

Canton of Vaud (1876).[5] The topic was symptomatic of the scientific preoccupation of young Kovalevsky, which had been the early history of institutions. His second work was devoted to the *Administration and Judicial Organization of English Counties up to the Death of Edward III* (1877); the next entitled, *Agrarian Communities* (1879), studied the formation and dissolution of that form of land tenure in colonial lands; the next covered *The Social Organization of England in the Later Middle Ages* (1880).

A booklet on the *Comparative Historical Method in Jurisprudence* (1880) led to one of Kovalevsky's most important contributions to the social sciences. In the hope of directly observing vestiges of early "Aryan" law, he spent three summers in the high valleys of the Caucasus; the result was three books: *Modern Custom and Ancient Law* (1886);[6] *Primitive Law* (1886); and *Law and Custom in the Caucasus* (1890).

Before the last-mentioned book was published, a catastrophe interrupted Kovalevsky's academic activity in Russia. Though a liberal (a typical member of the intelligentsia), he never was a revolutionary. His teaching on constitutional law in the university of Moscow was based on the idea of the similarity of political development in all countries and implied the assumption that, in his opinion, a constitutional reform in Russia was unavoidable. This could not be tolerated by the reactionary Ministry of Education of that time,[7] and Kovalevsky was suddenly dismissed from the university.

Because Kovalevsky was rich and independent and had never married, he was unhampered in immediately deciding to leave Russia and to continue his scientific activity in liberal surroundings. The decision was the easier for him as he spoke English, French, German, and Italian fluently. He first delivered a series of lectures in Stockholm[8] and then settled in France. He acquired a beautiful estate in Beaulieu on the shore of the Mediterranean and gradually collected a private library of fifty thousand volumes. There he spent about fifteen years, frequently leaving to lecture as a visiting professor (in Brussels, Oxford, and other places) or as a member of the Paris School of Social Sciences, which he created in 1900, or to study various societies and cultures. He twice visited the United States. He became vice-president of the International Sociological Institute in 1895 and its president in 1907 (after his return to Russia) and frequently contributed to the *Revue internationale de Sociologie*.

The French years were the most productive period in Kovalevsky's life. Three monumental works were written: *The Economic Growth of Europe up to the Rise of Capitalism,*[9] *The Origin of Modern Democracy,*[10] and *From Immediate to Representative Democracy.*[11]

During the same period he published several works in which he described Russian institutions for the use of non-Russian scientists. Two of these were *Le Régime économique de la Russie* (1898) and *Russian Political Institutions* (1902).

The great political changes which occurred in Russia in 1904-1906 permitted Kovalevsky to return to his fatherland and there to resume his academic activity. He became a professor at the University of St. Petersburg and in the Department of Economics of the Polytechnic Institute of the same city. At about the same time, Professor Bekhterev founded in St. Petersburg the "Psycho-neurological Institute" and created there a chair of sociology, the first in Russia. He offered it to Kovalevsky, who gladly accepted.

The last period of his academic and scientific activity was characterized by very much lecturing and much nonacademic activity. In 1906 he was elected member of the first Duma from his native city of Kharkov; he was defeated in the elections to the second Duma but was almost immediately elected one of the six representatives of Russian universities to the State Council (the upper chamber of Russia). He devoted much time and energy to legislative activity. At the same time he was president of numerous scientific and charitable institutions.

However, Kovalevsky did not abandon scientific activity. During the last period of his life his interest was concentrated on sociology. This was a logical crowning of a scientific life devoted mainly to the study of correlations between different aspects of social life in their historical development. In 1905 he published a book entitled *Contemporary Sociologists,* a fine review of the sociological theories of his time and, in addition to this, a brilliant criticism of all kinds of monism in sociology. In 1910 he published two volumes of *Sociology* (which were to be followed by others), the first being a discussion of the scope and methods of sociology and of its relation to the special social sciences, and the second, a monograph on *Genetic Sociology*. In 1913 he started editing (in cooperation with P. A. Sorokin and others) a series of monographs on "New Ideas in Sociology," to which he made several contributions.[12]

In the summer of 1914 Kovalevsky was living in Karlsbad, then in Austria, for treatment of heart disease. When the war broke out, he was considered a civil prisoner. His liberation was due only to the intervention of influential friends (among them, President Woodrow Wilson), but his health was definitely broken, and he died on March 23, 1916. His funeral was a national event, for Russia was aware that she had lost one of her greatest men of science. A symposium *In Memoriam of M. M. Kovalevsky* appeared in the next year with contributions by outstanding social scientists.

III. The scope and tasks of sociology

When Kovalevsky began his scientific activity, sociology was dominated by the theory of unilinear evolution and inevitable progress. During his lifetime the theory was gradually undermined and restated in new forms; Kovalevsky was not only aware of this change but contributed largely to it. However, he never was able to reject completely this theory, which was deeply ingrained in his mind; hence, there is a certain duality in his sociological ideas. On the one hand, he explained by "the unfortunate dominance of the organic theory of society" the tendency of his contemporaries to speak of the unilinear evolution as taking place in a similar way among all peoples and reproducing the different stages in the evolution of an organism; but, at the same time, he said that the basic law of sociology was that of progress[13] and that the similarities so frequently appearing between societies which did not interact or possess common ancestors could be explained only by the principle of the "unity of history," meaning that the evolution of humanity was progressive.[14] He frequently returned to this idea: "The similarity of economic conditions, the similarity of legal relations (closely related to the former), the similarity in the level of knowledge formed the cause of the fact that people of different races and belonging to different epochs began their development from identical stages." [15] This similarity continued in later stages: "Structures and institutions belonging to the *gens* structure, to the tribal duchy, to the estate monarchy can be discovered in the history of people who have nothing in common with each other and who never imitated each other. If the level of knowledge was similar, similar or identical legends evolved." [16]

Kovalevsky's vacillation concerning the very nature of the phenomena to be studied by sociology was reflected in his ideas concerning the scope and the purpose of sociology. In his earlier works he accepted Comte's definition, according to which sociology is the science of social order and of social progress.[17] Toward the end of his life, under the influence of American sociology,[18] Kovalevsky changed his mind and defined sociology as the "science of social organization and social change." It is impossible to assert," he said, "that evolution always tends to the cure of social diseases and to the increase of public welfare; it is also difficult to assume that every social organization is order; there is no order in Czarist Russia."[19]

Consequently, he assigned to sociology the task of studying the collective mentality of social groups in close connection with their organization and their evolution. Sociology must perform this task by abstracting trends from the mass of concrete facts and pointing out the general tendency; in this way it can discover the causes of social stability and social change.[20]

When sociology is assigned such tasks, a certain difficulty arises concerning the delimitation between its field and that of the special social sciences. Kovalevsky was aware of the difficulty and solved the problem in the following way: Sociology, as a generalizing science, cannot borrow its premises from the special social sciences; it has to elaborate them independently, taking into consideration the variability of human needs and sentiments distributed among the realms of religion, law, economics, politics, aesthetics, etc.[21] The special social sciences, although furnishing sociology with materials for its synthesis, must, at the same time, base their empirical generalizations upon the general laws of coexistence and development which sociology is called upon to establish.[22]

In Kovalevsky's opinion, sociology is related not only to the descriptive social sciences but also to the science of social policy.[23] Only sociology, said he, is able to discover all the causes on which depend the progress of societies and their interrelation.[24] Only sociology is able to teach us the lesson that order is impossible without progress and that progress consists of gradual changes in the social and economic structure, in close connection with the accumulation of knowledge and with the growth of population.[25] Only sociology may yield an objective criterion for estimating the value of positive law.[26]

IV. The methodology to be employed in studying social change

Kovalevsky's interest was concentrated on the study of social change. Whereas his great works on the history of economic, political, and legal institutions concerned later stages of development, the quest for the origin of society was never absent from his mind, as testified by numerous early essays, and it became his major preoccupation during the later years when he wrote his sociological works. This subject matter he called "social embryology," [27] or "genetic sociology"—the title of the second volume of his *Sociology*.

Kovalevsky's methods of studying social change (in regard to earlier and later stages) naturally depended on his fundamental hypothesis. In his opinion it is for genetic sociology to establish, first, the several stages of social evolution and, second, the laws governing it. Laws were understood by him as "necessary correlations of phenomena"; [28] they had to reflect the variability of the social nature of man, independent of climate or race.

The laws of this evolution can be discovered by the comparison of a number of parallel evolutions. The simple juxtaposition of phenomena is insufficient, and the use of the comparative historical method is necessary.[29] Being master of that method, Kovalevsky, in his sociological constructions, used materials acquired in his studies of the history of institutions and enlarged the perspective by adding data obtained through ethnology and the study of animal societies. Gradually he elaborated a methodology which may be formulated as follows:

1. Comparative ethnology and the comparative history of institutions must deal only with facts which had been correlated with all the past and present of the peoples among whom they occur, especially with their collective mentality.[30] "It is not sufficient," he said, "to present a large number of data which seem to confirm a hypothesis; it is necessary to show that the phenomenon, the existence of which is hypothetically asserted, was closely connected with the bulk of conditions given on a particular stage of social evolution."

2. Facts analyzed in this way must be studied in respect to their nature; in other words, it should be established whether, in the given stage of evolution, the fact belongs to the existing social structure or is a survival from the past, or perhaps, the germ of future development.[31]

3. However, the similarity of facts may be based on common descent or on imitation.[32] Therefore, before any conclusion is made regarding natural uniformities, these possibilities must be analyzed.

4. The arrangement of similar facts into systems corresponding to the stages of evolution presupposes the knowledge of these stages. Here arises the problem of the relative primitiveness of social forms. The difficulty is the greater as, according to Kovalevsky, it is impossible to see in contemporary savages a picture of the earliest stages of the evolution of historical people. One of the symptoms of primitiveness is analogy with the forms of social life among higher animals.[33] However, there is no human tribe which would be actually analogous to animal societies, for each possesses at least the germs of religion and government.[34] Therefore, those human societies must be considered the most primitive which know no limitation of sexual intercourse except the prohibition of intercourse with the mother; essential also is the recognized connection of the child with the mother only.[35]

5. Another criterion of primitiveness may be found by functional analysis: We cannot consider as primitive an institution which is incompatible with a low mental level and primitive material conditions.[36]

6. But the best guide is the principle of survival. Ethnographic material may yield results concerning the remote past only if there is reason to believe that it comprises survivals;[37] the same is correct in regard to early law.[38]

As has already been mentioned, the belief in the survival method induced Kovalevsky to spend three summers in the Caucasus. He explained his expectations in the following words: "Svanets and Ossets have lived for centuries in high mountains and have not been subjected to foreign influences; therefore, they might have preserved numerous survivals of early institutions." The study did not yield the expected results. Kovalevsky recognized his partial failure: "Not in respect to all problems did the law of the Ossets yield the expected answers. In many cases it proved to lack the intermediary links [for which he was looking], and therefore it frequently had to be interpreted by using data concerning other Aryan peoples." [39] However, he found what he especially wanted: vestiges of the matrilinear family; and this permitted him to make, much later on, the following conclusion: "Semites, Aryans, Polynesians, and American Indians have known the matrilinear family, the survivals of which have been preserved in ancient law and in the folklore." [40]

7. However, this result was relevant for genetic sociology only, because it was possible to establish many shifts from the matrilinear to the patrilinear family, whereas cases of the opposite development were unknown.[41] An important methodological rule is implied in this statement, a rule involving the use in ethnology of the statistical method, for which, in general, Kovalevsky had no great respect.[42]

8. Great caution is necessary, according to Kovalevsky, in all work with ethnological and comparative historical material. The greatest danger is that of groundless generalization. Thus, for instance, said Kovalevsky, the tendency to see in totemism a common stage of human evolution is refuted by the fact that no vestiges of it can be found in Russia.[43] Another danger is that of interpretation based on pre-established patterns of thought. Kovalevsky gave an illustration of this from personal experience:

> During my travels in the mountains of the Caucasus I frequently saw Christian chapels surrounded by high trees. Svanets have lost almost every recollection of having been Christians; the belief is vivid among them that woods are inhabited by spirits ready to punish anyone entering them. I immediately formulated the hypothesis that I had discovered a survival of ancestor worship in combination with the worship of trees. Fortunately, I did not publish anything on this question.

Further investigation showed that the Svanets had allowed trees to grow around the chapels in order to prevent the plundering of ikons and other valuable objects. The case of Svanet chapels was explained by accidental causes, irrelevant for general conclusions.[44]

9. Finally, Kovalevsky never denied the existence of variations. But in one of his earliest works[45] he stated that the study of the causes of variations must be considered a task for later generations of sociologists, to be carried out after the definite establishment of similarities and their reduction to one general law.

V. The pattern and nature of social evolution

Using the methods described, Kovalevsky formulated the following propositions concerning the stages of social evolution:[46] The most primitive form of social organization is the horde within which the matrilineal family evolves. The next stage (never reached by many tribes) was that of the gens, which is the primitive horde transformed by means of exogamy, taboo, and the prohibition of blood feud. The only mental link was the worship of common ancestors. The further development was closely related with the shift from the nomadic manner of life to a settled one; the clan became divided into "big families" (cognatic; later on, also agnatic), and these evolved, as the result of internal discord and of the growth of the population, into "small families." On the other hand, the gens was replaced by a more complicated structure which might be called the "feudal order." This has existed among nations widely distributed through time and space (western Europe, Byzantium, Russia, Moslem peoples, Japan): the possession of land and public service unified society as strongly as kinship. The shift from the feudal to the democratic order is the last stage of evolution which we know.[47] During this stage progress is manifested by the shift from inequality to equality and from governmental interference to private and collective initiative.[48]

The evolution from one stage to another is not, in Kovalevsky's opinion, a process imposed on men by destiny (to use a Spenglerian term) represented by any single factor, be it race, economic necessity, or anything else. Kovalevsky's lifetime was characterized by the dominance of monistic theories in sociology; but, having accepted Comte's doctrine about the interdependence of factors, he did his best to combat these theories and to formulate a pluralistic theory of social causation. "To accept the hypothesis of economic monism," he said, "or the opposite hypothesis of Stein and Gneist[49] would be admissible only if they were based, not on the study of one or another nation, but on the study of the total development of mankind; up to the present time this has not been done."[50] Despite his predilection for the study of the demographic factor (cf. below), he also combated demographic monism. When A. Coste explained the total processes of evolution merely by the growth of population, he was, in Kovalevsky's mind, guilty of the same onesidedness as the Marxists.[51]

Kovalevsky's personal views on the subject have been expressed in two frequently quoted passages:

Sociology will gain much if the attempt to find a first cause is eliminated from the number of its immediate problems and if it limits itself, in accordance with the complexity of social phenomena, to showing the simultaneous and parallel action and reaction of many causes.[52]

To talk about a central fact which would determine all others, is to me the same as to talk about the drops of water of a river which by their movement condition its current. I think that in the future the problem will not be solved, but simply suppressed. I explain the importance attributed to the problem in modern sociology by the desire to find a way out of the chaos of innumerable actions and reactions of which the social process consists.[53]

Kovalevsky's deep insight into the mutual interdependence of factors was largely based on his historical monographs, in which just this question was discussed. The central thesis of the *Economic Growth of Europe* was the connection between the growth of the population and the forms of economic life. The work entitled *From Immediate to Representative Democracy* was devoted to the study of the correlation between the political structure and the political ideals. The *Origin of Modern Democracy* stressed the interdependence between the economic structure, the political structure, and the political doctrine. In a number of cases Kovalevsky discussed the principle of interdependence in regard to particular factors. Thus, for instance, he denied that political and legal institutions would be more closely related to economic phenomena than to the accumulation of knowledge.[54] It is not always, said he, the richest man who becomes the boss; in many cases it is the strongest or the wisest.[55] It would be a great mistake to ignore the influence of the conflict of tribes and nations (political factor) on the creation of estates or classes, independent of the division of labor and the accumulation of riches (economic factor).[56]

Very stimulating was Kovalevsky's analysis of the problem of the apparent dominance of different factors in different epochs. All human needs, said he, are in constant interaction, which sometimes becomes partial antagonism. Temporarily, one or another need may become dominant.[57] In the times of Alexander of Macedonia, of the invasions of barbarians, of Napoleon, the political factor dominated; in the period of the struggle of the popes and the emperors or of the Reformation, as well as in certain periods of Chinese history, the religious factor played the major part; during the period of the shift from servitude to free labor the economic factor was of chief importance. However, deeper analysis shows that always every aspect of social life was subjected to important changes, naturally in close connection with changes in the dominant factor. The social process never stops, though at some times it is more, and at others less, apparent.[58]

The acceptance of the principle of plural causation creates well-known difficulties. Kovalevsky solved the problem by using patterns which might be considered analogous to those of "indeterminate equations": every situation is submitted to simultaneous influences in various directions and may evolve not in one, but in many, ways, though not at random: "It is impossible to explain all social phenomena," said he, "by applying abstract laws. In every concrete *milieu* these laws act simultaneously with a number of particular causes which partly accelerate, but partly inhibit, their influences." [59] Applying these general ideas to one of his favorite objects of study—the evolution of agrarian communities under the influence of the growth of population—he said:

> A social event may be the result of the summation or the subtraction of causes. Assume that the growth of population forces people to shift from the three-crop rotation to more complicated systems of agriculture. To do so men must abolish the system of hereditary leases and the scattering of allotments. What will be the actual course of events? Will not one factor check another? . . . We have no possibility of determining the magnitude of the convergent or divergent causes and deciding whether their action should be calculated in terms of arithmetic or geometric proportion.[60]

VI. The study of population and population changes

The full understanding of the plural character of social causation did not prevent Kovalevsky from choosing one such cause for close study. This was that of the growth of population and of its density, which seemed to him to give the most constant impulse to economic development. He wrote:

> In my Brussels lectures on the history of the economic development of Europe, as well as in my large work on the same subject, I have attempted to determine the influence of the density of population on the changes in the organization of production and exchange and on the structure of property. This factor has been responsible for the transition from a stage of hunters and fishermen to one of agriculture, and from a primitive system of agriculture to a more intensive one, with corresponding changes in the system of land ownership and land pos-

session. . . . The substitution of a manufacturing system of production in industry for a domestic one is due to the same factor. . . . Thus, the simple fact of the growth of population called forth a division of labor, a social differentiation into castes, orders and classes, and the evolution of the technique of production, as well as that of the economic regime.[61]

Illustrating this basic proposition, he showed that even in the thirteenth century the process of the emancipation of serfs had substantially advanced. But the Black Death of 1348 reduced the population by half, and the resultant rise in the cost of labor caused a legislative check on the processes of emancipation.[62] He maintained that the economic development of colonial lands also largely depended on the demographic factor:

> The economic process which had started in the mother countries continued in the colonies at a much slower rate, however, because of the lesser density of population and of the additional action of two secondary causes: (1) the necessity of using the labor forces of culturally backward races, and (2) the necessity of spending a part of the social forces for aggressive or defensive operations.[63]

However, Kovalevsky never exaggerated the role of the demographic factor and was never guilty of demographic monism.[64] In the first place, he always asserted that only economic evolution was directly influenced by the demographic factor, and this especially in the earlier stages: "Is it advisable," he asked, "to go further and to ascribe changes in state and church, the accumulation of technical knowledge, perhaps also of theoretical ideas, to the influence of the same factor? I do not think so." [65]

Second, he always stressed the fact that the demographic factor never worked alone. The growth of population (primarily a biological factor) increases or decreases its influence on social evolution in relation to numerous purely social causes: devastating wars, progress or regression in social hygiene, birth control (based on religious or moral principles or on individual or class egoism).[66] Incidentally, he mentioned the disturbances created by the settlement of newcomers (peaceful or as result of wars)[67] and by the interference of governments (permission or restriction of emigration).[68]

VII. Factors in social change

"Factors" were never considered by Kovalevsky as directly compelling men to act in a specific way. He elaborated a doctrine of the mechanism of social change in which the role of personality was stressed.[69] Thus, for instance, "when it appears that there is scarcity in food, the mind looks for a solution of the problem and finds it either in emigration, or in the domestication of animals, or in the first attempts to sow nourishing plants." [70] He explains in a similar manner the rise of political leadership (the creation of the political factor): "The necessity of making adjustment to new situations demands the use of additional psychic energy. In such circumstances actions of persons who possess initiative and creative spirit become necessary, whereas the masses are unable to do anything but submit to the leadership of the former." [71]

The process of social change, in Kovalevsky's opinion, may be described in two closely related ways: First, it is a sequence of inventions, imitations, and adjustments (secondary inventions); second, it is a gradual rise and development of rules of behavior.[72] Both aspects are related to each other as follows:

> Personal invention and imitation result in changes in custom and hence in law. In every legal institution it is possible to distinguish both elements. Thus, for instance, the private appropriation of land first appears as a personal invention; imitation and adjustment transform it into the institution of private property.[73]
>
> For a long time new rules lack any sanction and remain on the level of morals. . . . They may enter into conflicts with the existing legal order, but this does not prevent them from gradually becoming recognized in judicial decisions and, later on, being included in the system of legal rules.[74]

These ideas were mainly based on the direct observation of social and legal institutions in the Caucasus. This study, by the way, induced Kovalevsky to reject one of the fundamental ideas of the historical school, that of the superiority of custom in building legal codes: "Custom," says Kovalevsky, "frequently is the result of religious fanaticism, of violence and arbitrariness; frequently it is not the source of later law, but, on the contrary, the reflection of earlier law which ceased to comply with the exigencies of life." [75]

VIII. Kovalevsky's influence on social science

In an article devoted to the memory of Kovalevsky, René Worms wrote: "For French and English science he was the representative of the Russian social science, whereas everybody in Russia recognized that nobody knew better than he did the achievements of Western science. Thus he was a link between two worlds, Western Europe and Russia."

However, it would be difficult to trace his direct influence on Western science. Coste recognized his indebtedness to Kovalevsky for the understanding of the role of the demographic factor. Loria, who, for a certain time, stressed this factor in his works, disputed Kovalevsky's priority. Orthodox Marxists assailed those statements of Kovalevsky in which he denied the all-determining role of the economic factor.

In Russia, Kovalevsky was given the satisfaction of seeing the rise of a younger generation of sociologists directly influenced by him. But he died only eighteen months before the breach of continuity in Russian social science, which was due to the ascent to power of the Communists, which meant the establishment of the monopoly of Marxism. Most of his pupils were given no opportunity to display their talents and to continue his work. One of the most brilliant, N. D. Kondratiev, after a short period of leadership in Russian rural sociology, suddenly disappeared. The most prominent of them was permitted to escape and to become an outstanding American sociologist; this is P. A. Sorokin.[76]

However, theoretical systems exist independently of personalities. What has been the destiny of that of M. M. Kovalevsky?

One of its elements, the doctrine of the unilinear evolution toward progress, has been definitely abandoned. But it has to be remembered that Kovalevsky accepted it only with great reservations and modifications, and his teaching about the possible causes of cultural similarities is just the one that dominates social science in our day, perhaps with the addition of the principle of "the limitation of possibilities."

The other element for which he persistently fought and which, in his lifetime, was accepted only by an insignificant minority has gained a decisive victory; this is the idea of the plurality of social causation or of the interdependence of factors. Many of Kovalevsky's statements could be subscribed to by both followers of Pareto and modern functionalists. The idea certainly forms the foundation of the sociological doctrine of Sorokin.

Kovalevsky never asserted that he had been original on that subject; he recognized his indebtedness to Comte and to his predecessors. His greatest merit has been that of having preserved a sound idea through an age characterized by its almost wholesale rejection and of having accumulated overwhelming evidence in its favor.

In relation to social science as a whole, one may say that Kovalevsky's outstanding contribution was to introduce historical and anthropological concepts and data into sociology and to impress upon historians the importance of reckoning with sociological and anthropological materials. Among social scientists in other countries, those whose work and interests most resemble those of Kovalevsky have been Max and Alfred Weber in Germany, L. T. Hobhouse in England, and Alexander Goldenweiser, James T. Shotwell, Harry Elmer Barnes, and Hutton Webster in the United States.

Notes

1. As H. E. Barnes and H. Becker correctly say, "the parallelism is too close to be accidental" (*Social Thought from Lore to Science* [Boston, 1938], II, 1032-1033).

2. Cf. my article, "Die politische Lehre der Eurasier, *Zeitschrift für Politik*, XVIII (1929), 558-612.

3. This fact was pointed out, with some bitterness, by N. I. Kareev in his contribution to the symposium *In Memoriam of M. M. Kovalevsky* (Petrograd, 1917).

4. Up to the Communist Revolution, Russia adhered to the French system of academic degrees. A Master's degree was granted after the publication of at least one original monograph and a public disputation before the Faculty; the Doctor's degree was granted after the publication of a second (usually, larger) work and a similar disputation.

5. A German translation appeared the next year in Zurich.

6. French translation in 1893; abridged English translation in 1891.

7. The last two decades of the nineteenth century form a kind of "Dark Age" in the history of Russian education.

8. They were published in French under the following title: *Tableau de l'Origine de la Famille et de la Propriété* (1890); Russian translation (1891); Spanish translation (1913).

9. Three volumes (Moscow, 1898-1903). An enlarged German edition was published in seven volumes, (1901-1914).

10. Four volumes, published in Russian (1895-1897); large parts have been translated into French and published under different titles.

11. Three volumes in Russian, published in 1906.

12. A complete bibliography of the works of Kovalevsky, comprising eleven pages, is contained in the symposium, *In Memoriam*.

13. *Sociology,* pp. 261, 80.

14. *Contemporary Sociologists,* pp. 10-14.

15. *Sociology,* p. 35.

16. *Ibid.,* pp. 33-35.

17. Maintained in *Contemporary Sociologists,* p. 286.

18. With direct reference to an article "Sociology: Its Problems and Its Relations" by Charles Ellwood, *American Journal of Sociology*, XIII (1907), 300.

19. Kovalevsky obviously had in mind order in the "existential," not in the "procedural," meaning.

20. *Sociology,* p. 9.

21. *Contemporary Sociologists,* p. 286.

22. *Sociology,* p. 30.

23. The necessity of creating this science of social policy was vigorously stressed by Kovalevsky's famous contemporary, L. Petrazycki (ch. H. Babb, "Petrazhitsky's Science of Legal Policy," *Boston University Law Review*, XVII [1937], 793 ff.).

24. *Sociology,* p. 14.

25. *Ibid.,* p. 59.

26. *Ibid.,* p. 68.

27. *Ibid,* p. 84.

28. *Ibid.,* p. 33.

29. Many of Kovalevsky's contemporaries considered that method *the* method of sociology. Thus, for instance, Sir P. Vinogradov identified the sociology of law and the comparative history of law (cf. his article on "Comparative Jurisprudence" in the *Encyclopaedia Britannica* [11th ed.], Vol. XV).

30. *Sociology*, pp. 104-105.

31. *Ibid.*

32. *Ibid.*, pp. 36, 80.

33. *Genetic Sociology*, p. 18. The existence of such analogies was illustrated by the fact that the relation of hunters to the occupied territory is almost the same as that of a herd of animals or a flock of birds (*ibid.*, p. 125).

34. *Sociology*, p. 85.

35. *Genetic Sociology*, pp. 51, 76.

36. *Ibid.*, p. 19.

37. *Ibid.*, p. 2.

38. *Ibid.*, p. 17.

39. *Modern Custom and Ancient Law*, pp. iv and vi.

40. *Genetic Sociology*, p. 90.

41. *Ibid.*, p. 63.

42. *Sociology*, p. 90.

43. *Ibid.*, pp. 87-89.

44. *Genetic Sociology*, pp. 6-7.

45. *On the Comparative Historical Method in Jurisprudence* (1880). He repeated this statement in *Sociology*, p. 104.

46. In the monograph on the *Primitive Law;* repeated in *Genetic Sociology,* pp. 104 ff.

47. *Sociology*, pp. 44-50.

48. *Ibid.*, p. 58.

49. Both Stein and Gneist considered basic the political factor.

50. *Contemporary Sociologists*, p. 240.

51. *Ibid.*, p. 247.

52. *Ibid.*, chap. xiv.

53. *Ibid.*, chap. viii.

54. *Sociology*, p. 114.

55. *Ibid.*, pp. 102-103.

56. *Genetic Sociology*, p. 19.

57. *Contemporary Sociologists*, p. 286.

58. *Ibid.*, chap. xlv.

59. *Ibid.*, p. 59.

60. *Ibid.*, chap. xl.

61. *Ibid.*, pp. 200-201.

62. *The Economic Growth of Europe*, Vol. II, chaps. x, xiv, xv.

63. *Contemporary Sociologists*, p. 268.

64. In one of his later works he denied the honor of being the originator of the demographic school in sociology: according to him, Mercantilists, Physiocrats, and Comte had already had a full understanding of the importance of the density of population. Being accused by Marxists of having first recognized and then denied the determinant role of the demographic factor, he explained that the one-sidedness of his treatise on the *Economic Growth of Europe* had been voluntary (*Contemporary Sociologists*, p. 291). As explained by Sorokin, in that treatise the demographic factor was already treated as an "independent variable" (methodological procedure), not as "causa efficiens" (*In Memoriam*).

65. *Contemporary Sociologists*, p. 202.

66. *Ibid.*, chap. xiii.

67. *Ibid.*, p. 168.

68. *Ibid.*, p. 246.

69. Perhaps under the influence of the Russian school of sociology.

70. *Sociology*, p. 300.

71. *Genetic Sociology*, pp. 200, 215, with reference to an article by E. Mumford, "The Origin of Leadership," *American Journal of Sociology*, XII (1906), 216 ff.

72. *Contemporary Sociologists*, pp. 138-139.

73. *Sociology*, pp. 63-68.

74. *Contemporary Sociologists*, pp. 138-139.

75. In his work, *Modern Custom and Ancient Law*, Kovalevsky gave a detailed description of harmful customs. For a few illustrations cf. my *Introduction to the Sociology of Law* (Cambridge, Mass., 1939), p. 128.

76. Among other pupils of Kovalevsky should be mentioned E. Kulischer, also a political emigrant, who published (in German) a good book, A. and E. Kulischer, *Kriege- und Wanderzüge* (Berlin, 1932)

Perspectives on Lenin's organizational theory

SHELDON S. WOLIN

In the nineteenth century the anti-political impulses nurtured by classical liberalism took on a depth and pervasiveness unmatched in previous centuries. "The irksome situation" of today, Proudhon declared, was due to *"une certaine maladie de l'opinion . . . qu'Aristote . . . a nommé* POLITIQUE." The abolition of the political was proclaimed by almost every important thinker, and most projects for a future society excluded political activity from the routine of daily life. For, as Marx put it, "only *political superstition* believes at the present time that civil life must be held together by the State, when in reality the State is held together by civil life." Nor was this anti-political complex the private possession of any particular school. It was manifest in Saint-Simon, the Utopians, Proudhon, Comte, Durkheim, the Fabians, and the managerialists.

Now, as we have noted in previous chapters, the anti-political impulse was an old one, with roots deep in the very beginnings of political speculation. Consequently, our concern is not to re-emphasize old animosities but to isolate the peculiar manifestations of anti-politicism in the recent age and, more particularly, to indicate the unique substitutes that have been offered. Our inquiry, in short, is directed at the sublimation rather than at the elimination of the political.

The starting point of the nineteenth century was one which had been prepared by classical liberalism, the antagonism between "state" and "society," between institutions, authorities, and relationships that men believed to be political and the relationships of a social, economic, and cultural sort that men believed to be "private" or "outside" politics. In Proudhon's words:

From Sheldon S. Wolin, *Politics and Vision: Continuities and Innovations in Western Political Thought* (Boston: Little, Brown and Company, 1960), pp. 414-429. Extensive footnotes to this selection have been omitted.

We must understand that outside the sphere of parliamentarism, as sterile as it is absorbing, there is another field incomparably vaster, in which our destiny is worked out; that beyond these political phantoms, whose forms capture our imagination, there are the phenomena of social economy, which, by their harmony or discord, produce all the good and ill of society.

As the writers of the century reflected on the past, they gradually concluded that the eighteenth century, or, more accurately, 1789, marked the turning point to a future rid of the suffocating atmosphere of politics. The great revolution came to symbolize the time when the political order had mustered its failing forces for a last-ditch attempt to assert its general responsibility for the well-being of society. Proudhon claimed that the unintended result of the French Revolution had been to sharpen the identity of two incompatible entities, society and government. The latter, he asserted, was "a factitious order," out of harmony with the principles of "a natural order conceived in accordance with science and labor." The task allotted to the nineteenth-century revolution was to reverse and destroy the political tendencies nourished by 1789, but to do so with the *caveat* that "no question of touching society itself" should be entertained. Society was sacrosanct, "a superior being, endowed with independent life, and in consequence remote from any idea on our part to reconstruct it arbitrarily." "From the political order," Proudhon pleaded, "let us pass to the economic order."

By mid-century, however, the tone alters somewhat: political intervention into the affairs of society was not really dangerous, as Saint-Simon and the Utopian Socialists had believed, but merely trivial in its effects. Reality was socio-economic in nature; political action could not appreciably modify the fundamental character of reality, nor could political theory truly understand it. As Marx declared:

> *Political* thought is really *political* thought in the sense that the thinking takes place within the framework of politics. The clearer and more vigorous political thought is, the *less* it is able to grasp the nature of social evils.

Among later and less revolutionary writers than Marx there was the same belief in the ultimate futility of politics. At its very worst, they held, political action might pervert human affairs; at its best, it could only register social reality, but in no sense could political action supply a creative direction. Governments may crush an individual, Durkheim asserted, "but against the social condition (*état*) itself, against the structure of society, they are relatively powerless." Political action, he continued, operates from a point far too remote to penetrate the souls of the citizens and employs methods far too crude to be able to impose uniform regulations "against the nature of things."

To the writers of the late nineteenth century, as well as to their more recent successors, society presented a bafflingly complex structure held together by the cooperative efforts of millions of anonymous persons. This was the theme of Durkheim's famous concept of the division of labor, of Proudhon's idea of social solidarity, of Marx's vision of the future society. The common belief of all of these writers was that social cooperation stood as the complete antithesis to politics. Proudhon spoke for the age when he wrote that *"le dernier mot"* of politics is *"la* FORCE." The modern managerialist is equally emphatic: ". . . the political sphere deals with power. And power is only a tool and in itself ethically neutral. It is not a social purpose and not an ethical principle." Any political system, even democracy, declares another writer in the same tradition, is but an "artificial substitute for human cooperation," and one that "has brought all kinds of ills and abnormalities in its train." Politics has conflict as its *raison d'être,* and the politician feeds on these ills, exploits them by Machiavellian techniques, and traffics in popular passions and illusory grievances. "Political nostrums" supply no solution, because "the real problem is how to set each individual function to do its best for society."

In these criticisms the century articulated its ultimate longing: to commune with the underlying reality of society. What was truly human was the social condition. For Durkheim, for the English pluralists, such as Figgis and Cole, and for the American managerialists, as well as for psychoanalysts like Erich Fromm, the values of society were epitomized in small group relationships—just as they had been for Proudhon and the Utopian Socialists. Only private groups and occupational associations possess the power, Durkheim wrote, to "drag" isolated individuals "into the general torrent of social life." Locked deep in society was the life force for which the century searched.

At bottom the century desperately longed to transcend the political. The most powerful, and in many ways the most representative, expression of this point of view was to be found in Marx's writings. In previous ages, he wrote, political relationships had been supreme; they had pervaded all aspects of life and had overlaid the social and economic nature of groups with a political veneer. The emergence of the modern, centralized state constituted a "political revolution" which had shattered "the *political character of civil society."* What Marx meant by this paradox was that the State, on the one hand, had established a monopoly of power and authority, "a real State," by destroying the autonomy of corporations, guilds, and the feudal class structure; and, on the other hand, had drained "political" loyalties from these lesser associations and transferred them to the political order itself. In this way the political order became "a matter of general concern." But the effects of this development on society were momentous. Society was dissolved into a welter of isolated individuals, while the individual was deprived of contact with the rich life of community and association and left imprisoned in his own naked egotism. In the future the harmful effects of this "political" change would be repaired. The political dimension would be transcended; the concept of the citizen would be exchanged for that of the human person; the individual would be released from his artificially created status as a political animal and restored to his natural status of a social animal:

> The social life from which the worker is *shut out* is a social life very different in kind and extent from that of the *political* sphere. The social life . . . is *life itself,* physical and cultural life, human morality, human activity, human enjoyment, real *human* existence. Human life is the *true social life* of man. As the irremediable exclusion from this life is much more complete, more unbearable, dreadful and contradictory, than the exclusion from political life, so is the ending of this exclusion . . . more fundamental, as *man* is more fundamental than the *citizen, human life* more than *political life.*

Marx's attack on the state expressed a widespread conviction of the century that unless some drastic measures were taken to halt the progressive isolation of individuals, the growing power of the state would crush what was best and most promising in the human condition. While the nineteenth-century liberals had sought to diminish the threat by installing a variety of constitutional gadgets, other writers turned toward society to find havens of refuge for the individual. The Utopians found their solution to *étatisme* in the small self-sufficient community; de Tocqueville believed that democratic societies could avoid over-centralization only if they maintained a viable system of local self-government and encouraged the growth of voluntary associations; Durkheim and the English pluralists looked to a society of nearly autonomous vocational groups to offset the thrusts of state power. Thus there was widespread agreement that social isolation was the root-cause of *étatisme* and that if it could be overcome the power of the state would dry up at its source.

It would be ungenerous to doubt the genuineness of these anxieties or to imply that the century was following a spurious lead. Our concern, however, is with the consequences of the diagnosis and the remedy. To reject the state meant denying the central referent of the political, aban-

doning a whole range of notions and the practices to which they pointed
—citizenship, obligation, general authority—without pausing to consider
that the strategy of withdrawal might further enhance state power. Moreover, to exchange society or groups for the state might turn out to be a
doubtful bargain if society should, like the state, prove unable to resist
the tide of bureaucratization. Both of these possibilities have been realized. Suspicion of the state has reduced the codes of civility to the appearance of rituals which we follow half in shame and half in
embarrassment. At the same time, the discovery that precious little in
human life is immune to bureaucratization has dispelled some of the
magic of the group. These developments provide the contemporary setting for the re-enactment of political roles and the recital of political
ideas: with the discrediting of the political order and the retreat to
society which itself manifests growing symptoms of bureaucratization, the
political has re-emerged, but disguised in the trappings of organizational
life. What has been denied to the political order has been assimilated
to the organizational order. This transferral has not been difficult, for,
as Proudhon pointed out a century ago, the identity and the legitimacy
of the political consists only in "certain signs or ornaments, and in the
performance of certain ceremonies"; hence if modern man refuses to
believe in the importance of these symbols and rituals, he is free to shift
his support to other objects. And how easy the transition is: "the Rights
of Man can be made just as safe in corporate hands as they were in
individual hands."

The political life of organizations began with the discovery that a
private organization, like the modern business corporation, displayed
most of the distinguishing marks of a political order:

> The corporation is now, essentially, a monostatist political institu-
> tion, and its directors are in the same boat with public officeholders.

It was argued that a huge aggregate, such as General Motors, a cartel
like I. G. Farben, a monopoly like Standard Oil, all wield power equal
to that of many governmental bodies. They command enormous resources, human as well as natural; their wealth often exceeds that of
many governmental jurisdictions; their actions affect the lives and welfare of countless individuals; their influence extends beyond the merely
economic sphere, penetrating legislatures, governmental agencies, and
political parties. It follows that, if these entities seem to act like political
societies, they can be studied through the categories of political science.
For example, if the corporation is a political form, it must possess
"authority" over its members. According to one popular writer, the
"authority" of the governing group of a corporation is obtained by a

process identical with that depicted by the great contract writers of political theory:

> The modern corporation is thus a *political* institution; its purpose is the creation of legitimate power in the industrial sphere. . . . The political purpose of the corporation is the creation of a legitimate social government on the basis of the original power of the individual property rights of its shareholders. The corporation is the *Contrat social* in its purest form.

In keeping with this discovery of the "political" in organizations, the concepts and notions associated with the discredited political order are salvaged for use in describing its successor. Terms like "government," "kitchen-cabinet," "final judicial function," "Supreme Court," "representative institution," "order," "trustees for the community," and "just consent of the governed" are scattered about the literature of organization.

The culmination of this trend is most clearly revealed by Selznick's recent work, *Leadership in Administration*. The social world of today, he declares, is organized around "largely self-governing" organizations of huge size. Because of the enormous resources which they command, they have an inescapable responsibility, or rather their leaders do, for the "well-being of numerous constituents." These institutions are *"public in nature,"* because they are "attached to such interests" and deal "with such problems as affect the welfare of the entire community." As befits entities which have assumed the mantle of the political, the modern business executive "becomes a statesman" and, to a large degree, his organization sheds its technical or administrative character for the higher dignity of an "institution"; that is, "a responsive, adaptive organism" well-deserving of the time-honored name of "polity." The claim to a political status resides in the fact that the modern organization is confronted by the same type of problems familiar to the life of the political order. "There is the same basic constitutional problem" of accommodating "fragmentary group interests" to "the aims of the whole"; of elaborating statesmanlike policies which will "define the ends of group existence"; of ordering internal conflicts by establishing "consent" and maintaining a "balance of power." As the profile of leadership takes full shape, we find that we have run the full cycle and are back once more with the first of political philosophers—

> creative men . . . who know how to transform a neutral body of men into a committed polity. These men are called leaders; their profession is politics

Selznick's argument, which is a highly sophisticated and literal example of what can be found among many writers, is not concerned solely to establish the political character of business organizations. Rather the more general aim is to demonstrate that the politicalness of a corporation does not come from the fact that the corporation is a business enterprise, but from the fact that it is a large and powerful organization. In other words, the organization is the dominant and ubiquitous phenomenon of society, and whether it carries the adjective "business," "government," "military," or "educational" is largely irrelevant. All organizations are inevitably "political" in character, or, conversely, what is most politically significant in the modern world is contained in organizational life.

This being the case, the question naturally arises, how do these theorists view politics? A partial answer is that they perceive political problems from an elitist position. In Selznick's words, elites are "objectively necessary" for the maintenance and development of social institutions and culture. The form of elitism expressed in this literature has certain superficial affinities with, say, Platonism: it believes that those few who have the qualifications for exercising the highest social functions should be in the positions of highest authority. Fundamentally, however, contemporary elitism is indebted to a far different and more recent conception; namely, that an elite is a group whose superiority rests on its excellence in manipulation. The *locus classicus* of this formulation was in the writings of Pareto, but it has become commonplace in a wide variety of twentieth-century theorists: in Lenin's theory of the party elites; in Nazi and Fascist ideologies; in the various theorists of managerialism; and in Mannheim's conception of the role of social scientists in the planned society. Now the crucial theme in all of these writings, and the one which supplies the dialectical counterpoint to the elitist strain, is the emergence of the "masses." The concept of the masses haunts modern political and social theory: to disenchanted liberals like Ortega y Gasset, it represented the dreaded enemy of culture; to others, like Lenin and, more particularly, Fascist and Nazi writers, the masses represented the pliable stuff of revolutionary opportunity. Although there are a wide variety of definitions of the "masses," Selznick has given one which describes fairly well what most writers have in mind: "When the normal inhibitions enforced by tradition and social structure are loosened . . . the undifferentiated mass emerges." This kind of definition sets the stage for the dramatic confrontation between the "elite" and the "mass": the elite is a sharply defined group, possessing clear qualifications and performing a vitally useful role in the social system. The concept of the elite fits naturally with a tradition of political and social theory in which hierarchy, order, and differentiation are fundamental ideas: a tradition as old as political thought itself and as recent as modern sociology. The mass, in contrast, is undifferentiated, amorphous, banal in its tastes, lacking in a defined role and conscious purpose, the unattractive deposit of an age of rapid social change, the lost social battalion without ties of communication, affection, and loyalty. "Mass connotes a 'glob of humanity,' as against the intricately related, institutionally bound groupings that form a healthy social organism." The "disease" of contemporary society is "mass behavior."

The juxtaposition of "mass" and "elite" is highly informative of the present condition of theorizing, for it discloses that contemporary theory is, in a special sense, post-Marxian, and, in terms of mood, disenchanted. History has not only been unkind, it has been positively malicious. Instead of the highly self-conscious proletariat, the proud bearers of man's historical destiny, history has given us the vulgar mass; instead of Adonis, Quasimodo. Marx had depicted the working class as disciplined, purposeful, the symbolic representative of humanity's future triumph—"philosophy can only be realized by the abolition of the proletariat, and the proletariat can only be abolished by the realization of philosophy"—as well as the symbol of humanity's past. The proletariat had suffered on the cross of history for all humanity; "its sufferings are universal"; its present misery was "not a *particular wrong* but *wrong in general"*; its future emancipation promised to be "a *total redemption of humanity."*

Now if, instead of the proletariat, history has disgorged a "glob of humanity," it is not Marx who is teacher to the new age of mass society but Lenin; it is not the prophet of proletarian victory who speaks to the contemporary condition, but the strategist who perfects the instrument of action, the elite. If it is to be the elite, rather than the proletariat, who actually lead the way, the strategy is not to smash the pseudo-proletariat or masses, but to manipulate it. It is "our duty," Lenin wrote, "to go down *lower* and *deeper,* to the real masses."

What makes Lenin a central figure for our study is that he glimpsed sooner than most writers the possibilities of organization as the action medium best suited to a mass age. Organization was to mass in Lenin's theory what idea nad been to matter in Plato's: that which imparted form to the formless. Lenin was the first to seize the implications of transferring politics, political theory, political action—all that we have subsumed under the "political"—to the plane of organization. He taught that politics and the political had meaning only within an organizational setting. Industrialism and large-scale organization did not necessarily render political things unnecessary, nor did "administration" provide a complete substitute, as Saint-Simon and others had supposed. The trick was not to destroy the political but to absorb it into organization, to create a new compound. The measure of Lenin's success is that his lessons have become the common property of the age; the irony is that his prescription for revolution has also been used to preserve giant capitalism.

The central point of Lenin's argument was the refutation of an assumption common to classical liberalism, early socialism, and Marx as well: the primordial importance of economic phenomena. While other writers, professing to follow Marx, had also expressed anxieties about the continued and stubborn vitality of capitalism, Lenin not only rendered this problem irrelevant by turning the focus of revolutionary theory upon precapitalist societies, but, above all, he taught that the greatest danger to the revolutionary movement lay in allowing the workers to become preoccupied with economic issues. If the proletariat went whoring after material class interests, its tough revolutionary temper would surely soften and victory would be lost. Self-interest was self-interest, and it no more encouraged proletarian than capitalist heroics.

Lenin proceeded to discard the eighteenth- and nineteenth-century notion that significant action meant economic action. Political action was rescued from limbo and restored to a new primacy, new because revolution was proclaimed the quintessential form of political action. "The fact that economic interests are a decisive factor *does not in the least imply* that the economic [i.e., trade union] struggle must be the main factor, for the essential and 'decisive' interests in classes can be satisfied *only* by the radical *political* changes in general." For Lenin the "political" dealt with the comprehensive, with what transcended class horizons and interests; hence the workers had to rise above economic consciousness and acquire an "all-sided political consciousness" responsive to *"all cases* of tyranny, oppression, violence, and abuse, no matter *what class* is affected." He insisted that "political activity had its logic quite apart" from either terrorism or economic struggle, and he accused his opponents of committing "the fundamental error" of believing it possible "to develop the class political consciousness of the workers *from within* the economic struggle." "True" consciousness was political rather than economic, because revolutionary overthrow constituted a basically political act with a basically political objective. The workers, therefore, had to be educated to a political consciousness, which meant, in a very ancient notion, gaining a synthetic view of the whole:

> The consciousness of the masses of the workers cannot be genuine class consciousness, unless the workers learn to observe from concrete,

and above all from topical, political facts and events, *every* other social class and all the manifestations of the intellectual, ethical and political life of these classes; unless they learn to apply practically the materialist analysis and the materialist estimate of *all* aspects of the life and activity of *all* classes, strata, and groups of the population.

Having asserted the primacy of political action, Lenin then turned to the question of how best to pursue it. His answer, as we have already stated, was organization, and it was a choice which symbolized a crucial turning point in the Western tradition. When we look back on the late nineteenth and early twentieth century from the vantage point of what we know about Lenin's thought, it is possible to see in a clearer light what the protests of writers like Nietzsche, Kierkegaard, and Sorel had meant. Kierkegaard's lonely, desperate "leap" to God, Nietzsche's solitary superman struggling against the toils of a mediocre, bourgeois world, Sorel's "myth" of the spontaneous general strike by a proletariat welded to unity only by an heroic impulse—these were all last-ditch efforts to secure some place for unorganized individual action. They were last gasps of a romanticism doomed to expire before the age of streamlined organizations and rationally efficient bureaucracies. Nor was this a protest confined to deformed theologians and syphilitic philosophers, for nowhere was the anguishing tension between the world of organization and the creative individual more clearly revealed than in the thought of Max Weber, perhaps the greatest of sociologists.

No one saw more clearly than he that bureaucracy and large-scale organization were the fundamental phenomena of modern political, social, and economic life. No one was more unstinting in admiration for the routinized rationality, the impersonal fairness, the high level of expertise exhibited by these structures. Yet there was a strong note of ambiguity and soft whispers of pathos: "the fate of our times" is that man must dwell in the "disenchantment of the world." Mystery has been banished and "the bearing of man has been disenchanted and denuded of its mystical but inwardly genuine plasticity." Yet in his famous essay, *Politics as a Vocation,* along with its clear-eyed recognition of the way bureaucracy has invaded all political realms—party, government, and legislature—Weber plaintively pleaded for a conception of political leadership cut to truly classical proportions. Weber's leader is a political hero, rising to heights of moral passion and grandeur, harried by a deep sense of responsibility. But, at bottom, he is a figure as futile and pathetic as his classical counterpart. The fate of the classical hero was that he could never overcome contingency or *fortuna;* the special irony of the modern hero is that he struggles in a world where contingency has been routed by bureaucratized procedures and nothing remains for the hero to contend against. Weber's political leader is rendered superfluous by the very bureaucratic world that Weber discovered: even charisma has been bureaucratized. We are left with the ambiguity of the political man fired by deep passion—"to be passionate, *ira et studium,* is . . . the element of the political *leader"*—but facing the impersonal world of bureaucracy which lives by the passionless principle that Weber frequently cited, *sine ira et studio,* "without scorn or bias."

For Weber there remained one sanctuary of personal action, one province where man could affirm himself in a world otherwise dominated by rationalized and highly intellectualized processes. The area of choice or fundamental values was one which, by nature, stubbornly resists scientific method and other techniques of objectivity; it was the last preserve of passion. This casts a quite different light on Weber's endlessly labored and refined distinction between the scientifically knowable realm of "facts" and the subjective, nonscientific realm of "values." The wall between the two was not erected, as Weber's interpreters have sometimes implied, simply to shield the objective sphere of science from contamination by arbitrary values and personal idiosyncrasies. It was equally the result of a desperate effort on Weber's part to secure some sphere where affirmation was possible and, most important, where bureaucratic and scientific rationality were impossible. Yet the matter did not rest there, for Weber left a final irony for personal action to contemplate: each individual bore the awful responsibility for choice at this ultimate level but each was denied anything like the scientist's sense of certainty: "the ultimately possible attitudes towards life are irreconcilable, and hence their struggle can never be brought to a final conclusion."

Nostalgias such as these had no place in Lenin's thought. The latter was mesmerized by the potentialities of organization. One does not have to supply a gloss to say that Lenin looked upon organization as the Archimedean lever for overthrowing a whole society. He himself used the metaphor. "If we begin with the solid foundation of a strong organization of revolutionaries, we can guarantee the stability of the movement as a whole." Revolution, far from being the "spontaneous" uprising of an oppressed and exasperated mass, was an "art" requiring delicate timing; spontaneity rendered organization "more necessary." Only through organizational intelligence could the revolutionaries assess "the general political situation," develop "the ability to select the proper moment for the uprising," and enforce discipline among the local organizations so that the latter would "respond simultaneously to the same political questions." Thus organization provided preconceived direction and form to the bubbling ferment of "spontaneous" revolutionary forces;

it maintained "a systematic plan of activity" over time and preserved "the energy, the stability and continuity of the political struggle." Through organization the revolutionaries could "concentrate all these drops and streamlets of popular excitement" into "a *single* gigantic flood." Above all, the "all-sided and all-embracing political agitation" undertaken by organization helped to rivet the elite to the mass; organization brings the elite *"into closer proximity to, and merges* the elemental destructive force of the crowd with the conscious destructive force of the organization of revolutionaries."

As Lenin spelled out the details of revolutionary organization, a different, almost aesthetic note, crept into his writing. He began to look upon the "apparatus" with the jealous pride of the artist, heaping scorn on those who would "degrade" the organization by turning it towards tawdry economic objectives and "immediate goals," bemoaning the "primitiveness" of the existing organization which had "lowered the prestige of revolutionaries in Russia." The task of the organization was to raise the workers "to the level of revolutionaries," not to degrade the organization to the level of "the average worker." Above all, when the revolutionary situation ripened, special care must be taken to avert the danger of the party organization being "overwhelmed" by the revolutionary wave. For its own protection, the organization must be powerful enough to master the "spontaneity" of the masses.

Lenin's emphasis on the "small compact core" of professional revolutionaries as the vital cog of the organization led him to the question of what kind of democracy, and how much, could be permitted. His answer established a framework of argument that was to be duplicated by later writers concerned with the same broad question. It was the procedure adopted by Michels in his famous study of the oligarchical and bureaucratic tendencies in professedly democratic parties; by Chester Barnard in his analysis of the contradictions between the requirements of administrative leadership and democratic practices; by students of organization concerned at the way mass society, with its penchant for "radical leveling," "prevents the emergence of an effective social leadership." What is important here is the way that the question is posed: how much democracy can organization endure?—never the reverse. Lenin's answer was a model of candor:

> Bureaucracy *versus* democracy is the same thing as centralism *versus* [local] autonomism, it is the same organizational principle of revolutionary political democracy as opposed to the organizational principle of the opportunists of Social Democracy. The latter want to proceed from the bottom upwards. . . . The former proceed from the top, and

advocate the extension of the rights and powers of the center in respect
of the parts. . . . My idea . . . is "bureaucratic" in the sense that the
Party is built from the top downwards. . . .

Democracy, therefore, had to be re-defined in a way more consonant
with the imperatives of organization and elitism. Membership had to be
severely restricted so as not to compromise the highly professional quality of the leadership. At the same time, a type of bureaucratic democracy would encourage talented workers to rise to positions of leadership:
as in the modern corporation, there was to be room at the top. The
"real" guarantee of democratic responsibility to the membership lay in
the close-knit solidarity of the elite, the "complete, comradely, mutual
confidence among revolutionaries."

When Lenin came to consider the task of building the new order, he
relied once more on the same prescription: construction, as well as destruction, required systematic organization and a compact leadership
group. Like Calvin contending with the sectarians who believed that
"enthusiasm" alone could sustain the church, Lenin had to dispose of
the anarchist argument that, with the destruction of the old order, men
could proceed directly to a condition where power was unnecessary.
"The proletariat," Lenin asserted, "needs state power, the centralized
organization of force, the organization of violence. . . ." To be sure, the
old-style politics would be abolished, for, thanks to the advances of
capitalism, most governmental tasks had been so greatly simplified that
they could be discharged by the simple routines followed in post offices.
Gradually society would evolve towards the "non-political state," which,
while not the final phase, would be a definite advance over the past.

Lenin provided an illuminating glimpse into the workings of the
organizational mentality when he turned to consider what was to be
abolished of the political and what was to be retained. Politics, as represented by party rivalries, legislative maneuvers, the frictions generated
between governmental units, and the struggle for group advantage, was
to be suppressed: organization excluded politics. But those aspects of
the political congenial or necessary to organization were to be retained.
Thus the proletarian state was said to need "a certain amount of subordination" and "some authority or power." Above all, bureaucracy itself
would be perpetuated: "to destroy officialdom immediately, everywhere,
completely—this cannot be thought of." It was a mere "anarchist dream"
to hold that "all administration" and "all subordination" could be disposed of.

The affection which Lenin had lavished on the revolutionary organization was now transferred to the governmental machinery. He asserted

that revolutionary society would not only exploit the advanced techniques of capitalist administration but would perfect and purify them. No longer would public positions be degraded into being mere springboards for obtaining more lucrative posts in private industry; no longer would the careless, gentlemanly tradition of the civil service prevail. This was to be a pure organization, undisfigured by parasites. "Our problem here is only to *lop away* that which *capitalistically disfigures* this otherwise excellent apparatus. . . ."

In the light of his admiration for the beauties of organization and his faith in its creative power, there is small wonder that Lenin was eager to put it to the test. Like later theorists of organization, he was undismayed by the lack of resources available, the low level of skills and literacy, the appalling distance between reality and aspiration. To those faint-hearted followers who pleaded that the revolution should be postponed until human nature could be educated to the demands of the new age, Lenin replied with what was a classic statement of the faith of the new age of organization: "No, we want the Socialist revolution with human nature as it is now, with human nature that cannot do without subordination, control, and 'managers.' "

One final problem remained: how was organization to be squared with Marx's prophecy of a future society where the state would "wither away" and coercion would lose its rationale? For Lenin this was no problem. He agreed that ultimately there would be true or "primitive" democracy, but he conceived it to be democracy within the premises of organization, or, more accurately, he thought that the perfection of organization would be identical with true denocracy. The progressive simplification of work would obviate the need for expert talents and place all functions within the reach "of every single individual." Since "democracy means equality," the development of organization could satisfy this criterion by breaking down complex jobs into simple operations. "The whole of society will have become one office and one factory, with equal work and equal pay." In short, true organization *is* equality.

The prescience of Lenin's theories is confirmed by their reappearance in the conservatively oriented literature of organization theory. What Marx did to Hegel, writers like Selznick have done to Lenin; that is, turned him upside down. The new formula is not pure Leninism, but Leninism clothed in the language of Burke. The fondness for large-scale organization displayed by contemporary writers largely stems from anxieties provoked by the emergence of the mass. They see organizations as mediating institutions, shaping disoriented individuals to socially useful behavior and endowing them with a desperately needed sense of values. These large entities supply the stabilizing centers, which not only integrate and structure the amorphous masses, but control them as well. The role which Selznick assigns the elite seems more indebted to Burke than to Lenin. The ruling group, he warns, is not in a position analogous to the sculptor, free "to mould the organization according to his heart's desire. . . ." Instead, its posture is "essentially conservative." To preserve the life of the group was a task which could not be reduced to a question of balance sheets, any more than Burkean society could be treated as "a partnership agreement in a trade of pepper and coffee," or the Leninist revolutionary movement as a mere instrument to advance trade-union interests. The administrator is responsible for the life-processes of a "polity." To accomplish his ends effectively it is necessary that he win the "consent" of the members. But "consent" in the age of organization does not connote self-government, much less the idea of participation as practiced in the ancient "polity." It means, instead, "commitment," which is something far different. "Commitment" is the special prescription for a mass age where men are isolated and their lives depersonalized and bleak. Their wants are psychic and hence to be satisfied by "integration" rather than made more anxious by the demands of participation. The aim of the elite, therefore, is to convert "neutral men" into a "committed polity."

Now it is also true that Selznick sometimes uses commitment as a synonym for "loyalty" and "loyalty" is said to involve "rational, free-willed consent." While this might appear to be either a bit of careless usage or a deceptive strategy to exploit some "hurrah-words," it is also squarely in the manipulative tradition. Selznick's notions of "commitment," "loyalty," and "rational, free-willed consent" have as much of choice and spontaneity about them as Lenin's theory of "democratic centralism" has of democracy:

> By long habituation, sometimes also as a result of aggressive indoctrination, the individual absorbs a way of perceiving and evaluating his experience. This reduces his anxiety by lending the world of fact a familiar cast; and it helps assure an easy conformity with established practice.

As Selznick makes clear, "participation" is "prescribed . . . only when there is a problem of cohesion." Moreover, there is the cautionary reminder that the member must not be allowed to over-commit himself, for this builds up rigidities which limit "the freedom of the leadership to deploy its resources."

Other "political" aspects of the organizational "polity" are similarly transformed into ready counters of manipulation by the leadership. The rules or "laws" of the organization, the "pluralism" of its structure are all useful devices for facilitating the task of governing. The beliefs of the members are described as "ideologies," and they are the objects of a "technique" for manipulating "socially integrating myths." Although at one point "administrative ideologies" are said to emerge "in spontaneous and unplanned ways," our previous discussion has prepared us for the legerdemain which transforms "spontaneity" into direction. "A well-formulated doctrine," quite unsurprisingly, is discovered to be "remarkably handy for boosting internal morale, communicating the bases for decisions, and rebuffing outside claims and criticisms."

When we say that policy is built into the social structure of an organization, we mean that official aims and methods are *spontaneously protected or advanced*. The aspirations of individuals and groups are so stimulated and controlled . . . as to produce the desired balance of forces.

3 THE STALIN ERA

Introduction

The Stalinist period in Soviet history is one of decline in sociology and scholarship in general. Scholars who continued to form their judgments on the basis of objective evidence were eliminated. Social science was transformed into what the founder of sociology, Auguste Comte, had hoped it would become, a priesthood. Only those at the pinnacle of power had an opportunity to make innovations in social thought. Yet even they were limited in the kinds of departures they could undertake in their struggle with one another and in their newly acquired positions as guardians of the state. Their limitations did not stem from the fact that they were Marxists, for Marxist sociology maintained a respectable position in many countries. But Marxism transformed into official ideology became Marxist rhetoric.

The selections in the present section, in addition to a general analysis of Soviet Marxism, highlight the sociological ideas of men who had the most profound influence on Soviet social thought from 1924 to 1956: Bukharin, Trotsky, and Stalin.

The selection by Herbert Marcuse, Professor of Philosophy at the University of California at LaJolla, is part of a larger work of the same title which is the best objective sociological analysis of Soviet Marxism. After his discussion of Leninism, which set the stage for the development of Soviet Marxism, Professor Marcuse presents an analysis of Soviet society in the Stalinist period. It is a penetrating view of Soviet Marxist rhetoric. The rhetoric has its own rationality. Dogmatic and repetitious claims are not by themselves true but are "pragmatic directives for action." The truth of Marxist rhetoric lies in the effect it produces. Professor Marcuse concludes that "Soviet Marxism here shares in the decline of language and communication in the age of mass societies. It is senseless to treat propositions of the official ideology at the cognitive level: they are a matter of practical not theoretical reason."

The article by Sidney Heitman, Professor of History at Colorado State

University, discusses the life and work of N. I. Bukharin, whose biography he is presently finishing. Bukharin's most creative achievement was the reformulation of the theory of revolutions, which had been presented unsystematically throughout many of his works detailed by Professor Heitman. Although Bukharin is now "forgotten" in his own country, Lenin described him as "the most valuable and biggest theoretician of the party." Bukharin had proven himself valuable to Stalin, at the time of the latter's struggle with Trotsky, by supporting Stalin's thesis of "socialism in one country." One of Bukharin's major contributions to scholarship still survives in the Soviet Union today in the form of the first edition of the *Great Soviet Encyclopedia,* of which he was the editor.

The selection by Isaac Deutscher, author of the definitive three-volume biography of Leon Trotsky, is the finest discussion of Trotsky as a historian and sociologist of the Russian Revolution. Most of Trotsky's talents, however, were directed toward his professional political activities, first in the role of revolutionary and later as Stalin's opponent to succeed Lenin. As leader of the "left opposition," or as the originator of what was perjoratively dubbed as Trotskyism, Trotsky proposed a series of coercive measures to assure the victory of communism. These proposals involved the centralization of authority, the drive toward quick industrialization, and the centralization of planning. Despite Trotsky's defeat, these measures were later incorporated into Stalin's own program. Trotsky's banishment after his defeat forced him to become a scholar as well as a politician. As a result the world inherited Trotsky's discerning analysis of the Russian Revolution, which is critically reviewed here by Mr. Deutscher.

The article by George Allen Morgan, a U.S. diplomat trained as philosopher, was first published under the pen name of Historicus. It is one of the few available objective accounts of Stalin's social thought. Mr. Morgan takes Stalin's ideas seriously and refuses to deflate them. At a time when practically all of the writings on Stalin were tinged with personal evaluations of him as a cruel and ruthless despot, which he was, Mr. Morgan achieved an unbiased analysis of Stalin's work in the field of revolutionary ideas. The fact that Stalin's pronouncements were immediately canonized into a body of official dogma does not by itself necessarily invalidate all his ideas. Stalin was the first tyrant to rely heavily on a relatively systematic body of social theory in his guidance of the affairs of state. As Mr. Morgan points out, Stalin always shows a deep "conviction that correctness of theory is vitally important." Stalin is especially consistent and detached when pondering the nature, causes, and future possibilities of revolutions. This is probably because he considered these to be long-term trends over which he could exercise only limited influence through his own programs, which were designed to anticipate revolutionary developments abroad. Mr. Morgan's extremely thorough presentation of Stalin's ideas on revolution remains an important contribution to all sociologists working in the area of social change and social theory.

Soviet Marxism

HERBERT MARCUSE

I. Leninism

The emergence of Leninism as a new form of Marxism is determined by two main factors: (1) the attempt to draw the peasantry into the orbit of Marxian theory and strategy, and (2) the attempt to re-define the prospects of capitalist and revolutionary development in the imperialist era. The two main currents of Leninist thought are closely interrelated; the viability of advanced capitalism (unexpected from the traditional Marxist point of view) and, consequently, the continued strength of reformism among the proletariat in the advanced capitalist countries called almost inevitably for a shift in Marxist emphasis to the backward countries, which were predominantly agricultural and where the weakness of the capitalist sector seemed to offer better chances for a revolution. True, the notion that the capitalist chain must be broken at its "weakest link"—a notion stressed by Stalin after the revolution—was originally Trotsky's rather than Lenin's, but the whole trend of Leninist thought from the beginning is in this direction. When the "workers' and peasants' revolution," rather than the workers' revolution, becomes the center of Soviet Marxism, it is not only because the revolution happened to be successful in Russia but because the revolutionary potential of the industrial working class seemed to recede throughout the advanced capitalist world. It was this fact that, in the long run, decided the development of Soviet Marxism. We therefore take as a starting point Lenin's analysis of the situation of the proletariat at the imperialist stage.

Significant in this interpretation is the underestimation of the economic and political potentialities of capitalism, and of the change in

From Herbert Marcuse, *Soviet Marxism* (New York: Columbia University Press, 1958), pp. 29-37, 78-92.

the position of the proletariat. In fact, the refusal to draw the theoretical consequences from the new situation characterizes the entire development of Leninism and is one of the chief reasons for the gap between theory and practice in Soviet Marxism. For, while Lenin from the beginning of his activity reoriented the revolutionary strategy of his party in accordance with the new situation, his theoretical conception did not follow suit. Lenin's retention of the classical notion of the revolutionary proletariat, sustained with the help of the theory of the labor aristocracy and the avant garde, revealed its inadequacy from the beginning. Even prior to the First World War it became clear that the "collaborationist" part of the proletariat was quantitatively and qualitatively different from a small upper stratum that had been corrupted by monopoly capital, and that the Social Democratic party and trade union bureaucracy were more than "traitors"—rather that their policy reflected pretty exactly the economic and social condition of the majority of the organized working classes in the advanced industrial countries. And indeed, Lenin's strategy of the revolutionary avant garde pointed to a conception of the proletariat which went far beyond a mere reformulation of the classical Marxian concept; his struggle against "economism" and the doctrine of spontaneous mass action, his dictum that class consciousness has to be brought upon the proletariat "from without" anticipate the later factual transformation of the proletariat from the subject to an object of the revolutionary process. True, Lenin's *What Is to Be Done?* [1] where these ideas found their classical formulation, was written for the struggle of the Russian Marxists for leadership over a backward proletariat, but their implications go far beyond this context. The ultimate target is stated at the beginning of Lenin's pamphlet: it is the rising reformist camp in "international social democracy," represented for Lenin by Bernstein and Millerand, who demanded a "decided change from revolutionary social democracy to bourgeois reformism." Moreover, the phrase "class consciousness from without" did not originate from the Russian situation but was coined by Karl Kautsky in his polemics against the draft of the new program of the Austrian Social Democratic party.[2] Lenin aimed beyond the exigencies of the specific Russian situation, at a general international development in Marxism, which in turn reflected the trend of large sections of organized labor toward "class cooperation." As this trend increased, it threatened to vitiate the notion of the proletariat as the revolutionary subject on which the whole Marxist strategy depended. Lenin's formulations intended to save Marxian orthodoxy from the reformist onslaught, but they soon became part of a conception that no longer assumed the historical coincidence between the proletariat and progress which the notion of the "labor aristocracy" still retained. The groundwork was laid for the development of the Leninist party where the true interest and the true consciousness of the proletariat were lodged in a group different from the majority of the proletariat. The centralistic organization, which was first justified by and applied to the "immaturity" of backward conditions, was to become the general principle of strategy on an international scale.

The construction of the Leninist party (or party leadership) as the real representative of the proletariat could not bridge the gap between the new strategy and the old theoretical conception. Lenin's strategy of the avant garde acknowledged in fact what it denied in theory, namely, that a fundamental change had occurred in the objective and subjective conditions for the revolution.

In his *Finanzkapital*,[3] published in 1910, Rudolf Hilferding interpreted this change in terms of Marxian theory. He pointed out that, under the leadership of finance capital, the entire national economy would be mobilized for expansion, and that this expansion, through the collusion of giant monopolistic and semimonopolistic enterprises, would tend toward large-scale international integration, economic as well as political. On this new intercontinental market, production and distribution would be to a great extent controlled and regimented by a cartel of the most powerful capitalist interests. In the huge dominion of such a "general cartel," the contradictions of the capitalist system could be greatly controlled, profits for the ruling groups secured, and a high level of wages for labor within the dominion sustained—at the expense of the intensified exploitation of markets and populations outside the dominion. Hilferding thought that such international capitalist planning would require the abolition of democratic liberalism in the economy as well as in the political and ideological sphere; individualism and humanism would be replaced by an aggressive militarist nationalism and authoritarianism. Similar ideas were subsequently (1914) advanced by Karl Kautsky in his concept of "ultraimperialism." [4]

These developments were presented only as tendencies the realization of which for any length of time was doubted by Hilferding as well as Kautsky. Nor did these writers draw the full conclusions concerning the changing class situation of the proletariat. But the economic and political conditions had been outlined under which the capitalist world could be stabilized and hierarchically integrated—conditions which in Marxian theory appeared as utopian unless the actual forces which would supersede the contradictions and conflicts among the imperialist powers developed. Once they materialized, an economic basis for integration could indeed emerge. It did emerge, very gradually and with many regressions and breaks, under the impact of two world wars, atomic productivity, and the growth of Communist power. These events altered the structure of capitalism as defined by Marx and created the basis of a new economic and political organization of the Western world.[5] This basis came to be utilized effectively only after the Second World War. From then on, the conflicting competitive interests among the Western nations were gradually integrated and superseded by the fundamental East-West conflict, and an intercontinental political economy took shape—in extent much smaller than the former free world market, but susceptible to a planned regulation of that blind "anarchy" in which Marxism saw the root of capitalist contradictions. At the same time, the laboring classes were split on an international scale into (to use Toynbee's terms) an *internal* and *external* proletariat, the latter consisting of those (urban and rural) proletarian and semiproletarian classes, outside and inside the area of effective reconstruction, which did not benefit from it by higher wages, better living conditions, or greater political influence.

The external proletariat (including, as its largest part, the peasantry), which came to provide the Soviet leadership with a mass basis for the struggle against capitalism after the First World War, emerged as a historical "subject" seemingly by virtue of (from the Marxian viewpoint) an exogenous event, namely, by virtue of the fact that the revolution succeeded in backward Russia, failed to materialize in the advanced industrial countries, and subsequently spread from Russia into pre-industrial areas, while the advanced industrial countries continued to remain immune. But this event was not quite as exogenous as it seems. The gradual "immunization" of decisive areas of Western society had already begun to show its effectiveness prior to the First World War; the nationalist attitude of the Social Democratic parties in 1914—at that time the unchallenged Marxist organization of labor—was only its most conspicuous manifestation. The immunization then proved its power in the Central European revolutions from 1918 to 1923, where the majority of organized labor defeated the Communist assault in alliance with the bourgeoisie and the army. In England, the predominance of the reformist Labor party had never been seriously disturbed. In France and Italy, Communist strength continued to trail far behind that of Social Democracy; and in Germany, the only country where it came to a powerful resurgence after the defeat, Social Democratic as well as Communist labor succumbed quickly to the Fascist regime. The sustained weakness of the revolutionary potential in the advanced industrial countries confined the revolution to that area where the proletariat had not been thus affected and where the regime had shown political disintegration together with economic backwardness.

Marxian theory explained the rising standard of living, which lay at the economic roots of the immunization process, in terms of the growing productivity of labor, the effective organization of the industrial workers, which counteracted the pressure on the wage level, and in terms of monopolistic surplus profits in the most advanced capitalist areas. According to Marxism, none of these factors could neutralize for any length of time the inherent contradictions of the capitalist mode of production. The benefits for the working class were expected to be wiped out periodically by wars and crises since there was no basis for long-range international capitalist consolidation. This interpretation did not provide for the possibility (soon to become a fact) that such an international basis would materialize. On it, Western industrial society created its new economic and political institutions. The catastrophic violence, the unprecedented extent of physical and cultural destruction, and also the equally unprecedented growth of technical productivity which characterized the period after 1918, corresponded to the scope of the task. It was the very structure of the established civilization that was challenged and that had to be reaffirmed against a competing civilization. The technological and political potential developed in this struggle made it soon appear that minor adjustments would not suffice to meet the challenge. The need for the total mobilization of all material and mental forces necessitated the abolition of laissez-faire in economic and cultural life, the methodical control of the political process, and national regrouping under the actual hierarchy of economic power—at the expense of cherished traditional sovereignties. The overriding interest of Western society as a whole modified national and class interests: the national parties aligned themselves with the international economic and political forces. Labor was no exception and, at the end, Social Democracy became part of the Western, and Communism part of the Eastern, orbit. For Marxism, the capitalist world had never come closer to the dreaded specter of a "general cartel" which would replace the anarchy of capitalist production and distribution by ultraimperialist planning. And it was the very progress of the Soviet system which had promoted the realization of this dreaded possibility.

II. Stalinism

We shall begin with the attempt to define, in a preliminary way, the rationale of the civilization of "socialism in one country," that is to say, the principles which govern its construction and its inner dynamic. In doing so, we accept as guidance neither the term "socialism," nor its simple negation, nor "totalitarianism" and its synonyms—not socialism because the validation of the concept depends on agreement on definition and can even then only be the result of the examination; not totalitarianism because the notion is applicable to a wide variety of social systems with different and antagonistic structures. We shall rather try to arrive at the identification of these principles by assembling those features of the construction of Soviet society which have remained generally constant throughout all stages, regressions, and modifications. They may be restated, in summary form, as follows:

1. Total industrialization, on the basis of nationalized production, with priority of "main division I" (production of the means of production)

2. Progressive collectivization of agriculture aiming at the ultimate transformation of collective into state property

3. General mechanization of labor, extension of "polytechnic" training, leading to "equalization" between urban and rural occupations

4. Gradual rise in the general standard of living conditional on the maintenance of the goals set in Points 1-3

5. Building up of a universal work morale, competitive efficiency, elimination of all transcendent psychological and ideological elements ("Soviet realism")

6. Preservation and strengthening of the state, military, managerial, and party machinery as the vehicle for these processes (1-5)

7. Transition to the distribution of the social product according to individual needs after attainment of the goals set in Points 1-5

The goals are conditional upon the attainment of the productivity level of the advanced industrial countries; this is the termination point for the presently prevailing trends. Beyond this point, new and qualitatively different trends are stipulated. . . .

The following principles refer to the Soviet Marxist interpretation of this transition:

1. The development of Soviet society from socialism to communism takes place as the dialectical process of unfolding internal and external contradictions.

2. The internal contradictions can be solved rationally, without "explosion," on the basis of the socialist economy under the control and direction of the Soviet state.

3. The fundamental internal contradiction, which provides the motor power for the transition to communism, is that between the constantly growing productive forces and the lagging relations of production. Its rational and controlled development makes for a gradual and administrative transition to communism.

4. The gradual transition to communism occurs under conditions of capitalist encirclement (environment). The external contradictions involved in this situation can be finally solved only at the international

level—through a socialist revolution in some of the advanced capitalist countries.

5. This solution is itself a long-range process, covering a whole period of capitalist and socialist development. The weakness of the revolutionary potential in the capitalist world and the still prevailing backwardness of the Soviet orbit necessitate a new extended "respite" and "coexistence" of the two systems.

6. The Soviet Union must preserve this respite by utilizing conflicts among the imperialist powers,[6] avoiding a war with them, and discouraging revolutionary experiments ("seizure of power") in the advanced capitalist countries.

7. The solution of the external contradictions will ripen through (*a*) the inherent capitalist and intercapitalist contradictions, which will make the proletariat again the historical agent of the revolution; (*b*) the growing economic, political, and strategic power of the USSR.

8. The "main reserves" supporting these basic revolutionary forces are the semiproletarian and petty peasant masses in the developed countries, and the liberation movements in the colonies and dependent countries.

The social process guided by these principles is more than the industrialization of the backward areas of the East on the basis of nationalization under totalitarian administration. What is happening here extends beyond the borders of the Communist orbit. Communist industrialization proceeds through "skipping" and telescoping whole historical periods. The fundamental difference between Western and Soviet society is paralleled by a strong trend toward assimilation. Both systems show the common features of late industrial civilization—centralization and regimentation supersede individual enterprise and autonomy; competition is organized and "rationalized"; there is joint rule of economic and political bureaucracies; the people are coordinated through the "mass media" of communication, entertainment, industry, education. If these devices prove to be effective, democratic rights and institutions might be granted by the constitution and maintained without the danger of their abuse in opposition to the system. Nationalization, the abolition of private property in the means of production, does not, by itself, constitute an essential distinction as long as production is centralized and controlled over and above the population. Without initiative and control "from below" by the "immediate producers," nationalization is but a technological-political device for increasing the productivity of labor, for accelerating the development of the productive forces and for their control from above (central planning)—a change in the mode of domination, streamlining of domination, rather than prerequisite for its abolition.

By abrogating the individual as the autonomous economic and political subject, certain "obsolete" brakes on the development of the productive forces are eliminated. Individual units of production (material and intellectual) are no longer adequate instrumentalities for integrating society; technological progress and mass production shatter the individualistic forms in which progress operated during the liberalist era.

But, at the same time, technical progress and growing productivity threaten to counteract this trend. Increasing social capacity and wealth militate against the repressive organization and division of labor. Awareness of these counter-trends manifests itself in the recent policy changes and in the increased Soviet Marxist emphasis on the necessary transition to the "second phase of socialism. . . ."

The Soviet system seems to be another example of a late-comer "skipping" several developmental stages after a long period of protracted backwardness, joining and running ruthlessly ahead of a general trend in late industrial society. The skipped stages are those of enlightened absolutism and liberalism, of free competitive enterprise, of matured middle-class culture with its individualistic and humanitarian ideologies. The effort to catch up, in record time and from a state of backwardness, with the level of the advanced industrial countries led to the construction and utilization of a huge productive apparatus within a system of domination and regimentation incompatible with individualistic rationality and liberalism. Here lie the roots of the relentless struggle of Soviet Marxism against the liberal and idealist elements of "bourgeois ideologies"; the struggle reflects the societal organization of the productive forces as instruments of control rather than liberation.

The idea of Reason which was representative of modern Western civilization centered on the autonomy of the *Ego Cogitans,* whose independent thinking discovered and implemented the laws of the rational organization of nature and society. The Ego was itself subject to the objective laws of nature—but subjective and objective Reason were to coincide in a society that had mastered nature and transformed it into a practically inexhaustible material for the development of human needs and faculties. Attainment of this goal called for the emancipation of the individual as long as the state, the established authorities, were an impediment to technical and economic progress. The latter was expected to result from the reasonably free functioning of a multitude of individual enterprises (economic, political, cultural), and the rationality of the whole was to assert itself through the competitive process of these individual units. This process required a high degree of individual autonomy, foresight, calculability, perspicacity—qualities that had to be acquired not only in the actual business of living but also in the preparation for it: in the family, in school, in the privacy of thinking and feeling. Social progress thus depended to a large extent on the autonomy of the individual, that is, on the distinction and tension between subjective and objective Reason, and on a solution of this tension in such a way that objective Reason (the social need and the social interest) preserved and developed subjective Reason (the individual need and the individual interest).

Technological progress and the development of large industry contained two (antagonistic) tendencies which had a decisive impact on this process: (1) mechanization and rationalization of labor could free an ever greater quantum of individual energy (and time) from the material work process and allow the expenditure of this energy and time for the free play of human faculties beyond the realm of material production; and (2) the same mechanization and rationalization generated attitudes of standardized conformity and precise submission to the machine which required adjustment and reaction rather than autonomy and spontaneity.[7] If nationalization and centralization of the industrial apparatus goes hand in hand with counteracting the first of these tendencies, i.e., with the subjugation and enforcement of labor as a full-time occupation, progress in industrialization is tantamount to progress in domination: attendance to the machine, the scientific work process, becomes totalitarian, affecting all spheres of life. The technological perfection of the productive apparatus dominates the rulers and the ruled while sustaining the distinction between them. Autonomy and spontaneity are confined to the level of efficiency and performance within the established pattern. Intellectual effort becomes the business of engineers, specialists, agents. Privacy and leisure are handled as relaxation from and preparation for labor in conformity with the apparatus. Dissent is not only a political crime but also technical stupidity, sabotage, mistreatment of the machine. Reason is nothing but the rationality of the whole: the uninterrupted functioning and growth of the apparatus. The experience of the harmony between the individual and the general interest, between the human and the social need, remains a mere promise.

The Soviet Marxist self-interpretation of this rationality may serve to elucidate its function. According to this interpretation, the October Revolution has created a "conformity" between production relations and the "character of the productive forces" which eliminates the conflict between the individual and society, between the particular and the common interest. Consequently, Reason ceases to be split into its subjective and objective manifestations; it is no longer antagonistic to and beyond reality, a mere "idea"—but is realized in the society itself. This society, defined as socialist in terms of Marxian theory, becomes the sole standard of truth and falsehood; there can be no transcendence in thought and action, no individual autonomy because the Nomos of the whole is the true Nomos. To transcend that which is, to set subjective reason against state reason, to appeal to higher norms and values, belongs to the prerogatives of class society, where the Nomos of society is not the Nomos of its individuals. In contrast, Soviet society institutionalizes the real interests of the individuals—by this token, it contains all standards of true and false, rght and wrong. "Soviet realism" is not a mere matter of philosophy and aesthetics; it is the general pattern of intellectual and practical behavior demanded by the structure of Soviet society.

To be sure, outside the validity of Soviet Marxism, where the equation of the Soviet state with a free and rational society is not accepted, this notion of the "realization of Reason" is itself an ideology. Since in actuality the individual interest is still antagonistic to the interest of the whole, since nationalization is not socialization, the rationality of Soviet realism appears as utterly irrational, as terroristic conformity. However, to stop the evaluation of the new Soviet rationality at this point would be to overlook its decisive function. For what is irrational if measured from without the system is rational within the system. The key propositions of Soviet Marxism have the function of announcing and commanding a definite practice, apt to create the facts which the propositions stipulate. They claim no truth-value of their own but proclaim a pre-established truth which is to be realized through a certain attitude and behavior. They are pragmatic directives for action. For example, Soviet Marxism is built around a small number of constantly recurring and rigidly canonized statements to the effect that Soviet society is a socialist society without exploitation, a full democracy in which the constitutional rights of all citizens are guaranteed and enforced; or, on the other side, that present-day capitalism exists in a state of sharpening class struggle, depressed living standards, unemployment, and so forth. Thus formulated and taken by themselves, these statements are obviously false—according to Marxian as well as non-Marxian criteria. But within the context in which they appear, their falsity does not invalidate them, for, to Soviet Marxism, their verification is not in the given facts but in "tendencies," in a historical process in which the commanded political practice will *bring about* the desired facts.

The value of these statements is pragmatic rather than logical, as is clearly suggested by their syntactical structure. They are unqualified, inflexible formulas calling for an unqualified, inflexible response. In endless repetition, the same noun is always accompanied by the same adjectives and participles; the noun "governs" them immediately and directly so that whenever it occurs they follow "automatically" in their proper place. The same verb always "moves" the proposition in the same direction, and those addressed by the proposition are supposed to move the same way. These statements do not attribute a predicate to a subject (in the sense of formal or of dialectical logic); they do not develop the subject in its specific relations—all these cognitive processes lie outside the propositional context, i.e., in the "classics" of Marxism, and the routine statements only recall what is pre-established. They are to be "spelled," learned mechanically, monotonously, and literally; they are to be performed like a ritual which accompanies the realizing action. They are to recall and sustain the required practice. Taken by themselves they are no more committed to the truth than are orders or advertisements: their "truth" is in their effect. Soviet Marxism here shares in the decline of language and communication in the age of mass societies. It is senseless to treat the propositions of the official ideology at the cognitive level: they are a matter of practical, not of theoretical reason. If propositions lose their cognitive value to their capacity for bringing about a desired effect, that is to say, if they are to be understood as directives for a specific behavior, then *magical* elements gain ascendancy over comprehending thought and action. The difference between illusion and reality becomes just as obliterated as that between truth and falsehood if illusions guide a behavior that shapes and changes reality. With respect to its actual effect on primitive societies, magic has been described as a "body of purely practical acts, performed as means to an end." [8] The description may well be applied to formally theoretical propositions. The official language itself assumes magical character.

However, the contemporary reactivation of magical features in communication is far from primitive. The irrational elements of magic enter into the system of scientifically planned and practiced administration— they become part of the scientific management of society. Moreover, the magical features of Soviet theory are turned into an instrument for rescuing the truth. While the ritual formulas, severed from their original cognitive context, thus serve to provide unquestioned directives for unquestioned mass behavior, they retain, in a hypostatized form, their historical substance. The rigidity with which they are celebrated is to preserve the purity of this substance in the face of an apparently contradicting reality and to enforce verification in the face of apparently contradicting facts which make the pre-established truth into a paradox. It defies reason; it seems absurd. But the absurdity of Soviet Marxism has an objective ground: it reflects the absurdity of a historical situation in which the realization of the Marxian promises appeared—only to be delayed again—and in which the new productive forces are again used as instruments for productive repression. The ritualized language preserves the original content of Marxian theory as a truth that must be believed and enacted against all evidence to the contrary: the people must do and feel and think as if their state were the reality of that reason, freedom, and justice which the ideology proclaims, and the ritual is to assure such behavior. The practice guided by it indeed moves large underprivileged masses on an international scale. In this process, the original promises of Marxian theory play a decisive part. The new form of Marxian theory corresponds to its new historical agent—a backward population which is to become what it "really" is: a revolutionary force which changes the world. The ritualization of this theory has kept it alive against the power of factual refutation and communicated it, in ideological form, to a backward and suppressed population which is to be whipped into political action, contesting and challenging advanced industrial civilization. In its magical use, Marxian theory assumes a new rationality.

The paradoxical character of Soviet rationality is not confined to its own orbit; it also pertains to statements referring to the capitalist orbit. To be sure, straight falsehood may often be attributed to mere propaganda requirements. But here too, the recurrent pattern of falsehood beyond plausibility suggests the intent of defiance: the concerted struggle with facts which, measured against the world historical "truth," are accidental and to be negated. If, for example, *Pravda*'s special New York correspondent reports [9] that in the card catalog of the New York Public Library he did not find a single book "about Stalingrad or the Soviet army in general," the fact that the New York Public Library's catalog contains about "two dozen cards bearing directly on the Battle of Stalingrad" and "about 500 cards under 'Army, Russia' " is, for the Soviet reporter, "negated" by the essential context of systematic American hostility to the Soviet Union. Or, if William Z. Foster's *History of the Communist Party of the United States,* published in 1952—at a time when the party was practically without any popular support, its leadership in jail, its membership a negligible quantity—ends with a chapter headed "The Party of the Working Class and the Nation," and with a section headed "The Progress of the Communist Party," then the shattering unreality of these statements is itself part of their function: to refuse submission to the facts, to uphold and accomplish the true nature of the party as the "Leninist mass party" against its inadequate factual existence.

Hypostatized into a ritual pattern, Marxian theory becomes ideology. But its content and function distinguish it from the "classical" forms of ideology: it is not "false consciousness," [10] but rather consciousness of falsehood, a falsehood which is "corrected" in the context of the "higher truth" represented by the objective historical interest. This tends to cancel the ideological freedom of consciousness and to assimiliate ideology with the basis as part of consciously directed social action. As the contrast between ideology and reality sharpens with the growing contrast between the productive potential of society and its repressive use, the previously free elements of the ideology are subjected to administrative control and direction. The weakening of the relative independence of ideologies from established social needs, the ossification of their content, is characteristic of the present stage of civilization. In its ossified form, emptied of its meaning which was critical of and antagonistic to the established society, the ideology becomes a tool of domination. If ideas like human liberty and reason or individual autonomy of thought are no longer comprehended in their still unfulfilled claim but are items in the routine equipment of newspapers, statesmen, entertainers, and advertisers who betray them daily in their business of perpetuating the status quo, then the progressive notions of the ideology are deprived of their transcendent function and made into clichés of desired behavior.

The decline of independent thought vastly increases the power of words—their magical power, with whose destruction the process of civilization had once begun. Protected against the intellectual effort which traces the way back from the words to the ideas they once expressed, the words become weapons in the hand of an administration against which the individual is completely powerless. Through the means of mass communication, they transmit the objectives of the administration, and the underlying population responds with the expected behavior.

The rationality which had accompanied the progress of Western civilization had developed in the tension between thought and its object: truth and falsehood were sought in the relation between the comprehending subject and its world, and logic was the comprehensible development of this relation, expressed in propositions. Just as the object of thought was taken as something by and in itself (no matter how inseparable from thought), so the subject was held to be something "for itself"—free to discover the truth about its object—and especially the still hidden truth: its unrealized potentialities. Cognitive freedom was held to be an essential part of practical freedom, of the ability to act in accordance with the truth, to realize the subjective and objective potentialities. Where this relation between subject and object no longer prevails, traditional logic has lost its ground. Truth and falsehood then are no longer qualities of cognitive propositions but of a preestablished and predefined state of affairs to which thought and action are to be geared. Logic then is measured by the adequacy of such thought and action to attain the predetermined goal.

Notes

1. Lenin, *Chto delat'?* (What Is to Be Done?) appeared first in 1902.
2. See *What Is to Be Done?* (New York: International Publishers, 1929), p. 40.
3. *Das Finanzkapital; Eine Studie über die jungste Entwicklung des Kapitalismus* (Marx-Studien III; Vienna: Wiener Volksbuchhandlung, 1910). Hilferding's term designates not merely a specific form of capital, but a specific form of capitalist organization. He identifies its two essential elements as (a) the "abolition" (*Aufhebung*) of free competition by the formation of cartels and trusts, and (b) the ever closer amalgamation between "banking capital" and "industrial capital."
4. Kautsky, "Der Imperialismus," *Die Neue Zeit*, XXXII, 2, No. 21 (September 11, 1914), 921.
5. Soviet Marxism maintains—and indeed must maintain .if the Marxian conception is to be preserved—that these events are intrinsically related: the "permanent war economy," as the sole outlet for the imperialist contradictions, leads to atomic productivity, and the latter enforces economic as well as political integration of the Western powers. According to this conception, the events which bring about the transformation of the Western world are not extraneous but rather internal to the dynamic of the capitalist system, and the same forces that make for war make for progress in productivity and for "temporary stabilization."
6. The last two points summarize Lenin's conception for the "third historic phase of the Russian Revolution" (beginning with the victory of the October Revolution and lasting into the present), as paraphrased by Stalin. See Stalin, *Sochineniia* (Works), (13 vols.; Moscow: Gospolitizdat, 1946-1951), VI, 153; also L. F. Shorichev, *Voprosy strategii i taktiki v trudakh I. V. Stalina perioda 1921-1925 godov* (Problems of Strategy and Tactics in the Writings of J. V. Stalin, 1921-1925) (Moscow: Pravda, 1950).
7. Thorstein Veblen, *The Instinct of Workmanship* (New York: B. W. Huebsch, 1922), pp. 306 ff.
8. Bronislaw Malinowski, *Magic, Science and Religion* (Anchor Books; New York: Doubleday, 1954), p. 70.
9. *New York Times,* February 2, 1953.
10. Engels, Letter to Franz Mehring, July 14, 1893, in Marx and Engels, *Selected Works* (2 vols.; Moscow: Foreign Languages Publishing House, 1949-1950), II, 451.

Between Lenin and Stalin: Nikolai Bukharin

SIDNEY HEITMAN

Among the outstanding figures in the history of Marxism, few occupy a more prominent place than Nikolai I. Bukharin. As one of the foremost theoreticians in the early history of the Bolshevik movement, he played a major role in the formation and development of Communist revolutionary thought. Although today his significant contributions to Bolshevik theory and practice are officially repudiated in the Communist world, their enduring impact has long survived his time in power.

A brief summary of the highlights of Bukharin's career in the Russian Communist movement reveals the source of his ideological influence.[1] Born in 1888, Bukharin was one of the youngest of the leading Bolsheviks. He joined the Social Democratic party while still a student in Moscow University and worked for several years as a party organizer and propagandist among Moscow workers. After his third arrest for revolutionary activity, Bukharin escaped to Europe, where in 1912 he met Lenin and became one of his associates. After four years of exile in various European countries, where he continued his studies in economics and worked with left-wing socialist groups during the First World War, he emigrated to the United States in 1916. In New York he became co-editor with Leon Trotsky of a Russian language newspaper and helped to organize a group of radical socialists who later founded the American Communist party.

Bukharin returned to Russia in April 1917 following the fall of the Tsarist government and worked closely with Lenin in planning and carrying out the November Revolution. In the summer of that year, Bukharin assumed the first of the many high positions he would come to hold when he became a member of the Central Committee of the party and editor of *Pravda*. After a short break with Lenin in 1918 over the issue

From Leopold Labedz, ed., *Revisionism* (London: Allen and Unwin, 1962), pp. 77-90.

of a separate peace with Germany, Bukharin was made a member of the Politbureau in 1919. In the same year he played a major role in the founding of the Communist International and was elected to its Executive Committee. In 1926 he succeeded Zinoviev as its highest officer. Other important organizations in which he acquired leading positions at various times in his career include the Central Executive Committee of the Congress of Soviets, the Komsomol, the Central Council of Trade Unions, the Red International of Trade Unions, the Supreme Council of the National Economy, the Institute of Red Professors, the Communist Academy and the Academy of Sciences of the USSR, the Marx-Engels-Lenin Institute, and numerous other Soviet economic, cultural, scientific, and educational organizations.

At the same time, Bukharin also achieved outstanding prominence as one of the foremost Communist theoreticians. From the time he first joined Lenin in exile, Bukharin rose rapidly to first-rank importance among those who formulated and spread Bolshevik ideas. Possessed of a fertile mind, great erudition, and a prolific pen, he wrote hundreds of important books, pamphlets, and articles which influenced and expressed the party's attitude towards a multitude of problems lying in such diverse areas as philosophy, economics, social and political theory, science, literature, art, and education. At the peak of his career in the 1920's, Bukharin was widely regarded as the leading theoretician and the foremost authority on Marxism in the party, a distinction which had been acknowledged by Lenin himself.[2]

By virtue of his high posts, varied and widespread activities, and authority as a theoretician, Bukharin exercised greater influence in the Communist world during the middle and late 1920's than any other individual until that time except Lenin, and after Lenin's death in 1924 many Soviet and foreign observers came to regard him as the legitimate heir and successor to Lenin's political and ideological leadership of the international Communist movement. Bukharin's triumph was short-lived, however, for in 1928 Stalin launched his attack against the "right-wing" of the party, and in the following year Bukharin lost most of his important offices in the party and the Comintern. Later he was compelled to repudiate his earlier contributions to the Communist movement and to pay degrading homage to Stalin. In 1937 he was arrested and charged with treason, and after a spectacular trial he was executed on March 15, 1938. Since his death, Bukharin's name has been considered anathema in the Communist world. One of Bukharin's most significant accomplishments was his contribution to the evolution of Communist revolutionary thought. Bukharin's career spanned a period in the history of Bolshevism when its ideology was in a state of transition. In the decade preceding and following the Revolution of 1917, the party still lacked a coherent body of revolutionary theory, considered essential to the success of its cause. Although the Bolshevik leaders subscribed generally to Marxism as the sole scientific doctrine capable of guiding the proletariat in its historically ordained mission to overturn capitalism and supplant it with communism, they also recognized the need to modify the doctrine and to accommodate it to the conditions of their day, while intent upon preserving its revolutionary content.

Foremost among the party's revolutionary "revisionists" was Bukharin, determined from the outset of his career as a Bolshevik leader to transform Marxian doctrine into an operative weapon in the struggle for world communism, in the light of his times and the needs of the party. By 1928 his effort to provide a version of Marxism applicable to twentieth-century conditions had taken shape in a comprehensive reformulation of the classical Marxian theory of proletarian revolution which represented a major landmark in the history of Marxian thought. One measure of the success of his efforts was the adoption in 1928 by the Communist International of his modified conception of the causes, processes, and goals of proletarian revolution as its official operative ideology.

Bukharin's revision of the classical Marxian scheme of proletarian revolution did not proceed in a systematic, orderly manner. Rather, it evolved gradually out of the complex interplay of ideas, personalities, and events of the early years of the Bolshevik movement and was developed and expressed in scores of articles, books, and speeches produced between 1912 and 1928. Among these numerous works several merit special mention as outstanding landmarks in the development of Bolshevik thought. These include:

Mirovoe Khoziaistvo i Imperializm,[3] written in 1914–1915, in which he first formulated his revision of Marx's doctrine of capitalist development and laid down his theory of imperialism, as well as its implications for the proletarian revolution—a year before Lenin produced his own version of imperialism;

K Teorii Imperialisticheskovo Gosudarstva,[4] written in 1916, in which Bukharin developed his theory of the state both before and following a proletarian revolution—subjects left vague and ambiguous by Marx and Engels and also not treated by Lenin until a year later;

Programma Kommunistov (1918),[5] a popular pamphlet outlining the program of the Communist party in Russia, written shortly after the November Revolution and distributed in millions of copies to all parts of the country; it was subsequently translated into every major Western language and reprinted in many editions;

Azbuka Kommunizma (1919),[6] written jointly with E. Preobrazhensky, which became the standard textook for an entire generation of party members in the 1920's;

Ekonomika Perekhodnovo Perioda (1920), the first detailed analysis by any Marxist of the transition period between capitalism and communism, which became a classic in its day;

Teoriia Istoricheskovo Materializma (1921), Bukharin's major philosophical work, giving his distinctive interpretation of dialectical and historical materialism; it gave rise to an historic controversy in the party over its implications for Soviet social and economic theory; [7]

Imperializm i Nakoplenie Kapitala (1925), a restatement and modification of the Marxian theory of the accumulation of capital, which Marxists generally agreed stood in need of correction;

Kapitalisticheskaia Stabilizatsiia i Proletarskaia Revoliutsiia (1927), originally a report delivered to the Executive Committee of the Communist International[8] and subsequently published separately and widely distributed; it formulated the official Soviet and Comintern theory of the dynamics of proletarian world revolution during the current stage of "capitalist stabilization";

a series of articles and pamphlets produced in the middle 1920's which spelled out the theory of "socialism in one country" and the policy of gradualism in building socialism in Soviet Russia, and which were instrumental in defeating Trotsky and his supporters;[9]

the *Programme of the Communist International* (1928),[10] one of the basic documents in the history of communism, which intended to be, but failed to become, a modern, twentieth-century version of the original *Communist Manifesto.*

In these and other works, Bukharin achieved a remarkable synthesis between classical Marxian social theory and Bolshevik revolutionary experience. While retaining in his modified conception of proletarian revolution the core of the original doctrine, he enlarged and elaborated it in a way that transformed it into a highly flexible, adaptable ideology that could be invoked under a wide variety of conditions unforeseen by Marx and Engels. Thus, Bukharin not only reaffirmed the essential claims of classical Marxism, but also converted it into a pragmatic instrument of social action.

The similarities and differences between Bukharin's revised version of the theory of proletarian revolution and the original doctrine of Marx and Engels may best be seen by summarizing the main provisions of Bukharin's thought as it finally crystallized by 1928. His point of departure was an expansion of the Marxian theory of capitalist development. Even before Lenin turned his own attention to this problem, Bukharin advanced the concept of a "higher" stage of capitalist development beyond that of industrial capitalism, which Marx and Engels had been unable to foresee. In the normal course of evolution, Bukharin held, industrial capitalism, characterized by the domination of productive capital and free competition within individual states, leads to the rise of "monopoly," or "state capitalism," which is characterized by the "organization" of production within single "state trusts," by the rise of imperialism, and by the formation of a unified, global system of "world capitalism."

Bukharin argued that the progressive accumulation of capital and its centralization led in time to the transfer of ownership of the means of production to the hands of a few powerful bankers and financiers. As the contradictions of capitalism and competition inevitably result in a decline of the rate of profit, these finance capitalists, content at first simply to extract profit from competitive production, attempt to overcome the anarchy of production by means of monopolistic organization of the national economy. Partial organization leads to complete organization, and ultimately the capitalist state is employed to exercise centralized regulation and control of the entire economy from a single center dominated by the finance capitalists. Thus, Bukharin held, industrial capitalism inevitably leads to "organized state capitalism," in which the formerly anarchic productive economy becomes rationally ordered by the new "Leviathan" state.

Although these measures succeed for a time in overcoming the consequences of the declining rate of profit, they do not eliminate the basic anarchy and contradictions of the capitalist system. The ceaseless growth of the organic composition of capital still compels the finance capitalists to seek new ways of earning profit. One solution of this problem is to intensify exploitation at home, which has limits set by the minimum needs of labor. Another is to seek foreign outlets for investment, where returns are greater than at home. Yet another is to market goods abroad, while a last measure is to employ and exploit foreign labor in underdeveloped areas of the world where lower wages yield huge "super-profits." Part of the profits of overseas expansion is shared with the labor elite at home, thereby winning it to the side of the capitalists, dividing the ranks of the workers, and repressing class struggle.

Although the contradictions of capitalism are thus overcome in the advanced capitalist states, the emergence of a world-wide capitalist economy as a result of the extension of capitalist relations simply transfers—"reproduces"—the contradictions to the "higher" level of the world economy. There the contradictions are expressed at first in the form of peaceful economic competition among capitalist state trusts, which then extend political and military control over their economic zones of influence in order to exclude competitors, and in time the underdeveloped areas are converted into outright colonies. Continuing competition for empire leads inevitably to imperialist wars. At first they are limited in scope and intensity, but as the weaker states are conquered and annexed together with their empires by the larger ones, war becomes more frequent and destructive, encompassing finally the entire earth.

Just as ruinous competition during the earlier stage of capitalist development impels the capitalists to organize their national economies, so the emergence of a few huge super-powers as a result of imperialist war leads to efforts by the victorious finance capitalists to divide and exploit the entire world in an amicable, organized manner. At this point, where all of mankind is threatened with total subjection to finance capitalism, the contradictions of the system generate an insurmountable crisis and lead inevitably to its downfall. For when the world economy becomes susceptible to conscious, organized regulation from a single world center, it becomes ripe also for its revolutionary transformation into a communist system. At this point, both the necessity and the feasibility of proletarian world revolution and communism are present. The inherently anarchic and contradictory character of capitalism prevents the finance capitalists from completing the process of organization of the world economy. Only the proletariat is capable of achieving this in a system of communism. Imperialist wars continue, and in the midst of one, or between wars, the system of world capitalism reaches its end. The destruction of productive forces and the increasing misery caused by imperialism and war end in a crisis, in which world capitalism breaks down.

The first breach in the system may come in an advanced capitalist state, where intensified exploitation, political oppression by the state, and the suffering caused by war lead to a classic proletarian revolution. It may occur first in a semi-developed capitalist state, where exploitation of the proletariat by the capitalists and of the peasantry by both the capitalists and the remaining feudal landlords leads to a combination of proletarian revolution and peasant revolt. Or it may occur first in a colonial or an oppressed national minority area, where it takes the form of a revolt against imperialism by various classes. The determining factor in each instance is the relative strength of the forces of world capitalism and the forces of anti-capitalism and anti-imperialism. Breaches in the system occur first and successively thereafter wherever world capitalism is most vulnerable and the forces of revolution strongest.

Bukharin contended that although a "weak link" in the chain of world capitalism may exist in an advanced capitalist state, in reality such links develop first in the colonial periphery. In the finance capitalist centers, the repression or elimination of anarchy, contradiction, and class struggle by the capitalist state effectively forestalls revolution for some time. In the colonial and semi-colonial areas, however, where the contradictions of world capitalism concentrate in the combined form of economic exploitation, national oppression and colonial tyranny, and where, consequently, misery, unrest, and hostility to capitalism are greatest, revolutions mature first. There also, Bukharin added, capitalism is weakest, for these areas lie far from the imperialist centers of the world and have not yet developed their own advanced forms of state capitalism. Thus the First World War, brought on by imperialist competition, led to the first breach in the world capitalist system at its most vulnerable spot—Russia, which was both an object of capitalist imperialism as well as a capitalist state itself. There the combination of proletarian revolution against capitalism, peasant revolt against capitalism and the vestiges of feudalism, and wars of liberation by national minorities severed the chain of capitalism at what was then its most vulnerable link.

An initial break in the system may be followed, as it was after 1921, by a period of recovery and reorganization of the forces of world capitalism. The system does not collapse as a whole or all at once. Revolutions against capitalism and imperialism rise and fall in uneven waves of crisis, breakdown, and recovery. Periods of recovery between crests of the revolutionary tide are only temporary, however, for after the first breach the system as a whole exists in a state of permanent crisis. Each successive break in the system compels the finance capitalists to restore the "equilibrium" of the network on a diminished basis, which leads inevitably to an intensification of the basic contradictions of the system. Thus, although contemporary world capitalism had recovered after 1921 from the initial revolutionary crisis caused by the war and had succeeded in stabilizing itself, the recovery was only "temporary" and "partial," and new waves of revolution would inevitably follow.

Ultimately, Bukharin concluded, as additional areas of the world are successively detached from the capitalist network, the equilibrium of the system becomes completely undermined, and even the capitalist state trusts come down in ruin. Following a period of transition, during which the proletariat reorganizes the world into a system of universal communism, a new epoch dawns for mankind in which the way is opened for the unlimited and unprecedented flourishing of man and society.

Thus world capitalism leads inevitably to world communism by means of revolution. The process, however, in contrast to the classical Marxian view, proceeds in a complex manner and fills an entire historic epoch. In his words, quoting from the *Programme of the Communist International:*

Between capitalist society and communist society lies a period of revolutionary transformation, during which the one is transformed into the other. . . . The transition from the world dictatorship of imperialism to the world dictatorship of the proletariat extends over a long period of proletarian struggles with defeats as well as victories; a period of continuous general crisis in capitalist relationships and growth of social revolutions, that is, of proletarian civil wars against the bourgeoisie; a period of national wars and colonial rebellions, which, although not in themselves revolutionary proletarian socialist movements, are nonetheless objectively, insofar as they undermine the domination of imperialism, constituent parts of the world proletarian movement; a period in which capitalist and socialist economic and social systems exist side by side in "peaceful" relationships as well as in armed conflict; a period of formation of a union of soviet states; a period in which the ties between the soviet states and colonial peoples become ever closer.

. . . Hence it follows that the international proletarian revolution cannot be conceived as a single event occurring simultaneously all over the world. At first socialism may be victorious in a few, or even in one single capitalist country. Every such proletarian victory, however, intensifies the general crisis of capitalism. Thus, the capitalist system as a whole reaches the point of its final collapse; the dictatorship of finance capital gives way to the dictatorship of the proletariat.[11]

Bukharin's revision of the classical Marxian theory of the causes of proletarian revolution led necessarily to modifications of his conception of the revolutionary process itself. Since the prerequisite for the transformation of world capitalism into world communism is the creation first of a dictatorship of the proletariat throughout the world, and since the world dictatorship of the proletariat is established as the result of revolutions in countries at various levels of economic and social development, the general process by which the proletariat comes to power throughout the world and utilizes such power for the purpose of realizing communism is also varied and complex.

In semi-capitalist states and colonial areas, where revolutions mature first, the proletariat inevitably finds itself a minority of the population. If it is to overturn capitalism and sever the chain of imperialism, it needs allies in the struggle. The peasant masses in such countries, living under a combination of both capitalist and feudal exploitation, represent a potential reservoir of revolutionary power which can be mobilized if the revolution promises to benefit them. Accordingly, in order to secure the support of the peasantry and retain its support after a revolution, when the proletariat is small in numbers and requires allies in the struggle against counter-revolution and for socialism, it must advance revolutionary objectives that correspond with the interests of the peasants. This means, Bukharin maintained, that revolutions in semi-capitalist countries cannot proceed directly towards a pure proletarian dictatorship or the immediate introduction of complete socialism. The political alliance that brings the proletariat to power must be maintained indefinitely in the form of a "democratic dictatorship of the proletariat and peasantry," a political partnership in which the proletariat dominates while sharing power with the non-proletariatian masses. Only after a period of economic development under the democratic dictatorship which broadens the socialized base of society and permits a transition to a true proletarian dictatorship does the revolution proceed towards pure socialist objectives. Hence the economic program in such countries must take into account the most pressing demands of the peasantry, which does not at first desire socialism, but rather an equitable distribution of land and liberation from the exploitation of feudalism and capitalism. Moreover, since the proletariat will be confronted in such countries with many vestiges of pre-capitalist economic forms, it will be unable for this reason also to proceed directly toward socialist construction in all areas of the economy. Rather, the proletariat may introduce socialist forms only in the large-scale enterprises inherited from the previous regime, while employing entirely different measures in the private, small-scale sector. There, it must strive by means of peaceful, evolutionary methods to eliminate private enterprise and supplant it with socialist enterprise, lest the political alliance that brings the proletariat to power and retains it in power be destroyed by class war. Accordingly, the proletariat must tolerate the indefinite existence of private production, attempting only by means of incentives, economic competition, propaganda, and example to eliminate the private sector of the economy and attract its members to the socialist forms of the future. Thus the transitional form of democratic dictatorship of the proletariat and peasantry must carry out transitional economic policy.

For all these reasons, Bukharin concluded, socialism in underdeveloped countries is established only slowly and gradually, governed in its pace of development and methods by the material legacy inherited from the previous regime, by the relative strength of the proletariat and other class forces, and by the extent and tenacity of small-scale, private enterprise. Any effort to accelerate or force the pace can lead only to a disruption of the inherent equilibrium of forces in transitional society and to a rift in the worker-peasant bloc.

In more advanced capitalist states, however, where the material base of society inherited from the bourgeois regime is broader, and where fewer pre-capitalist economic and social vestiges remain, the transition will be proportionately more rapid and direct. In such countries the revolution will take more nearly the form of a pure, classical proletarian revolution with only a minimum of "bourgeois-democratic" tasks to complete and will move directly and rapidly toward socialism.

Finally, in areas where revolutions against imperialism break out but where capitalism has been only recently introduced, or not at all, and where, consequently, there is no proletariat and no base on which to construct socialism, the process of advancing towards communism will be far different. Such areas, he held, will be annexed directly into the growing proletarian-socialist sector of the world and advanced immediately towards socialism, thereby enabling them to "skip the stage of capitalism."

Summarizing his view of the process of revolution under the conditions of finance capitalism and imperialism, Bukharin stated, in the words of the Comintern Programme:

> The international proletarian revolution represents a combination of processes which vary in time and character: pure proletarian revolutions, revolutions of a bourgeois-democratic type which grow into proletarian revolutions, wars for national liberation, and colonial revolutions. The world dictatorship of the proletariat comes about only as the final result of this revolutionary process.
>
> The uneven development of capitalism, which becomes more accentuated in the period of imperialism, gives rise to various types of capitalism, to different shades of ripeness of capitalism in different countries, to a variety of specific conditions of the revolutionary process. These circumstances make it historically inevitable that the proletariat will comes to power in a variety of ways and degrees of rapidity and that a number of countries must pass through certain transitional stages leading to the dictatorship of the proletariat and must adopt varied forms of socialist construction.[12]

From this brief summary of the major revisions introduced by Bukharin into the classical Marxian scheme of revolution it may be seen that his efforts to expand the original body of social and revolutionary theory and to incorporate within it both post-Marxian world developments and the experience of the Russian Revolution resulted, in effect, in the creation of a substantially new revolutionary doctrine that diverged considerably from the letter of the original. Whereas Marx and Engels had been concerned primarily with the problem of proletarian revolution in the most advanced capitalist states and had developed their theories with this in mind, Bukharin broadened the conception of proletarian revolution to encompass many other types of revolutionary movements in countries at various levels of economic and social development. Moreover, in modifying the classical Marxian scheme, Bukharin placed far greater emphasis than Marx or Engels had upon the role of conscious leadership by dispensing with the traditional Marxian prerequisites of a minimum level of economic development and the presence of a majority proletariat, substituting instead the actions of the Communist parties as primary determinants of revolution.

While departing in this way from the traditional Marxian conception of proletarian revolution, Bukharin permitted its application to a wider variety of specific conditions.

While the historic significance of Bukharin's revisions of classical Marxian revolutionary theory is obvious, two important questions relating to his thought logically arise—namely, the extent to which his views on revolution were original and the precise extent to which they influenced the development of Communist theory and practice. In considering these questions, it may be noted, first of all, that there is a close affinity between Bukharin's version of revolutionary Marxism, and ideas that have come to be known as "Leninism" and "Stalinism," implying a source of authorship other than Bukharin. While many similarities between Bukharin's views and those of Lenin and Stalin undoubtedly exist, it should be recalled that in the case of Lenin, Bukharin anticipated the former in at least two important instances—namely, the theory of imperialism and the theory of the state before and following a proletarian revolution—and in other instances directly influenced Lenin's own ideological development, as Lenin himself acknowledged. This in no way implies that Bukharin did not borrow heavily from the Leninist store of ideas as well, for he freely admitted this. At the same time, however, it is also true that in so doing, Bukharin did not simply take over Leninist ideas intact, but rather carried their implications and meaning further than Lenin had and ultimately achieved, as Lenin had not before his death, a system of thought that neatly integrated classical Marxism and the new Bolshevik concepts and which became the official outlook of the international Communist movement from the late 1920's onward.

With respect to the similarities between Bukharin's thought and that of Stalin's, it should be noted that, apart from a number of specific theoretical innovations introduced by Stalin before and after 1928 into the body of Bolshevik doctrine, his primary contribution to the development of Communist ideology was to harden the doctrine that had emerged by 1928 into a rigid dogma and to apply it to areas of Soviet life not yet fully affected by it in Bukharin's day. Stalin made two major ideological contributions before 1928, one on the nationality problem and the other on the theory of "socialism in one country." In the former instance, some Soviet specialists attribute all but the actual writing of Stalin's initial article on the nationality question in 1913 to Bukharin,[13] while the historical record clearly reveals that although Stalin first advanced the theory of "socialism in one country" late in 1924, it was Bukharin, and not Stalin, who gave it its full theoretical expression and integrated it into the body of Bolshevik ideology. On the other hand, although Stalin added new doctrines after 1928 to the official body of Communist theory, in some instances these were merely reaffirmations or reformulations of ideas advanced earlier by Bukharin. An example of this is Stalin's theory of "revolution from above" by which he justified his programs of enforced industrialization and collectivization in the 1930's. The precedent for this theory, however, had been laid down as early as 1920 by Bukharin, when he characterized the dynamics of the transition period as an extraordinary process of "reverse influence of the superstructure on the base," arising from the revolutionary, "cataclysmic nature of the transitional process."

It should be remembered, too, in estimating the influence of Bukharin's views on Stalin, that between Lenin's death in 1924 and Stalin's rise to unrivalled power after 1928, the ideology of the party was still in a process of evolution. During this time, Stalin and Bukharin were political allies and held essentially similar views, but it was Bukharin, not Stalin, who dominated the Soviet scene in the ideological sphere. Accordingly, it is far more probable to assume that Bukharin provided the theoretical leadership of their political alliance, rather than the other way round. Later, although Stalin turned against Bukharin and repudiated some of his specific policies applicable to the late 1920's, he retained the essential core of Bukharin's thought without, however, crediting him any longer with its origin.

Summarizing the historical significance of Bukharin's role in the development of Bolshevik revolutionary doctrine, it may be seen that, among other things, Bukharin filled the ideological gap between the death of Lenin and the rise of Stalin. For although it is axiomatic in the Communist world to portray the evolution of Soviet ideology as a direct, continuous line of orthodox doctrinal descent running from Marx through Lenin to Stalin, there are important differences as well as similarities between Leninism and Stalinism. Both the differences and similarities, however, cannot be adequately understood without taking into account Bukharin's intervening influence between the years 1924 and 1928. It may well be for this reason, among others, that Stalin thought it necessary not only to break Bukharin's political authority as a prerequisite to his own unchallenged leadership of the Communist world, but also to destroy both him and his image in the party as well.

Notes

1. There is no comprehensive biography of Bukharin. The material in this essay is based on the research of the writer for his doctoral dissertation, "Nikolai I. Bukharin's Theory of World Revolution" (Russian Institute of Columbia University). The only specialized works dealing primarily with Bukharin or some phase of his career and produced in the West are: Peter Knirsch, *Die Ökonomischen Anschauungen Nikolai I. Bucharins* (Berlin: East European Institute of the Free University of Berlin, 1959); John E. Flaherty, "The Political Career of Nicholas I. Bukharin" (unpublished doctoral dissertation, New York University, 1954); Daniel J. Nelson, "The Views of N. Bukharin on the Future Communist Society" (unpublished master's thesis, Russian Institute of Columbia University, 1952); Sidney Heitman, "Bukharin's Conception of the Transition to Communism in Soviet Russia: An Analysis of His Basic Views, 1923-1928" (unpublished Certificate Essay, Russian Institute of Columbia University, 1952). Two bibliographies of Bukharin's works have been published: Sidney Heitman, *An Annotated Bibliography of Nikolai I. Bukharin's Published Works* (Fort Collins, Colorado: privately printed, 1958), and Sidney Heitman and Peter Knirsch, *N. I. Bucharin*, Vol. I. in *Bibliographische Mitteilungen des Osteuropa-Instituts an der Freien Universität Berlin* (Berlin: East European Institute of the Free University of Berlin, 1959).

There are only two reliable and fairly detailed biographical sketches of Bukharin's life and work emanating from Soviet sources. One is an autobiographical article written in the early or middle 1920's and published in *Entsiklopedicheskii Slovar Russkovo Bibliographicheskovo Instituta Granat* (52 vols.; Moscow: Granat Russian Bibliographical Institute, 1910-1934; XLI, Part 1, 51-56). The other is an article written by one of Bukharin's followers, D. P. Maretskii, and published in 1927 in *Bolshaia Sovetskaia Entsiklopediia* (1st ed.; 65 vols.; Moscow, 1926-1931; VIII, 271-283).

2. In his so-called "testament," Lenin is purported to have characterized Bukharin as "the most valuable and biggest theoretician of the Party." It should be noted, however, that Lenin also added, "But Bukharin's views can only with the very greatest doubt be regarded as Marxian, for there is something scholastic in him (as he has never learned and, I think, never fully understood the dialectic)." Leon Trotsky, *The Suppressed Testament of Lenin*, New York, 1935, p. 6.

3. Moscow, 1918. An English translation was published in 1929 under the title, *Imperialism and World Economy*.

4. Published in *Revoliutsiia Prava* (Moscow, 1925), Part I, pp. 5-32.

5. Petrograd: Petrograd Soviet of Workers' and Red Army Deputies.

6. Translated into English as *The ABC of Communism*.

7. See Raymond Bauer, *The New Man in Soviet Psychology* (Harvard University Press, 1952), for a brief discussion of this controversy and a more detailed analysis of its consequences for the development of Soviet psychological theory and practice.

8. See *Puti Mirovoi Revoliutsii. Sedmoi Rasshirennyi Plenum Ispolnitelnovo Komiteta Kommunisticheskovo Internatsionala. Stenograficheskii Otchet* (2 vols.; Moscow-Leningrad, 1927).

9. Novoe Otkrovenie o Sovetskoi Ekonomike, ili Kak Mozhno Pogubit Rabochii-Krestianskii Blok; K Voprosu ob Ekonomicheskom Obosnovanii Trotskizma," in *K Voprosu o Trotskizme* (Moscow-Leningrad, 1925); *K Kritke Ekonomicheskoi Platformy Oppozitsii, op. cit.; Kak Ne Nuzhno Pisat Istoriiu*

Oktiabria; Po Povodu Knigi Tov. Trotskogo "1917 g.," *op. cit.; K Voprosu o Trotskizme; Teoriia Permanentnoi Revoliutsii, op. cit,;* "O Kharaktere Nashei Revoliutsii i o Vozmozhnosti Pobedonosnovo Sotsialisticheskovo Stroitelstva v SSSR," in *V. Zashchitu Proletarskoi Diktatury; Sbornik* (Moscow-Leningrad: State Publishing House, 1928); *Put k Sotsializmu i Rabochii-Krestianskii Soiuz* (Moscow-Leningrad, 1927); "O Novoi Ekonomicheskoi Politike i Nashikh Zadachakh," *Bolshevik* (No. 7-8, 1924).

10. *International Press Correspondence*, VIII, No. 92, December 31, 1928, 1749-1768. While the authorship of the Programme adopted in 1928 by the Sixth World Congress of the Communist International was officially attributed to the committee which prepared and submitted it for consideration, it was written by Bukharin, and amended in the program commission.

11. *The Programme of the Communist International, op. cit.,* p. 1756. Minor changes have been made in the original wording and punctuation which do not change the meaning.

12. *Ibid.,* p. 1761. Minor changes have been made in the original.

13. Abdurakhman Avtorkhanov, supporter of Bukharin, states in his *Stalin and the Soviet Communist Party; A Study in the Technology of Power* (New York, 1959), for example, that Bukharin "helped Stalin to compile his *Marxism and the National Question,* which first appeared under the title of *Social Democracy and the Problem of Nationalities. . . .* Bukharin found and translated for Stalin suitable quotations . . . and edited the entire book before it was accepted by Lenin for publication in 1913. . . ." (p. 23)

It should be noted, however, that while some writers sustain Avtorkhanov's contention, for example Bertram Wolfe in *Three Who Made a Revolution* (New York, 1948, p. 582); others deny that Bukharin's views influenced Stalin in the writing of this article (see Isaac Deutscher, *Stalin; A Political Biography,* New York, 1947, p. 119, for example).

Leon Trotsky as a historian
and sociologist of revolution

ISAAC DEUTSCHER

Like Thucydides, Dante, Machiavelli, Heine, Marx, Herzen, and other thinkers and poets, Trotsky attained his full eminence as a writer only in exile, during the few Prinkipo years. Posterity will remember him as the historian of the October Revolution as well as its leader. No other Bolshevik has or could have produced so great and splendid an account of the events of 1917; and none of the many writers of the anti-Bolshevik parties has presented any worthy counterpart to it. The promise of this achievement could be discerned in Trotsky very early. His descriptions of the revolution of 1905 provide till this day the most vivid panorama of that "general rehearsal" for 1917. He produced his first narrative and analysis of the upheavals of 1917 only a few weeks after the October insurrection, during the recesses of the Brest Litovsk peace conference; and in subsequent years he went on working at his historical interpretation of the events in which he had been a protagonist. There was in him a twofold *vis historica:* the revolutionary's urge to make history and the writer's impulse to describe it and grasp its meaning.

All banished men brood over the past; but only a few, very few, conquer the future. Hardly any one among them, however, has had to fight for his life, morally and physically, as Trotsky fought. Stalin at first inflicted exile on him in the way the Romans used to inflict it—as a substitute for the death penalty; and he was not to remain content with the substitute. Even before Trotsky was assassinated physically, his moral assassins were at work for years, first effacing his name from the annals of the revolution and then reinscribing it as the eponym of counter-revolution. Trotsky the historian was therefore doubly embattled: he defended the revolution against its enemies; and he defended his own place

From Isaac Deutscher, *The Prophet Outcast* (New York: Oxford University Press, 1963), pp. 218-221, 230-247.

in it. No writer has ever created his major work in similar conditions, designed to inflame all his passions, to rob him of every calm thought, and to distort his vision. In Trotsky all passions were aroused, but his thought remained calm and his vision clear. He often recalled Spinoza's maxim: "Neither weep nor laugh but understand"; but he himself could not help weeping and laughing; yet he understood.

It would not be quite right to say that as historian he combined extreme partisanship with rigorous objectivity. He had no need to combine them: they were the heat and the light of his work, and as heat and light belonged to each other. He scorned the "impartiality" and "conciliatory justice" of the scholar who pretends "to stand on the wall of a threatened city and behold at the same time the besiegers and the besieged." [1] His own place was, as it had been in the years 1917–1922, within the revolution's threatened city. Yet his involvement in the struggle, far from blurring his sight, sharpens it. His antagonism to Russia's old ruling classes and their willing and unwilling supporters makes him see clearly not only their vices or weaknesses but also such feeble and ineffective virtues as they possessed. Here, as in the best military thinking, extreme parti sanship and scrupulously sober observation indeed go hand in hand. To the good soldier nothing is of greater importance than to get a realistic picture of the "other side of the hill," unclouded by wishful thinking or emotion. Trotsky, the commander of the October insurrection, had acted on this principle; and Trotsky the historian does the same. He achieves in his image of the revolution the unity of the subjective and the objective elements.

His historical writing is dialectical as is hardly any other such work produced by the Marxist school of thought since Marx, from whom he derives his method and style. To Marx's minor historical works, *The Class Struggle in France, The 18th Brumaire of Louis Bonaparte,* and *The Civil War in France,* Trotsky's *History* stands as the large mural painting stands to the miniature. Whereas Marx towers above the disciple in the power of his abstract thought and gothic imagination, the disciple is superior as epic artist, especially as master of the graphic portrayal of masses and individuals in action. His socio-political analysis and artistic vision are in such concord that there is no trace of any divergence. His thought and his imagination take flight together. He expounds his theory of revolution with the tension and the *élan* of narrative; and his narrative takes depth from his ideas. His scenes, portraits, and dialogues, sensuous in their reality, are inwardly illumined by his conception of the historical process. Many non-Marxist critics have been impressed by this distinctive quality of his writing. Here, for instance, is what a British historian, A. L. Rowse, says:

The real importance of Trotsky's *History* does not lie in his power of word painting, either of character or of scene, though indeed his gift is so brilliant and incisive that one is continually reminded of Carlyle. There is something of the same technique, the same mannerism even, in the way the rapid lights shift across the scene and particular odd episodes are brought out in singular sharpness of relief and made to bear general significance; something of the same difficulty in following the sequel of events—the lights are so blinding—one may add. But where Carlyle had but his magnificent powers of intuition to rely on, Trotsky has a theory of history at his command, which enables him to grasp what is significant and to relate things together. The same point can be illustrated more appositely by comparison with Winston Churchill's *The World Crisis,* for the two men are not dissimilar in character and gifts of mind. But here again one notices the difference; for Mr. Churchill's history, for all its personality, its vividness, and vitality, points which it has in common with Trotsky—has not a philosophy of history behind it.[2]

The remark about the similarity between Trotsky and Churchill is correct: at their opposite poles the two men represent the same blend of realism and romanticism, the same pugnacity, the same inclination to look, and to run, ahead of their class and milieu, and the same urge to make and to write history. One need not deny Churchill a "philosophy of history" even if he holds it only instinctively; but it is true that Trotsky's is a fully formed and elaborate theory. What is important is that his theoretical *Weltanschauung* permeates his sensitivity, amplifies his intuition, and heightens his vision. And, although he has in common with Carlyle the intensity and dazzling brilliance of imagery, he also has the compactness and clarity of expression and the balance of the greatest classical historians. He is indeed the only historian of genius that the Marxist school of thought has so far produced and so far—rejected.[3]

Of Trotsky's two major historical works, *My Life* and the *History,* the former is, of course, the less ambitious. He wrote it too early in a sense, though if he had not written it in 1929, or shortly thereafter, he might not have written it at all. It tells in the main one half of his story, that of his revolutionary triumph; it only sketches the beginning of the other half, which was still unfolding. He concluded the book after a few months in exile, only five years or so after the struggle between him and Stalin had begun in earnest. The conflict was still too fresh, and in relating it he was handicapped by tactical considerations and lack of perspective. . . .

The *History* is his crowning work, both in scale and power and as the fullest expression of his ideas on revolution. As an account of a revolution, given by one of its chief actors, it stands unique in world literature.

He introduces us to the scene of 1917 with a chapter "Peculiarities of Russia's Development" which sets the events in deep historical perspective; and one recognizes in this chapter at once an enriched and mature version of his earliest exposition of Permanent Revolution, dating back to 1906.[4] We are shown Russia entering the twentieth century without having shaken off the Middle Ages or passed through a Reformation and bourgeois revolution, yet with elements of a modern bourgeois civilization thrust into her archaic existence. Forced to advance under superior economic and military pressure from the West, she could not go through all the phases of the "classical" cycle of western European progress. "Savages throw away their bows and arrows for rifles all at once, without travelling the road which lay between those two weapons in the past." Modern Russia could not enact a Reformation of her own or a bourgeois revolution under bourgeois leadership. Her very backwardness impelled her to advance politically all at once to the point western Europe had reached and to go beyond it—to socialist revolution. Her feeble bourgeoisie being unable to cast off the burden of a semi-feudal absolutism, her small but compact working class, eventually supported by a rebellious peasantry, came forward as the leading revolutionary force. The working class could not content itself with a revolution resulting in the establishment of a bourgeois democracy—it had to fight for the realization of the socialist program. Thus by a "law of combined development" the extreme of backwardness tended towards the extreme of progress, and this led to the explosion of 1917.

The "law of combined development" accounts for the force of the tensions within Russia's social structure. Trotsky, however, treats the social structure as a "relatively constant" element of the situation which does not account by itself for the events of the revolution. In a controversy with Pokrovsky, he points out that neither in 1917 nor in the preceding decade did any fundamental change occur in Russia's social structure—the war had weakened and exposed that structure but not altered it.[5] The national economy and the basic relations between social classes were in 1917 broadly the same as in 1912–1914, and even in 1905–1907. What then accounted directly for the eruptions of February and October, and for the violent ebb and flow of revolution in between? The changes in mass psychology, Trotsky replies. If the structure of society was the constant factor, the temper and the moods of the masses were the variable element which determined the flux and reflux of events, their rhythm and direction. "The most indubitable feature of a revolution is the direct intervention of the masses in historic events. The revolution is there in their nerves before it comes out into the street." The *History* is therefore to a large extent a study in revolutionary mass psychology. Delving into the interconnection between the "constant" and "variable" factors, he demonstrates that what makes for revolution is not merely the fact that the social and political institutions have long been in decay and crying out to be overthrown, but the circumstances that many millions of people have for the first time heard that "cry" and become aware of it. In the social structure the revolution had been ripe well before 1917; in the mind of the masses it ripened only in 1917. Thus, paradoxically, the deeper cause of revolution lies not in the mobility of men's minds, but in their inert conservatism; men rise *en masse* only when they suddenly realize their mental lag behind the times and want to make it good all at once. This is the lesson the *History* drives home: no great upheaval in society follows automatically from the decay of an old order; generations may live under a decaying order without being aware of it. But when, under the impact of some catastrophe like war or economic collapse, they become conscious of it, there comes the gigantic outburst of despair, hope, and activity. The historian has therefore to "enter into the nerves" and the minds of millions of people in order to feel and convey the mighty heave that overturns the established order.

The academic pedant burrowing in mountains of documents in order to reconstruct from them a single historical incident may say that no historian can "enter into the nerves" of millions. Trotsky is aware of the difficulties: the manifestations of mass consciousness are scrappy and scattered; and this may lead the historian to arbitrary constructions and false intuitions. But he points out that the historian can nevertheless verify the truth or untruth of his image of mass consciousness by certain severely objective tests. He must follow faithfully the internal evidence of the events. He can and must check whether the motion of mass consciousness, as he sees it, is consistent with itself; whether every phase of it follows necessarily from what went before it, and whether it leads clearly to what comes after it. He must further consider whether the flow of mass consciousness is consistent with the movement of events: are the moods of the people reflected in the events and do they in turn reflect these? If it be argued that the answers to such questions must be vague and subjective, Trotsky replies by referring, in the Marxist manner, to practical action as the final criterion. He points out that what he is doing as an historian, he and other Bolshevik leaders did while they were making the revolution: relying upon analysis and observation they made guesses about the state of mind and the moods of the masses. All their crucial political decisions rested on these "guesses"; and the course of the revolution is there to show that, despite trial and error, these had been broadly correct. If in the heat of battle the revolutionary was able to form an approximately correct image of the political emotions and thoughts of millions, there is no reason why the historian should not be able to form it after the event.

The manner in which Trotsky depicts the mass in action has much in common with Eisenstein's method in the classical *Potemkin*. He picks out of the crowd a few individuals, exposes them in a moment of excitement or apathy, and lets them express their mood in a phrase or gesture; then he shows us the crowd again, a dense and warm crowd, swayed by a tidal emotion or moving into action; and we recognize at once that this is the emotion or action which the individual phrase or gesture had foreshadowed. He has a peculiar gift for overhearing the multitudes as they think aloud and for letting us hear them for ourselves. In conception and image he leads perpetually from the general to the particular and back to the general; and the passage is never unnatural or strained. Here one is again reminded of the comparison between Trotsky and Carlyle; but the comparison lights up a contrast rather than a similarity. In the histories of both much of the ethos depends on the mass scenes. Both make us feel the elemental force of an insurgent people, so that we view it as if we were watching landslides or avalanches on the move. But whereas Carlyle's crowds are driven only by emotion, Trotsky's think and reflect. They are elemental; yet they are human. Carlyle's mass is enveloped in a purple haze of mysticism, which suggests that the revolutionary people of France are God's blind scourge bringing retribution upon a sinful ruling class. His mass fascinates us and repels us. He "enters into its nerves," but only after he has worked himself up into a frenzy—he himself is all nerves and hallucinatory fever. Trotsky draws his mass scenes with no less imaginative *élan,* but with crystalline clarity. He lets us feel that here and now men make their own history; and that they do it in accordance with the "laws of history," but also by acts of their consciousness and will. Of such men, even though they may be illiterate and crude, he is proud; and he wants us to be proud of them. The revolution is for him that brief but pregnant moment when the humble and downtrodden at last have their say. In his eyes this moment redeems ages of oppression. He harks back to it with a nostalgia which gives the re-enactment a vivid and high relief.

He does not, however, overstate the role of the masses. He does not oppose them to the parties and leaders as, for instance, does Kropotkin, the great anarchist historian of the French Revolution, who seeks to prove that every advance of the revolution is due to spontaneous popular action and every setback to the scheming and the "statesmanship" of politicians. Trotsky sees the masses as the driving force of the upheaval, yet a force which needs to be concentrated and directed. Only the party can provide direction. "Without a guiding organization the energy of the mass would dissipate like steam not enclosed in a piston box. But nevertheless what moves things is not the piston or the box but the steam." The great contrast which he draws between the two revolutions of 1917 is based on this idea. The February revolution was essentially the work of the masses themselves, whose energy was powerful enough to force the Tsar to abdicate and to bring the Soviets into existence, but then dissipated before having solved any of the great issues, allowing Prince Lvov to become the head of the government. The October Revolution was primarily the work of the Bolsheviks who focused and directed the energy of the masses.

The relationship between classes and parties is much more complex in Trotsky's presentation, however, than any mechanistic simile might suggest. He shows the subtle interplay of many objective and subjective factors. What guides a party in its action is basically a definite class interest. But the connection between class and party is often involved and sometimes ambiguous; in a revolutionary era it is also highly unstable. Even if a party's behavior is ultimately governed by its nexus with one particular class, it may recruit its following from another, a potentially hostile, class. Or it may represent only one phase in the development of a social milieu, a phase to which some leaders remain mentally fixed, while the milieu has left it far behind. Or else a party may be ahead of its class and expound a program which the latter is not yet ready to accept, but which events will force it to accept; and so on and so forth. In a revolution the traditional political balance collapses, and new alignments take shape abruptly. Trotsky's *History* is a grand inquiry into the dynamic of these processes.

We have said that Trotsky does not disguise his hostility towards the enemies of the October Revolution. To put it more accurately, he confronts them before the tribunal of history as Counsel for the Prosecution; and there he inflicts upon them for a second time the defeat he had inflicted on them in the streets of Petrograd. As a rule this is not a role that fits the historian. Yet in history as in law it happens that the Counsel for the Prosecution may present the fullest possible truth of a case—namely, when he charges the men in the dock with offences they have actually committed; when he does not exaggerate their guilt; when he enters into their conditions and motives and gives due weight to mitigating circumstances; when he supports every count of the indictment with ample and valid evidence; and, finally, when the defendants, having full freedom to refute the evidence, not only fail to do so, but loudly quar-relling among themselves in the dock only confirm it. Such is the manner in which Trotsky discharges his duty. When his *History* was published, and for many years thereafter, most of the chiefs of the anti-Bolshevik parties, Miliukov, Kerensky, Tseretelli, Chernov, Dan, Abramovich, and others were alive and active as émigrés. Yet none of them has exposed a single significant flaw in the fabric of fact which he presented; and none, with the partial exception of Miliukov, has seriously attempted an alternative account.[6] And so (since no history worthy of the name has so far been produced in the Soviet Union either), Trotsky's work is still, in the fifth decade after October, the only full-scale history of the revolu-tion. This is no accident. All the other major actors, again with the partial exception of Miliukov, were so entangled in their contradictions and failures as to be incapable of presenting in full their own more or less coherent versions. They refused to go back as historians to the fatal battlefield where every landmark and indeed every inch of land reminded them of their disgrace. Trotsky revisits the battlefield, his conscience clear and his head up.

Yet his story has no real villains. He does not, as a rule, depict the enemies of Bolshevism as corrupt and depraved men. He does not strip them of their private virtues and personal honor. If they nevertheless stand condemned, it is because he has shown them as defending inde-fensible causes, as lagging behind the times, as elevated by events to heights of responsibility to which they had not risen mentally and mor-ally, and as perpetually torn between word and deed. The villainy he exposes lies in the archaic social system rather than in individuals. His determinist view of history allows him to treat adversaries, not indul-gently indeed, but fairly, and at times generously. When he depicts an enemy in power he shows him complacent, talking big, throwing his weight about; and he crushes him with irony or indignation. Not rarely, however, he stops to pay a tribute to an adversary's past achievement, integrity, even heroism; and he sighs over the deterioration of a character worthy of a better destiny. When he describes a broken enemy, he dwells on the necessity of what had happened and exults in its historic justice; but sometimes the exultation subsides and he casts a commiserating glance—usually his last glance—at the prostrate victim.

He never paints the enemies of the revolution blacker than they have painted one another. Often he paints them less black, because he dissects their mutual animosities and jealousies and makes allowance for exag-geration in the cruel insults they exchanged. He treats the Tsar and the Tsarina no more mercilessly than Witte, Miliukov, Denikin, and even more orthodox monarchists have treated them. He even "defends" the

Tsar against Liberal critics who have held that by means of timely concessions the Tsar might have averted the catastrophe. Nicholas II, Trotsky argues, made quite a few concessions, but could not yield more ground than self-preservation permitted. As in Tolstoy's *War and Peace,* so in Trotsky the Tsar is a "slave of history." "Nicholas II inherited from his ancestors not only a giant empire, but also a revolution. And they did not bequeath him one quality which would have made him capable of governing an empire, or even a province, or a county. To that historical flood which was rolling its billows each one closer to the gates of his palace, the last Romanov opposed only a dumb indifference." [7] He draws a memorable analogy between three doomed monarchs: Nicholas II, Louis XVI, and Charles I, and also between their Queens. Nicholas's chief characteristic is not just cruelty, of which he was capable, or stupidity, but "meagerness of inner powers, a weakness of the nervous discharge, poverty of spiritual resources." "Both Nicholas and Louis XVI give the impression of people overburdened by their job, but at the same time unwilling to give up even a part of those rights which they are unable to use." Each went to the abyss "with the crown pushed down over his head." But, Trotsky remarks, "would it be any easier . . . to go to an abyss which you cannot escape anyway with your eyes wide open?" He shows that at the decisive moments, when the three sovereigns are overtaken by their fate, they look so much like each other that their distinctive features seem to vanish, because "to a tickle people react differently, but to red hot iron alike." As for the Tsarina and Marie Antoinette, both were "enterprising but chicken-headed" and both "see rainbow dreams as they drown." [8]

And here is how he portrays the Cadets, the Mensheviks, and the Social Revolutionaries. Miliukov: "Professor of history, author of significant scholarly works, founder of the Cadet Party . . . completely free from that insufferable, half-aristocratic and half-intellectual, political dilettantism which is proper to the majority of Russian Liberal men of politics. Miliukov took his profession very seriously and that alone distinguishes him." The Russian bourgeoisie did not like him because "prosaically and soberly, without adornment [he] expressed the political essence of the Russian bourgeoisie. Beholding himself in the Miliukov mirror, the man of the bourgeoisie saw himself grey, self-interested, and cowardly; and, as often happens, he took offense at the mirror." Rodzianko, the Tsar's Lord Chamberlain who became one of the leaders of the February regime, cuts a grotesque figure: "Having received power from the hands of conspirators, rebels, and tyrannicides, [he] wore a haunted expression in those days . . . sneaked on tiptoe round the blaze of the revolution, choking from the smoke and saying: 'Let it burn down to the coals, then we will try to cook up something.' " [9]

Trotsky's Mensheviks and Social Revolutionaries have, of course, little in common with the faceless counter-revolutionary phantoms usually shown in Stalinist and even post-Stalinist literature. Each of them belongs to his species, but has his individual traits of character. Here is a thumbnail sketch of Chkheidze, the Menshevik President of the Petrograd Soviet: "He tried to consecrate to the duties of his office all the resources of his conscientiousness, concealing his perpetual lack of confidence in himself under an ingenious jocularity. He carried the ineradicable imprint of his province . . . mountainous Georgia . . . the Gironde of the Russian revolution." The "most distinguished figure" of that Gironde, Tseretelli, had for many years been a hard labor convict in Siberia, yet

remained a radical of the southern French type. In conditions of ordinary parliamentary routine he would have been a fish in water. But he was born into a revolutionary epoch and had poisoned himself in youth with a dose of Marxism. At any rate, of all the Mensheviks, Tseretelli . . . revealed the widest horizon and the [strongest] desire to pursue a consistent policy. For this reason he, more than any other, helped on with the destruction of the February regime. Chkheidze wholly submitted to Tseretelli, although at moments he was frightened by that doctrinaire straightforwardness which caused the revolutionary hard labor convict of yesterday to unite with the conservative representatives of the bourgeoisie.[10]

Skobelev, once Trotsky's disciple, looks like an undergraduate "playing the role of a statesman on a home-made stage." And as for Lieber:

If the first violin in the orchestra . . . was Tseretelli, the piercing clarinet was played by Lieber, with all his lung power and blood in his eyes. This was a Menshevik of the Jewish Workers' Union (the Bund) with a long revolutionary past, very sincere, very temperamental, very eloquent, very limited, and passionately desirous of showing himself an inflexible patriot and iron statesman . . . beside himself with hatred of Bolsheviks.

Chernov, the ex-participant in the Zimmerwald movement, now Kerensky's Minister:

A well-read rather than educated man, with a considerable but unintegrated learning, Chernov always had at his disposition a boundless assortment of appropriate quotations, which for a long time caught the imagination of the Russian youth without teaching them much. There was only one single question which this many-worded leader could not answer: Whom was he leading and whither? The eclectic formulas of Chernov, ornamented with moralisms and verses, united for a time a most variegated public who at all critical moments pulled in different directions. No wonder Chernov complacently contrasted his methods of forming a party with Lenin's "sectarianism.". . . . He decided to evade all issues, abstaining from the vote became for him a form of political life. . . . With all the differences between Chernov and Kerensky, who hated each other, they were both completely rooted in the pre-revolutionary past—in the old, flabby Russian society, in that thin-blooded and pretentious intelligentsia, burning with a desire to teach the masses of the people, to be their guardian and benefactor, but completely incapable of listening to them, understanding them, and learning from them.[11]

What distinguishes Trotsky's Bolsheviks from all other parties is precisely the ability to "learn from the masses" as well as to teach them. But it is not without reluctance and inner resistance that they learn and rise to their task; and when Trotsky concludes with an apotheosis of the revolution and its party, he leaves us wondering for just how long the Bolsheviks will go on "learning from the masses." The party he shows us is very different from the "iron phalanx" which, in the official legend, marches steadfastly and irresistibly, free from all human frailty, towards its predetermined goal. It is not that Trotsky's Bolsheviks lack "iron," determination and audacity; but they possess these qualities in doses appropriate to the human character and distributed rather unevenly among leaders and rankers. We see them in their finest moments, when isolated, insulted, and battered, they hope and struggle on. In selfless devotion to a cause none of their adversaries is their equal. Greatness of purpose and character is ever present in their picture. But we see them also in disarray and confusion, the leaders shortsighted and timid, the rankers groping tensely and awkwardly in the dark. Because of this Trotsky has been accused of presenting a caricature of Bolshevism. Nothing is further from the truth. His picture is superbly true to nature precisely because he exposes all the weaknesses, doubtings, and waverings of Bolshevism. At the decisive moment the hesitancy and the divisions are subdued or overcome, and doubt gives place to confidence. That the party had to struggle with itself as well as with its enemies in order to rise to its role does not derogate from its accomplishment—it makes the accomplishment all the greater. Trotsky does not detract from the political honor even of Zinoviev, Kamenev, Rykov, Kalinin, and the others who shrank from the great leap of October; if his narrative brings discredit upon them, it is only because after the event they posed as the unflagging leaders of the iron phalanx.

The *History* highlights two great "inner crises" of Bolshevism in the year of the revolution. In the first Lenin, just returned from Switzerland, presents his April Theses and politically "rearms" his party for warfare against the February regime; in the second, at the penultimate stage of the revolution, the advocates and opponents of insurrection confront each other in the Bolshevik Central Committee. In both crises the limelight rests for a long time on a narrow circle of leaders. Yet the scenes engrave themselves on our mind as deeply as do the broader, majestic images of the February rising and of the October Revolution or as does the somber interval of the July days, when the movement is shown at its nadir. In both crises we are made to feel that it is on the few members of the Central Committee that the fate of the revolution hangs: their vote decides whether the energies of the masses are to be dissipated and defeated or directed towards victory. The problem of masses and leaders is posed in all its acuteness; and almost at once the limelight is focused even more narrowly and intensely on a single leader—Lenin.

Both in April and October, Lenin stands almost alone, misunderstood and disavowed by his disciples. Members of the Central Committee are on the point of burning the letter in which he urges them to prepare for insurrection; and he resolves to "wage war" against them and if need be to appeal, disregarding party discipline, to the rank and file. "Lenin did not trust the Central Committee—without Lenin. . . ," Trotsky comments; and "Lenin was not so wrong in his mistrust." [12] Yet in each crisis he eventually won the party for his strategy and threw it into battle. His shrewdness, realism, and concentrated will emerge from the narrative as the decisive elements of the historic process, at least equal in importance to the spontaneous struggle of millions of workers and soldiers. If their energy was the "steam" and the Bolshevik party the "piston box" of the revolution, Lenin was the driver.

Here Trotsky is grappling with the classical problem of personality in history; and here he is perhaps least successful. His factual account of Lenin's activity is irreproachable. At no stage is it possible to say that here, at this or that point Lenin did not act and the other Bolsheviks did not behave as Trotsky tells us they did. Nor is he out to present Lenin as a self-sufficient maker of events. "Lenin did not oppose the party from outside, but was himself its most complete expression," he assures us; and he repeatedly demonstrates that Lenin merely translated into clear formulas and action the thoughts and moods which agitated the rank and file, and that because of this he eventually prevailed. Leader and mass act in unison. There is a deep concord between Lenin and his party, even when he is at cross purposes with the Central Committee. Just as Bolshevism had not made its historic entry by chance, so Lenin's part was not fortuitous: he was "a product of the whole past . . . embedded in it with the deepest roots. . . ." He was not "a demiurge of the revolutionary process"; but merely a link, "a great link," in a chain of objective historic causes.[13]

However, having placed Lenin as a link in this chain, Trotsky then intimates that without the "link" the "chain" would have fallen to pieces. He asks what would have happened if Lenin had not managed to return to Russia in April 1917—"Is is possible . . . to say confidently that the party without him would have found its road? We would by no means make bold to say that. . . ." It is quite conceivable, he adds, that "a disoriented and split party might have let slip the revolutionary opportunity for many years." If in the *History* Trotsky expresses this view with caution, he dots the i's elsewhere. In a letter he wrote to Preobrazhensky from Alma Ata he says: "You know better than I do that had Lenin not managed to come to Petrograd in April 1917, the October Revolution would not have taken place." In his French Diary he makes the point categorically: "Had I not been present in 1917 in Petrograd the October Revolution would still have taken place —*on the condition that Lenin was present and in command*. If neither Lenin nor I had been present in Petrograd, there would have been no October Revolution: the leadership of the Bolshevik Party would have prevented it from occurring—of this I have not the slightest doubt!" [14] If Lenin is not yet a "demiurge of history" here, this is so only in the sense that he did not make the revolution *ex nihilo:* the decay of the social structure, the "steam" of mass energy, the "piston box" of the Bolshevik party (which Lenin had designed and engineered)—all these had to be there in order that he should be able to play his part. But even if all these elements had been there, Trotsky tells us, without Lenin the Bolsheviks would have "let slip the revolutionary opportunity for many years." For how many years? Five—six? Or perhaps thirty— forty? We do not know. In any case, without Lenin, Russia might have continued to live under the capitalist order, or even under a restored Tsardom, perhaps for an indefinite period; and in this century at least world history would have been very different from what it has been.

For a Marxist this is a startling conclusion. The argument admittedly has a flavor of scholasticism, and the historian cannot resolve it by reference to empirical evidence: he cannot re-enact the revolution, keep Lenin out of the spectacle, and see what happens. If the issue is nevertheless pursued a little further here, this is done not for the sake of the argument but for the light it throws on our chief character. On this point the views of Trotsky, the historian, are closely affected by the experience and the mood of Trotsky, the leader of the defeated Opposition—it is doubtful whether earlier in his career he would have expressed a view which goes so strongly against the grain of the Marxist intellectual tradition.

Of that tradition Plekhanov's celebrated essay *The Role of the Individual in History* is highly representative—like Plekhanov's other theoretical writings it exercised a formative influence on several generations of Russian Marxists. Plekhanov discusses the issue in terms of the classical antinomy of necessity and freedom. He does not deny the role of the personality; he accepts Carlyle's dictum that "the great man is a beginner": "This is a very apt description. A great man is precisely a beginner because he sees *farther* than others and desires things *more strongly* than others." Hence the "colossal significance" in history and the "terrible power" of the great leader. But Plekhanov insists that the leader is merely the organ of an historic need or necessity, and that necessity creates its organ when it needs it. No great man is therefore "irreplaceable." Any historic trend, if it is deep and wide enough, expresses itself through a certain number of men, not only through a single individual. In discussing the French Revolution, Plekhanov asks a question analogous to that which Trotsky poses: what would have been the course of the revolution without Robespierre or Napoleon?

> Let us assume that Robespierre was an absolutely indispensable force in his party; but even so he was not the only one. If the accidental fall of a brick had killed him in, say, January 1793, his place would, of course, have been taken by someone else; and although that other person might have been inferior to him in every respect, events would have nevertheless taken the same course as they did with Robespierre. . . . The Gironde would probably not have escaped defeat, but it is possible that Robespierre's party would have lost power somewhat earlier . . . or later, but it would have certainly fallen. . . .[15]

What Trotsky suggests is that if a brick had killed Lenin, say in March 1917, there would have been no Bolshevik revolution in that year and "for many years after." The fall of the brick would consequently have diverted a tremendous current of history in some other direction. The discussion about the individual's role turns out to be a debate over accident in history, a debate with a close bearing on the philosophy of Marxism. Plekhanov concludes his argument by saying that such accidental "changes in the course of events might, to some extent, have influenced the subsequent political . . . life of Europe," but that "in no circumstances would the final outcome of the revolutionary movement have been the 'opposite' of what it was. Owing to the specific qualities of their minds and their characters, influential individuals can change the *individual features of events and some of their particular consequences,* but they cannot change their general *trend,* which is determined by other forces." Trotsky implies that Lenin's personality changed not merely the "individual features of events," but the general trend—without Lenin the social forces that made that trend or contributed to it would have been ineffective. This conclusion accords ill with Trotsky's *Weltanschauung* and with much else besides. If it were true that the greatest revolution of all time could not have occurred without one particular leader, then the leader cult at large would by no means be preposterous; and its denunciation by historical materialists, from Marx to Trotsky, and the revulsion of all progressive thought against it would be pointless.

Trotsky evidently succumbs here to the "optical illusion" of which Plekhanov speaks in his argument against historians who insist that Napoleon's role was decisive because no one else could have taken his place with the same or a similar effect. The "illusion" consists in the fact that a leader appears irreplaceable because, having assumed his place, he prevents others assuming it.

> Coming forward [as the "saviour of order"] . . . Napoleon made it impossible for all other generals to play this role; and some of them might have performed it in the same or almost the same way as he did. Once the public need for an energetic military ruler was satisfied, the social organization barred the road to this position . . . for all other gifted soldiers. . . . The power of Napoleon's personality presents itself to us in an extremely magnified form, for we credit him with the power of the social organization which had brought him to the fore and held him there. His power appears to us quite exceptional because other powers similar to his did not pass from the potential to the actual. And when we are asked: "What would have happened if there had been no Napoleon?" our imagination becomes confused, and it seems to us that without him the social movement upon which his strength and influence were based could not have taken place.[16]

Similarly, it may be argued, Lenin's influence on events appears to us greatly magnified because once Lenin had assumed the post of the leader, he prevented others from assuming it. It is, of course, impossible to say who might have taken his place had he not been there. It might have been Trotsky himself. Not for nothing did revolutionaries as important as Lunacharsky, Uritsky, and Manuilsky, discussing, in the summer of 1917, Lenin's and Trotsky's relative merits, agree that Trotsky had at that time eclipsed Lenin—and this while Lenin was there, on the spot; and although Lenin's influence on the Bolshevik party was decisive, the October insurrection was in fact carried out according to Trotsky's, not to Lenin's, plan. If neither Lenin nor Trotsky had been there someone else might have come to the fore. The fact that among the Bolsheviks there was apparently no other man of their stature and reputation does not prove that in their absence such a man would not have emerged. History has indeed a limited number of vacancies for the posts of great chiefs and commanders; and once the vacancies are filled, potential candidates have no opportunity to develop and achieve "self-fulfilment." Need it be held that they would not have achieved it in any circumstances? And could Lenin's or Trotsky's part not have been played by leaders smaller in stature, with this difference perhaps that the smaller men instead of "allowing destiny to direct" them would have been "dragged" by it?

It is a fact that almost every great leader or dictator appears irreplaceable in his lifetime; and that on his demise someone does fill his place, usually someone who to his colleagues appears to be the least likely candidate, a "mediocrity" "destined to play second or third fiddle." Hence the surprise of so many at seeing first Stalin as Lenin's successor and then Khrushchev as Stalin's heir, the surprise which is a by-product of the optical illusion about the irreplaceable colossus. Trotsky maintains that only Lenin's genius could cope with the tasks of the Russian Revolution; and he often intimates that in other countries too the revolution must have a party like the Bolshevik and a leader like Lenin in order to win. There is no gainsaying Lenin's extraordinary capacity and character, or Bolshevism's good fortune in having him at its head. But have not in our time the Chinese and the Yugoslav revolutions triumphed under parties very different from that of the Bolsheviks of 1917, and under leaders of smaller, even much smaller, stature? In each case the revolutionary trend found or created its organ in such human material as was available. And if it seems implausible to assume that the October revolution would have occurred without Lenin, this is surely not as implausible as is the opposite assumption that a brick falling from a roof in Zurich early in 1917 could have altered the fortunes of mankind in this century.

Let us add that this last view accords so ill with Trotsky's basic philosophy and conception of the revolution that he could not uphold it consistently. Thus, in the *Revolution Betrayed,* written a few years later, he asserts:

> The quality of the leadership is, of course, far from being a matter of indifference . . . but it is not the only factor, and in the last analysis

is not decisive. . . . The Bolsheviks . . . conquered . . . not through the personal superiority of their leaders, but through a new correlation of social forces. . . . [In the French Revolution too] in the successive supremacy of Mirabeau, Brissot, Robespierre, Barras, and Bonaparte, there is an obedience to objective law incomparably more effective than the special traits of the historic protagonists themselves.[17]

As indicated, Trotsky's "optical illusion" about Lenin sheds a light on himself and his state of mind in these years rather than on Lenin. He produced the *History* after the orgy of the Stalinist "personality cult" had begun; and his view of Lenin was a negative reflex of that cult. He appealed against the "irreplaceable" Stalin to the "irreplaceable" Lenin. Moreover, in view of the apathy and amorphousness of Soviet society, the leader did indeed loom incomparably larger in those years than in 1917, when the whole mass of the nation was seething with political energy and activity. On the one hand Stalin was emerging as autocrat; on the other, Trotsky was of necessity exercising a sort of ideal, moral autocracy as sole mouthpiece of the Opposition. He too, in his defeat, loomed as an individual exceptionally, even uniquely, large. As historian, he projected the leader's huge apparition back on to the screen of 1917, and drew this self-defensive moral: "From the extraordinary significance which Lenin's arrival acquired, it should only be inferred that leaders are not accidentally created, that they are gradually chosen out and trained up in the course of decades, that they cannot be capriciously replaced, that their mechanical exclusion from the struggle gives the party a living wound, and in many cases may paralyze it for a long period." [18] In his Diary he draws the moral even more explicitly:

> . . . I think that the work on which I am engaged now [the opposition to Stalin and the foundation of the Fourth International], despite its extremely insufficient and fragmentary nature, is the most important work of my life—more important than 1917, more important than the period of the civil war, or any other. . . . I cannot speak of the "indispensability" of my work, even in the period of 1917 to 1921. But now my work is "indispensable" in the full sense of the word. There is no arrogance in this claim at all. The collapse of the two Internationals has posed a problem which none of the leaders of these Internationals is at all equipped to solve. The vicissitudes of my personal fate have confronted me with this problem and armed me with important experience in dealing with it. There is now no one except me to carry out the mission of arming a new generation with the revolutionary method. . . . I need at least about five more years of uninterrupted work to ensure the succession.[19]

He needed to feel that the leader, whether Lenin in 1917 or he himself in the 1930's, was irreplaceable—from this belief he drew the strength for his solitary and heroic exertions. And now, when alone of a whole Bolshevik generation he spoke against Stalin, no one indeed was in a position to take his place. But, precisely because he was alone and irreplaceable did so much of his labor run to waste.

Notes

1. Trotsky referred in particular to L. Madelin, "the reactionary and therefore fashionable" French historian. Preface to *History of the Russian Revolution*, Vol. I.

2. A. L. Rowse, *End of an Epoch*, pp. 282-283.

3. This is true, however, only to the extent to which it may be permissible to characterize the communist movement under Stalin and Khrushchev as Marxist.

4. See *The Prophet Armed*, chapter VI.

5. Preface to vol. I and introduction to vols. II and III of the *History*.

6. Miliukov, however, himself partly renounced his own work as being from an historical viewpoint inadequate. Miliukov, *Istorya Vtoroi Russkoi Revolutsii*, Preface. The main, or rather the only, point of fact on which Kerensky seeks to refute Trotsky is in reiterating the old accusation that Lenin and the Bolshevik party were spies in German pay. Kerensky, *Crucifixion of Liberty*, pp. 285ff.

7. Trotsky, *op. cit.*, I, 71.

8. *Ibid.*. pp. 108-118.

9. *Ibid.*, pp. 197-198.

10. Trotsky, *op. cit.*, I, 243.

11. *Ibid.*, pp. 244-246.

12. *Op. cit.*, III, 131.

13. *Op. cit.*, I, 341-342.

14. *Trotsky's Diary in Exile*, pp. 53-54. The letter to Preobrazhensky, written in 1928, is in the Trotsky *Archives*.

15. G. Plekhanov, *Izbrannye Filosofskie Proizvedenya*, II, 325. (In English: *The Role of the Individual in History*, pp. 46-47.)

16. Plekhanov, *op. cit.*, pp. 325-326. (English ed., *loc. cit.*)

17. Trotsky, *The Revolution Betrayed*, pp. 87-88. Characteristically, Sidney Hook in his reaction against Marxism (and Trotskyism) leaned on the subjectivist note in Trotsky's treatment of Lenin, and concluded that the October Revolution "was not so much a product of the whole past of Russian history as a product of one of the most event-making figures of all time." Hook, *The Hero in History*, pp. 150-151.

18. *History of the Russian Revolution*, I, 342. There is, however, a *non sequitur* in this moral, for if leaders are "not accidentally created" they are not accidentally (or "capriciously") eliminated either.

19. *Diary in Exile*, p. 54.

Stalin on revolution

GEORGE ALLEN MORGAN

The stress laid by Stalin on the importance of theory is so foreign to American habits of mind that we are prone to underestimate the influence which theory plays in determining his action. Any such tendency would lead us into especially grave error when we come to estimating the importance of his theoretical conception of the nature of revolution; for on this he has been amazingly consistent.

In a preface to the first volume of his collected works, Stalin takes the trouble to point out deficiencies in certain views expressed in his youthful writings, years before the October Revolution.[1] Since then eight volumes of the collected works have appeared, but they contain no more prefaces by Stalin; the inference is that he considers the rest doctrinally correct. Stalin exhibits the same meticulous care about doctrine in a letter to members of the Politburo in which he opposes the re-publication of an obscure article of Engels' in *Bol'shevik* unless the errors in its conception of imperialism are pointed out. Publication of an article in "our fighting magazine," he holds, means that it is to be taken "as directive or at least deeply informative for our party workers."[2] Back of such pains about detail on the part of so busy a man lies a conviction that correctness of theory is vitally important. Stalin denies that "Leninism is the primacy of practice over theory." On the contrary, "the tendency of practical workers to brush theory aside contradicts the whole spirit of Leninism and is pregnant with great dangers for the cause." And again: "None other than Lenin said and repeated tens of times the well-known thesis that: *'Without revolutionary theory there can be no revolutionary movement.'* "[3]

The present study summarizes the body of ideas on revolution which has presumably played a part in Stalin's thought and action, as revealed in his published writings and statements. Except for two reports of interviews with Stalin published in the United States but apparently not in the Soviet Union, it makes use of Russian sources only. The author

From *Foreign Affairs*, January 1949, pp. 215-255.

believes that he has discovered and examined for relevant material nearly everything by Stalin originally published between January 1, 1929, and March 28, 1948; and, in addition, he has read all of Stalin's writings likely to be of central importance as far back as February 1919. Much of the material was republished on a large scale during the periods investigated. The general character of Communist thought makes it extremely unlikely that this would have happened if the statements were considered out of date or in any way inconsistent with current ideology, and, above all, if the outmoded features were not at the same time pointed out clearly. The sacredness in which the faithful hold every word of Stalin's makes it doubly improbable that anything of his which was obsolete would be republished without proper correction. "Voprosy Leninizma" ("Problems of Leninism," the basic collection of Stalin's writings, hereafter referred to in this study as "Voprosy") has gone through eleven editions to date and has been reprinted in many millions of copies; the 1947 printing of the eleventh edition (first published in 1939) states, on the last page, that it amounts to 4,000,000 copies. Stalin's "Istoriia vsesoiuznoi kommunisticheskoi partii" ("History of the All-Union Communist Party," hereafter referred to in this study as "Istoriia"), first published in 1938, is still being reprinted; in 1946, *Pravda* stated that the total number of copies exceeded 31,000,000.[4] The fundamental role played by these two volumes in the indoctrination of party workers and in the compulsory courses in Marxism-Leninism justifies us in attributing high value to their testimony on matters of current orthodoxy according to Stalin.

The few instances where passages in republished works are (or at first sight appear to be) inconsistent with passages in new publications will be discussed on their merits when occasion arises. In view of the acknowledged Communist practice of pursuing long-range strategy by means of highly variable tactical lines, the presumption is by no means necessarily in favor of the new statements. The burden of proof must rather fall on whoever maintains that the new statement represents a permanent change in doctrine and not a mere temporary shift in the "line."

The cornerstones of "Voprosy" are found in two works by Stalin published in 1924, "Ob osnovakh Leninizma" and "Oktiabr'skaia revoliutsiia i taktika russkikh kommunistov." They contain the essence of his revolutionary theory, which he attributes to Lenin. This theory has been clarified or supplemented from time to time with respect to particular points. Thus it received more explicit Marxist-Leninist philosophical setting in the "Istoriia." But it has never been abandoned or altered in fundamentals.

Americans, though of course admitting the role of science in engineering, industry, and similar fields, will be surprised by Stalin's conviction that in Leninist-Marxism he has a science of human society and its development in history which makes possible the prediction—and, within limits, the engineering—of the course of history. Thus he writes in his history of the party: "Marxist-Leninist theory is science of the development of society, science of the workers' movement, science of proletarian revolution, science of the construction of Communist society." And again: "The strength of Marxist-Leninist theory consists in the fact that it enables the party to orient itself in a situation, to grasp the internal connection of surrounding events, to foresee the course of events and to discern not only how and when events are developing in the present but also how and when they must develop in the future." [5]

Only such a view could explain the strong language Stalin uses on the ideological training of party cadres:

> One can say with confidence that if we could prepare our cadres in all branches of work ideologically and temper them politically to such a degree that they can easily orient themselves in the domestic and international situation, if we could make them fully mature Marxist-Leninists, able to solve the problems of running the country without serious errors—then we would have reason to consider nine-tenths of all our problems already solved. And we are absolutely able to accomplish this task.[6]

II. The science of revolution

In outlining Stalin's revolutionary theory, we shall first consider his views on those determinants of revolution which he calls "objective," i.e., those historical forces which, though modified by the action of conscious human wills, determine the basic pattern of history regardless of human will.

Stalin calls the philosophical framework of his theory "dialectical and historical materialism." It is, in effect, revolution writ large into the cosmos; its basic postulates are so many reasons why "the bourgeoisie" are on the way down and "the proletariat" on the way up, why "capitalism" must inevitably give way to "Socialism" everywhere, and why this must occur by violent revolution. It is sufficient for our present purposes to state briefly those postulates which are most important for Stalin's theory of revolution.

Relativity. Nature is a "connected, single whole" in which "phenomena are organically related to each other, depend on each other, and condition each other." Applied to human society, this means "that every social system and every social movement in history must be evaluated not from the point of view of 'eternal justice' . . . but from the point of view of the conditions which gave birth to that system and that social movement with which they are connected." Thus a slave-owning economy, which would be absurd for modern conditions, was once a "step forward" in comparison with the primitive communal system; and "a bourgeois-democratic republic," though it would have represented a "step forward" for Russia in 1905, would be a "step backward" for the USSR today.

Change. Nature is constantly changing; "there is always something arising and evolving, something declining and living out its time." This means that "the dying off of what is old and the growth of something new is the law or evolution," hence that there are no " 'stable' social orders" or " 'eternal principles' of private property." It means further that "only that which is rising and developing is invincible," i.e., that a rising class, though yet relatively weak, is a better bet politically than one which has had its rise and, though still relatively powerful, is beginning to decline. Hence, according to Stalin, the Marxists were right in basing their policy on the proletariat even in Russia in the 1880's, because it was evolving as a class, while the peasantry, though in the enormous majority, was declining as a class.

Sudden qualitative change. The process of evolution is not simply one of quantitative growth; "insignificant and hidden quantitative changes" repeatedly accumulate to a point at which radical and "open" "qualitative changes" suddenly occur. For human society this means that "revolutionary overturns, produced by oppressed classes, are a perfectly natural and inevitable phenomenon." In contemporary terms, "it means that the transition from capitalism to Socialism . . . can be accomplished not by means of slow change, not by means of reform, but only by means of qualitative change of the capitalist system, by means of revolution."

Progress. The previous postulate, according to Stalin, implies that evolution is progress, i.e., that nature moves not in a circle but in an upward direction, from "the simple to the complex, from the lower to the higher." [7] We state this here as a separate postulate, because on it depends the claim that revolution is not merely inevitable but right, since it leads to a "qualitative change for the better." Stalin does not go into this, preferring, as Marxists generally do, to stress the "scientific" rather than the ethical aspects of his theory. But that he has deep convictions on the matter is evident from the general tone of his writings. When in an interview with Stalin, Emil Ludwig compares him to Peter the Great, Stalin replies: "The task to which I am dedicating my life consists in elevating . . . the working class. That task is not the strengthening of any national state but the strengthening of a Socialist, and that means international, state. . . ." [8]

Contradiction and struggle. ". . . the process of evolution from the lower to the higher takes place not as a harmonious unfolding of phenomena but as a disclosure of the contradictions inherent in things and phenomena, as a 'struggle' of opposite tendencies which operate on the basis of these contradictions . . . in order to overcome these contradictions." This means that "the class struggle of the proletariat is a perfectly natural and inevitable phenomenon," that "we must not cover up the contradictions of the capitalist system but uncover and draw them out, not extinguish the class struggle but carry it to its conclusion." Here, and in the theory of sudden qualitative change, is Stalin's philosophical ground for his position that a basic policy (as distinguished from temporary tactics) of compromise and reform is a mistake.

Materialism. Objective reality is material; consciousness is a "reflection" of matter and a product of it. From this Stalin infers that "the material life of society . . . is primary, and its spiritual life secondary, derivative," i.e., that "one must look for the source of social ideas, social theories, political views and political institutions . . . in the conditions of the material life of society," of which the ideas and institutions are a "reflection."

The means of production. Of the various factors composing "the material life of society," the one which determines "the character of the social system and the evolution of society from one system to another" is "the means of production of material goods." This in turn consists of "productive forces"—the instruments of production and the people who operate them—and "productive relations," i.e., the relations between people in the productive process, such as master-slave, capitalist-laborer. "Changes in the means of production inevitably evoke change of the whole social system," including political institutions.

The primary contradiction of capitalism. The prime mover of social progress is change in the productive forces, especially tools: as new types of tools develop they enter into "contradiction" or "nonconformity" with the increasingly outmoded productive relations, until the latter are demolished and new ones created to correspond with the requirements of the productive forces. With this "sudden, qualitative" change comes a change in the whole social system. Such is the inmost dynamic of revolution. Capitalism, for example, develops large-scale industrial plants as productive forces; but "by gathering millions of workers together in enormous factories and plants, capitalism gives a social character to the process of production and thereby undermines its own basis," namely, the productive relations that center around private ownership of industry.

Thus the primary contradiction that develops inside capitalism as it evolves is that between actual private ownership and the new productive forces which require social ownership for their full expansion. This maladjustment expresses itself in the periodic crises of overproduction familiar to capitalism, and finally in revolution which resolves the contradiction by socializing the means of production.[9]

The foregoing is not a complete summary of Stalin's dialectical and historical materialism, but it gives the basis of his claim to know with "scientific" certainty that Socialist revolution must come sooner or later in capitalist countries. It should be stressed that for Stalin the decisive issue is the substitution of Socialist ownership and operation for private ownership and operation of the means of production: all other differences in modern social systems are of subordinate importance. This is the basis of his insistence to H. G. Wells, in 1934, that the New Deal reforms in the United States cannot affect the ultimate necessity for revolution, and to Harold E. Stassen, in 1947, that the United States and Nazi Germany had the same kind of economic systems.[10]

The next step in our inquiry is to analyze in greater detail Stalin's conception of the social forces, apart from conscious leadership, which contribute to the build-up and final achievement of revolution. These forces are formed around four secondary contradictions, which are aggravated by the primary contradiction between productive forces and productive relations.

The class struggle. Antagonism between classes is not peculiar to capitalism, in Stalin's view. It is inherent in slave-owning and feudal social systems as well—in short, wherever one class monopolizes ownership of the means of production and thereby "exploits" the rest. Under capitalism the chief protagonists of class struggle are the "capitalists" and those who must sell their labor to the capitalists in order to live—the "proletariat." The rest of society—petty bourgeois, peasants, intelligentsia—form a comparatively amorphous and fluctuating mass, gravitating now to one side, now to the other.[11]

Hence the proletariat is the inevitable vehicle for the Socialist revolution. In contrast to the peasantry, it is connected with the most advanced form of economy and therefore has "more future." Further, "the proletariat as a class is growing year by year, is developing politically, is easily accessible to organization by reason of its work in large-scale production, and is most revolutionary because of its proletarian position, as it has nothing to lose by revolution except its chains." [12] In contrast to the intelligentsia, on the other hand, the proletariat has the mass necessary for revolutionary power: "for that, a large class is needed, which would replace the class of capitalists and become just as sovereign a

master as it is. . . ." [13] Thus arises the central Leninist doctrine that
Socialist revolution can occur only through substitution of the dictator-
ship of the proletariat for the dictatorship of the bourgeoisie (which, in
Stalin's view, is the essence of all capitalist states). [14]

It is ultimately from the growing contradiction between social productive forces and private property productive relations that the class
struggle receives the dynamism, the increasing tension, which impels it
toward revolution. [15] Just how this occurs is not fully clear from Stalin's
writings. The earlier Marxist doctrine of "increasing misery" of the
proletariat was modified by Lenin and others in view of the observable
fact that workers were not getting poorer. Stalin does not discuss this
topic; but possibly, he, too, as a disciple of Lenin, does not hold the
earlier view. What certainly does increase, according to Stalin, is tension
between the two classes—the bourgeoisie put more and more "pressure"
on the proletariat, which the proletariat meets with growing resistance
and resentment. The "pressure" or "oppression" by the bourgeoisie takes
various forms. One is the effort to reduce wages or hold them down,
which becomes ever more powerful as capitalism enters its monopoly
stage. Another is the actual misery caused by falling wages and unemployment in times of economic crisis—the recurrent crises being due to
the fact that the capitalists do not allow wages to rise in proportion to
production, thus curtailing purchasing power and resulting in "overproduction." Another form of pressure by the bourgeoisie is Fascism,
which deprives workers of important means of resistance—labor unions,
parliaments, the freedom to form labor or Communist parties. [16]

As will be explained later, the tension between bourgeoisie and proletariat does not increase uniformly but in a wave-like ebb and flow.
While tension mounts, the social system nears the flash-point of revolution: there is "aggravation of the revolutionary crisis inside the capitalist
countries, accumulation of explosive elements on the internal, proletarian
front." [17]

The imperialist stage of capitalism. Stalin, following Lenin, holds that
capitalism in its last stage, when it becomes ripe for revolution, turns
monopolist and imperialist. The scene is dominated by giant trusts and
combinations of international finance which rival each other for control
of world markets, raw materials, and opportunities for investment of
surplus capital. This means that there is no longer an assortment of
capitalist systems, one for each country, but one world capitalist system.
Revolution accordingly occurs in particular countries as a result of the
total interplay of forces within the world system and not, as earlier Marxists expected, simply as the result of local conditions. "Formerly it was
usual to speak of the presence or absence of objective conditions for

proletarian revolution . . . in one or another well-developed country. . . . Now we must speak of the presence of objective conditions of revolution in the entire system of world imperialist economy as an integral whole; the existence within this system of some countries that are not sufficiently developed industrially cannot serve as an insurmountable obstacle to revolution . . . *because* the system as a whole is already ripe for revolution." [18]

From this it follows that revolution need not occur first in the countries that are most advanced industrially, as Marx's historical materialism seemed once to imply. Revolution occurs rather as a break in the world "front" of the capitalist system, and therefore at the point where the chain has its weakest link. So in 1917 it came first in Russia, an admittedly backward country, and in 1924 Stalin said it might occur next in Germany or in India—in any case, again at the weakest point in the world system. In a later comment Stalin points out that the weakest point in the world system of capitalism is not the point where industry is *least* developed, else revolution would have begun somewhere in central Africa. A "certain minimum" of industrial development and of culture is prerequisite for revolution. [19]

The direct effect of the rise of monopoly capitalism on the contradiction between bourgeoisie and proletariat has been mentioned. In addition, two further contradictions are now generated within the capitalist system.

One of these is the international counterpart of the class struggle: the great monopolies seek to exploit the foreign as well as the domestic field, which leads to a few powerful capitalist countries dividing up the world as colonial possessions and spheres of influence. Thus arises a contradiction within the capitalist world economy between the exploiting imperialists and the exploited colonies. As tension rises, a revolutionary crisis develops in the exploited countries, taking the form primarily of movements for national liberation from imperialism. [20]

The other contradiction develops between rival capitalistic countries. Since some evolve more rapidly than others, they come to demand a larger share of colonies and spheres of influence than the one allotted on the basis of their former power. Since no country will voluntarily hand over part of its present share, tension mounts until imperialist war—for example, the First and Second World Wars—inevitably breaks out as the sole means of re-dividing the world and restoring equilibrium. [21] In Stalin's thinking, the importance of war as a midwife of revolution can scarcely be exaggerated.

The contradiction between capitalists and socialist systems. According to Stalin, the contradictions above described created the "objective" basis for the October Revolution of 1917, but in so doing they helped to generate yet another contradiction, that between the capitalist and Socialist systems. For henceforth the system of world capitalism has lost its monopoly of the world and its claim to be the latest work in progress. Beside it grows a Socialist system which "by the very fact of its existence demonstrates the rottenness of capitalism and shakes loose its foundations." [22] This predicament, together with the loss both of economic equilibrium and of authority in colonial areas occasioned by the war of 1914, constitutes what Stalin calls the "general crisis of capitalism," a condition of permanently impaired health. The capitalist system will never recover its pre-1914 stability and self-assurance.

Increasing tension grows from both sides of this contradiction between the social systems. It is an axiom with Stalin that capitalists are filled with envy and hatred, and that whenever they can and dare they will seek to intervene in the Socialist country and restore capitalism. This danger he dramatizes as "capitalist encirclement," declaring that Socialism cannot be considered finally achieved as long as this danger of intervention and restoration persists.[23] From the other side of the contradiction, every triumph of the Soviet Socialist system is considered by Stalin to have a profoundly revolutionizing effect on capitalist countries. In 1933 he states: "The successes of the Five Year Plan are mobilizing the revolutionary forces of the working class of all countries against capitalism. . . ." [24] In addition, there are various kinds of deliberate aid on the part of the Socialist system for revolutionary movements inside the capitalist system. These are, properly speaking, not part of the "objective" determinants of revolution.

The primary and secondary contradictions of capitalist society, which we have just described, interact upon one another to produce revolution. There are three chief types of interaction.

Productive forces vs. productive relations: economic crises. The effects which the fundamental capitalist contradiction and economic crises have on the class struggle were briefly discussed above. The most striking feature of Stalin's treatment of the contradiction between productive forces and productive relations under capitalism is how little he has to say about it. He does not formulate it expressly until 1938, in his exposition of historical materialism. We have found only one brief earlier allusion to it, as the cause of economic crises.[25]

It would nevertheless be unsafe, as in other cases, to infer from Stalin's comparative silence on this subject that he considers it of minor importance or that he only half believes in it. On the contrary, this doctrine is an integral part of the bedrock of Marxist "scientific" certainty about the future course of history on which Stalin evidently bases his entire life work. It is his cardinal reason for holding that, no matter what happens, in the long run all the contradictions of capitalism will get worse and worse until revolution cures the source of trouble by substituting Socialism. Indeed, the chief function which this central contradiction of capitalism performs in Stalin's thinking may be to impart certainty to the doctrinal framework. If so, that would explain the brevity of its role in his published writings.

If, however, the idea also operates directly in Stalin's concrete estimates of the pattern of forces in the capitalist world system, this should find expression as some definite relationship between the increasing disparity between productive forces and productive relations—the ultimate mainspring of the trend to revolution—and resultant increases of tension in the derivative contradictions of capitalism. The sole clue of this kind discovered during the present investigation is Stalin's explanation of economic crises. Noting that they have occurred in capitalist countries every eight to twelve years for a century, he claims that they are "an example of the non-correspondence of productive relations to productive forces," in other words, of the contradiction between "the social character of production and the capitalist form of appropriating the results of production." As capitalism evolves, productive forces (i.e., productive capacity) are dynamically expanded but wages are kept as low as possible in order to make more profits. The result is a "relative curtailment of purchasing power"; goods accumulate for which there is no market and a crisis of overproduction is precipitated; finished goods and even productive forces are destroyed, factories are closed, and millions suffer unemployment and hunger not because goods are scarce but because they are plentiful. Stalin stresses the destruction of productive forces as conspicuous evidence of the way in which their development is hampered by capitalist productive relations. His account in 1930 concludes: "If capitalism could adapt production not to getting maximum profit but to the systematic improvement of the material conditions of the masses of the people . . . then there would not be any crises. But then also capitalism would not be capitalism." [26]

The role of economic crises in Stalin's writings must be stated carefully. He pays almost no attention to them until after 1929 and, as his writings show, probably did not expect the world depression. The emphasis given to economic crises after 1929—notably in the reports to the Party Congress in 1930, 1934, and 1939—suggests that the lesson of 1929 actually produced an important change in Stalin's thinking about the capitalist world. However, that change appears to have been a modification not in fundamental theory but on an intermediate level between it and concrete data. The doctrine of the contradictions of capitalism remains the basic framework. Within it, after 1929, economic crises play a very prominent role as *symptoms* of the progressive decay of capitalism at its roots—namely, of the increasing contradiction between productive forces and relations—and as added *causes* of greater tension in the four secondary contradictions. In 1930 Stalin sums up his first analysis of the world economic crisis by saying: "The most important results of the world economic crisis are to uncover and aggravate the contradictions inherent in world capitalism." [27]

The fact that Stalin depicts the crisis of 1929 as the worst so far in capitalist history, and that of 1937 as worse still,[28] together with his general picture of capitalism as now in its decadent phase, suggests that such crises do in fact play an important diagnostic role in Stalin's estimates of the degree of deterioration reached at a given time by the capitalist system, and also that he would expect each future crisis—at the customary interval of eight to twelve years—to be worse than the last. The principle indices used in his discussions of particular crises are statistics of production and of unemployment. These are further possible clues to his method of diagnosis.[29]

The "objective" conditions for revolution: war. We have seen that, for Stalin, capitalism in its imperialist stage has become a single world system in which the total interplay of forces determines the ripeness of conditions for revolution in particular countries, revolutions actually occurring where the world front of capitalism is weakest in relation to the forces of revolution. The foregoing discussion of capitalist contradictions has provided a ground-plan of the lines along which the revolutionary forces are organized. The next step is to consider the criteria for judging the ripeness of the revolutionary situation. Stalin writes that "the proletarian revolution must be regarded primarily as the result of the development of the contradictions within the world system of imperialism, as the result of the snapping of the chain of the imperialist world front in one country or another." [30] How does Stalin estimate when and where the chain is ready to break?

Pointing out that there are "several absolutely necessary conditions, in the absence of which seizure of power by the proletariat is not to be thought of," Stalin quotes Lenin's formulation of them:

> The fundamental law of revolution . . . consists in this: for revolution it is not enough that the exploited and oppressed masses should feel the impossibility of living in the old way and demand change; for revolution it is necessary that the exploiters should not be able to live and rule in the old way. Only when the *"lower classes" do not want* the old way and when the "upper classes" *cannot carry on in the old way*—only then can revolution conquer. This truth may be expressed

otherwise in the words: *revolution is impossible without a nation-wide crisis (affecting both the exploited and the exploiters).*[31]

"Revolutionary crisis" is accordingly Stalin's usual name for the total complex of forces constituting the "objective" conditions necessary for revolution.[32]

Two features stand out in the above quotation: the power of the bourgeoisie is shaken; the proletariat is aroused. More detail is supplied by a sketch written in 1921 but first published in 1947:

> How define the arrival of the moment for revolutionary outbreaks? . . . When the revolutionary mood of the masses . . . brims over and our slogans for action and directives lag behind the movement of the masses. . . . When uncertainty and confusion, disintegration and dissolution in the adversary's camp have reached the highest point . . . when the so-called neutral elements, all that mass of many millions of city and village petty bourgeoisie, begin definitely to turn away from the adversary . . . and seek alliance with the proletariat.[33]

This introduces a third feature of the "objective" conditions for revolution: the masses (other than the proletariat) swing away from the bourgeoisie and toward the proletariat, thus isolating the former and becoming allies or "reserves," as Stalin's military phraseology often puts it, of the proletariat. The above quotation mentions petty bourgeoisie, but in other passages Stalin stresses even more the role of the peasantry as ally of the proletariat.[34] In the present context only the general point is important: the bourgeoisie proper must be bereft of mass popular support and the proletariat must have it.

Support is not confined to the boundaries of one country: the local bourgeoisie must to a considerable degree be isolated internationally, while the proletariat receives direct or indirect support from the proletariat of other capitalist countries and from the proletarian state already in existence—the USSR. Hence a further condition for successful revolution is that the balance of potential outside aid for revolution as against potential outside aid for counterrevolution must be sufficiently favorable.[35]

To sum up, Stalin's necessary "objective" conditions for revolution are: bourgeoisie isolated and disorganized, proletariat aroused to revolt and supported by the masses, and a favorable balance of proletarian as against bourgeois aid from outside the country. With these as a frame of reference, we are now able to indicate how, according to Stalin, the contradictions of capitalism interact to produce revolutionary crises. Only certain main lines of influence will be described; details vary endlessly with the concrete configuration of forces.

The primary contradiction, both chronically and in its acute manifestation as economic crisis, impels the bourgeoisie to increase pressure against the proletariat, against colonial peoples, against each other (in rivalry for spheres of influence), and against the Soviet Union. The culmination of these trends is war of one kind or another: the colonies fight for liberation, the capitalist nations who demand greater spheres of influence fight to get them or capitalist countries attack the Soviet Union as the major threat to their whole system and also as another big area to be exploited. Preparation for war on the part of the bourgeoisie further arouses the proletariat and the other masses who desire peace and resent having to die for their masters, and who also resent the added economic and political pressures—including Fascism, in some cases—which are imposed in order to prepare for war. When the war is to be directed against the Socialist Fatherland, this fact of course greatly adds to the resentment of the proletariat, whose deeper sympathies are on the side of the Soviet Union. Bourgois preparation for war likewise leads to increased pressure on colonies, with a correspondingly greater tendency of colonies to rebel.[36]

Actual war, however, is the crux of the matter. Stalin writes of the relation of the First World War to the contradictions of capitalism that "the imperialist war . . . gathered all these contradictions into one bundle and threw them onto the scales, thereby accelerating and facilitating the revolutionary battles of the proletariat." [37] War between capitalist countries further intensifies the resentment of the masses and at the same time both exhausts the strength of the bourgeoisie at home and makes it difficult for them to intervene against revolution abroad. Again writing in 1924 of the First World War, Stalin speaks of "the enormous significance of the fact of mortal war between the chief groups of imperialists in the period of the October Revolution, when the imperialists, occupied with war among themselves, lacked the ability to concentrate forces against the young Soviet power, and the proletariat just for that reason was able to get down to the work of . . . consolidating its power. . . . It must be presumed that now, when the contradictions among the imperialist groups are becoming more and more profound, and when a new war among them is becoming inevitable, reserves of this description will assume even greater importance for the proletariat." [38]

Thus for the past quarter-century, according to the overwhelming testimony of his writings, Stalin has expected the next crop of revolutions to come during, or in the immediate aftermath of, the Second World War. To the Seventeenth Party Congress in 1934 he stated that a new imperialist war "will surely turn loose revolution and place in jeopardy the very existence of capitalism in a number of countries, as happened in the course of the first imperialist war." [39] His history of the party makes explicit the connection between war and the development of a "weak link" in the chain of world imperialism: "Lenin showed that precisely in consequence of this unevenness in the development of capitalism imperialist wars occur, which weaken the forces of imperialism and make possible a break-through in the front of imperialism at the point where it proves to be weakest." [40]

Imperialism, he maintains, is the fundamental antagonist of the Soviet Union, and Fascism only its worst reactionary form. "Hitler, Goebbels, Ribbentrop, Himmler, and the other administrators of present-day Germany are the chained dogs of the German bankers." [41] The capitalist, not the Nazi, is the ultimate enemy. The theoretical framework is made fully explicit in Stalin's election speech of February 1946: "It would be incorrect to think that the Second World War arose accidentally or as a result of the mistakes of some statesmen or other. . . . The war in fact arose as the inevitable result of the development of world economic and political forces on the basis of contemporary monopolistic capitalism." [42]

The case of a war against the Soviet Union, according to Stalin, presents an additional factor favorable to revolution. To the Seventeenth Party Congress in 1934 he declares: "It can hardly be doubted that this war will be the most dangerous for the bourgeoisie. . . . The numerous friends in Europe and Asia of the working class of the USSR will endeavor to strike from the rear their oppressors who have started criminal war against the Fatherland of the working class of all countries." [43] Though Stalin hopes for proletarian revolutions in certain colonial areas, he values all local movements for national liberation, whether proletarian or not: in any case, each step they take toward emancipation is "a steam-hammer blow against imperialism" and thus has "objective" revolutionary significance, i.e., weakens the bourgeoisie of imperialist countries by depriving them of markets and raw materials.[44] Hence a colonial war would become an added factor promoting a revolutionary crisis in the metropolitan country.

The law of ebb and flow. According to Stalin, the October Revolution of 1917 ushered in "a new era in the history of humanity—the era of proletarian revolutions," in fact, "the epoch of world revolution." [45] This means, in terms of his theory, that the contradictions in the world system of capitalism have evolved to the point where revolutions are generally in order. Actual revolution, however, occurred first in only one country, and Stalin expects further revolutions usually to occur in one country at a time, as state after state breaks away from the capitalist system and joins the Socialist one.[46]

But the course of the revolutionary movement is not expected to be uniform. Stalin notes that it has always moved in a wavelike rhythm of ebb and flow, rise and fall. For example, one wave reached its crest in the 1905 Revolution and subsided in the Stolypin reaction. Another rise occurred in the years 1912–1914. Under the stress of the First World War a major crest came with the two revolutions of 1917—though in the short interval between them there were also rapid changes of ebb and flow—and the wave spread out to Europe in the years immediately following. In 1925 Stalin announces that another decline has set in, corresponding to a "partial and temporary stabilization of capitalism," but he now generalizes the alternation of ebb and flow in a prediction of the future: "The epoch of world revolution . . . is a whole strategic period, embracing a whole series of years and, I dare say, even a number of decades. In the course of this period there can and must be ebbings and flowings."

Though an ebb tide has set in, Stalin goes on to say, the contradictions of capitalism will inevitably bring on a new flood tide in due time. With the flood tide new victories may be won for the revolution; if they do not complete world revolution, there will follow another ebb, and so on until revolution has spanned the globe.[47] In 1927 Stalin announces that the "stabilization of capitalism" is drawing to a close, a new "crisis of world capitalism" is gathering, and with it is beginning another revolutionary rise. In 1930 and 1934, successive reports to Party Congresses continue the same line of thought: the contradictions of capitalism, accentuated by the world economic crisis of 1929, are converging inevitably on another imperialist war. Therefore "a revolutionary crisis is ripening and will continue to ripen." [48] In his report to the Party Congress in 1939 he announces that the imperialist war has already begun and is gradually becoming a world war.[49]

Up to March 1948, Stalin has published nothing to indicate that the revolutionary wave—so long expected in connection with World War II —has passed its crest, though his doctrine of ebb and flow suggests that he must expect another ebb within a few years unless capitalism collapses completely in the meantime. Thus the entire period from 1929 to March 1948 moves before Stalin's eyes on a rising tide of revolutionary opportunities.

III. The art of revolution

Having outlined Stalin's conception of the "objective" determinants of revolution, our inquiry now turns to the "subjective" side: the role of conscious organization.

Communist leadership. Notwithstanding the remorseless and unavoidable evolution of the contradictions of capitalism, making Socialist revolution sooner or later inevitable, Stalin holds that actual revolution can occur only through conscious human efforts. In this he is a disciple of Lenin, and his history of the party records with sympathy Lenin's battles against "reformist" Marxists, compromisers, opportunists, gradualists—any and all who held that the "objective" factors would automatically bring about the change to Socialism, or that anything short of the most resolute and uncompromising revolutionary policy should be adopted.[50]

Stalin's ultimate reason for this position lies in his dialectical and historical materialism. As has been noted, one postulate of this theory is that objective reality is material, and consciousness only a "reflection" of it. This view now requires further elaboration. Stalin does not mean that consciousness plays no casual role, but only that its role is secondary. The direction of history, its movement from one mode of production to another, with consequent changes in class structure, social institution and ideas, is indeed determined by the evolution of the means of production, and no conscious human effort can change this direction. But consciousness does have a positive and important function: it affects not the pattern of history, but its pace. It can accelerate or retard the coming of the inevitable. Social theories which accelerate historical evolution do so because they "reflect the needs of the development of the material life of society" and by mobilizing the masses lead them in the direction of revolutionary change. Social theories arise "because they are necessary for society, because without their organizing, mobilizing and transforming work the solution of the problems which have come to a head in the evolution of society is *impossible.*"

This is Stalin's ground for holding that conscious leadership is necessary for revolution. The primary contradiction in capitalism gets worse and worse, and increasing strain works out from it through the secondary contradictions, causing suffering, war and destruction: but conscious effort, following correct theory, is necessary to help these blind forces produce the readjustment which alone can bring relief. Hence arises the necessity for the Communist party. Stalin writes that "Socialist ideology arises not from the spontaneous [working class] movement but from science." The party is that vanguard of the working class which, because it is guided by "scientific" insight into the ills of capitalism and the sole means of cure, can and must organize the proletariat and lead it to revolutionary victory: "The Marxist party is a part of the working class. . . . The party differs from other detachments of the working class primarily in that it is . . . the *leading* detachment, the *class-conscious* detachment . . . armed with knowledge of social life, knowledge of the laws of the class struggle, and for this reason able to lead the working class and to direct its struggle."

Stalin's conception of Marxist theory is likewise his justification for the character and organization of the Bolshevik party as opposed to Marxist parties of the Western type. Because the party is the embodiment of "scientific" truth, and because that truth is uncompromisingly revolutionary —teaching that class war must be fought to a finish—the party must be "monolithic," a centrally controlled army under strict military discipline, tolerating no other parties except for temporary reasons of expediency, hunting down and destroying compromisers—all who are disposed to take the edge off the revolutionary drive, to let things move more gradually—both in society at large and within its own ranks. The same claim to infallible "science" lies at the base of Stalin's theory of the party purge, so strange to Western modes of thought: "The party strengthens itself by purging itself of opportunist elements. . . ." A procedure that to Western minds is a sign and a further cause of weakness is for Stalin a means to strength because strength derives ultimately, not from numbers, but from "knowledge" which harnesses revolution to the laws of history: the purge eliminates those whose allegiance to this "knowledge," and the program based on it, is dubious.[51]

From Stalin's point of view "democratic liberties" have always been compatible with strict Communist party control. In his report on the Draft Constitution, he claims that the Soviet system is more democratic than any other. And in reply to foreign critics who object that the one-party system is undemocratic, he praises the constitution because it leaves in force the dictatorship of the working class and "the present directing position of the Communist party."[52] Further, Stalin is on record as holding that proletarian revolution may legitimately be carried out when the proletariat is only a minority of the population—the party, of course, being only a minority of the proletariat.

Stalin expresses the contrast between Bolshevism and Western Socialism most vividly in his 1934 interview with H. G. Wells, already mentioned. Wells approaches Stalin from the point of view of a Western Socialist; he states that conceptions of violent class war are obsolete; leading businessmen are not ruled wholly (or even primarily in many cases) by the profit motive and there is therefore no radical conflict of interest between capital and labor; modern technology makes Socialism inevitable through gradual extension of government controls; hence the need is for intelligent direction, not violent revolution; Eastern and Western Socialists should develop a common language and work together rather than emphasize their historic antagonisms. Stalin replies with denial on all points and puts the crux of the matter as he sees it thus:

"... the replacement of one social system by another social system is a complicated and protracted revolutionary process. It is not a merely spontaneous process. ... No—revolution ... has always been struggle, an excruciating and cruel struggle, struggle for life and death."

Communists, he continues, do not idealize force and violence: they would gladly dispense with them if the bourgeoisie would consent to turn things over peaceably to the proletariat. But abundant historical experience teaches (as he said to Wells) that "classes which have had their day do not leave the stage of history voluntarily." His history of the party picks up this theme in describing (p. 125) how the revolutionary period comes after social forces have evolved spontaneously to a certain point:

> After the new productive forces have matured, the existing productive relations and their bearers, the ruling classes, turn into that "insurmountable" obstacle which can be removed only by means of the conscious action of the new classes, by the forcible acts of these classes, by revolution. ... The masses are welded into a new political army, create a new revolutionary authority and use it to abolish by force the old system of productive relations and establish the new system. The spontaneous process of development gives place to the conscious action of men, peaceful development to violent upheaval, evolution to revolution.

The "combat staff" of the new political army is the Communist party.[53] Effective Communist party action is Stalin's "subjective" condition for revolution which, when timed with the "objective" conditions previously described, actually brings revolution to pass. As he puts it to the Seventeenth Party Congress: "Some comrades think that as soon as there is a revolutionary crisis the bourgeoisie must be in a situation from which there is no way out . . . that the victory of revolution is thus secure. . . . This is a profound mistake. The victory of the revolution never comes of itself. It must be prepared for and won. And only a strong proletarian revolutionary party can prepare for and win it. Moments occur when the situation is revolutionary, the power of the bourgeoisie is shaken to its very foundations, and yet the victory of the revolution does not come, because there is no revolutionary party of the proletariat sufficiently strong and authoritative to lead the masses and take power in its own hands." [54]

World strategy: the Soviet Union as base. Before we proceed to examine Stalin's views on how revolution is "prepared for and won" by the Communist party, a word of caution is in order. As generals are not accustomed to publish their operational directives, so it is unreasonable to expect Stalin to publish his. From his writings it is possible to reconstruct certain main lines of strategy and tactics, but the writings also contain definite acknowledgment that "illegal" or underground activities play a major role in Communist operations. Speaking of the revolutionary uses of compromise and reform, he states: ". . . in revolutionary tactics under a bourgeois regime, reform naturally becomes an instrument for disintegrating this regime, an instrument for strengthening revolution. . . . The revolutionary accepts reform in order to use it as a means of meshing the legal work with the illegal work, in order to use it as a cover for the strengthening of the illegal work which aims at revolutionary preparation of the masses for the overthrow of the bourgeoisie." [55] Therefore it must remain a question to what extent Stalin's published views on Communist strategy and tactics are supplemented or modified by doctrine reserved for the Communist high command.

In any case, Stalin's approach is characteristically military, and it is hardly by accident that his writings are strewn with military figures of speech—tactics and strategy; staff, cadres, vanguards, reserves; strong points, forward positions; advances, assaults, retreats, maneuvers; encirclement, flanking movement, regrouping of forces, etc.[56] An early sketch not published until 1947 shows most succinctly the connection between theory and strategy: "The *theory* of Marxism, studying primarily the objective processes . . . defines the tendency of evolution, points out the class or classes which are inevitably rising to power or which are inevitably falling, must fall. . . . The *program* of Marxism, basing itself on the conclusions of the theory, defines the goal for the movement of the rising class, in this case of the proletariat. . . . *Strategy,* guiding itself by the directives of the program and resting on a calculation of the contending forces, internal . . . and international, defines that . . . general direction along which the revolutionary movement of the proletariat should be directed with a view to achieving the biggest results with the . . . developing correlation of forces. . . ." [57]

The program thus defines the objectives at which strategy aims. Stalin distinguishes the "maximum program"—"Socialist revolution, overthrow of the capitalists' rule, establishment of the dictatorship of the proletariat" —from the "minimum program" formulated for a particular phase of the total process.[58] Stalin writes in "Voprosy" that "Strategy has to do with the main forces of revolution and their reserves. It changes with the passage of revolution from one stage to another, remaining essentially without change for the whole period of a given stage." The first stage was 1903 to February 1917, the second March to October 1917. The third stage began after the October Revolution: *"The goal is to consolidate the dictatorship of the proletariat in one country, using it as a base for the overthrow of imperialism in all countries.* Revolution spreads beyond the limits of one country; the epoch of world revolution has begun." [59]

The fundamental, not merely incidental, intention to use the Soviet Union as the base for world revolution has thus been on the record in Stalin's most important doctrinal work, repeatedly republished for mass circulation from 1924 to the present time. In another passage which has had similar authoritative distribution from 1924 to the present Stalin elaborates his view:

> . . . the very development of world revolution . . . will be more rapid and more thorough, the more thoroughly Socialism fortifies itself in the first victorious country, the faster this country is transformed into a base for the further unfolding of world revolution, into a lever for the further disintegration of imperialism.
>
> While it is true that the *final* victory of Socialism in the first country to emancipate itself is impossible without the combined efforts of the proletarians of several countries, it is equally true that the development of world revolution will be the more rapid and thorough, the more effective the aid rendered by the first Socialist country to the workers . . . of all other countries.
>
> In what should this aid be expressed?
>
> It should be expressed, first, in the victorious country "carrying out the maximum realizable in one country *for* the development, support, awakening of revolution in all countries" . . .
>
> It should be expressed, second, in that the "victorious proletariat" of the one country . . . "after organizing its own Socialist production, should stand up . . . *against* the remaining, capitalist world, attracting to itself the oppressed classes of other countries, raising revolts in those countries against the capitalists, in the event of necessity coming out even with armed force against the exploiting classes and their governments" . . .[60]

This passage deserves detailed comment. The supreme aim of world revolution is the logical outcome of Stalin's entire theoretical position as outlined in the present study—notably the thesis that capitalism is a single *world-system* fatally torn by contradictions which can be cured only by a consciously directed Socialist revolution. Granted these assumptions, the determination to use the foothold won in the Soviet Union as a base for world revolution is elementary common sense. This outlook is confirmed by many other passages in widely published statements by Stalin.[61] The sole contradictory passages—unless cunningly interpreted—are remarks made by Stalin to two foreigners, under circumstances where it is obviously to his advantage to convey another impression. For example, he tells Roy Howard in 1936 that the Soviet Union has never had plans for fostering revolution in other countries because exporting revolution is nonsense.[62] The other statement, made to Mr. King, of Reuters, in May 1943, will be described in a moment. These two statements are not republished in "Voprosy" or otherwise for wide and lasting distribution in the Soviet Union. When they are weighed against the mass of contrary evidence on Stalin's views presented above, the only conclusion is that they are misleading.

In 1938 the party history appears with the revolutionary motto on its title page: "Workers of all countries, unite!" And the introduction declares: "Studying the history of the CPSU (b) strengthens confidence in the final victory of the great cause of the party of Lenin and Stalin, the victory of Communism in the whole world." The history also repeats the fundamental quotation from Lenin on the country of Socialism "rising against" the capitalist world after organizing its own production; states that "the victory of proletarian revolutions in capitalist countries is a vital interest of the toilers of the USSR"; and quotes Stalin's "great vow" of "fidelity to the principles of the Communist International." All these points, it should be remembered, are made in a work used for mass indoctrination down to the present time.

In 1936 Howard asks Stalin if he has not to some extent abandoned his plans for world revolution. Stalin replies, "We never had such plans and intentions," thus excluding the interpretation that what he is saying to Howard represents in any way a change of mind.[63] He then declares that "we Marxists hold that revolution will occur in other countries too. But it will occur only when the revolutionaries of these countries find it possible or necessary. The export of revolution—that is nonsense." But this statement says nothing about ways in which local revolutionaries may be used, directed, and aided by outside agencies; the only "export" of revolution which it denies would be the very crudest kind, which dispensed with forming even a minimum of local Communist leadership. Carefully analyzed, then, Stalin's remarks turn out to be a sort of legalistic quibble used to convey a general impression which is in fact false.

It has at times been thought that some of Stalin's statements during the current period indicated a change of mind on his part with regard to long-term relations with the "capitalist" democracies. A careful search through all his published statements from July 1941 to March 1948 yields only one case which appears to warrant such a belief—a letter in May 1943 to King, Reuters correspondent (mentioned above), about the dissolution of the Comintern. The interview with Stassen merely says that the important point is not whether coexistence is possible but whether both sides desire it. If "one side" does not want cooperation, "the result will be conflict, war." [64] In other words, if "one side" does not like the terms of the Soviet Union, it is lacking in desire to co-operate. Also, when Stassen asks if wartime experience has changed things, Stalin denies that he ever said the two systems could not cooperate; he thus implies that his views remain unchanged and makes it impossible to attribute to his current statements on cooperation a more generous meaning than to his earlier ones. Stalin's remark that the post-war international security organization "will be effective if the Great Powers . . . continue to act in a spirit of unanimity" [65] is another expression of this same conception of "cooperation"; when queried by Hugh Baillie about the veto, Stalin denies that the Soviet Union has abused it in the United Nations or the Council of Foreign Ministers.[66]

But the letter to the Reuters correspondent on the dissolution of the Comintern is an explicit contradiction of Stalin's earlier statements of revolutionary methods and aims. Here he says that the dissolution of the Comintern is right because, among other reasons: "(a) it exposes the lie of the Hitlerites that 'Moscow' intends to intervene in the life of other states and 'bolshevize' them. Henceforth an end is put to that lie. (b) It exposes the slander of the enemies of Communism in the workers' movement to the effect that the Communist parties of the various countries act not in the interests of their own nation but according to orders from outside. Henceforth an end is put to that slander too." [67]

These propositions, reminiscent of the 1936 Howard interview, can be reconciled with Stalin's established revolutionary doctrine only by very special pleading. Since they are made to a foreign correspondent and contain no express disavowal of pertinent basic writings currently republished in quantity in the Soviet Union, the balance of evidence is that they are merely part of the current tactical and propaganda line and do not reflect a fundamental change. The most decisive evidence to this effect is the republication of Stalin's vows of fidelity to Lenin and his cause originally made before the Second Congress of Soviets on January 26, 1924. Toward the close Stalin says that "Lenin was the leader not only of the Russian proletariat, not only of the workers of Europe, not only of the colonial East, but also of the earth's entire toil-ing world." Then he makes his last vow, set off in boldfaced capitals from the rest of the text: "In departing from us, Comrade Lenin be-queathed to us fidelity to the principles of the Communist International. We swear to thee, Comrade Lenin, that we will not spare our life in order to strengthen and expand the union of toilers of the whole world —the Communist International." [68] In the light of this vow, repeatedly republished, Stalin's real view evidently is that the Comintern was dis-solved only in form, not in spirit. Stalin's charge that the United States and Great Britain are not interested in agreement and cooperation with the USSR, made in the interview by a *Pravda* correspondent, are also to be read against this background.[69] The passages in Stalin's various interviews in which he indicates the possibility or desirability of coexistence and cooperation between capitalist and Socialst systems do not really contradict the strategic aim of world revolution because they refer to a temporary tactic.

The second paragraph in the long passage quoted above places the problem of the "final" victory of Socialism in one country within the wider context of world revolution, thus excluding the hypothesis that the more limited objective—involving merely enough additional revolutions to end "capitalist encirclement" and provide security for the Soviet Union—marks the outer limit of Stalin's program for Communist expansion. Further, the passage quoted indicates that the Soviet Union will first be prepared as a base, and only then, "*after* organizing its own Socialist production," will be used more aggressively to aid revolution abroad. This tallies with the predominant absorption of the Soviets with internal affairs during the earlier five-year plans. Further, the phrase does not define the stage at which production is to be considered adequately organized. Hence the prospect of three or more additional five-year plans, as announced in 1938 and again in 1946, may indicate that the base is still not ready for contemplated operations.

Finally, the passage definitely states that armed force will be used against capitalist governments if necessary. There thus is nothing except expediency to limit the aid which Stalin contemplates giving to revolutions abroad. However, the phrase "if necessary" indicates that armed force is not to be used by preference; ahead of it come propaganda and Communist party control, by which is meant that the Soviet Union should attract to itself "the oppressed classes of other countries, raising revolts in these countries against the capitalists." [70]

The ultimate resort to armed force is a logical development of the Leninist thesis that only consciously led revolution can drive the capitalists from the stage of history, as explained in the preceding section. The assumption that the world has been fundamentally divided into two camps since the October Revolution runs through Stalin's writings from his early days and is grounded in his Marxist philosophy.[71] Stalin pictures the long-range evolution of the two camps as follows:

Most probably, in the course of development of the world revolution, side by side with the centers of imperialism in individual capitalist countries and the system of these countries throughout the world, centers of Socialism will be created in individual Soviet countries and a system of these centers throughout the world, and the struggle between these two systems will fill up the history of the development of the world revolution.[72]

The systems are expected to be organized around two centers:

Thus in the course of further development of international revolution two centers will form on a world scale: a Socialist center, binding to itself the countries that gravitate to Socialism, and a capitalist center, binding to itself the countries that gravitate to capitalism. The struggle between these two centers for the possession of the world economy will decide the fate of capitalism and Communism in the whole world.[73]

The plan to make the Soviet Union the base for world revolution implies that it will be one of the two centers. Evidence will be presented later that the United States is expected to be the other. The ultimate inevitability of war to the finish between the two camps is made clear in one of Stalin's favorite quotations from Lenin: "We live . . . not only in a state but in a system of states, and the existence of the Soviet Republic side by side with the imperialist states for a long time is unthinkable. In the end either one or the other will conquer. And until that end comes, a series of the most terrible collisions between the Soviet Republic and the bourgeois states is inevitable." [74] Stalin appended to this forecast of inexorable wars a succinct, "Clear, one would think." Thus Stalin expects not merely one but several world wars before the end of capitalism.

At the very close of the struggle the forces of Socialism will be so superior that Stalin foresees an exception to the general rule that revolutionary violence is necessary to overthrow capitalism: "Of course, in the distant future, if the proletariat wins in the most important capitalist countries and if the present capitalist encirclement is replaced by a Socialist encirclement, a 'peaceful' path of development is fully possible for some capitalist countries, whose capitalists, in view of the 'unfavorable' international situation, will consider it expedient to make serious concessions to the proletariat 'voluntarily.' " [75] The technique of "cold revolution," as it has been called, illustrated recently in eastern Europe, may be interpreted as a variety of "Socialist encirclement" in that it also dispenses with the need for overt violence. In any case, the passage quoted excepts "the most important capitalist countries," and so does not apply to the United States.

Flexibility of strategy and tactics. We are now in a position to link Stalin's strategy and tactics with his conception of the "objective" conditions making for revolution. It is the business of strategy and tactics, he holds, to prepare the "subjective" conditions of revolution—i.e., the mobilization of the proletariat and its allies—and bring them into action at the most favorable times and places as determined by the development of the "objective" conditions.[76] More than this, preparation of the "subjective" conditions really involves gaining leadership of social forces which often in the first place develop spontaneously. Describing the skill shown by the Communist party in Russia in 1917 in uniting "in one common revolutionary stream such different revolutionary movements as the general democratic movement for peace, the peasant democratic movement for seizure of the landed estates, the movement of the oppressed nationalities for national liberation and national equality, and the Socialist movement of the proletariat for the overthrow of the bourgeoisie and the establishment of the dictatorship of the proletariat," Stalin declares that "undoubtedly, the merging of these diverse revolutionary streams in one common, powerful revolutionary stream decided the fate of capitalism in Russia." [77]

In general, despite his comparatively rigid doctrinal framework, Stalin's conception of Communist strategy and tactics is highly flexible. It rests on a continual assessment of the status of forces in both the capitalist and the Socialist systems. Thus he writes: *"Tactics,* guiding itself by the directives of strategy and by experience of the revolutionary movement . . . calculating at every given moment the state of forces inside the proletariat and its allies (greater or less cultivation, greater or less degree of organization and class-consciousness, presence of particular traditions, presence of particular forms of movement, forms of organization, *basic* and *secondary*), as well as in the camp of the adversary, profiting by discord and every kind of confusion in the camp of the adversary— marks out those *concrete courses* for winning the wide masses to the proletarian side and leading them to battle stations on the social front . . . which most surely pave the way for strategic successes." [78]

In view of this flexibility, and of the way in which Stalin expects Communist leadership to win control of many movements which originate spontaneously, it must be concluded that the "objective" conditions of revolution are not fixed quantities in Stalin's thinking, but rather interdependent variables which are to be manipulated to satisfy just one equation: revolution occurs where the Communist command concentrates superiority of forces at a point on the capitalist front where the bourgeoisie can be isolated and overwhelmed. In other words, "revolutionary crises" do not have to be waited for; they can to some extent be organized; and an extremely favorable balance of outside aid can compensate to a considerable degree for a deficiency in favorable internal conditions.

For the period of world revolution, Stalin's grand strategy is to use the Soviet Union as a base linking the proletariat of the West with the movements for national liberation from imperialism in the East into "a single world front against the world front of imperialism." In this way he harnesses two of the major contradictions of capitalism to his chariot —contradictions between proletariat and bourgeoisie, and contradictions between capitalist and colonial countries. The front thus formed is to be used to exploit the third contradiction of capitalism—that between capitalist countries, whose rivalry for spheres of influence must lead periodically to war, the event most propitious for revolution.[79]

One of the chief conditions to which tactics must be adjusted, according to Stalin, is the ebb and flow of the forces favoring revolution. Aggressive tactics should be timed with a rising tide; tactics of defense, the assemblage of forces, and even retreat go with an ebbing tide.[80] The importance of gauging the direction of the tide is illustrated by Stalin's remarks in 1929 concerning a controversy with Bukharin, who apparently held that the "stabilization of capitalism" was persisting unchanged: "This question, comrades, is of decisive importance for the sections of the Comintern. Is the capitalist stabilization going to pieces or is it becoming more secure? On this the whole line of the Communist parties in their day-to-day political work depends. Are we in a period of decline of the revolutionary movement . . . or are we in a period when the conditions are maturing for a new revolutionary rise, a period of preparing the working class for coming class battles—on this depends the tactical position of the Communist parties." Stalin holds that it is a period of revolutionary upswing.[81]

Stalin's insistence on flexibility of tactics is ground for a very important maxim in the interpretation of his public statements; one must avoid, if possible, mistaking a change in tactics for a change in fundamental doctrine and strategic objectives. The example of a change in tactics often thus mistaken is Stalin's remarks about peaceful coexistence of and cooperation between the Socialist and capitalist systems. The whole body of mutually reinforcing propositions in Stalin's philosophy adds up to a veritable religion of conflict and contradiction. This is described as not only inevitable but desirable, until revolution is achieved. Here we find further strong evidence that Stalin's statements on cooperation represent nothing deeper than a tactic.

Stalin first announced a period of "peaceful coexistence" for proletarian and bourgeois worlds in 1925, saying that the revolutionary movement was ebbing and capitalism achieving a temporary stabilization. But the context of his statement makes plain that he expected peaceful coexistence to be as temporary as the stabilization.[82] In 1927 he stated that capitalist stabilization was coming to an end and that the period of "peaceful coexistence" was likewise giving way to one of imperialist attacks. But he added that the Soviet Union must continue to pursue a policy of maintaining peace for the following reason:

> We cannot forget the saying of Lenin to the effect that a great deal in the matter of our construction depends on whether we succeed in delaying war with the capitalist countries, which is inevitable but which may be delayed either until proletarian revolution ripens in Europe, or until the colonial revolutions come fully to a head, or, finally, until the capitalists fight among themselves over division of the colonies. Therefore the maintenance of peaceful relations with capitalist countries is an obligatory task for us.
>
> The basis of our relations with capitalist countries consists in admitting the coexistence of two opposed systems.[83]

This concern for peaceful relations in order to build the Socialist economy at home should be read in the context of the previous discussion in this paper of the Soviet Union as a base for world revolution; in that light, a peace policy is an intelligible tactic. Stalin continues to advocate it in the years after 1927, while at the same time urging the Communist parties to adopt aggressive tactics in keeping with the end of capitalist stabilization.[84] Thus appears an important variation of tactics on different levels of activity: peaceful coexistence for the Soviet government, preparation for attack by Communist parties.

The peace policy has another tactical function in Stalin's strategy of revolution. He notes how successfully the Communists capitalized on the general popular craving for peace during the October Revolution; accordingly he maneuvers the Soviet Union and the Communist parties into position as apostles of peace, unmasking the imperialist "warmongers" in order to profit by popular sentiments for peace in the future. Particularly interesting in this connection is the way Stalin combines his peace stand with verbal onslaughts on Social Democratic pacifism as a mere mask of the warmongers.[85]

Apart from their bearing on peace, the tasks of developing trade and obtaining technological assistance from capitalist countries have a direct relationship to building the industrial base of the Soviet Union, expecially during the early stage of the five-year plans. Stalin makes several unsentimental and businesslike proposals for improved relations along these lines, particularly with the United States.[86] His fullest and frankest statement on cooperation between Soviet and capitalist worlds is made in 1927, shortly before his announcement that the capitalist stabilization is coming to an end. To the American Workers' Delegation, who asked to what extent such cooperation is possible and whether it has definite limits, Stalin replies:

The matter concerns, obviously, temporary agreements with capitalist states in the field of industry, in the field of trade, and, perhaps, in the field of diplomatic relations. I think that the presence of two opposed systems . . . does not exclude the possibility of such agreements. I think that such agreements are possible and expedient under conditions of peaceful development. . . .

The limits of these agreements? The limits are set by the opposition of the two systems, between which rivalry and struggle go on. Within the limits permitted by these two systems, but only within these limits, agreements are fully possible. . . .

Are these agreements merely an experiment or can they have more or less lasting character? That depends not only on us; that depends also on those who contract with us. That depends on the general situation. War can upset any agreement whatever. . . .[87]

A few pages later the same interview reads: "Thus in the course of further development of international revolution two centers will form on a world scale: a Socialist center . . . and a capitalist center. . . . The struggle between these two centers for the possession of the world economy will decide the fate of capitalism and Communism in the whole world." This passage places cooperation clearly as a temporary tactic on the way to world revolution. When read against the foregoing as background, Stalin's statements to Howard, Duranty, Lyons, Werth, Elliott Roosevelt, and Stassen, to the effect that the two systems can coexist and compete peacefully, appear not so much inconsistent with his basic principles as merely elliptical: he neglects to specify how long and on what terms. To that extent the effect is misleading, as we have seen, and properly comes under the heading of propaganda.

IV. Revolution in the United States

In a speech in the Comintern in May 1929, Stalin rebukes representatives of the American Communist party for exaggerating the "specific traits" of American capitalism. The basis for the activities of all Communist parties, he states, is the "common traits" of capitalism, which are fundamentally the same for all countries—the specific traits of capitalism in a particular country merely supplement the general traits. This implies that Stalin makes no major exceptions on behalf of the United States in regard to the application of his theory of capitalism and his objective of world revolution. In April 1947 Stalin presents an unchanged view in his talk with Stassen: he even says that the economic systems of the United States and of Nazi Germany are identical—namely, monopoly capitalism. When Stassen argues that the American system is really very different, he is politely but firmly parried.

As we have noted, Stalin's portrait of the capitalists paints them as utterly unprincipled and ruthless men, dominated by the lust for profits, to which they are willing to sacrifice all else. In his interview with Lyons (intended for publication in America and appealing for better business relations) he remarks, apropos of the alleged sanctity of the old war debts, which were a stumbling block: "Since when has the bourgeoisie placed principle above money?" In his report to the Eighteenth Congress in 1939, he complains of the policies of the United States and other countries toward Germany and Japan, and declares: "Far be it from me to moralize on the policy of nonintervention, to talk of treason, of treachery. etc. It is naive to read a moral to people who do not recognize human morality." [88] To Wells in 1934 he says that American or other capitalists will never permit abolition of unemployment because they need a "reserve army of unemployed" to ensure cheap labor; capitalists are "riveted to profit" and "see nothing except their own interest." The government is merely their tool: if Roosevelt seriously threatens private property and the profit system, they will put in another president.

How does Stalin regard Americans in general? His admiration for American technological prowess and business efficiency are well known. To Ludwig in 1931 he also mentions the democratic simplicity of American manners; but he denies "worship of everything American." As far as Soviet sympathies with the majority of any other nation are concerned, those with the Germans are beyond comparison with "our feelings toward Americans." [89] On no occasion does Stalin appeal to lasting ties of sentiment or culture as a basis for cooperation with the United States. Even to Howard in 1936 he specifies that neither of the rival systems will evolve into the other. "The Soviet system will not grow into American democracy, and vice versa." The utterly unsentimental basis of Stalin's approach to cooperation despite ideological differences is made particularly clear by his statement to Stassen in 1947 that the Soviet Union would have cooperated with Germany as much as with any other capitalist country if Germany had desired. Stalin bids for cooperation on the basis of interest, such as maintaining peace and securing profitable trade.

Stalin has long evinced a belief that proletarian forces are backward in the United States. To the American Labor Delegation in 1927 he comments that American labor leaders are "reactionary" and "reformist," and points to the small fraction of workers who are unionized. He also observes that both political parties are bourgeois, and asks: "Don't you Comrades consider that the absence of your own mass workers' party, if only one like the English [Labor party], weakens the strength of the working class in its political struggle with capitalism?" In 1947 he remarks to Stassen that he sees little difference between Democrats and

Republicans. Likewise in speaking to American Communist party representatives in 1929 he attacks them for "rightist factionalism," saying: "It cannot be denied that American life offers an environment which favors the Communist party's falling into error and exaggerating the strength and stability of American capitalism." [90] He has said nothing since to indicate a change of opinion. Thus such evidence as his writings afford points to an expectation that the United States will be one of the last countries to go Communist.

This conclusion is reinforced by Stalin's views on the American economy. He notes that the United States—"the chief country of capitalism, its stronghold"—is hardest hit by the economic crisis of 1929, and that the crisis of 1937 originates here. But he also observes that the country leads world recovery in 1925 and 1933, and in 1939 he implies that it will pull out of the later crisis.[91] Thus the United States is the center of the capitalist world system, its "stronghold," and, though affected by the general decadence of capitalism, shows some remnants of health in its powers of recovery. As early as 1925 Stalin observes that the center of capitalist financial power is moving across the Atlantic, and he describes how the United States, with England as partner, is becoming the hub of the capitalist system; ". . . two chief, but opposed, centers of attraction are being formed," he writes, "and, in conformity with this, two directions of pull toward these centers throughout the world: Anglo-America . . . and the Soviet Union. . . ." [92] In the years immediately following, Stalin sees the United States and England becoming rivals rather than partners, but at no time up to the present has he implied that the United States has ceased to be the center of world capitalism. To Stassen in 1947 he comments on the unique opportunities for rapid economic development enjoyed by this country from the beginning, and also points out that with the elimination of Germany and Japan as competitors it has access to world markets as never before, and thus has opportunity for further development.

Thus Stalin's conception of the United States as the "stronghold of capitalism" dovetails with his picture of the future course of world revolution. The United States is expected to be the center of the rival world system which finally must clash with the Soviet system until capitalism goes down and Socialism conquers the world. This means that Stalin expects revolution in the United States only near the end of the "epoch of world revolution." [93] As he declares to the American Commission of the Comintern in 1929, "when a revolutionary crisis has developed in America, that will be the beginning of the end of all world capitalism."

V. The next phase

Thus it is probable that Stalin hardly expected revolution to occur in the United States during World War II or its aftermath. But the evidence presented in the present article makes it likely that his perspective on this period was (and is) as follows:

(1) The time for the next harvest of revolution is at hand. The world war, predicted since 1927, has come to pass, and the upheaval it has created will bring to a climax the contradictions of capitalism in a way that will make revolution possible in "a number of countries in Europe and Asia." [94] Precisely such revolution is required to guarantee once and for all that the forces of capitalism will not obliterate Socialism (even in the USSR itself) and compel the whole process to begin again from scratch. Therefore the minimum revolutionary objective for World War II and its aftermath is to bring enough countries into the Soviet camp to effect such a guarantee.

(2) The "law of ebb and flow" implies that unless the whole of capitalism collapses under the present revolutionary wave, the surviving remnant will temporarily stabilize itself a few years after the end of the war and an ebb in the tide of revolution will set in: the revolutionary objective for World War II must therefore be consolidated before the tide begins to ebb. This imparts a certain urgency to revolutionary tactics in the immediate postwar period.

(3) Though the Soviet Union has not yet equaled the United States in industrial production per capital, its industrial and military strength has increased greatly since 1928, and with the defeat of Germany and Japan its relative strength among the powers of Europe and Asia will be enormous. Therefore the Soviet Union will be in position to serve as base for much more active fostering of revolutionary movements in other countries, though not ready to establish Communism throughout the world. This indicates a much more aggressive tactic toward other countries, but not so aggressive as deliberately to bring on war for world hegemony in the immediate future.

The success of this tactic would depend in part, according to Stalin's theory of revolution, on the extent to which the critical areas were isolated from foreign influences hostile to revolution. This gives a major clue to Stalin's war and postwar policies toward Britain and the United States. Many of them can be regarded as a delaying action: by retarding realization on the part of these countries of what is really going on, then minimizing efforts to intervene as realization gradually dawns, they, in effect, tend to isolate the "bourgeoisie" in the countries singled out for revolution until Communist control is established. Stalin's profession of nonaggressive war aims served to lull suspicion. So did the dissolution of the Comintern and his comments thereon. So did his statements on the possibility of coexistence and cooperation and the necessity for unanimity among the big powers after the war. These and similar moves imposed a serious reluctance on the part of the Allies to do or say anything that could be construed as a breach in the spirit of wartime collaboration. When at last Allied public opinion began to denounce Soviet or Communist actions, the same statements served as a basis for propaganda counterattack. Stalin launched this attack with his comments on Churchill's speech at Fulton, declaring it a "dangerous act," sowing discord among the Allies, harming the cause of peace and security, in short, warmongering.[95] Thereafter those who like Churchill object to Soviet policies in eastern Europe and elsewhere are denounced as "warmongers," and an attempt is made to mobilize against them the popular craving for peace.

Even the United Nations has to some extent been exploited by Stalin's tactics. The possibility of using the veto to cripple Allied action in revolutionary areas is obvious. But if, as some think, Stalin might prefer a deal based on spheres of influence to the United Nations pattern, such an arrangement could be depended on to further, not to limit, revolutionary operations. Within his sphere Stalin would have a free hand, and Communist action would also continue across the demarcation line into the other sphere.

When Stalin looks to the most distant future, the United States, which has emerged from the last war more truly than ever the "stronghold of capitalism," probably continues to figure in his thinking as it has done in his basic writings since the mid-1920's—as the center around which the capitalist system will form for the final war to the death between the two systems. Meanwhile, Stalin (*Pravda,* February 10, 1946) projects further industrial expansion in the Soviet Union on a scale which suggests, other factors aside, that the climactic struggle will not be risked before fifteen or twenty years have elapsed. Stalin's theory of "ebb and flow" would lead him to expect a new stabilization of capitalism within a few years, followed some years later by another wave of crisis and revolution generated by capitalism's inexorable contradictions. He apparently is timing completion of the Soviet base of operations for the crest of this next wave. Tactics of the moment may swing this way or that, but the Marxist doctrine to which he is committed is uncompromisingly revolutionary. In that doctrine, world Communism is the supreme aim, Soviet power the major instrument by which it will be achieved.

Notes

Note: Where the period of republication of particular items for mass consumption is relevant to the discussion, this information is supplied in parentheses in the footnotes. (Thus (1925-1939) means "originally published in 1925, republished until 1939," and (1925 to present) means "originally published in 1925, republished up to the present time."

1. "Sochineniia," I, 1946, xi. The author of the present study found only one other instance in which Stalin in his mature years modified an earlier statement. "K voprosam Leninizma" (1926) quotes the original version of one paragraph in "Ob osnovakh Leninizma" (1924), relating to the victory of Socialism in one country, and points out its inadequacy; and subsequent versions of "Ob osnovakh Leninizma" contain a revised wording of the passage. ("Voprosy Leninizma," 11th ed., 1945, pp. 25, 137.)

2. *Bol'shevik,* May 1941, p. 1.

3. "Ob osnovakh Leninizma" (1924 to present), "Voprosy," 11th ed., 1945, p. 14.

4. *Pravda,* October 2, 1946, p. 2.

5. "Istoriia" (1938 to present), p. 339; "Voprosy," 11th ed., 1945, p. 598.

6. "Otchetnyi doklad t. Stalina na XVIII s"ezde partii o rabote TsK VKP (b)" (1939 to present), "XVIII s"ezd. Stenograficheskii otchet," Moscow, 1939, p. 31.

7. This quotation and the quotations used in the preceding three paragraphs are from "Istoria" (1938 to present), pp. 101, 102, 104, 105.

8. "I. Stalin, Beseda c nemetskim pisatelem Emilem Liudvigom," *Bol'shevik,* April 30, 1932, p. 33.

9. The quotations in this paragraph and the preceding three paragraphs are from "Istoriia" (1938 to present), pp. 103, 105, 106, 110, 114, 117.

10. "Beseda t. Stalina s angliiskim pisatelem G. D. Uellsom" (1934-1939), *Bol'shevik,* September 15, 1934, p. 8; "Zapis' besedy tov. I. V. Stalina s deiatelem respublikanskoi partii SShA Garol'dom Stassenom," *Pravda,* May 8, 1947, p. 1.

11. "Istoriia" (1938 to present), pp. 120, 15; "Ob osnovakh Leninizma" (1924 to present), "Voprosy," 11th ed., 1945, pp. 54, 60, 74.

12. *Ibid.,* p. 14.

13. To Wells, *loc. cit.,* p. 13.

14. "Ob osnovakh Leninizma" (1924 to present), "Voprosy," 11th ed., 1945, p. 26; "Istoriia" (1938 to present), p. 11.

15. "Istoriia" (1938 to present), pp. 117, 121.

16. "Ob osnovakh Leninizma" (1924 to present), "Voprosy," 11th ed., 1945, pp. 3, 17; "XVI s"ezd" (1930-1939), *Pravda,* June 29, 1930, p. 1; "XVII s"ezd" (1934) to present), *Pravda,* January 28, 1934, p. 1; "Istoriia" (1938 to present), pp. 117, 121, 288.

17. "Ob osnovakh Leninizma" (1924 to present), "Voprosy," 11th ed., 1945, pp. 17, 55.

18. *Ibid.,* p. 18.

19. *Pravda,* December 18, 1929, p. 3.

20. "Ob osnovakh Leninizma" (1924 to present), "Voprosy," 11th ed., 1945, pp. 3, 17.

21. *Ibid.,* pp. 3, 17; *Pravda,* February 10, 1946, p. 1.

22. "XVI s"ezd" (1930-1939), *Pravda,* June 29, 1930, p. 1.

23. "Ob osnovakh Leninizma" (1924 to present), "Voprosy," 11th ed., 1945, pp. 25, 32; "K voprosam Leninizma" (1926 to present), *ibid.,* p. 140; "O nedostatkakh partiinoi raboty i merakh likvidatsii trotskistskikh i inykh dvurushnikov," *Pravda,* March 29, 1938, p. 2; "Otvet t-shchu IVANOVU Ivanu Filippovichu," *Pravda,* February 14, 1938, p. 3; "Otchetnyi doklad" (1939 to present), "XVIII s"ezd. Sten. otchet," p. 32; "Istoriia" (1938 to present), p. 261.

24. "Itogi pervoi piatiletki" (1933 to present), *Pravda,* January 10, 1933, p. 1.

The example of the Stalin Constitution is likewise expected to exert such a revolutionizing force. *Pravda,* November 26, 1936, p. 3.

25. "XVI s"ezd" (1930-1939), *Pravda,* June 29, 1930, p. 1.

26. *Ibid.,* p. 1; "Istoriia" (1938 to present), pp. 117, 121; to Wells (1934-1939), *Bol'shevik,* September 15, 1934, p. 9.

27. "XVI s"ezd" (1930-1939), *Pravda,* June 29, 1930, p. 1. See also "XVII s"ezd" (1934 to present), *Pravda,* January 28, 1934, p. 1; "Otchetnyi doklad" (1939 to present), "XVIII s"ezd. Sten. otchet," p. 11.

28. "XVI s"ezd" (1930-1939), *Pravda,* June 29, 1930, p. 1; "Otchetnyi doklad" (1939 to present), "XVIII s"ezd. Sten otchet," p. 9.

29. Stalin mentions, but does not give statistics on, bankruptcies, ruin of peasants, falling prices, maintenance of monopoly prices at the expense of restricting production, bank failures, trade wars, dumping, currency wars. In 1939 he gives statistics on gold reserves as evidence that the avoidance of economic crisis in Fascist countries is only temporary. See "XVI s"ezd" (1930-1939), *Pravda,* June 29, 1930, p. 1; "XVII s"ezd" (1934 to present), *Pravda,* January 28, 1934, p. 1; "Otchetnyi doklad" (1939 to present), "XVIII s"ezd. Sten. otchet," p. 10.

30. "Ob osnovakh Leninizma" (1924 to present), "Voprosy," 11th ed., 1945, p. 19.

31. *Ibid.,* p. 25.

32. Stalin uses the term "crisis" in so many ways that we must not jump to conclusions from a particular statement. Besides "revolutionary crisis" he speaks of "economic crises," "general crisis of capitalism," "crisis of world capitalism," etc. So "crisis" does not necessarily mean "revolutionary crisis." Moreover, "revolutionary crisis" does not necessarily mean revolution, for leadership may fail to take advantage of the situation. Again, "revolutionary crisis" sometimes means the full ripeness of the objective conditions for revolution, sometimes the long period of rising tensions which in some cases culminates in ripeness, for which Stalin sometimes employs a special term, "the immediate revolutionary situation." On the latter see *Pravda,* February 10, 1930, p. 2.

33. "Sochineniia," V, 73.

34. "Ob osnovakh Leninizma" (1924 to present), "Voprosy," 11th ed., 1945, pp. 23, 56, 60; "Istoriia" (1938 to present), p. 65.

35. Stalin does not formulate this condition definitely, but it is a clear implication of: 1, his thesis that capitalism is now a world system and revolution the product of forces throughout the system; 2, his emphasis on the international ties of the bourgeoisie and the constant threat of intervention from that quarter (e.g., "Ob osnovakh Leninizma," "Voprosy," 11th ed., 1945, p. 26); 3, his statement that the proletariats of capitalist states, and the state in which Socialism has already won, will assist the proletariats in other countries to achieve revolution. See "Oktiabr'skaia revoliutsiia i taktika russkikh kommunistov" (1924 to present), *ibid.,* p. 104. The topic of outside aid for revolution includes conscious leadership and will be dealt with later in this study.

36. "Politicheskii otchet TsK (1927), "XV s"ezd. Sten. otchet," p. 44; "Ob itogakh iiul'skogo plenum TsK VKP (b)" (1928), "Voprosy," 9th ed., 1932, p. 336; "XVI s"ezd" (1930-1939), *Pravda,* June 29, 1930, p. 1; "XVII s"ezd" (1934 to present), *Pravda,* January 28, 1934, p. 1.

37. "Ob osnovakh Leninizma" (1924 to present), "Voprosy," 11th ed., 1945, p. 4.

38. *Ibid.,* p. 56. Stalin here used the term "reserves" to include all favorable factors, not merely men.

39. "XVII s"ezd" (1934 to present), *Pravda,* January 28, 1934, p. 1. The inevitability of war is the central theme of the foreign affairs section of each of Stalin's reports to the Party Congresses from 1925 to the last one in 1939; the direct connection with revolution is obvious in each case, and made explicit in most.

40. "Istoriia" (1938 to present), p. 162.

41. *Pravda,* May 1, 1942.

42. *Pravda,* February 10, 1946, p. 1.

43. "XVII s"ezd" (1934 to present), *Pravda,* January 28, 1934, p. 1.

44. "Ob osnovakh Leninizma" (1924 to present), 'Voprosy," 11th ed., 1945, pp. 48, 3, 17, 54; "XIV s"ezd. Sten. otchet," p. 12; "XV s"ezd. Sten. otchet," p. 44; Sochineniia," IV, 166, 238, 378.

45. "Istoriia" (1938 to present), pp. 214, 338; "Ob osnovakh Leninizma" (1924 to present), "Voprosy," 11th ed., 1945, p. 54.

46. "Oktiabr'skaia revoliutsiia i taktika russkikh kommunistov" (1924 to present), "Voprosy," 11th ed., 1945, p. 102.

47. "K itogam rabot XIV konferentsii RKP(b)" (1925-1934), "Voprosy," 9th ed., 1932, pp. 109, 111; "Ob osnovakh Leninizma" (1924 to present), "Voprosy," 11th ed., 1945, p. 55; "Beseda s inostrannymi rabochimi delegatsiiami," "Voprosy," 9th ed., 1932, p. 301; "XV s"ezd. Sten. ochet," p. 44; "Istoriia" (1938 to present), pp. 27, 80, 84, 127, 138, 140, 221, 258.

48. "XVII s"ezd" (1934 to present) *Pravda,* January 28, 1934, p. 1; "Politicheskii otchet TsK" (1927), "XV s"ezd. Sten. otchet," pp. 38, 44; "XVI s"ezd" (1930-1939), *Pravda,* June 29, 1930, p. 1.

49. "Otchetnyi doklad" (1939 to present), "XVIII s"ezd," p. 11.

50. For references in this and the following two paragraphs, see "Istoriia" (1938 to present), especially pp. 11, 36, 105, 337, 343, 110, 111, 16, 45, 339.

51. "Istoriia" (1938 to present), pp. 40, 45, 135, 337, 343; see also "Ob osnovakh Leninizma" (1924 to present), "Voprosy," 11th ed., 1945, pp. 64-75.

52. "O proekte konstitusii Soiuza S.S.R." (1936 to present), *Pravda,* November 26, 1926, p. 3.

53. "Ob osnovakh Leninizma" (1924 to present), "Voprosy," 11th ed., 1945, p. 66.

54. "XVII s"ezd"(1934 to present), *Pravda,* January 28, 1934, p. 1; see also "Beseda s pervoi amerikanskoi rabochei delegatsiei" (1927-1939), "Voprosy," 9th ed., 1932, p. 266; "Istoriia" (1938 to present), p. 337.

55. "Ob osnovakh Leninizma" (1924 to present), "Voprosy," 11th ed., 1945, p. 63. See also "Istoriia" (1938 to present), pp. 127, 133, 136, 151.

56. Stalin remarks that he and other younger members of the Central Committee were required by Lenin to study the fundamentals of warfare. ("Otvet tov. Stalina na pis'mo Razina," *Bol'shevik,* February 1947, p. 6.)

57. "Sochineniia," V, 62; see also p. 162.

58. "Istoriia" (1938 to present), pp. 40, 38; "Sochineniia," V (1947), 63, 162.

59. "Ob osnovakh Leninizma" (1924 to present), "Voprosy," 11th ed., 1945, p. 54 (italics added); see also "Sochineniia," V, 173-180; "K itogam rabot XIV konferentsii RKP(b)" (1925-1934), "Voprosy," 9th ed., 1932, p. 110.

60. "Oktiabr'skaia revoliutsiia i taktika russkikh kommunistov" (1924 to present), "Voprosy," 11th ed., 1945, p. 104. The latter part of this passage, including the reference to using armed force, is a quotation from Lenin which Stalin employs also in "K voprosam Leninizma" (1926 to present), *ibid.,* p. 142, and in "K itogam rabot XIV konferensii RKP(b)" (1925-1934), "Voprosy," 9th ed., 1932, p. 122. This repetition in widely circulated works is added evidence that Stalin means every word.

61. See the statement to Ludwig above, and the vow of fidelity to the principles of the Comintern quoted below; also "Mezhdunarodnyi kharakter oktiabr'skoi revoliutsii" (1927, 1934 to present), "Voprosy" 11th ed., 1945, p. 179; "Sochineniia," IV, 166, 238, and V, 85, 169, 179; "K itogam rabot XIV konferentsii RKP (b)" (1925-1934), "Voprosy," 9th ed., 1932, p. 132. This list of corroborating passages is by no means exhaustive.

62. "Beseda tovarishcha Stalina s predsedatelem amerikanskogo gazetnogo ob"edineniia 'Skripps-Govard N'iuspeipers' g-nom Roi Govardom," *Pravda,* March 5, 1936, p. 2.

63. The denial that the USSR ever had "such plans and intentions" amounts to denying that it had ever given aid to revolutions abroad, e.g., to China. The import of the statement for the future can be no greater than its application to the past.

64. *Loc. cit.,* p. 1.

65. "XVII godovshchina velikoi oktiabr'skoi sotsialisticheskoi revoliutsii," *Pravda,* November 7, 1944, p. 2.

66. "Otvety tov. Stalina I. V. na voprosy prezidenta amerikanskogo agentstva Iunaited Press g-na Kh'iu Beili," *Pravda,* October 3, 1946, p. 1.

67. "Otvet tov. I. V. Stalina na vopros glavnogo korrespondenta angliiskogo agentstva Reiter," *Pravda,* May 30, 1943, p. 1.

68. "Po povodu smerti Lenina," in V. I. Lenin, "Izbrannye proizvedeniia v dvukh tomakh," 4th ed., Moscow, printing of 1946, I, 8, which in turn refers to Stalin's "O Lenine," 1942, pp. 17-22. The vow is also quoted in "Istoriia" (1938 to present), p. 257. Thus it has been widely circulating in at least three authoritative versions during the current period.

69. *Pravda,* October 29, 1948.

70. Stalin's belief in the necessity for strict party discipline on an international and not merely a national scale is illustrated in his speeches in the Comintern in May 1929, in which he castigates members of the American Delegation for refusing to accept a decision of the Presidium disciplining American party leaders: debate and criticism are permissible in advance of decision, he concludes, but once a decision is made all must accept it, else there can be no "collective direction." ("O pravykh fraktsionerakh v amerikanskoi kompartii," *Bol'shevik,* January 15, 1930, pp. 8-26).

71. "Sochineniia," IV, 232, 380; "Ob osnovakh Leninizma" (1924 to present), "Voprosy," 11th ed., 1945, pp. 26, 54; "K voprosam Leninizma" (1926 to present), *ibid.,* pp. 113, 140; "Itogi pervoi piatiletki" (1933 to present), *Pravda,* January 10, 1933, p. 1; "Privetstvie tov. I. V. Stalina," *Pravda,* September 7, 1947, p. 1. These are only a few of the many passages which reflect a two-world conception.

72. "Oktiabr'skaia revoliutsiia i taktika russkikh kommunistov" (1924 to present), "Voprosy," 11th ed., 1945, p. 105.

73. "Beseda s pervoi amerikanskoi rabochei delegatsiei" (1927-1939), "Voprosy," 9th ed., 1932, p. 287; also reproduced in the introductory section of a popular edition of Lenin's works, "Izbrannye proizvedeniia v dvukh tomakh," 4th ed., Moscow, printing of 1946, 1, 28. See also "K itogam rabot XIV konferentsii RKP (b)" (1925-1934), "Voprosy," 9th ed., 1932, p. 111; "Politicheskii otchet TsK" (1925), "XIV s"ezd. Sten. otchet," p. 19; "Ob itogakh iiul'skogo plenuma TsK VKP (b)" (1928-1934), "Voprosy," 9th ed., 1932, p. 338.

74. "K voprosam Leninizma" (1926 to present), "Voprosy," 11th ed., 1945, p. 140; see also p. 113. Quoted again in "Otvet t-shchu IVANOVU Ivanu Filippovichu," *Pravda,* February 14, 1938, p. 3.

75. "Ob osnovakh Leninizma" (1924 to present), "Voprosy," 11th ed., 1945, p. 32. On Socialist encirclement see also "XVIII s"ezd. Sten. otchet" (1939 to present), pp. 33, 36.

76. "Sochineniia," V, 62, 74, 161; "O pravykh fraktsionerakh v amerikanskoi kompartii," *Bol'shevik,* January 15, 1930, pp. 13, 23; "Voprosy sverdlovtsev i otvet t. Stalina," *Pravda,* February 10, 1930, p. 2.

77. "Istoriia"(1938 to present), p. 204.

78. "O politicheskoi strategii i taktike russkikh kommunistov" (written 1921, first published 1947), "Sochineniia," V, 63.

79. "Ob osnovakh Leninizma" (1924 to present), "Voprosy," 11th ed., 1945, pp. 17, 54; "Sochineniia," IV, 166, 238, 378.

80. "Ob osnovakh Leninizma" (1924 to present), "Voprosy," 11th ed., 1945, p. 55; "Sochineniia," V, 64.

81. "O pravom uklone v VKP (b)" (1929 to present), *Bol'shevik*, December 1929, p. 20.

82. "XIV s"ezd. Sten. otchet," pp. 8, 10, 17; "K itogam rabot XIV Konferentsii," "Voprosy," 9th ed., 1932, p. 110.

83. "XV s"ezd. Sten. otchet," p. 47.

84. On aggressive tactics, see "O pravom uklone v VKP(b)" (1929 to present), *Bol'shevik*, December 1929, pp. 15-49 (including passage quoted immediately above in text); "O pravykh fraktsionerakh v amerikanskoi kompartii," *Bol'shevik*, January 15, 1930, pp. 8-26.

85. "Ob itogakh iiul'skogo plenuma TsK VKP(b)," "Voprosy," 9th ed., 1932, p. 336; "Otchetnyi doklad" (1939 to present), "XVIII s"ezd. Sten. otchet," p. 15; "Oktiabr'skaia Revoliutsiia" (1924 to present), "Voprosy," 11th ed., 1945, p. 78.

86. "Gospodin Kempbell priviraet," *Bol'shevik*, November 30, 1932, p. 12; interview reported by Eugene Lyons, *New York Herald Tribune*, November 24, 1930, pp. 1, 2.

87. "Beseda s pervoi amerikanskoi rabochei delegatsiei" (1927-1939), "Voprosy," 9th ed., 1932, pp. 280, 287.

88. "Otchetnyi doklad" (1939 to present), "XVIII s"ezd. Sten. otchet," p. 14.

89. To Emil Ludwig, *Bol'shevik*, April 30, 1932, p. 38.

90. "O pravykh fraktsionerakh v amerikanskoi kompartii," *Bol'shevik*, January 15, 1930, p. 8.

91. "XVI s"ezd" (1930-1939), *Pravda*, June 29, 1930, p. 1; "Politicheskii otchet (1925), "XIV s"ezd. Sten. otchet," p. 11; "Politicheskii otchet" (1927), p. 38; "VII-omu s"ezd" (1934 to present), *Pravda,* January 28, 1934, p. 1; "Otchetnyi doklad" (1939 to present), "XVIII s"ezd. Sten. otchet," p. 9.

92. "XIV s"ezd. Sten. otchet," pp. 10, 19.

93. The factor of geographical position obviously supports such a view also. Stalin recognizes that proximity is an important factor in assisting revolution in another country from the Soviet base. Among the unfavorable circumstances of the October Revolution in Russia he mentions "the absence, next to it or in its neighborhood, of a Soviet country which it could lean upon. Undoubtedly, a future revolution, in Germany for example, would be in a more favorable situation in this respect, for it has nearby so powerful a Soviet country as our Soviet Union." "Voprosy" (1924 to present), 11th ed., 1945, p. 79.

94. "XVII s"ezd" (1934 to present), p. 1.

95. "Interv'iu tov. I. V. Stalina s korrespondentom 'Pravdy' otnositel'no rechi g. Cherchillia," *Pravda*, March 14, 1946, p. 1.

4 THE POST-STALIN ERA

Introduction

The re-emergence of Soviet sociology in the post-Stalin era can be only partially explained in the present volume. The process of its revival is not yet complete, and we thus lack the historical perspective to evaluate these events. Nevertheless, certain suggestions can be made to clarify the rise of the new sociology. Changes in the various spheres of Soviet life nurtured its comeback. While the death of Stalin brought on a subsequent reduction in the powers of the secret police, and the attack on the cult of personality brought on changes in ideological orientations, new areas of inquiry were opened and the possibility of reform was suggested. Such reforms were especially desirable, at least as far as the men of power were concerned, in the areas of rational economic planning, which has always been part of a socialist tradition but which was seriously undermined in the Stalin era. The selections in this section are designed to document the slow and painful path of development of Soviet sociology over the past decade. These contributions will remain indispensable for any future systematic analysis of Soviet sociology.

The paper of Leopold Labedz, editor of *Survey* and editor-in-chief of the Library of International Studies, takes us to the beginning of Soviet sociological stirrings. It provides an excellent perspective for judging the progress of the discipline today. In 1956 Soviet "sociologists," who appeared for the first time at the World Congress of Sociology, held in Amsterdam, were full of misconceptions about the practice of sociology in the West. Their abysmal ignorance of the subject, rather than the fact that each side represented a different ideological camp, prevented a serious discourse between the delegates. Nor were the Soviets prepared to concede that their socialist society had any problems that could be studied by Soviet sociologists. According to Labedz, the question of empirical research to be conducted by Soviet sociologists "was hardly mentioned." The conclusion reached by Mr. Labedz is that in 1956 Soviet sociology had "not so far emerged as a science."

Labedz's second article is an appraisal of Soviet sociology through the year 1962. He finds Soviet performance at the Fifth World Congress of Sociology, in Washington, D.C. in 1962, quite appalling and little different from its appearance on the world scene in 1956. Considerable change, however, occurred on the domestic scene with the introduction of the so-called concrete sociological research. Mr. Labedz is perceptive in distinguishing between the terms "concrete" and "empirical" investigations. The original meaning of the "concrete" studies is indeed "designed to uphold a dogma, not to test hypothesis." Despite the various restrictions placed upon the conduct of inquiry by Soviet sociologists, Mr. Labedz points out that these studies should provide us with some data on Soviet society which is otherwise unavailable. He concludes that since Soviet sociologists will be forced to analyze their data from a very narrow ideological standpoint, it will be up to sociologists outside the Soviet Union to make a more objective assessment. Under these circumstances Soviet sociologists would be contributing in their own way to the development of an international sociology.

The contribution by Arvid Brodersen, Professor of Political Science at the New School for Social Research, was written early in 1957 and represents one of the earliest accurate assessments of the possible development of Soviet sociology. Professor Brodersen argued that whatever future events might bring, social scientists in the West "should act on the assumption that the answer will be affirmative, and pursue the goal of a systematic internationalization of their discipline." Despite Mr. Brodersen's sage advice, Western social scientists have been surprised by the new developments in Soviet sociology and many still refuse to take Soviet sociology seriously, interpreting its rise as purely a propaganda maneuver by the Soviet government. Fortunately, it is still not too late to consider seriously Mr. Brodersen's policy proposal for Western social scientists, stated at the conclusion of his article.

The article by Lewis S. Feuer, Professor of Social Science and Philosophy at the University of California at Berkeley, details his personal impression of Soviet sociology and philosophy while on a four-and-a-half month visit to the Soviet Union in 1963. It is a highly informative description of the intellectual limitations and problems of Soviet scholars. Professor Feuer contributes a new word, "protivism," to describe the state of Soviet sociology and philosophy. According to Feuer, the Russian word "protiv," meaning "against," is used repeatedly by Soviet scholars to denounce undesirable ideas emanating from the West and is "the most characteristic word in Soviet philosophical essays." In Feuer's use, the term has a negative connotation reflecting the stifling atmosphere of Soviet scholarship imposed by the party. But in the perspective of recent history it is possible to interpret "protivism" as a positive force in the development of Soviet social sciences. It is through the "protivist" literature that Soviet readers learn of Western ideas, even if this knowledge is falsely interpreted. Nevertheless, Professor Feuer gives us a vivid description of the continued isolation of Soviet scholars from the rest of the world.

The selection by George Fischer, Professor of Sociology at Columbia University, comes from the only presently available monograph devoted to an analysis of Soviet sociology. Professor Fischer made the term "new Soviet sociology" popular. In the first part of the selection he presents a discussion of the party decisions which made "concrete" sociological research possible in the Soviet Union, followed by a summary of the first studies conducted by Soviet social scientists. The second part is devoted to a discussion of the social, intellectual, and political profiles of men who are in the forefront of Soviet sociology. The party's support of sociology can only be sustained with the backing of scholars with exceptional political and academic influence.

The Soviet attitude to sociology

LEOPOLD LABEDZ

There is no Soviet counterpart of Western sociology. The Department of Social Sciences established in 1919 at Moscow University, which included a Chair of Sociology, was closed in 1924. Ethnography survived in the new Department of Ethnology until 1930. From then until 1939, when a Chair of Ethnography was established in the Department of History, there was no academic teaching on topics even distantly related to sociology.[1] The Chair of Anthropology, which existed in the Department of Biology, represented physical anthropology.

There were similar developments elsewhere. The subject-matter of sociological inquiry was removed from the context of academic life and placed under direct party supervision. It was subsumed under Marxism-Leninism, which was taught either as Political Economy or Philosophy, or as part of general political education. Various institutions of academic standing occasionally engaged in investigations of a social character (such as surveys of working-class family budgets), but they did not survive the holocaust of 1930, when a purge hit most of the economic and statistical institutes.

The administrative division of the social sciences which emerged reflects *raison d'état,* or rather party reasons. The Marxist-Leninist substitute for sociology is not subject to academic control but is under the supervision of a party institution, the Academy of Social Sciences attached to the Central Committee of the CPSU. There are neither departments of sociology nor separate institutes of sociology. The Academy of Sciences of the USSR has a section on social sciences, but this comprises only institutes of philosophy, economics, ethnography, law, and history. None of the institutions which prepare for the degree of candidate in the various sciences has sociology among them. Dissertations for such a degree in the social sciences [2] may include subjects bordering on sociological topics, but their ideological character is at variance with sociol-

From *Soviet Survey,* 1956, No. 10.

ogy. It would be difficult to learn much about the Soviet social structure from a thesis entitled: "Defense of Socialist Society—A Sacred Task and Honorable Duty of the Citizens of the USSR." [3] There can be little empirical interest for Western sociologists in dissertations on: "Intensification of the Impoverishment of the British Working-Class after the Second World War (1945–1953)," [4] or "Militarization of the Economy and Deterioration of the Conditions of the Working-Class in the USA in the Post-War Period (1946–1954)." [5]

Since the abolition of the "cult of personality," some of the favorite topics have naturally been replaced by others. In the lists of dissertations one no longer encounters such once popular subjects as "J. V. Stalin on Historical Peculiarities in the Formation of the Russian National Character" [6] (thesis in psychology). Instead one finds "Marxism-Leninism on Freedom of Personality." [7] But otherwise the style has not changed much. As before there is a monotonous repetition of the current propaganda clichés, and the themes still include such dreary slogans as "Cosmopolitanism—the Ideology of Imperialist Reaction." [8]

There is no empirical research. Sociological field-work in the form of social surveys, participant observation, or any other technique of social investigation, is neither known nor applied to any sphere, from social stratification and mobility to family and industrial relations. The reasons are too obvious to need elaboration.

Ethnography is perhaps the Soviet academic discipline closest to the non-existent empirical sociology. Yet it is hardly comparable to Western social anthropology or even cultural anthropology. It is confined mainly to the material aspects of the culture of various Soviet peoples, to "folklorism," social history, and the investigation of various tribes living on Soviet territory. As a study of historical cultures it is largely a handmaiden of history and archaeology.[9]

During the Stalinist period ethnography was frankly employed for patriotic purposes. Ethnographic studies of the Scythians were added to the denunciation by the historians of the "Norman theory of the origin of the Russian State," in order to free Soviet historiography from alien tendencies and establish it on an autochthonous basis free from foreign influences. Not all Soviet ethnographers were happy to deal with history for current consumption (the historians have no choice). Recently some of them have been trying to sever their close connection with the historians.[10] Unlike the latter, they had already been given limited freedom to move into the contemporary field. The second conference of ethnographers, which took place in Moscow in January–February 1951, after an interval of twelve years, placed before them the task of "investigating the decisive transformation of the kolkhoz village." [11] The resulting studies [12] are not without some sociological interest. Although they concern themselves mainly with such items as dress, forms of housing, and patterns of settlement, they nevertheless adduce some evidence on changes in the extended family in the village and deal with some aspects of non-material culture. A proposal to investigate more of them was made by some Soviet ethnographers.[13]

While the "reactivation of the superstructure" by Stalin widened the ethnographers' margin of study, they had to make the necessary obeisances on the occasion of the publication of his "work" on linguistics.[14] They also duly censured the so-called "Veselovsky school" allegedly connected with the views of the condemned philologist N. Ya. Marr.

Stressing all the time that they are "armed with Marxist-Leninist methodology," Soviet ethnographers use a conceptual framework which is still dominated by the views of Morgan [15] and Tylor. They stick to the enumerative concept of culture and concentrate on its material aspects. It is a case of arrested development. Ideology prevented the scientific progress which has taken place in Western anthropological thought, where new field-work contributed to the development of more refined concepts and to the abandonment of many false assumptions held by earlier ethnographers and "armchair anthropologists." Soviet psychology, being another example of arrested development, had no influence on the ideas of Soviet ethnographers.

These are not the only contrasts with the West. The mere fact that Marx and Engels used some of the ideas of the early pioneers of anthropology to develop their own historical schemes set a conceptual barrier to the development of Soviet anthropology. The teleological outline of history in the scheduled march of humanity from primitive communism to the classless society cannot be tampered with. It would be politically imprudent if this dialectical construction inducing the certainty of "ultimate victory" were to be qualified by the consideration that Engels' notions of primitive society were based on inadequate evidence and some fancy assumptions. Consequently, the new data collected by Western anthropologists during half a century are simply ignored by Soviet ethnography which is compelled to stick to obsolete conceptions.

As Sovetskaya Etnografiya put it: "Linked to the positive task of developing the problems of Soviet ethnography is the struggle against reactionary bourgeois science which has placed itself in the service of the warmongers." [16]

In executing this task Soviet ethnographers have produced a crop of publications in which ignorance of Western anthropology is surpassed only by the arrogance with which it is condemned. It is difficult to convey to the Western reader, accustomed to the normal language of scientific controversy, an idea of the resulting mixture of abuse and mis-information. The level of these "works" on Western social sciences can be judged from a few examples published by the Academy of Sciences of the USSR, the highest scientific institution. One such treatise, entitled *Anglo-American Ethnography in the Service of Imperialism,*[17] includes chapters on "Cosmopolitanism in American Ethnography," "The Func-tional School of Ethnography in the Service of British Imperialism," "Psycho-racism in American Ethnography," and so on. The resulting picture of American anthropology is summarized as follows in a review in *Sovetskaya Etnografiya:* "It is well known to everybody that some American 'ethnographers' support the bandit-terrorist anti-Negro organi-zation, the Ku Klux Klan. Hence on the basis of well-founded evidence it can be said, in the literal and not the metaphorical sense of the word, that the contemporary reactionary bourgeois ethnographers are hired mercenaries of Wall Street." [18] Other writings are in the same vein.

Criticism of Western sociology is equally ill-informed. M. P. Baskin declares in his "Apologia for Imperialism in American Sociology" [19] that "American sociologists are not only ideologically but organizationally linked with the most reactionary strata of American finance-capital . . . [they] are above all the propagandists of a new world war . . . [they] justify and glorify the zoological punishment of other nations. . . . Fol-lowing Hitler, who proclaimed in his time the slogan that 'the German should not think' . . . [they] are leading a crusade against free human thought, against reason and science."

No less startling are his pronouncements on individual American sociologists: "Their leader, F. Ogburn, cynically compares their function to that of the managers of war factories. . . . The sociologist Ross tries to show the existence of races with a predominance of 'animal desires' and others with a predominance of 'desires of an emotional and intel-lectual order,' The latter comprise all 100 percent Americans, i.e., in the first place financial kings and plutocrats. . . . The sociologist Bo-gardus, paid by Wall Street, advocates on the basis of racial 'theory'—genocide, the physical extermination of whole nations. He pours out tor-rents of dirty slander on Negroes, Chinese, Indians, and other nations which are not convenient to Wall Street."

The list of American sociologists mentioned is too long to be quoted, but it includes certain unexpected names among other "lackeys with diplomas" and "rotten idealist-metaphysicians." Not only G. Santayana ("self-confessed obscurantist"), John Dewey ("enthusiastically glorifying fascism"), or Professor Davidson (". . . who with the passion of a stock-exchange swindler . . . wants to turn into slaves not only the black but also the white workers") are attacked as sociologists but even such unlikely persons as Mr. Green ("the Fuehrer of the American trade unions") and Mr. Herbert Hoover, the ex-President, who "tries as a 'sociologist' to justify 'theoretically' the reactionary lunatic claims of the American monopolies to world hegemony." However, "a stubborn struggle is being fought against reactionary bourgeois sociology in the USA by the American Communists . . . [who] are supported by leading American scientists and millions of American people." There is little point in multiplying these examples of Soviet writings published during the Stalin epoch. In style and content they do not vary much,[20] and in comparison with them criticism of "bourgeois" sociological theories published in the early Soviet era, though sharply polemical, looks in retrospect almost like models of *bon ton*.[21]

Have the post-Stalinist developments affected the situation? The attempts to subordinate science to party control were never uniform. Their fate depended at any given time on a curious combination of ignorance, ideological legacy, current political circumstances, and pragmatic considerations. Thus after 1929–1930, when the economists Kondratyev and Groman were purged, statisticians were nevertheless permitted to pursue a "bourgeois" heresy, namely, the mathematical theory of probability. They again suffered personally during the Great Purge, when the directors of the Central Statistical Bureau were executed and many others imprisoned for the "sabotage" of perpetrating the suppressed 1937 census. But their theories were not fundamentally attacked until 1949–1950, when statisticians were told to become "class-conscious and party-conscious." Pragmatic implications were then disregarded in the ideological frenzy. One result was that the possibilities of "quality control" in Soviet industry were neglected since the old definition of statistics as "a science dealing with mass phenomena in *both* society and nature" was condemned in favor of statistics as a "social science."

On the other hand, Soviet physicists, who in the thirties were forced to distort or soft-pedal the theoretical significance of relativity and quantum physics, were comparatively unmolested even during the Zhdanov era, when it became imperative to incorporate heresies which might help in the atomic race. The vulnerability of a doctrine to empirical social research currently sets narrower limits to the revival of the social sciences than of the natural sciences. The requirements of efficiency are making their greatest impact in the technological sphere. However, some relaxation has been felt in other fields. One such domain is that of economic and vital statistics. Thus the grip of the 1947 State Secrets Decree has been loosened, following a joint session of the Presidium of the Academy of Sciences, of the Central Statistical Administration, and of the Collegium of the Ministry of Higher Education to discuss the development of statistics.[22]

Ever since 1930 the blackout on statistics had become worse. Not only were no statistics published on the cost of living, prices, or real wages (penal statistics were an early casualty), but even the Five-Year Plan figures were becoming steadily thinner in each subsequent plan. The last figures of professional distribution were given in 1937. Demographic data ended with the publication of the 1939 census, of which only the crude results were given. The Soviet demographers, led by Ryabushkin and Kuzminov, who attended the World Population Conference in 1954, could not even produce figures of the Soviet population. But in 1956, for the first time in almost twenty years, a statistical yearbook [23] was published, disclosing this [24] and some other statistical information. The social statistics it provides are most inadequate, but they are certainly more abundant than in the preceding period. Some Soviet statisticians who had to eat humble pie at the February 1950 conference in Moscow [25] but never quite recanted, such as I. Yu. Pisarev and V. S. Nemchinov, [26] could again press the universalist view of statistics at a Conference in March 1954.[27] Although the concept of statistics as a social science was retained, it was acknowledged that it can be applied to both nature and society.

The ethnographers boldly announced that the primary task placed before their May 1956 conference by the XXth Congress of the CPSU was "to put an end to Talmudism and uncritical attitudes." [28] *Sovetskaya Etnografiya* demanded "a strictly objective analysis of facts" and diagnosed a shift from the investigation of archaic cultures to the contemporary life of peoples, adding sadly that "this new orientation even now unfortunately sometimes meets with the opposition of some scientists." Whether resistance to objectivity and contemporary interests comes only from scientific quarters is an interesting question. One result of the new orientation is a research project on the family life of the kolkhoz peasantry.

Perhaps to stress the continuous interest in matters of "superstructure," N. Ya. Marr has again been condemned, this time without reference to his original destroyer.

The new objectivism does not amount to much in practice. It moves within a familiar circle. The abusive style *vis-à-vis* Western anthropology has been mitigated a little, and there is perhaps a little less heavy irony, the favorite weapon of ignorance in the Stalinist intellectual armory. But factual writings are a very rare exception [29] and none of them displays a really critical attitude. It is stressed, as before, that "with the problems of ethnogenesis are closely connected the problems of cultural relations between nations, and particularly of the influence of the culture of the Russian people on the numerous peoples of the Soviet Union." [30] Ethnographical dissertations are still confined to the same limited and/or propagandistic concepts. Their scope, however, has widened. There has been an expansion of studies on certain societies outside the Soviet Union, more particularly the African peoples.

The prevailing attitudes towards Western anthropological and sociological thought have not changed much. There is a slightly more civilized reporting of it, but hardly an accurate one. "Labeling" is still a substitute for argument. It is enough to call George Gurvich a Machist, or Claude Lévy-Strauss a reactionary, to settle the problem.[31] The works of Ruth Benedict or Margaret Mead are dismissed quite simply as "openly dictated by the attempts of reactionary circles to stir up hostility among peoples, to facilitate the policy of domination over the Asiatic nations, the policy of colonialism." [32] The list could be continued.

Comments on Western social psychology and political sociology are disarming in their doctrinaire naiveté. Informing its readers about the conference of the British Sociological Association on problems of public opinion, *Voprosy Filosofii* remarks pontifically: "When analyzing the state of public opinion in capitalist countries, it is necessary to note that in the conditions of an antagonistic social system there can be no unanimity about any problems. The exploiting minority and the exploited majority have different interests and tasks. Therefore in capitalist countries there is not and cannot be one public opinion about various problems: to the public opinion of the working-class and of all toilers stands opposed the public opinion of the bourgeoisie." [33] Because they do not understand this, psephologists such as Mr. D. Butler, Mr. R. T. McKenzie, and others, are solemnly taken to task.

Psychoanalysis is condemned and so, in consequence, is its possible contribution to social analysis. This is because "the basic reactionary significance of psychoanalysis consists in the tendency of its propagandists (such as Sullivan, Fromm, Kardiner, and others) to lead the average American astray into the realm of subjectivism." [34]

In the most recent publication on 'bourgeois sociology" [35] another author discovered in the West the existence of "a pseudo-science, so-called 'atomic sociology,' which is a part of bankrupt atomic propaganda." [36] Another system, the "sociology of espionage and subversion," is said to be advocated by Professor Jessie Bernard, who "justifies the use of any means, including espionage and subversion, to achieve a goal. She praises Hitler as a practical 'expert in the theory of strategic games.' " [37] Although "there are different tendencies and schools in contemporary bourgeois sociology... bourgeois sociologists only pretend that they oppose each other. . . ." [38] "Bourgeois sociology has suffered bankruptcy. . . . It is passing through a deep crisis." [39] Nevertheless, "whereas at the end of the nineteenth century and at the beginning of the twentieth the ideological struggle with Marxism was conducted mainly in the realm of gnosiology, it has now been transferred to sociology." For this reason 'bourgeois sociology calumniates Marxism." [40] It is also accused of distorting facts and slandering the popular masses. Its representatives, such as Professor F. Ogburn, "prefer not to notice such phenomena in the USA as the impoverishment of millions of toilers on the one hand, and the increasingly fabulous profits of the monopolists on the other." [41] In short, "contemporary reactionary sociology sees its basic orientation in the defense of the foundations of capitalist society." [42] With this purpose it "propagates the imperialist theories of racism and of race inequality, the cosmopolitan theories of the abolition of national sovereignty and the subjugation of nations to foreign domination, the reactionary Malthusian philosophy of over-population according to which all evils are caused not by the bourgeois system of exploitation but by the 'surplus' of population, the theory of geopolitics, etc." [43]

The new line in Soviet foreign policy has, however, resulted in a widening of scientific contacts. Soviet scientists, including social scientists, have begun to attend international conferences. Thus, despite the "anti-scientific character of bourgeois sociology" and the various sins of Western sociologists so forcibly described, it was decided to send a Soviet delegation to the World Congress of Sociology held in Amsterdam in August 1956. The fact that sociology as a separate discipline does not exist in the Soviet Union was no obstacle.

Inevitably, the composition of the delegation was mixed; it did not include, as might be expected, persons who in the Western world would be regarded as sociologists. Instead it was headed by the director of the Institute of Philosophy, P. Fedoseyev.[44] Other members of the delegation were Professor V. S. Nemchinov (already mentioned for his heresies in biology and statistics), Professor M. Kammari, editor of *Voprosy Filosofii,* Professor A. Kuznetsov, editor of *Sotsialisticheski Trud,* Professor A. Rumiantsev, the present editor of *Kommunist* and a member of the Institute of Economics, and various lecturers in Marxism-Leninism. Not one of the "specialists" on Western sociology quoted above was sent to the Congress. The theme of the Congress was "Problems of Social Change in the Twentieth Century." Characteristically, the Soviet contributions [45] included nothing on capitalist developments. All the papers submitted dealt with internal changes in the Soviet Union. Their intellectual level was poor, and considering their general propagandist tone they might just as well have been published by *Pravda* or *Izvestia.* Their content and style were in striking contrast to the contributions of the "bourgeois sociologists." Papers submitted by the latter, whatever their merits or demerits, were concerned with analysis and not with propaganda.

Despite the fact that the Soviet delegates tried to be as agreeable as possible, abstained from name-calling, and in their public speeches and private conversations stressed the necessity of international scientific cooperation, there were few indications how such cooperation is to emerge. Indeed, it is not quite clear why cooperation between the "only true science of society" and "bourgeois sociology," which is described not only as "un-scientific" but as "anti-scientific," should be desired at all. One could sympathize with the Soviet delegates, torn between personal amiability, intellectual crudity, and party directives. But that does not alter the fact that their application of the concept of science to sociology is still dominated by scholastics. Their attitude, both at plenary sessions and smaller meetings, revealed to the Western delegates the gap which exists between sociology and Soviet historical materialism. It was not a question of rival theories. There is no official doctrine in the West, and many Western sociologists have incorporated a good deal of Marxian thinking. It was not a question of "fact-finding approach" versus "global theory," or even of "value-free sociology" versus "partiinost" in sociology. The epistemological controversies on the thorny problem of "value-judgment" in sociology cannot in practice prevent Western sociologists from trying to eliminate bias in their research. And finally, the obstacles to the development of Western sociology are not being concealed but can be critically approached.

The gulf, which became so obvious, resulted from the fact that the Soviet delegates simply did not grasp what sociology is about. In their contributions they dwelt on the superiority of the Soviet system and hardly touched on the problems of sociological studies, not realizing that the question of the relative merits of various systems is primarily a political and not a sociological one. Sociologists *qua* sociologists have to study *all* social systems. But the problem of empirical sociological studies in the Soviet Union was hardly mentioned [46] by those who sometimes referred to themselves as Soviet sociologists. Not only were sociological problems not within their sphere of interest, but in their constant praise of "socialism" they did not indicate any social problems which have to be *studied* in socialist society. If problems of social policy arise there, they are within the competence of the Politbureau. The acute social problems of the USSR (as of any country undergoing an industrial revolution)—urban migration, juvenile delinquency, and so forth—were not faced by the Soviet delegates, who showed hardly any interest in (or knowledge of) Western urban sociology, criminology, or any other specialized subdivision dealing with relevant subjects.

The mentality of the Soviet delegates, their uniform speeches without any individual ideas, their monotonous repetition of Party slogans at a scientific congress, without any attempt at deviation—suggest that the development of the Soviet social sciences is not just a matter of the "thaw" in the Stalinist institutional glacier but also concerns the petrified minds which emerged from the Stalinist era, whatever their intellectual level.[47] To what ridiculous lengths they can go could be judged by such small manifestations as for instance the choice of literature displayed during the Congress in the Soviet part of the bookstall. That it did not comprise any sociological works is, after all, understandable; but it also included such treatises as *Paul Langevin—Fighter for Democracy* and other pamphlets having hardly any relation either to the Congress or to sociology in general.

In contrast to the Soviet delegates, those from the satellite countries in some cases displayed individual differences of opinion and the standard of their papers was higher. This applies above all to the Polish delegates who were quite critical of their Soviet colleagues. Some of them were authentic sociologists, who complained at being cut off for such a long time from the West. Others expressed a desire to learn Western techniques of social investigation and statistical analysis, of which they were ignorant because of their earlier cultural isolation, and tried to arrange for a few Polish students to go to Western universities (including American ones) for that purpose. They also reported on some empirical research, in the form of a factory survey, rural investigations, and a study of the cultural integration of Polish settlers. One of the papers submitted by them was particularly striking. Its author indicated that "while the fact that humanitarian or national slogans frequently mask a class interest was known long ago, new experience has disclosed that it is no less possible to mask the interests of an organization by class slogans." There can be little doubt to which organization this refers. He also stressed that the "Marxian concept of social class . . . seems today much less adequate, even in regard to the capitalist countries." [48] Only when such daring breaches in the conceptual barrier have been made in the Soviet Union will sociology emerge from the pre-scientific age.

The perspectives of development of Soviet science depend only partly on political changes. In the case of sociology, however, the dependence is almost total. The problem is not so much that it is indistinguishable from social philosophy, as that it is imprisoned by a party doctrine which has been turned into a state religion. In this respect its position is rather different from that of other sciences. All of them were exposed to various stages of pressure by the party, but at different times individual disciplines were subject to different degrees of political interference because their ideological relevance was unequal. The risks involved in writing on contemporary or ancient history were not the same, neither were the dangers for party policy in the findings of radio astronomy and in research on present social phenomena. Sociology obviously was at the wrong end of the spectrum. Questions relating to the problems of its theory and methods were identified with the problems of Marxism [49] and were soon put under direct party control. It is this identification which has resulted in the absence of sociology as a separate discipline in the Soviet Union.

The Soviet view of scientific method was thus summarized in *Voprosy Filosofii:* "The true and completely correct method of every science is nothing other than the concrete application of dialectical materialism to that science." [50] The case of sociology was peculiar in this respect. *Diamat* was to be applied to other sciences as an unspecific method. Sociology, identified with historical materialism, was indissolubly linked with it. Epistemology and the subject-matter of knowledge were less easily separable here than elsewhere. Marxism *tout court* thus became a sort of substitute for sociology. As an ideology, however, it served as a legitimation of the system, and this made its position as a theory of social analysis hopelessly ambiguous. The contrast (which existed in nuclear form in Marx himself, in his roles of social analyst and social revolutionary) became institutionalized in the Soviet Union, where political needs quickly overruled the critical necessities of study. In effect, the desire to change the world outran the necessity to understand it. One consequence of this was that sociology failed to develop from a concept into a discipline. Any independent social research might reveal facts difficult to reconcile with the current party dogma, or even strike at the roots of its ideological legitimation.

When demographers reveal population deficiencies, that is bad enough, but if sociologists were permitted to find out whether Soviet society is becoming classless, they might undermine the position of a party claiming an historical mandate for its monopoly of power in terms of what is partly a sociological theory. It is not surprising that the party is not interested in empirical investigation which might disclose errors in doctrine. This does not exclude the possibility that such auxiliary techniques as the methodology of social surveys based on sampling could eventually be adopted for limited purposes. But it is inconceivable that, for instance, "Gallup polls" of political opinions, or other forms of research dealing with political attitudes, will be acceptable, as long as the façade of political unanimity is the form.

At various times, the changes in the margin of rationality in the treatment of sociological themes have depended on the laxity or rigidity permitted in the interpretation of the ruling doctrine. At different periods there were smaller or greater outlets for the manifestation of various attitudes, by means of changing emphasis on Marxian scriptures. But even those Soviet scientists who press for the relaxation of "partiinost" in their disciplines have to use suitable quotations from Marx or Lenin (Stalin is in eclipse as a source of quotations) to justify their positions.

While for other sciences in the Soviet Union the problem of the application of Marxism is contingent, for sociology it is fundamental. It has not so far emerged as a science, for reasons similar to those which prevented natural science from freeing itself from the shackles of theological scholasticism in the Middle Ages as long as the hold of the Church on the State remained unshaken.

Notes

1. *Cf.* K. I. Kozlova and N. N. Cheboksarov: "Ethnography at the University of Moscow," *Sovetskaya Etnografiya,* 1955, No. 2, pp. 100-111.
2. They are prepared not only at the universities but at various economic and pedagogical institutes, at the Military-Political Academy, at the Higher Party School, etc.
3. *Vestnik Akademii Nauk SSSR,* 1956, No. 5, p. 115.
4. *Vestnik vysshey shkoly,* 1956, No. 5, p. 62.
5. *Ibid.*
6. *Ibid.,* 1953, No. 8.
7. *Ibid.,* 1956, No. 4.
8. *Ibid.,* 1956, No. 4.
9. The first professor of the re-established Chair of Ethnography at Moscow University, S. P. Tolstov, is engaged on a work on the history of Khorezm, based on excavations in Soviet Central Asia.
10. *Sovetskaya Etnografiya* (1955, No. 3) published a letter suggesting that the teaching of ethnography be separated from history.
11. *Ibid.,* 1951, No. 2.
12. *Cf.* Lawrence Krader: "Recent Studies of the Russian Peasant," *American Anthropologist,* 1956, Vol.58, No. 4, pp. 716-719.
13. L. A. Pushkarova in *Sovetskaya Etnografiya,* 1953, No. 1, p. 174.
14. "The work of Comrade Stalin on linguistics played an important part in the development of ethnography"—*Sovetskaya Etnografiya,* 1951, No. 2, p. 4.
15. *Cf.* P. Tolstoy: "Morgan and Soviet Anthropological Thought," *American Anthropologist,* 1952, Vol 34, No. 1.
16. 1951, No. 2, p. 6.
17. Institute of Ethnography, Academy of Sciences of the USSR, Vol. XII, Moscow, 1951.
18. 1952, No. 1, p. 212.
19. *Against the Philosophizing Warriors of Anglo-American Imperialism,* Institute of Philosophy, Academy of Sciences of the USSR, Moscow, 1951, pp. 102-140.
20. *Cf.* O. I. Sayapina: *Anglo-American Sociologists in the Struggle Against Progress, ibid.,* pp. 173-200; G. E. Glezerman: "Classes," *Great Soviet Encyclopedia,* xxi, 338-392; A. P. Gagarin, *American Bourgeois Philosophy and Sociology in the Service of Imperialism,* Moscow, 1951; M. P. Baskin: *Contemporary Amer-*

ican Bourgeois Sociology in the Service of Expansionism, Academy of Sciences of the USSR, 1952.

21. *Cf.* F. Telezhnikov, "Durkheim on the Subject and Method of Sociology," *Vestnik Kommunisticheskoi Akademii,* 1928, Vol. 30 (6), pp. 159-188.

22. *Pravda,* June 2, 1954. p. 4.

23. *Naradnoe Khozyaistvo SSSR,* Central Statistical Administration, Moscow, 1956.

24. The figure turned out to be more than fifteen million less than the estimates of Western demographers.

25. *Cf.* Stuart T. Rice: "Statistical Conceptions in the Soviet Union," *The Review of Economics and Statistics,* 1952, XXXIV, No. 1, 82-86.

26. He defended the chromosome theory of heredity at the August 1948 session of the Soviet Academy of Agricultural Science against Lysenko and his followers.

27. *Cf. Vestnik Akademii Nauk SSSR,* 1954, No. 8.

28. This and subsequent references: *Sovetskaya Etnografiya,* 1956, No. 1, pp. 3-8.

29. A unique example of such a soberly informative article free from abuse is a short outline on "Sociological Societies and Periodicals in the USA," by V. S. Semenov (*Voprosy Filosofii,* 1956, No. 3, pp. 246-248).

30. *Sovetskaya Etnografiya,* 1955, No. 2, p. 111.

31. *Ibid.,* 1956, No. 1, pp. 140-149, "The Influence of Contemporary Reactionary American Sociology on French Ethnography."

32. E. Bagramov and B. Lavrentiev: "Racist Inventions about the Japanese Nation," *Kommunist,* 1956, No. 9, pp. 113-120.

33. 1956, No. 3, p. 252. *Cf. The British Journal of Sociology,* 1955, No. 2.

34. *Kommunist,* 1956, No. 7, p. 115.

35. G. L. Episkoposov: *On Some Aspects of Contemporary Reactionary Bourgeois Sociology,* All-Union Society for the Dissemination of Political and Scientific Knowledge, Moscow, July 1956.

36. p. 10.

37. p. 38.

38. p. 6.

39. p. 42.

40. p. 5.

41. p. 21. *Cf.* L. M. Tsyrlin and I. Petrov: *Bourgeois Statistics Conceal the Truth,* Moscow, 1953. "Even the falsified US statistics had to admit that in October 1951 three-quarters of the total population of the U.S.A. were below the subsistence level" (p. 123).

42. p. 15. Defending Soviet Marxism at one of the meetings of the Sociology Congress, Professor Kuznetsov claimed that not one of the "bourgeois sociologists" present defended capitalism.

43. *Kratkii Filosofskii Slovar,* Ed. M. Rozental and P. Yudin, Moscow, 1955, p. 452.

44. Fedoseyev, purged from the position of editor of the theoretical organ of the party, *Kommunist,* reappeared after Stalin's death.

45. *Cf. Transactions of the Third World Congress of Sociology,* Amsterdam, 1956, International Sociological Association, Vols. I-VII.

46. In a private conversation a family budget was mentioned, the results of which are not, however, being published.

47. The leader of the Soviet delegation, P. Fedoseyev, expressed the opinion during the meeting of the social science section of the Academy of Sciences on January 31, 1956, that "Soviet scientists taking part in international congresses make an indelible impression on bourgeois scientists by the clarity of their opinions and their devotion to the ideas of Marxism-Leninism" (*Voprosy Ekonomiki,* 1956, No. 3, p. 189).

48. *Transactions of the Congress,* III, 23. In a report in the official Polish Communist party paper *Trybuna Ludu* it was emphasized that "the paper aroused special interest among the Congress participants" (October 4, 1956, p. 4).

49. "The real science of development of society is nothing but historical materialism—the theory of Marx, Engels, Lenin, and Stalin," *Politicheskii Slovar,* Ed. G. Alexandrov *et al.,* Moscow, 1940, article: "Sociology," p. 531. "Only the ideologists of the proletariat, Marx, Engels . . . established the real science of society and its laws," *Kratkii Filosofskii Slovar,* Ed. M. Rozental and P. Yudin, Moscow, 1955, article: "Sociology," pp. 451-452.

50. No. 5, 1952 p. 203.

Sociology as a vocation

LEOPOLD LABEDZ

> In the lecture-rooms of the university no other virtue holds but plain intellectual integrity.
>
> —MAX WEBER, *Science as a Vocation*

The new member of the Executive Committee of the International Sociological Association, F. V. Konstantinov, wrote a report on the Fifth World Congress of Sociology which he attended in September 1962 in Washington as the head of the Soviet delegation.[1] In his time Konstantinov has performed many functions, as political commentator, ideological interpreter of Marxism, and until recently the editor-in-chief of the Soviet Communist party's theoretical journal *Kommunist;* but this was the first time he had dealt with sociology. In his report he defined "the conditions of a genuinely scientific sociology":

> Strictness, objectivity, many-sidedness, good faith—these are the demands which the party puts before the sociologists and all theoretical workers. In the Soviet Union political figures are armed with a profound theoretical knowledge. They are guided in their activity by the principles of Marxist-Leninist sociology. . . . Nikita Sergeyevich Khrushchev, with all his tireless and versatile activity, shows how to develop creatively the Marxist theory, how to enrich it by new experience, how to link it with practice, how to make use of the laws of social development . . . (p. 17).

Not everywhere are conditions so favorable for scientific sociology. In the United States, for instance, when C. Wright Mills objected to the American policy towards Cuba, "he was persecuted by the reactionary politicians and died prematurely" (p. 5).

With reference to the congress itself, Konstantinov wrote [2]:

> It was not easy for us to defend our views from our opponents, enemies, and vacillating people. But we overcame with honor all

From *Survey,* 48, July 1963, pp. 57-64.

the difficulties and complexities of the struggle. We were armed with Marxist sociology and truth was on our side. We knew that we represented a great power, the Soviet Union. This inspired us in the difficult and complex struggle with bourgeois ideology.

When Konstantinov said that there is only one sociology, this was taken by some participants to mean that the eschatological frontier between "Marxist" and "bourgeois" sociology was no longer stressed. But when, at a subsequent session, Professor Daniel Bell referred to this statement, Konstantinov explained that indeed there was only one sociology, namely, Marxist sociology.

Other recollections by Soviet participants at the congress are equally triumphant about their successes on the battlefield.[3]

> Feldman and Moore (in their paper on "Industrialisation and Industrialism") repeated, without any arguments or understanding, the hackneyed slander about "forced collectivization" and "compulsory labor" as the "means taken to solve" the labor-force problem in the USSR. . . . It is quite symptomatic that the "display of their wares" by Feldman and Moore received no support or sympathy from the audience.

The Soviet sociologists themselves "convincingly exposed" all these "sophisms," they "literally smashed" the arguments of their opponents "with the help of statistics and other material." The chairman of the section on "Education and Formation of Elites," Madame Floud, "was forced to conclude that Soviet sociologists gave a full and well-founded account of the problem of the Soviet intelligentsia."

It would be a waste of space to give more examples of the triumphant unmasking of the "servants of capitalism" by the Soviet sociologists. The passages quoted may not faithfully represent the role of the Soviet delegates at the congress, but they do represent their intellectual style.

At the Amsterdam congress, where a Soviet delegation attended for the first time, there was some novelty in their appearance. At the following congress in Stresa there was still an air of expectation about the development of Soviet sociology. Now, in Washington, these expectations were to be put to the test: Soviet sociologists were at last going to provide information and data about Soviet society based on the "concrete" investigations to which so many references had been made. But they did nothing of the kind. Western sociologists who were hopefully looking for some new sociological data about Soviet developments were to be disappointed. Instead, the Soviet delegates repeated their customary eulogies about everything Soviet and this became so boring that finally Raymond Aron asked them whether they had *any* social problems in Soviet society.

It would however be misleading to conclude from this that no change in the field of sociology had occurred in the Soviet Union between the Stresa and Washington congresses. When attending such congresses Soviet delegates are duty bound to engage in an ideological struggle with "bourgeois sociology" and to present, for both patriotic and doctrinal reasons, the most immaculate picture of Soviet achievements. This turns all of them, including the non-professionals, into simple propagandists. But at home the situation is more complex and the roles more differentiated: there they stress that their activity is or should be directed "towards the amelioration of practical problems," [4] the same problems which almost disappear from sight in the eschatological battle abroad.

What then are the main characteristics of the developments in the field of sociology since about 1958–1959?

In respect to "bourgeois sociology" the attitude has remained intransigently hostile, in line with the principle that there cannot be any coexistence in the field of ideology. Their knowledge of the subject they criticize has slightly improved but remains painfully limited. This applies not only to the ideological functionaries, like Fedoseyev or Konstantinov, "nominated" sociologists, but also to those who now specialize in sociology and to writers who purport to study "bourgeois sociology." Whatever the theoretical orientation of the particular Western sociologist in question, the conclusion drawn from an examination of his work is monotonously similar; only his political orientation can sometimes make a difference in the harshness or relative lenience of the assessment. Occasionally mildness can be displayed, on account of such extra-sociological factors as the attitude towards "peace appeals," unilateral disarmament, or Cuba. But in the realm of theory, where such considerations are not operative, the judgment is simple and definite:

> In Parsons' analysis the conclusion is reached that without "the American way of life," without the bourgeois state and capitalist business, without the bourgeoisie and the proletariat, the existence of a social system, of social life, is altogether impossible. Such are the trivial conclusions attained by functionalism, conclusions limited by the bourgeois framework. . . . According to Merton, functionalism may now "serve equally well [as a vehicle] for ideological poison or for ideological nectar." By such reasoning, the functionalists break completely with science. . . . To say that social life can be integrated on the basis of any "values" or "interests" means to liken society to a football which can be sent in any direction, if it happens to be one

where the "values" may, for instance, be "interesting" to the American monopolies.[5]

Bourgeois sociology continues to be presented simply as a reflection of capitalist interests:

Frank admissions about the social significance of American sociology were made by Professor B. Barber of Columbia University. He stressed that the government and the capitalists support sociological investigations.[6]

Whether it is empirical, positivistic, or historical, "bourgeois sociology has been in a state of crisis in the last few years."[7] Some Soviet comments, repeating critical Western arguments about certain aspects of contemporary sociology, are not altogether off the mark. But they are more concerned with the inexorable phrase "Even so and so is forced to admit . . ." than with the argument itself. Ironically, at the same time as some Western objections to the "quantification mania" are quoted, and the mathematical models of Lewin, Dodd and others criticized, Soviet sociologists themselves are now told that "mathematics and its methods can give real results only on the basis of an analysis of all aspects of real social processes with the aid of various scientific methods in the light of the materialist theory of social development." Once the obstacle has been removed, the mathematical "Model Building in Sociological Research" can go very far indeed:

One can surely foresee the compilation of a balance for the utilization of people's lives: a balance of resources and their utilization, expressed in man-days of life, work, rest, and self-cultivation.[8]

A "balance for the utilization of people's lives" will be a great contribution to social planning, but fortunately this splendid vision, in the best tradition of Huxley and Orwell, is still far off. The claims made at the congress that mathematical computers are used on a large scale in Soviet sociology are to be taken with a grain of salt. One cannot get out of a computer more than is fed into it. In the meantime it is the "concrete sociological investigations" which are to help the party in its social engineering. "Sociological investigations should lighten the road for the practice of building communism."[9] This, according to G. V. Osipov and M. T. Yovchuk, is being done by the study of the following areas [10]:

1. Investigation of the general laws of the growth of socialism into communism.

2. Social problems of building the material and technical base for communism.

3. The problem of the development of communist social relationships.

4. Problems of the development of the ideology and culture of communist society, of the formation of the new man and the all-round development of the personality.

5. Applied social research.

It is misleading to define the general orientation of Soviet "concrete sociological investigations" as "practical empiricism," an effort to obtain just enough systematic information on which to base recommendations for policy and action.[11] It may or may not be practical, but it certainly is not empirical in orientation, and it is strange to see the Soviet type of "mirror image" perception now displayed by the American sociologists projecting their familiar concepts on an unfamiliar situation. Investigations whose basic results are invariably known in advance, and research which can only confirm what has already been proclaimed by the party, are not exactly empirical in orientation. Therefore it is incorrect to suggest, as Merton and Riecken do, that "since the differences between manual and mental workers in the USSR have not been erased, this becomes a prime target for research." There is no such causal connection. All Soviet research on this question consists in "proving" that such differences are in fact disappearing, and the findings always miraculously confirm it. It is not without reason that these investigations are called "concrete" and not "empirical." They are designed to uphold a dogma, not to test hypotheses.

This is not to say that such investigations may not yield new data on the Soviet social scene, however limited their scope may be because of all the historical inevitabilities of social change postulated by the doctrine. Nor is it suggested that "concrete" investigations, by the mere fact of dealing with the concrete phenomena of social life, may not act corrosively on the purity of the doctrine. But this is precisely what the party is trying to avoid by imposing a rigidly controlled doctrinal orientation designed to make them strictly instrumental in helping to improve economic performance and social control, while rendering them ideologically innocuous and therefore politically safe. This is a far cry from "practical empiricism." The label is not applicable to Soviet sociological investigations.

At present "concrete investigations" are conducted in the following places:

Moscow. In the Institute of Philosophy of the Soviet Academy of

Sciences there is a section for sociological research under G. V. Osipov. It is concerned with the study of the "new forms of labor and daily life." Investigations were made in factories and enterprises in Moscow and Gorki on the rationalization of work, the adjustment of workers to the conveyor-belt system, and the factors affecting the efficiency and productivity of labor, such as the level of education, the character and length of work, and so on. Another study has been conducted in a Moldavian village which had previously been studied by Rumanian sociologists.

Another Moscow center, the "Laboratory of Sociological Studies," attached to the philosophical faculty of Moscow University, is concerned with the problem of "the abolition of the differences between mental and manual labor," and with this in view investigated the social effects of automation in the Moscow Ball-Bearing Plant No. 1. A study of management is in preparation. The laboratory has also conducted an investigation of the resettlement problem in one of the newly created agricultural sites in the "virgin lands" in Kazakhstan.

Leningrad. The "Laboratory of Sociological Studies" at Leningrad University is doing research into workers' attitudes and the effect on them of technological change. About 2,000 workers answered a questionnaire. It was quite an elaborate questionnaire, and although it avoided some sensitive areas, was quite competently done in line with Western methodological practice. If the answers were candid, it must have elicited quite an interesting amount of information. Nothing has so far been published.

A new "Institute of Human Studies" is shortly to be published in Leningrad to coordinate the work of sociologists, economists, psychologists, and educationalists.

Urals. The philosophy department and the sociological laboratory of the Ural State University published a study of the rise in the cultural and technical level of the working class based on an investigation in several enterprises and factories of the Sverdlovsk *sovnarkhoz.*

Another investigation on changes in the educational level of the working class was conducted in the Karaganda coal mines. A heavy concentration on the problems of industrial efficiency is reflected in other studies: one on the adaptation of work to the rhythm of automated machine production; another on the conditions of work and automation by the Moscow Institute of Labor Research, and so on.

Sociological laboratories either exist or are being established in Kiev, Voronezh, Novosibirsk, and Rostov. Pedagogical institutes conduct some school studies.

The only "Institute of Public Opinion" was set up by the paper of the Young Communist League, *Komsomolskaya Pravda.* It started as a purely journalistic venture and then established contact with the Academy. It has conducted five opinion polls on subjects ranging from the attitudes to peace to the problems of marriage and divorce. A survey on the profile of contemporary youth based on answers by 18,000 people has been recently published by B. Grushin and W. Chikin.

Other subjects studied in Soviet "applied social research" are time-budgets and leisure activities, and what is called "education in atheism and the survival of religious beliefs."

All this sounds impressive enough. But it looks different when not only the scope but also the methodology of these investigations is subjected to scrutiny. Whatever snippets of information can be derived from them, few of these studies would pass the most elementary methodological tests in the West. Apart from the Leningrad inquiry already mentioned, the other studies were not carefully prepared and none of them deals with the question of representativeness; to disregard this makes the basic predetermination of the results easier to handle.

In an article on "Methods of Sociological Study of Specific Phenomena," M. N. Rutkevich and L. N. Kogan, put the problem succinctly, if somewhat obliquely:

> Bourgeois sociologists conduct interviews with persons selected at random, and sometimes "prepare" the desired result by the selection of those to be questioned. . . . For Marxist sociologists conducting interviews or gathering data through questionnaires, it is unthinkable to pose questions provocative in nature, designed to suggest a particular, desired response, or demeaning to human dignity.[12]

But the Soviet interviewers also have their problems, as this "simplified" dialogue quoted in an article on "The Methodology of Studying Religious Survivals" testifies:

> *Interviewer:* Will you tell me, please, do you believe in God?
> *Answer:* Well, how can I tell you . . . I don't know myself whether there is a God or not.
> *Interviewer:* And do you go to church?
> *Answer:* When do we have time to go to church?
> *Interviewer:* Then why do you keep ikons?
> *Answer:* My parents hung them there. Why should the corner be empty? Let them hang.

The reasearcher concludes that this is a person "of wavering faith." [13] It takes a great deal of ingenuity to argue, as the author of the article does, that it depends on the interviewer whether the responses of religious persons "come as close as possible to what they actually think," without mentioning that the lack of candor in responses is a result of the state's policy towards religion (which is taken as a premise and a point of departure of the inquiry itself).

It is obvious that, despite the boast that "concrete investigations are nothing new for Marxism," [14] Soviet sociologists have a lot to learn, even with the limited framework determined by the party; and it is now admitted that they may borrow from "bourgeois sociology" some of its techniques, provided that they "show the falsity of its theoretical constructions." [15]

The question arises why the decision to introduce "concrete investigations" was taken in the first place, despite the dangers of ideological erosion which they may present. The answer is not entirely clear, but it is indicative:

> Life itself, and in particular the needs of construction of communism, imperatively demand the development of concrete sociological investigations.[16]

This answer may perhaps be elaborated. To maintain party rule and to preserve its authority it is necessary to control social change in the USSR. This means both the ability to engineer change and to adapt to it. The first depends on manipulating motives and incentives, and this in turn depends on the means available for influencing the situation. The present stage of Soviet social and economic development made the mass terror economically less practical and politically more risky. To maintain the party's dominating position, when Stalin's authority disappeared, required more subtle means, the balancing of social forces rather than total control over them. And to maintain economic growth the crude Stalinist combination of big stick and very small carrot was no longer suitable. In this situation the party leadership needed more information for devising suitable political motives and economic incentives, and sociologists are there to provide it. The shift from control by naked terror to control through such additional means as "voluntary organizations" and "self-government of the masses" requires some knowledge of the working of primary groups in society which are no longer completely atomized. Under Khrushchev the Stalinist "revolution from above" is supplemented by manipulated "control from below," and, as an organizational corollary of this, the "permanent purge" is replaced by permanent reorganization.

Admittedly, it is an unstable equilibrium. But precisely because of this, more "concrete" information on the social and economic background is necessary in order to maintain it through the establishment of suitable incentives, appropriate motivations, and new mechanisms of control.

It is extremely unlikely that the new Soviet sociologists will provide more than marginal elements of such information. Not just because they are too crude in their methods to realize such a technocratic dream, but basically because party rule itself renders impossible too close an insight into the workings of a society which is continually adapting itself to this rule through informal organization. The potentialities of "concrete" investigations are thus circumscribed not only by ideological considerations, but also by the nature of the social realities with which they have to deal. The legitimacy of the party rests on the myth of a classless society. This myth is not only socially but also sociologically relevant. As long as it prevents social reality from coming to the surface, the basic elements of the situation are not susceptible to "concrete investigations," which are thus limited in more than one way.

There is little doubt, however, that "concrete investigations" will increase the amount of information on Soviet society, even though not all of it will be published. In the Soviet Union it will be interpreted ideologically; sociologically, it will still have to be studied from outside, where those who study it are not prisoners of a sociological myth.

Social change in the Soviet Union must be studied for its own sake and for its wider implications. The evidence is scanty and unsatisfactory, but there is no choice but to use whatever is available. Paleontologists are not in a better position. And counsels of methodological perfection will not prevent the curious from asking for tentative answers. Where they cannot be given, relevant questions themselves contribute to understanding.

Notes

1. *Voprosy Filosofii*, No. 11, 1962.
2. *V. Mezhdunarodny Sotsiologicheskii Kongress* (Moscow, 1963), p. 13.
3. *Voprosy Filosofii*, No. 11, 1962, p. 26.
4. Cf. Robert K. Merton and Henry W. Riecken, "Notes on Sociology in the USSR," in *Current Problems in Social-Behavioral Research* (Washington), March 1962.
5. M. Sh. Bakhitov, *Amerikanskaya funktsionalnaya teoriya obshchestva* (Moscow, 1962), pp. 40–41. Cf. also N. V. Novikov, "Ideologicheskii smysl teorii sotsialnovo deistva," *Filosofskie Nauki*, No. 4, 1961, p. 4.
6. B. A. Chagin in *Voprosy Marksistskoi Sotsiologii* (Leningrad, 1962), p. 54.
7. V. S. Semenov in *Voprosy Filosofii*, No. 11, 1962, p. 31.
8. P. P. Maslov in *Voprosy Fliosofii*, No. 3, 1962.
9. B. P. Rozhin in *Voprosy Marksistskoi Sotsiologii*, p. 18.
10. *Voprosy Filosofii*, No. 12, 1962, p. 23.
11. R. K. Merton and H. Riecken, *loc. cit.*
12. *Voprosy Filosofii*, No. 3, 1961.
13. L. N. Mitrokhin in *Voprosy Filosofii*, No. 3, 1962.
14. *Filosofskie Nauki*, No. 5, 1962, p. 21.
15. *Kommunist*, No. 2, 1963, p. 103.
16. V. P. Rozhin, *Vvedenye v marksistskuyu sotsiologiyu* (Leningrad, 1962), p. 30.

Soviet social science and our own

ARVID BRODERSEN

Western observers have recently expressed urgent concern over a new and to most people unexpected challenge from the Soviet Union: its mighty forward stride in science and technology. "Russia is turning out two scientists to our one, two engineers to our one, in ten years it will be four to one" (Dr. Alvin Johnson), and "Ten years from now the best scientists in the world will be found in Russia" (Dr. Edward Teller)—these are representative comments.

A considerable amount of research has been devoted to the situation of the natural and technological sciences in the Soviet Union, but the social sciences, hardly a less important subject, have received less attention from students in the West. The present paper, based exclusively on Western sources, cannot pretend to fill this gap. It can offer only a preliminary exposition of the problem, as far as this is within the field of vision of one who is not a Russian scholar, and it can perhaps identify some areas in particular need of research.[1]

Social vs. natural science in Soviet higher education

Soviet higher education, generally speaking, offers vocational training keyed to a large number of specific occupations in industry, agriculture, administration, and society at large. This is true of the universities as well as of the many hundreds of specialized institutes of education in the Soviet Union. University students are not, as in the West, educated for general culture, for personality development, for "getting along with other people," or for intellectual leadership in general. They are to become workers, in the sense of technicians mastering a specific job and functionaries serving the state. For this the individual student is trained

From *Social Research*, XXIV, No. 3 (1957), 253-286.

intensively in his own chosen or assigned discipline, and this latter often covers a far more limited and specialized field than would typically be the case in the West, particularly in Europe. Thus there seem to be no institutes of technology as we know them, teaching technological subjects in general. Instead, the Soviet system provides a large number of institutes for single subjects, such as communications, light metals, electrical engineering, and the like.

For the vocational training intended to produce technicians for the various higher functions in industry, agriculture, and the health services the Soviet policy-makers apparently see no need to spend much time on extraneous subjects. The curricula of study leading into these three professions provide far less time for topics from the social sciences (6 to 8 percent of the total) than do the corresponding curricula in the Western system (12 to 15 percent). Apart from this quantitative difference there are also, of course, important differences in the kind and quality of offerings in these fields, but this matter I shall discuss later.

The three professional groups I have mentioned (engineering, agricultural science, and medicine) account for over half, 52 percent, of the total professional manpower available in the Soviet Union (1954). The other, smaller half is made up of two groups, the teaching profession, which is by far the largest of them all, 42 percent, and the one referred to as the "socio-economic" profession, which is the smallest of them all, 6 percent. By their very nature and their functions in society these two groups are likely, under any system, to receive considerably more social science training than the other professions just referred to. Thus for Soviet teachers the program of general subjects, mostly political indoctrination, takes up to 20 percent, or more than twice the maximum time devoted to these subjects in the technological or medical schools. More significant, a sizable proportion of the student body, both at the universities and at the teachers' institutes, take social or humanistic disciplines as major subjects of study.

Soviet universities, numbering at present thirty-three, typically have six divisions or faculties: physical and mathematical sciences, philology, history, geography, biology, and chemistry. In addition some of them have separate faculties in jurisprudence, economics, and "Eastern and Pacific cultures."

Of the total class of about 18,000 students leaving Soviet universities in 1954, as many as 55 to 60 percent were graduated with a major in a subject other than natural science. Among these majors, however, the proportion of social science subjects, properly speaking, appears to be relatively small, since philology (Russian and foreign languages and literature) probably accounts for more than half the total, while the remainder is divided between such subjects as political science and philosophy, economics, history, geography, and jurisprudence, to name them in order of decreasing frequency. This is suggested by the information available on the relative proportions of subjects for the "aspirantura" examination and for dissertations.

Of the university graduates in human and social sciences, about 50 percent enter the teaching profession, by way of which some of them may join the ranks of what we would call professional social scientists, combining, more or less, research and writing with their principal activity of teaching. Very few indeed are likely to make social science research their principal work and full-time activity. University graduates in the non-natural sciences, if they do not go into teaching, are likely to be employed as interpreters, translators, journalists, or in other intellectual jobs of a practical kind in government enterprises. Facilities for pure research in the social sciences, apart from teaching or other applied fields, are extremely scarce in the Soviet Union.

By far the main supply of teachers comes from the many specialized training centers—the pedagogical institutes, teachers' institutes, foreign-language institutes, institutes for librarians, archivists, and the like. Of about 70,000 new teachers who were graduated in 1954, these institutes supplied 65,000, with only about 5,000 coming from the universities. Usually about half of these institute graduates have majored in mathematics and natural sciences, the other half majoring in a variety of other subjects in which, again, the share of the social sciences proper is modest, the preponderant emphasis going to such subject matters as philology, librarianship, and archival science, and also to the theory and methodology of education (pedagogy).

The other main professional group where we would naturally look for a considerable training in, and concern with, social science subjects is the socio-economic profession. As I have mentioned, this group is numerically far smaller, comprising in 1954 a total of 125,000 individuals, or about 6 percent of the total professional labor force. In comparison, teaching and engineering accounted in that year for 857,000 and 541,000 professionals, respectively. While the large majority of this group is trained for technical jobs as accountants or statistical or archival experts, a minority is educated for higher-level activities in such fields as banking, trade and distribution, jurisprudence, planning, and economic management. The main burden of training students for the socio-economic profession is carried by about 35 institutes of higher education, of which nine specialize in planning and managerial economics, nine in finance, five in trade, three in industrial, technical, and engineering economics, and nine in jurisprudence. Again the Soviet Union does not seem to have the type of single institution which, like our schools of business administration, covers more or less the entire range of socio-economic disciplines in a comprehensive, articulated program. Nor do these disciplines occupy more than a modest place in Soviet universities; for example, only eight out of 33 universities have a faculty of economics.

To sum up the situation in global figures, it appears that the ratio of professionally skilled manpower produced year by year by Soviet higher education in the natural and applied sciences, on the one hand, and, on the other hand, in the humanities and social sciences, pure and applied, is in the order of 70–75 percent to 25–30 percent, while in the United States the comparable figures are in the order of 30–35 percent to 65–70 percent, that is, much the same in reverse. As far as the social sciences proper are concerned, this justifies DeWitt in stating that "the Soviet Union trained only about one-tenth as many persons as were trained in these fields in the United States"; and similarly, "In the humanities, liberal arts, and other non-specialized fields, Soviet higher education trained but a small fraction of the number of persons trained in American colleges and universities in these fields."

Figures alone do not, however, tell the full story. Far more important are the qualitative aspects, both generally, in the selection of personnel (teachers and students) and the standards of teaching and research, and, more specifically, in the types and content of the material handled. In the field of natural and applied sciences, qualitative comparison between Soviet and Western performance has been a subject of keen interest and considerable study in recent years, particularly in the United States and Britain. The DeWitt report devotes most of its space to this problem.

In general the picture looks somewhat like this. Soviet science and technology compare favorably with their Western counterparts in the selection of the students and in their secondary-level preparation in basic science, mathematics, and foreign languages. The training and quality of teachers are probably not inferior to the average in the West. Standards and methods of teaching, though in certain respects somewhat inferior to those in the United States, especially in availability of instruments and of teaching equipment, are in other respects superior to the West, as in methods for training in mathematics. On balance, it seems that Soviet science and technology compete with those of the West on about an even level, as far as general quality goes. And also in the matter of specific quality, that is, the types and content of materials that are treated in teaching and study, Soviet science and technology are substantially similar to their Western counterparts, and in fact are, to a large extent, operating with knowledge of Western performance and attempting to match or emulate it. The Western scientific literature is widely read, in the original or in translations, and there is an abstracting service in Russian, covering almost 7,000 foreign scientific periodicals and reporting regularly on the current production in such fields as mathematics, mechanics, astronomy, geodesy, physics, chemistry, biology, machine building, electrical engineering.

There are two notable exceptions to this basic similarity or near-identity in content. One, which is a difference in emphasis and specialization, reflects the differences of Soviet from Western society, particularly American, in economic structure and development. The other is a substantive difference in scientific theory itself, and is far the most important and most commonly noted qualitative difference between Soviet science and our own. The Lysenko doctrine is its *cause célèbre*.

That particular deviation from well-established theory, with its assumption that even the genes, the foundations of living nature, are subject to willful manipulations by the state through science, caused considerable deterioration in certain areas of Soviet science. It should be noted, on the other hand, that these areas—mainly genetics, in part agricultural biology and biochemistry—although they are extremely important, do not by any means include all of the scientific disciplines. The extent of the damage was therefore far from total. Luckily it was also of limited duration. With the demise of Mr. Lysenko, after Stalin's death, Soviet biology was free to go back to normal and again share the basic theory of genetics.

At present there remains scarcely any difference of major intellectual or theoretic importance between Soviet natural science and our own. Thus, for instance, Dr. G. E. Brown, of the University of Birmingham, in a paper dealing with the discussion on physics in the Soviet Union, makes the following observation *(Soviet Studies,* vol. 6, 1954–1955, p. 132; italics mine): "Radically different results and theories from those in Western physics ... have fallen into disrepute and are no longer believed in the USSR. *Physical theories and physical laws have been international* in this period" (that is, during the past thirty years).

The picture changes, however, when we consider Soviet social science, for this is in a category qualitatively different from that of the natural and applied sciences, East and West, as well as from Western social science. This is particularly striking in regard to specific and substantive quality.

The situation with respect to general quality is more difficult to evaluate with certainty. In regard to the recruitment, selection, and training of Soviet social scientists there is, to my knowledge, no material available like the Sibley Report published by the American Social Science Research Council in 1948, analyzing problems pertaining to the general quality of United States social scientists. On indirect evidence, however, it seems hardly an unfair assumption that the best academic talent in the Soviet Union is channeled or attracted into natural science and related applied fields, rather than into human and social science. In the latter fields, also the quality of the training seems inferior to that in the former, if availability of training materials such as textbooks is a valid criterion. In the list of Soviet textbooks published between 1938 and 1948, the distribution by fields is shown for a total of 2,165 books. Of these, 1,835 were in natural and applied sciences, and only 330 in human and social sciences. Of the latter, 132 were in finance and economics, 113 in foreign languages, leaving only 85 to be distributed as follows: pedagogy 32; history 32; geography 17; and philosophy 4. An indication of the comparative standards of learning and research may be seen also in the availability of the aforementioned abstracts in many scientific and technical fields, and their absence in the humanities and social sciences.

Obviously far more important, as well as more easily documented, are the specific and substantive quality differences, involving the types and content of material treated in Soviet social science as compared with our own. Here the differences are substantial, even though most of the disciplines taught and studied in the West have their opposite numbers in Soviet social science. Among the total of eighteen major areas of learning officially recognized as fields of specialization for the advanced degrees (doctorate and "candidatura"), five social science disciplines are listed: economics, history, jurisprudence, geography, political science (including general philosophy).

Sociology does not exist as a separate discipline, but the implication of this is not immediately evident, since sociology is still quite unevenly and inadequately represented in many countries of the West, and since in Soviet social science, as often in our own, it may be present more or less incognito, included in or subsumed under kindred disciplines like economics, philosophy, ethnology, or even geography. Further reflection indicates, however, that the absence of sociology as a separate discipline, in a system otherwise given to almost excessive specialization, can be no mere accident. This was demonstrated when the chair of sociology at Moscow University, established in 1919, was abandoned in 1924, and more recently, in the Soviet zone of Germany, when in the process of *Gleichschaltung* of universities and other institutions of higher learning to bring them into line with the Soviet Russian system, all existing chairs of sociology were either abandoned or converted into chairs of dialectical materialism, Marxism-Leninism, or recent history. Considered primarily a political discipline, this subject matter has been carefully removed from the context of Soviet academic life and placed under direct party supervision.

We shall presently examine further the situation of sociology, but let us now turn again to the officially recognized social science disciplines, and consider their relative quantitative importance as academic subjects. A general criterion to go by here is the number of completed study careers, that is, final examinations absolved and academic dissertations defended. On the basis of figures reported by DeWitt, the proportions for each of these disciplines—in relation to the total for all fields—appear to be as follows, for the periods 1925–1946 (examinations) and 1934–1946 (theses):

	Examinations	Theses
Political science and philosophy	5.1%	2.9%
Economics	3.0	2.9
History	2.7	2.5
Geography	1.1	1.1
Jurisprudence	.6	.5
Total	12.5	9.9

This picture checks only in part with the figures previously noted regarding textbooks. The discrepancy between the prominence of political science and philosophy, as shown here, and the absence of special textbooks in political science and their scarcity in philosophy may be explained, however, by the fact that the abundant party literature on Marxism-Leninism serves as textbook material for students in these disciplines. The textbook figures for history and geography are approximately in line with the relative importance of these subjects in terms of reported examinations and dissertations. The general order of magnitude for the five disciplines taken together is evident from the fact that their combined proportions are considerably lower than the individual figures for such disciplines as philology (19.4 and 11.4 percent), medicine (16.5 and 16.5), and engineering (15 and 20.8).

The prominent position of philology, evident throughout the educational system of the Soviet Union, is explained by the pluralism of languages existing inside the Union and the sphere of Soviet power as well as outside them, in the world-wide areas of communist penetration and propaganda. The communication problems of the Soviet Union and of world communism are formidable. Wherever the Soviets are masters they drive for the adoption of Russian as a common language, by making it a compulsory major subject of instruction. At the same time they need a large number of specialists in other languages. It is hardly an accident that Stalin himself devoted an important political and ideological statement to the subject of linguistics.

A few remarks are needed also on the organization and content of Soviet universities and other higher education, particularly in the social sciences. Generally, the total period required to complete a program of study for a diploma at a university or institute varies from three or four to six years. The academic year lasts ten months (September 1 to July 1), and the number of instruction hours ranges from 32 to 40 per six-day week (with attendance compulsory), which is about twice the average in the United States system. The programs of study provide for a high degree of specialization, offering choices among a large number of major subjects. In addition, certain recurrent items are included in every social science program, regardless of specialization: a basic course in political subjects or Marxism-Leninism; introductory courses in mathematics and natural science; and courses in Russian and selected foreign languages.

As a fairly typical example of a study program leading to a specialist degree at Soviet universities we may consider the work required in economics, recently described by Professor Meek of the University of Glasgow.[2] The standard five-year course in economics impressed that Western observer as "extremely thorough." Its main offerings may be summarized as follows. First year: political economy of capitalism; economic geography; higher mathematics; Russian; a foreign language; "the foundations of Marxism-Leninism." Second year: political economy of capitalism completed; political economy of socialism started; economic geography, Russian, and the foreign language continued; new course in statistics started. Third year: courses in political economy of socialism, the foreign language, and statistics completed; new courses started in history of economic thought and principles of economic planning; work begun on the student's special subject, selected from a list including such fields as industrial economics, trade, finance and credit, planning and managerial economics, statistics, economic theory. The fourth and fifth years are devoted to the special subject; a semester of reading is followed by a period of paid practical work, related to the subject, in some appropriate institution, such as the Ministry of Finance, and the final months are reserved for the writing of a thesis and advanced seminars. At the end of each course there is an oral examination of about twenty minutes, and a term paper. Comprehensive examinations occur at the end of the five-year period.

The four-year standard program in history involves first a two-year period of preparatory study in general historical subjects and the usual political, linguistic, and mathematical "must" courses. The second two years are devoted to a special subject, such as the history of slave-economy societies, history of feudalism, modern history, recent and contemporary history, history of individual peoples (according to choice), methodology of historical research. In jurisprudence there is a four-year course for specialists in Soviet law and a five-year course for those specializing in international law. The curriculum in the former includes a total of thirty-three subjects, of which two are purely political and eight general (Latin, history, foreign language, logic, and the like); the remainder, involving about 75 percent of the period of instruction, are technical law subjects. The curriculum in geography includes, besides topography and physical geography, a particularly heavy component of social science subjects, such as economic geography, demography, human resources, and even geopolitics. DeWitt notes that in no other field are there so many subjects in general education; this is true if "general" is read as meaning "social science."

Finally, the critical Soviet discipline called "politics and philosophy" is taught on two different levels: in basic courses for all students, regardless of their chosen major subjects; and in extended courses for specialists. The basic courses vary in length and scope, depending on the major subject; for engineering students they may take 6 to 8 percent of the total instruction period, for social science students and prospective teachers as much as 20 percent. The specialized courses normally require three years of study at universities or institutes, the most prominent of which is the Academy of the Social Sciences, an institution under the immediate direction of the Central Committee of the party. The topics of instruction here include the general theory of Marxism-Leninism, as well as its applications in a number of special fields, chosen from such subjects as political economy, economics and politics of foreign countries, theory of state and law, history of the USSR, international relations, history of Russian and Western philosophy, logic, psychology.

Fact vs. doctrine

Because of the systematic political bias in all Soviet study programs, the Western observer inevitably introduces here a distinction between fact and doctrine. In analyzing the content of Soviet social science study programs and publications, he will grant that certain components belong in the category of fact. And this is true not only of largely descriptive disciplines, such as geography or ethnology, but also of the more interpretive, like political science and philosophy. Obviously the Soviet student, during his years of training, acquires knowledge in the technical sense, as does his Western counterpart. As to how much and what type of knowledge he acquires, I believe, though only on the basis of second-hand impressions, that the West probably underestimates the opponent in this regard: he may be better informed and know more than we think. On the other hand, however, the factual components of Soviet social science are always treated in a context of political doctrine. Fact never stands straight and plain, but is always distorted by a biased philosophic interpretation.

In their efforts to explain the mental basis for this, some Western writers have applied analogies from religious experience, like a belief in revealed truth, obedience to spiritual authority, and communism itself has been termed religion or pseudo-religion. Whatever the usefulness of such analogies in other respects, the best key to our particular problem lies rather, I believe, in the theory of science itself, or, to be more precise, in the epistemology of Marxism-Leninism-Stalinism. The operative elements of that theory are, very briefly, the following. First, knowability (*Erkennbarkeit*) of the total universe (nature, society, and human mind) and of the regularities (laws) in the process of its evolution. Second, materialist realism, which views the universe as matter, and consciousness (thought, knowledge) as an *Abbild* or reflection of it in the mind. Third, pragmatism, which finds the criterion of realistically correct judgment only in the practice of socio-political action. And fourth, Sovietism; according to Marx and Marxist-Leninist theory, valid until about 1933, the chance of correct judgment (*Erkenntnis-Chance*) rests on the struggling proletariat and the Communist party, but according to the subsequently dominant Stalinist theory it rests on the existence of the Soviet Union, whose actions and policies are now the sole criterion of scientific truth and correct judgment (see Lange for further elaboration of this last point).

The consequences of this Marxist-Leninist-Stalinist epistemology for Soviet science, both natural and social, and for Soviet education are far-reaching. First of all, in contrast to Western science and education, there can be no intellectually relevant difference between fact and doctrine; the two are identical in the correct teachings of Soviet science and education. In Western terms, doctrine is fact, and fact is doctrine. In Soviet terms, both are truth (*pravda*), and the distinction is not at all valid or necessary, as it must be under the conditions of capitalist society. And secondly, it follows that Soviet policymakers have a responsibility, a duty, to control the operations of science, not only administratively, in the manner of some Western governments, but intellectually, by way of decision and command regarding scientific theories, the content of teaching, the priorities in research. This is a duty in the interests not only of the state and the people, but of scientific correctness and truth as such, and it applies in principle to all scientific and scholarly activities, that is, to mathematics no less than to Marxism. The workings of Soviet theory-control are by now well known through numerous studies (Ashley, Huxley, Zircle, Counts, Bauer, Moore, and others), and need no further elaboration here.

In the realm of educational techniques and practices the consequence of this epistemology is an authoritarian-disciplinarian approach to the activities of teaching, whereby factual information and political indoctrination are inseparably fused. Since it is a working assumption of the system that the truth is one and is known, the way of imparting truth to the new generation is principally by making use of the mnemonic aptitudes of the brain. This involves heavy emphasis on knowledge as acquired by learning and retaining given data, rather than by thinking as developed by the individual's free logical operations. The method relies, in other words, on conditioning and memorizing, more than on any other mental process; and a remarkable feature is that it is followed regardless of the intrinsic character of the data themselves, whether they are exact and quantitative, as in mathematics, or in the nature of purely political ideology, as in the theory of imperialism. In Western terms, one may say with equal justification that facts are being taught by methods of indoctrination, and political doctrines by methods of factual information.

It has recently been maintained that Soviet instruction in science and mathematics is superior to the Western average. A question that suggests itself is whether this superior efficiency may have one of its sources, or even its main source, in the realm of general educational philosophy, and if so, whether it is attributable to the stricter discipline of learning, to the emphasis on memory, or to the "propaganda-type" approach to teaching, or to all of these elements of the total technique. An answer to this question would repay further study. One result of recent debate about it is another sharp revision of the West's stereotyped estimate of Soviet strength. Previously it was widely taken for granted that Soviet society, for political reasons, is poor in intellectual capabilities for both knowledge and thinking, but the assumption now is that, for similar reasons, it is rather strong in the knowledge department and weak in thinking, as compared with Western societies, notably the United States, where the reverse is believed to be true. The West assumes that its own superiority in wisdom and ideas, being a product of the free mind, is unassailable from the position of Soviet strength in information. It considers the latter an attainment it can, with effort, continually emulate. Therefore, even with the revised estimate, most Western peoples view the situation without serious concern.

The question of Soviet efficiency in social science instruction has so far scarcely been raised in Western discussion. How much and how well do Soviet students learn in such subjects as economics, history, geography? What is the scope and volume of their knowledge here, in terms of facts and figures? How do they compare with students in the West? As I have already suggested, I suspect that we would once more do well to revise our estimate upward. I shall presently come to the problem of how political indoctrination and control affect scientific and scholarly attitudes and production, especially in the social sciences, but first a few remarks on their practical effect on political attitudes and behavior.

It has been noted by Moore, DeWitt, and others that the political instruction of natural science professionals (engineers, agricultural scientists, physicians), which constitutes anyway only a small part of their total curriculum, is not very effective in penetration, is received "passively and mechanically," and frequently results in "outward conformity only." This is a well documented observation. One may wonder, however, whether the actual effect of this indoctrination program is fully evaluated in these terms. Whatever the political effect, properly speaking, there is probably another effect, of value to both the state and the individual. What I mean to suggest is that the political instruction, however passively and mechanically it is received, may well have the "latent function" of training and conditioning Soviet professionals precisely in the outward conformity required for safe travel in the dangerous political landscape of that society, somewhat in the same sense as instruction in motor traffic rules is indispensable to the driver moving on our highways—as well as to the community at large.

Nor should there be a mistake about the political importance of outward conformity and passivity. Most modern regimes, and especially the totalitarian ones, feed on conformity and passivity. If by tediously repetitive "mechanical propaganda" a major part of the brains that are trained for technical skills can be rendered passive, or even cynically indifferent toward politics, "fed up" with it, so much the better for those who hold power. The more conformity, the less trouble they will have; the less independent thinking, the less risk that some of the intelligentsia will listen with interest to the voices of opposition. It is a paradox, but likely to be true, that a political indoctrination program has on many people the effect of psychological compartmentalization: it produces technicians, pure and simple, who are content to leave the business of politics to others, and therefore are that much easier to manipulate, that much more serviceable to the state. The personality type of the unpolitical expert at the core of totalitarian society is only too well known from recent history in Germany and Italy. Should anyone be surprised to meet it again in the maturing Soviet society? Even in Western democracies a certain relationship is evident, although in a different way, between conformity and power.

Nor is this all. Among the hundred thousand Soviet students at any time going through the various institutions of higher education in order to enter professional life—as engineers, doctors, scientists, teachers, socio-economic managers, and the like—there are always some to whom the political subject matters mean a great deal more than they do to others. With them the effect of indoctrination is one of conditioning not merely for passive functioning or conformity, but for active political participation. The Soviet power apparatus needs and gets a certain current influx of new blood from among the professional intelligentsia. It is important to keep in mind, however, that, in the interest of the ruling group and the Soviet state itself, this influx must be both selective in quality and limited in number. Therefore if we find, as we do, that the politically activated professionals are a minority, this should be read not as a failure but rather as a success, and perhaps the intention of the Soviet rulers.

On this point I disagree, for once, with the judgment of DeWitt. He states, from Soviet sources, that party membership of professionals increased from about 7 percent of all professionals in 1929 to about one-third in 1947; in spite of this almost fivefold increase he finds it "surprising that in 1947, after thirty years of Communist rule in Russia, only about one-third of all professionals had been recruited into the party." On the contrary, it seems surprising that this stratum, which constitutes not quite eight-tenths of one percent of the nation, should have such a high representation in the party, when less than 5 percent of the total population belong to the party, and only 5 to 10 percent of the working class, allegedly the backbone of the Soviet state. The party membership itself is composed to an increasing and, by now, predominant degree of professional people. In 1925 they made up less than 10 percent of the total membership (over 78 percent being workers, over 12 percent peasants), but by 1948 they were more than 50 percent of the total, and their representation in the more influential and important brackets of the party was, and is, much higher still. Thus among the members of the Party Congress the proportion of people with professional and secondary education is reported to have been over 50 percent even in 1934, and to have reached over 85 percent in 1952, with more than 90 percent of the Moscow delegation consisting of members from that stratum.

From these and other figures it is evident that the Soviet Union today may recruit "only" one-third of its professional manpower into politically active positions and still be sure that this group remains a dominating element in the apparatus. This one-third proportion, incidentally, indicates the average for all professions. A group-by-group breakdown shows an interesting inequality of distribution. According to DeWitt, the largest proportion of party members, about 38 percent, is found among engineers, the lowest, about 16 percent, among professionals in the fields of education, while among medical doctors and agricultural professionals the proportion is about 19 percent.

The relatively high degree of political activity among engineers might perhaps be expected in view of the policy priorities of the Soviet Union during the current period of grand-scale industrialization. This group's political potency is indicated not only by its party membership but also by its prominence among Soviet policymakers. As Meissner has said,[3] "It is not without significance that Malenkov and Khrushchev, the leading representatives of the state and party bureaucracy, are engineers by training." A number of other names also come to mind, like Pervukhin, Saburov, and, among notables of the past, Beria and Vosnezensky. Among the delegates to the 19th Party Congress (1952) the numerical prominence of engineers — 282 delegates — is particularly striking when compared with the figures for the other professions listed by Meissner: teachers 98, agricultural experts 68, economists 18, doctors 11, and jurists 7. It appears that the engineering profession occupies a position in Soviet politics today somewhat comparable to that of the legal profession in Western politics.

It may be noted, too, that it is largely from Soviet leaders with a background in engineering that new, and in part deviant, political ideas have emerged, envisaging a major policy-making role for engineers ("technocracy"). The Vosnezensky and Yaroshenko deviations, for example, basically involved a technocratic proposition advocating a changeover from political control to a purely administrative management by economic technicians, industrial leaders, and scientists, a "managerial revolution" of a sort. Both of these, incidentally, ended badly for their instigators. Vosnezensky's deviation led to his execution on Stalin's orders, and Stalin directed against Yaroshenko's heresies an elaborate and scornful polemic throughout a good part of his "Economic Problems in the USSR" (1952).

In sum, one might say that political indoctrination has both a conformity effect (for the majority of individuals) and an activization effect (for a minority). From the point of view of the Soviet rulers, both are useful and desirable. How far there may be boomerang effects in terms either of latent hostility toward the regime, rather than conformity, or of political heterodoxy, as in the deviations mentioned, is another matter.

A question more specifically relevant to our present topic is whether there is a significant difference in the effects on the two groups of professionals, the natural science and the social science groups. Social science and related types of training involve much the heaviest doses of instruction in socio-political subjects; also, these subjects are here more directly related to the other major topics of study. Yet if party membership represents a valid index of political participation and activity, the figures quoted point to the engineers as a far more political group than the teachers. How is this apparent contradiction to be explained? I suggest, partly by the nature of the training of the engineers, but mostly by the nature of their occupational relatedness to socio-economic matters.

In the first place, the Soviet educational system trains two types of higher engineering personnel, pure technologists and "engineer-economists," the latter being prepared for managerial as well as purely technical tasks. And second, the actual day-to-day occupational problems of the engineer, regardless of his specific training, inevitably bring him face to face with the social, economic, and political facts of life in a more realistic fashion than is likely in the context of the teacher's daily duties. From these two points it may be assumed, first, that some engineers receive more of a social science type of training than do others, and second, that whatever social science and political instruction is given will generally have a relatively high rate of salience to the engineers in practical-occupational terms. This contains no implication, however, regarding the intensity of the propaganda effect. A high degree of practical occupational meaningfulness is quite compatible with a low degree of psychological penetration. Doctrines may well be assimilated as matters of routine rather than of political faith. From internal evidence (Soviet self-criticism) this indeed appears to be the case. The rank and file, as well as the officers of the party, are to a large extent practical men rather than political believers.

Turning now to the effect of political indoctrination and control on scientific and scholarly attitudes, and on actual performance (theory and research) in Soviet science, especially social science, a few general remarks are first in order. As was mentioned in an earlier context, the operative doctrine of the Soviet state is one of scientism, in the sense that it assigns overriding socio-political importance to science, and in fact presents itself as science, claiming scientific truth and validity for its every judgment. In consequence, we find political authority operating with acknowledged legitimacy in the substantive realm of theory and research. On grounds of principle there is no difference among the various disciplines in this regard. In actual fact, however, the exercise of political authority, in terms of interference with scientific and scholarly theory, is far more comprehensive in the area of human and social sciences than in that of the natural sciences and their applied disciplines. Although the difference may seem to be only one of degree, it is large enough to set the two groups of disciplines rather radically apart, both intellectually, as regards the conditions of professional operations, and socially, as regards the prestige attached to the two groups in Soviet society.

The Soviet public, as well as the scientific community, tends to be far more aware of the positive than of the restrictive aspect of the policy-makers' concern with natural science and technology. The "cult of science," as expounded and practiced by the party, is perceived as the dominant feature of the situation, completely overshadowing the restrictions and interferences. In the social sciences and humanities, the situation is the very opposite, as Soviet public opinion cannot possibly fail to observe. Here the policy-makers' positive concern, expressed in allocation of funds, priorities, and other active encouragements, is only a fraction of what it is in the natural sciences. Moreover, it is entirely subordinate to the restrictive aspects of policy. As a consequence, the natural sciences and the professions related to them enjoy a greater autonomy, expressed in less rigorous restrictions, and also a considerably higher prestige in Soviet society, than do the social and human sciences.

What all this adds up to is obviously that the intellectual and social climate in which Soviet social and human science operates must be unfavorable and unproductive compared to the conditions prevailing in regard to Soviet natural science, or Western science, natural and social. Consequently, while Western observers watch the developments in Soviet natural science and technology with respectful and even anxious interest, they mostly tend to dismiss Soviet social science as more or less unworthy of their attention.

There are exceptions to the second part of this rule, as evidenced in Meek's report, mentioned above, on conversations with Soviet economists, and in Jean Piaget's "Some Impressions of a Visit to Soviet Psychologists" (*International Social Science Bulletin*, vol. 8, no. 2, 1956). On the whole, however, the Western attitude is one of contempt or ignorance in the face of a performance that is considered to be poor in intellectual quality, narrow in scope, and biased in outlook. From a strictly "academic" point of view there may be some validity in this judgment, but is there any validity in the implied assumption that the West can get along without being concerned with Soviet social science, while Soviet technology and physics are matters of vital concern to us?

I shall presently set forth my own answer to this question, but various developments that may bear on it should first be discussed.

Possible new factors in the situation

Is there any reason for believing, as is sometimes contended, that new factors in the world situation—such as Stalin's death and the emerging new post-Stalinist Soviet leadership, the atomic stalemate, the upsurge of nationalism within the Soviet power bloc as well as in the Western spheres of interest—are bringing about a change in the historical situation, gradually dissolving the East-West or Soviet-West separation, thus setting the stage for overt, active, world-wide competition, over a much broader area than heretofore? And especially, what are we to make of the expectation, held by many intellectuals on both sides, that this extension of the competitive field—which here means the field of mutual discourse and scrutiny—would also include the sciences of man and society?

These questions are here to be considered briefly in terms of four major trends: first, pressures within Soviet society for new approaches to social science and socio-political problems; second, new developments in Soviet social theory and ideology; third, satellite opposition to Soviet dominance in the social and political sciences; and fourth, the thaw in international scholarly relations.

As for the first of these developments, outspoken public criticism ("self-criticism"), in keeping with current trends, has been directed against the state of affairs in Soviet social science. Several speakers at the 20th Party Congress emphasized this subject, which was then treated with unreserved frankness in the press. A representative contribution to this debate was an article published in a Soviet journal early in 1956.[4] Its authors point to the decline in the quantity of output in Soviet social science over the last twenty years, citing for illustration the number of economic periodicals—a total of eight published in 1956, as against 85 in 1936—stating that at present only one (*Voprosy ekonomiki*) is concerned with problems of economic theory, and adding: "The condition of the law and philosophical presses is by no means better." In sum their verdict is that "our present does not compare favorably with the past in the scope and volume of publications devoted to social sciences, although the problems of these sciences have become much larger and more complex in the past 20 years."

Far worse, however, than the decrease in volume of output is the deterioration in quality. The authors base their devastating criticism here on various criteria. In the first place, they maintain that Soviet social science at present lacks positive foundations in the reality of life (hence the title of the paper), having timidly withdrawn from any relationship to practitioners and to practical problems. "Unwilling to tackle contemporary problems," it has turned to the past. Of 33 books published in 1955 in various social science fields, the authors find that 29 are "devoted to historical problems." This is certainly not for lack of important tasks in the present. The authors mention such problems as "bureaucracy, alcoholism, and other negative phenomena that have not yet been overcome," as well as shortcomings in agriculture and problems in social legislation (for example, abortion laws), to which social scientists should be able to contribute, but fail to do so.

Other "gaps and omissions" are attributed to the social scientists' failure to appraise the importance of major intellectual discoveries, such as the theory of relativity and cybernetics, and to study foreign societies. "Competition with the capitalist countries that we are striving to outstrip economically also poses sharp problems before our social sciences. It is of great importance to us to know what happens in the capitalist countries, what their economic power is, what are the peculiarities of their development and the distribution of class forces. For this we need not those superfluous pamphlets where the authors have made it easy for themselves by pouring reality into a ready-made mold, but profound analytical works based on reliable factual material."

The authors candidly diagnose the causes of this general timidity and mediocrity as being, first, the prevailing atmosphere of "negativistic criticism" (read: political terror), and second, the social scientists' poor knowledge of research methods, especially statistics. They have become compilers and commentators dealing with doctrines, rather than students working with data based on first-hand observation and measurement. The critics do not hesitate to put the blame for this situation where it belongs, nor do they fail to name the only real remedy: "Unfortunately, publication of such data is in an extremely unfortunate state; this was brought out by some speakers at the 20th Party Congress. It is indicative that the 1939 census is still the source for all kinds of ethnic data and indexes of nationality, class, and population factors. Nor is data which can be easily obtained from election materials being published. Information on the dynamics of migration, marriage, divorce, mortality, the birth rate, and so on and so on, is still at the prewar level. It is quite obvious that the systematic publication of statistical data is important to the further development of the social sciences."

The second of the trends I have noted is the new developments in Soviet social theory and ideology itself. The general assessment of capitalism, for instance, has changed in important respects, and so has the conception of the role of war in history and the inevitability of war in the future relations between the camp of capitalism and that of socialism. There is a new look regarding the role of the Communist party and its leadership. While these shifts in political beliefs have obvious general implications for operative Soviet views on world relations at large, certain new developments in theory and doctrine on a higher level of abstraction are probably more important with regard to the specific problems of the internationalization of Soviet social science.

I refer here, above all, to the fundamental change in Soviet social and cultural theory inaugurated by Stalin in his pronouncements on linguistics (1950). What was at stake there (and still is, for this particular piece of "Stalinism," unlike the Lysenko doctrine in genetics, has been confirmed rather than repudiated since Stalin's death) was not merely an academic re-evaluation of a hitherto dominant trend, the Marr school, in the study of languages, but a matter of consequence to the general Soviet interpretation of culture and society. Its full implications are not yet manifest, but as the debate continues they are becoming revealed as profound and far-reaching, extending into such fields as general logic, epistemology, and general social science theory. Moreover, they seem likely to involve a trend toward systematic positions similar to those of Western social science, closer, in other words, to a universal theory and methodology.

N. Y. Marr's theory had for many years completely dominated the science of linguistics in the Soviet Union when in 1950 Stalin's *Pravda* letters suddenly abolished it and introduced entirely different ideas in its place. Marr (who died in 1934) was a competent scholar, specializing in the languages of the Caucasian region, and besides a convinced Marxist. In accordance with his political philosophy, he held that languages belong to the ideological superstructure in any given society, and therefore express or reflect the class struggle; the nationally dominant language of any society is that of the ruling classes. This theory was applied by the Communist and other Marxist parties in and outside the Soviet Union in support of linguistic minorities' strivings for power in a multi-lingual situation. An example outside the Soviet Union is Norway, where the Marxists of the 1920's and 1930's, identifying language-striving with class struggle, banded together with the populist movement in favor of the underlying folk dialect against the supremacy of the Dano-Norwegian national language.

Stalin rejected the Marr school from the position that the class-character-of-language formula is "erroneous and non-Marxist." "National languages" (such as Russian, as developed over time in speech and literature) "are not class, but common languages, common to the members of each nation and constituting the single language of that nation," to which the existing "offshoots," "dialects," and "jargons" are subordinate.[5] In practical terms this Stalin thesis claims (in the name of Marx!) a position of hegemony for Russian as the national language, over the minority dialects of the Union. It also reaffirms the already existing trend of cultural nationalism, that is, identification with traditional Russian culture, its classical art and literature.

In terms of social theory the Stalin thesis involves a radical revision of the doctrines of historical materialism. If the language, with its grammatical system and vocabulary, is not a part of the ideological superstructure, and therefore is a common property of all members of the society, regardless of the historical process of class struggle, then what is the nature of such long-term historical products as man's capacity for logical thinking and, indeed, the accumulated wealth of scientific knowledge itself? Stalin declared that "Grammar is the outcome of a process of abstraction performed by the human mind over a long period of time; it is an indication of the tremendous achievement of thought," and he added: "In this respect grammar resembles geometry." Would this not be equally true of general logic and science? In the debate that followed Stalin's *Pravda* letters, and still goes on, this question was raised with great insistence.

In regard to the controversy on logic, an authoritative statement by the Soviet journal *Problems of Philosophy* settled the issue (at least for the time being) in 1952: "There are not two formal systems of logic— an old, metaphysical one, and a new dialectical one, no more than there are two arithmetics or grammars, one metaphysical and one dialectical. There is only one formal logic and that is universally human; this is a collection of the elementary rules of thinking and the simple theory of these rules."

The problem of the sciences seems more complicated. Here the recent debate has tended to acknowledge that the exact and natural sciences are: first, per se materialistic; and second, universal, in the sense of being a product not only of any particular type of society, but of the intellectual progress of mankind as such. In practice, Soviet natural science operates by and large on this basic assumption, and today is, in fact, predominantly international.

As regards the social and human sciences, the recent debate still assumes that they are part of the superstructure (here socialist, here capitalist), and therefore belong in a different category from the natural sciences, but there seems to be a new mobility in the positions taken. The dichotomy is no longer quite so sharp and absolute as before. M. G. Lange, observing the lively debate in the Soviet Zone of Germany, remarks that "mathematics and the natural sciences were not the only disciplines the social impact of which was redefined after 1950," and, more specifically, "all the social sciences were affected by Stalin's pronouncements" on linguistics.

What this means is not that Soviet social science has yet reached the point where it is, or will overnight become, universal and international in character, similar to the natural sciences. But it does indicate quite a few "broken windows," and a state of philosophic crisis and fermentation in which definite tendencies toward a convergence with Western social science are discernible.

A case in point, to mention but one instance, is the current controversy among Soviet social scientists over the problem of statistics. The issue here is whether or not statistics is a universal method, equally applicable to both nature and society. The official view was expressed by Academician K. V. Ostrovitianov (described as "the chief organizer of Soviet economists") in his account [6] of the Moscow Conference on Statistics, March 1954, to the effect that there are two different kinds of statistics: "mathematical statistics," applicable to nature; and simply "statistics," applicable to society. The report does not conceal the fact, however, that this view met with considerable opposition among Soviet statisticians, and that there is a universalist school of thought, represented by Professors Pisarev, Nemchinov, and others, considerably closer to the Western way of thinking in these matters.

The debate discloses a sharp division among Soviet social scientists, as Ostrovitianov's choice of language indicates: "The comrades who regard statistics as a universal science which studies nature and society make of it some kind of science over and above the classes, coldly indifferent to good and to evil, without any preference at all as between classes and between social structures." The fact that the political chief of Soviet economists admits that this overt division exists may partly be due to a relative increase in intellectual tolerance. Probably, however, it is attributable in great part to the fact that the divergent views have by now become too strong and too widespread to be categorically suppressed. The crisis in social theory has arrived.

The third trend I mentioned is satellite opposition to Soviet dominance in the social and political sciences. This has become particularly evident in recent years, especially in East Germany, Poland and Hungary. There the previous claim that the Soviet Union and its leadership is the ultimate source of truth and authority in the social sciences is no longer accepted as axiomatic by intellectuals, as is evidenced by the many defections of students and professors from East German universities and the uncompromising deviations of others, like Professor Georg

Lukács of Hungary and Professor Wolfgang Harich of the Soviet university in East Berlin. The revolt against Soviet monopoly control involves an active reorientation among satellite social scientists, toward intellectual freedom and, specifically, free communication with the West.

The fact that the open revolt has been momentarily crushed (Lukács, for instance, was forcibly exiled, Harich condemned to ten years in jail) will hardly remove its deeper causes, nor is it likely to enable the Soviet rulers and their puppets to return all the way back to the policy of total Iron Curtain control, keeping the satellite peoples in isolation. For that, too many windows have been broken, too many doors opened, and sooner or later the Soviets will have to adjust to the new situation, permitting or even promoting the exchange they can no longer prevent.

Finally, we come now to the fourth trend, the thaw in international scholarly relations. Evidence of this has been seen recently in the increased interest shown by Soviet and Western social scientists in each other's published output; in the participation of Soviet representatives at international social science congresses; in the new opportunities for exchange visits by individual students crossing the dividing line from both sides.

In familiarity with the other's published production the Soviets are ahead of us, in that they have adopted a definite policy of studying Western output while we hold on to a careless indifference toward what they are doing. Thus Professor Meek found in his visits at Soviet universities that the economics students were reading Keynes' *General Theory* as well as authors like Marshall, Fisher, and J. B. Clark, all in Russian translations, and that many other standard works were available and eagerly read in the original. Other reports indicate that Soviet economists are seeking instruction from Western sources on certain strategic problems, such as those of underdeveloped countries. In fields like political science and sociology the Soviet students are probably, at present, far less versed in the writings of their Western counterparts, but here again the policy is definitely to encourage study of "bourgeois" literature.

In part this increased familiarity with Western social science is obviously intended to improve Soviet capabilities in the ideological conflict, both defensively, in countering Western critique of the Soviet system, and in offensive terms, by sharpening the instruments of attack against capitalism. In part, however, this knowledge is sought also for the help it can give in coping with pressing internal problems in Soviet society itself. Both these aims are clearly stated in the following sentences with which Academician P. Fedoseyev, the leader of the Soviet delegation at the World Congress of Sociologists (August 1956), concluded his report on the lessons of that meeting (*Pravda,* October 19, 1956):

Something which attracts attention is the enormously rich literature existing in the capitalist countries in various fields and on different questions in sociology. It must be said that this literature is not subjected to a critical analysis by the workers in the social sciences in the Soviet Union or the countries of the People's Republics. Of these problems, extremely few scientific works are published with us, especially there is little research done on questions that belong in the borderline areas between, on the one hand philosophy and historical materialism, on the other hand, economics, law, technology, and geography. The sociological problems concerning labor, culture, ways of life, family, morals, urban and rural living, require more profound study and elucidation from all angles. It is the duty of the workers in the social sciences to liquidate this serious shortcoming in their work.

If this statement reflects a genuine policy resolution for Soviet sociology, it seems to call for a reappraisal of the value of the Amsterdam Congress, and particularly of the Soviet-Western encounter that took place there. Comments by Western participants have been negative, expressing annoyance and frustration over a deadlocked dialogue and over the fact that our partners showed so little professional grasp of modern sociology and the subjects under debate.[7] In the light of Fedoseyev's interpretation of what the Congress meant to him and his Soviet colleagues, we may have to revise our judgment somewhat.

Is it likely that events and factors like the four trends I have discussed will eventuate in the Soviet Union in a more universal (Western type) approach to social and human problems and to the social sciences? Will these and other major forces currently at work in Soviet society produce a desire or even an objective necessity for an undoctrinaire reality-orientation toward the social universe, similar to that sought by Western social science? The answer can be provided only by future events themselves. I suggest, however, that Western social scientists should act on the assumption that the answer will be affirmative, and pursue the goal of a systematic internationalization of their disciplines. This will involve a deliberate, consistent policy in relation to our Soviet counterparts.

A policy proposal

I contend that Soviet social science, be it rich or poor, is an eminently political factor of strategic importance in the total East-West situation. It is this not as "propaganda" but because it conceptualizes the dominant Soviet ideas of man and society, of power and history, of capitalism and socialism, of international relations and the world conflict. In other words, it sets the framework in which the rulers and the ruled interpret the political universe and define their own actions within that universe. Thus it is a guiding force in Soviet politics.

When I say Soviet social science I refer to the total body of propositions in the various disciplines, a body that is in Western terms a hybrid of fact and doctrine, with the second always the core of the whole. This means that in dealing with Soviet social science we shall, whether we like it or not, have to deal with the doctrine called Marxism-Leninism-Stalinism. There is considerable reluctance in the West, and especially in the United States, to spend time and brain power on understanding communist doctrine. The highbrows dismiss it as "intellectual fabrications" hardly worth the candle. The lowbrows reject it as the devil's own work, and brand as a traitor anyone who tries to understand what it is about. Even among special students of Soviet affairs there are some who ignore the communist doctrine. Another and more general bias, among American social and political scientists, seems to operate against the economic and historical approach to society, in favor of a psychological-behavioral approach, hardly an adequate tool in dealing with this particular subject matter.

If Western social science is to relate itself meaningfully to its Soviet counterpart, it will have to master communist doctrine—that is to say, devote serious study to it and produce an adequate number of specialists who, without being "believers," know and understand it from within. There is merit in the idea once suggested by an American social scientist, that every university in this country ought to have on its teaching staff at least one first-rate specialist in Marxism, one who, without fear of suspicion, would teach the new generation how to master intellectually the doctrine that is the heart of communist power. Only with this knowledge can the West hope to master it, or indeed survive it politically.

On the basis of a better intellectual mastery of communist doctrine and ideology, Western social scientists should actively study the work of their Soviet counterparts in the various disciplines. This means systematic research in various directions: studies of the institutional establishments, the personnel, the mode of operations, the published production of Soviet social science. We should become fully as familiar with the situation there as we are, through the DeWitt report and other studies, with Soviet natural science and technology. The objective, however, would be different. Unlike that of the earlier studies the primary aim would not be political intelligence, that is, an assessment of Soviet strength, but rather the substantive policy objective of internationalizing the social sciences. The term "internationalize" is to be understood here as a development toward social science theories and methods that are equally valid east and west of the great divide.

Western social scientists should set for themselves the very objective that Academician Fedoseyev envisaged for Soviet sociologists, and "liquidate a serious shortcoming in their work" by discovering what the fellows in the other camp are doing. While the two operations, Soviet and Western, would not be strictly reciprocal, either in motives or in procedures, they still should offer mutual opportunities and challenges. If the Soviets are eager, the West has all the more reason to proceed vigorously.

On our part, one important aim would be simply to see what we can learn from Soviet social science on the substance of general theoretical and other problems in the various disciplines. This might or might not amount to much of a net gain—in some fields, like economics, probably more than in others, like sociology. In any case, it would be only the first and immediate objective of our effort. In addition, we stand to gain in knowledge of Soviet society itself, the status and structure of its intellectual and professional population, the particular conditions and roles of its social scientists, and numerous similar questions. Far more important, however, is a still further objective, that of establishing an "exchange situation" with Soviet social science. What would this require of us?

It would require that our receptivity to Soviet output be not merely specialized, that is, limited to expert groups and special journals, but generalized, covering both a wider public and more numerous channels of communication. Concretely, the professional magazines and other technical literature in Western languages should deal more with past and current Soviet writings, review and summarize their content, and subject them to rigorous, specific, and constructive criticism in terms of our own standards. We would benefit from this ourselves, and Soviet students reading our publications would discover not only the ideas and findings of Western social science as such, but also their application and relevance to the teachings and problems of Soviet social scientists.

With regard to the published output of our own social science, the "exchange situation" could best be established by improving communication through already available media, especially by adding Russian-language summaries and abstracts to some of our leading social science periodicals, and by publishing occasional articles designed for the Soviet reader, surveying large areas of recent work in Western social science. If Western production is to be actively received and have an effect on the other side, it is not irrelevant for us to wonder whether, or how far, we answer their questions, or indeed, whether we even ask them.

As a means of developing the "exchange situation" I have deliberately stressed communication through the impersonal mass medium of print, and through the conventional, existing channels available to the profession. This does not imply that other means should be excluded. To the extent that government policies, East and West, permit other modes of contact and communication—by exchange of visitors, by study abroad, by international meetings and conferences, and by individual correspondence and exchange of publications—these should be employed. Yet it should be remembered that confrontation through the mass medium of print is usually a necessary first step before a real dialogue can take place. Also, the mass medium reaches a far wider circle of people, including many individuals who may not be accessible to person-to-person encounters with foreigners, especially among the younger students and those who do not enjoy Communist party favors, like a passport or an appointment for travel abroad.

Whether the conventional channels of publication already available to Western social science should be supplemented by other media, like radio, is problematic. It would not be difficult to design programs of social science subjects, variously addressed to specialists, teachers, individuals in the socio-economic managerial professions; and there is no reason why such programs should not in themselves be objectively good and also interesting to listeners. There is a danger, however, that the context in which they would appear, if transmitted by a Western international broadcasting agency, would make them suspect as items of political propaganda. This result would be quite contrary to the intention that should guide Western social scientists in their communication with the Soviets.

That intention would be not merely to make friends and meet people, but to end the state of insulation between the Soviets and ourselves, and establish communication in a limited area of crucial importance. Our aim would emphatically not be to "manipulate" or even to "liberate," but simply to establish a common universe of discourse and research, within which we could together develop an international social science.

Notes

1. The principal sources in this paper are: Nicholas DeWitt, *Soviet Professional Manpower*, published by the National Science Foundation (Washington, 1955) (although primarily devoted to manpower problems in the natural and applied sciences, this study also contains valuable information on the situation of the social sciences in the Soviet Union); "The Social Sciences in the USSR," a special issue, no. 10 (November 1956), of the periodical *Soviet Survey*, published by the Congress for Cultural Freedom, London; Max Gustav Lange, *Wissenschaft im totalitären Staat* (Stuttgart and Düsseldorf, 1955), referred to as Lange (this study indirectly sheds new light on the present problem by examining in detail the Sovietization of the social sciences in the East Zone of Germany). References to other sources are given in full in the text.

2. R. L. Meek, "Conversations with Soviet Economists," in *Soviet Studies,* VI (1954-1955), 238 ff.

3. Boris Meissner, *The Communist Party of the Soviet Union* (New York, 1956) p. 10.

4. F. Burlatsky and G. Shakhnazarov, "Social Sciences and Life," in *Literaturnaya Gazeta,* March 24, 1956. The following references to this paper are based on an English translation, printed in *Current Digest of the Soviet Press,* vol. 8, no. 15 (1956).

5. J. V. Stalin, "Concerning Marxism in Linguistics," English translation (London, 1950) pp. 9, 15, 16.

6. Reprinted in English in *Soviet Studies,* VI (1954-1955), 321-31.

7. See especially *Soviet Survey,* pp. 12-15; also Norman Birnbaum, "Science, Ideology and Dialogue," in *Commentary* (1956), pp. 567-575.

Meeting the Soviet philosophers

LEWIS S. FEUER

I make no claim to being an "area specialist" on the Soviet Union, but for many years I have read the literature on Soviet society and ideology. For several years I attended courses in the Russian language, and acquired a stuttering knowledge. My hope in going to the Soviet Union was to do what I had once done in Japan—namely, to engage in discussions with its philosophers, sociologists, and students, to speak with them while their doubts and searchings had not yet been blue-penciled out of existence by editorial committees, administrators, and bureaucrats. I was to find that it took a month or more to learn in the Soviet Union what needed only a week in Japan. One could meet readily in Japan, for instance, with a variety of factions in the Zengakuren, but in the Soviet Union my meetings with free student circles had to be arranged with caution. Where Marxist professors in Japan would speak freely of their different tendencies, among Soviet professors there was a conditioned preliminary response to profess a unanimous consensus in dialectical materialism, even when their differences were patently straining the consensus into a dissensus, and tearing the ideological garments at the seams.

During four and a half months, I talked with upwards of 150 Soviet philosophers and social scientists, sometimes for an hour, sometimes for five hours. At the Institute of Philosophy of the Soviet Academy of Sciences in Moscow, I gave five lectures to the research workers, ranging in number from twenty to fifty. I went to Tashkent to talk with the Institute of Philosophy and Law in Uzbekistan, and to Tbilisi, for long discussions with scholars at the Georgian Institue of Philosophy. At Leningrad, I inquired into the projects of the hard-working sociologists of the Social Research Laboratory. Most of all, I learned from discussions with Soviet philosophers who raised objections and questions at my lectures.

From *Survey*, April 1964, pp. 60-74.

My first lecture was on "The Development of Dewey's Pragmatism." The audience consisted largely of the Institute's Section on Bourgeois Philosophy and Sociology. I suggested this subject because I thought it would enable me to raise directly what I regarded as shortcomings and misstatements in the studies by Soviet ideologists of American philosophy. The discussion which followed showed how hard the Soviet ideological stance makes it for them to approach the history of ideas in an empirical spirit.

In the last few minutes of the lecture, I considered the allegation which I found in Soviet books that Dewey was the philosopher of American imperialism. I said that from his first political writings, Dewey had been a critic of all imperialist ideology; that his essay on savage mind in 1902 had been directed against racist imperialism in the aftermath of the Spanish-American War; that he had lived in China for two years and had witnessed the May Fourth movement in 1919, and had written a series of remarkable articles defending its anti-imperialist program; that he had been a critic of American imperialism in Mexico; that he had been personally invited by Krupskaya, presumably on Lenin's behalf, to help in reorganizing Soviet education; that he had visited the Soviet Union in 1928 and written a series of warmly enthusiastic reports concerning the Soviet experiment; that, finally, the Soviet attacks on Dewey as an imperialist philosopher had begun only in the mid-thirties when Dewey criticized the Moscow trials and purges. "You yourselves," I said, "have since then come to recognize that with regard to these trials Dewey was right and Stalin was wrong."

The young philosophers in the audience listened intently and did not challenge these observations. But the chairman cautioned everybody to remember that I was giving my "personal opinions," and that they should bear in mind that Dewey had supported Trotsky, and that Trotsky had been trying to restore capitalism in the Soviet Union. It was amazing. These were not illiterates; these were the picked Soviet research workers on Western thought, and all had to acquiesce in this nonsense. Questions on my findings and method followed, and then the floor was taken by the Soviet authority on American pragmatism, Yuri Melvil. Dewey, he asserted, *was* the philosopher of American imperialism, and all the facts I had adduced were trivial; for "objectively" Dewey was a supporter of imperialism; he quoted from an American book which said that Dewey had become anti-communist long before it was fashionable to be so.

I prevailed on the chairman to allow me a few minutes to reply (it is the custom of the Communist party to allow its spokesman the last word). I pointed out what a "dogmatic Marxist" he was, for his dogmatism was such that no set of facts could possibly move him from his belief that Dewey "objectively" was a philosopher of imperialism; this was using "objectively" in an unverifiable sense to conform to dogmatic preconceptions. (There was a round of pleased laughter from the younger side of the room.) I then tried to show how the history of American philosophy did not confirm the Marxist formula that materialism was the progressive philosophy, and idealism the reactionary. Transcendentalism, for instance, was the philosophy of the most radical group of reformers in American history—the New Englanders, who, before the Civil War, dedicated themselves to socialist and abolitionist movements. I said I had once been a Marxist, but that my experience, and philosophical and sociological studies, had persuaded me there were basic limitations to Marxism.

Obliteration of Soviet philosophical past

It would be hard to exaggerate the degree to which the Stalinist era extirpated original philosophy and social science, and how its effects still persist. The sense of a continuing and supporting tradition of philosophical discussion is absent. I asked one young philosopher, the author of a work on English intuitionist ethics, if he could give me the title of a good history of Soviet philosophy; I remarked that in the United States we had several histories of American philosophy. He replied, after a moment's thought, that no such history of Soviet philosophy existed. The reason, he said, was simple: they had no need of one because, unlike America, they had no different schools of ideas; everybody worked within the framework of Marxist philosophy. This struck me as tantamount to admitting that the philosophical life of his country was so uninteresting that it didn't deserve to be written; why bother writing a history of commentaries and explications of the Truth which was already written clearly enough by Marx and Lenin? The young philosopher went on to add that a chapter on philosophy during the Lenin period had been prepared for the sixth volume of their collective history of philosophy, but it had been so much criticized that it had never been published. Clearly, silence about the destroyed generation of Soviet thinkers is still regarded as judicious.

An incident during the discussion of my second lecture on "The Sociology of Science" illustrated vividly the official obliteration of the Soviet philosophical past. I was presenting material which was published the following month in a book, *The Scientific Intellectual*. In reply to a question, I said that I disagreed with a seminal Marxist essay in this field. Someone asked to what essay I was referring. I answered it was an article by the Soviet scholar, B. Hessen, "The Social and Economic Roots of Newton's *Principia*," published in 1931 in a book called. . . . The chairman looked at my interpreter, an unspoken message seemed to flash between them, and the interpreter interrupted me: "We do not know anything of the author. I do not know his name." The chairman nodded assent. I looked at the audience. Not a word, not a question about the Soviet scholar to whom I had referred. In any normal gathering the scholars would have been eager to get the exact reference to an important, neglected essay of one of their own countrymen. But with one glance they had been warned: Do not ask about this man. No doubt the book *Science at the Crossroads* was known to both the chairman and interpreter; its opening essay was by the still unrehabilitated Nikolai Bukharin, and Hessen himself evidently vanished during the Stalinist era. Their names are still enveloped in the collective repression of Soviet memory; references to their writings are to be avoided by the prudent Soviet scholar.

My third lecture was on "Contemporary American Thought." I chose this subject because I wanted to emphasize the tremendous variation in American philosophies, the "law of the spectrum," I called it, according to which the distribution of philosophies was primarily the outcome of differences in individual temperament, and the "law of the wings," in accordance with which every philosophical movement, whether pragmatism, idealism, or materialism, tended to evolve into right, left, and center wings. I spoke of the generational differences among American philosophers—how the older philosophers were idealist, realist, or pragmatist, the middle-aged ones naturalist or positivist, and the younger ones, existentialist or ordinary linguisticians, and suggested that under normal conditions such a spectrum of philosophies would manifest itself in the Soviet Union, that this was typical of societies where the spectrum was not deflated by external pressure.

I was promptly challenged at that meeting and at subsequent discussions to apply these "laws" to Soviet philosophy. When I first did so, and pointed to the emerging diversity which I had encountered among Soviet philosophers, I was told that a few weeks of discussions were no sufficient basis for such a judgment; all Soviet philosophers were dialectical materialists. As the months went by, and the discussions accumulated, it became still more evident to me that a variety of conflicting philosophies is emerging in the Soviet Union, and that they are housed together under the rubric "dialectical materialism" in an unstable equilibrium. Dictatorial power, not intellectual agreement, imposes the harness of a planned ideology on recalcitrant temperaments. Nevertheless, even within the framework of the mandatory creed, one discerns the workings of the law of the spectrum. In the Soviet Union, the counterpart exists for every philosophical movement in western Europe and America. If planned ideology was eliminated, one might expect a flowering of these diverse philosophical trends.

Among the young philosophers, I found chiefly three trends: scientific realism, existentialism, and pragmatism. The scientific philosophers are (what I called) "scientific realists," that is, their "materialism" is simply a belief in the reality of the physical world. They are engaged in catching up with problems and readings which were central in American philosophy thirty-five years ago. I found circles, for instance, studying such works of Bertrand Russell as *Introduction to Mathematical Philosophy,* and the more recent *Human Knowledge.* They are intrigued by the concepts of "structure" and "isomorphism," and talk very much in Russell's terms about how only the structure of the physical world can be known. They tend to reject Engels' theory of sensation as a "reflection" of the world, and find this to be "mirror-magic." They take the basic meaning of "reflection" to be "isomorphism." The scientific realist group is on friendly political terms with the Soviet existentialists, that is, they regard them as "moral people." They do not, however, think highly of the philosophical merits of the existentialists, who in their opinion have not yet broken with the Hegelian concept that contradictions can exist in reality.

What characterizes the Soviet existentialists? In the first place, they prefer to study the humanistic Marx of the *Economic-Philosophic Manuscripts,* the Marx of the concept of alienation. As one professor observed: "They are interested in Marx when he was not yet a Marxist." When I noted that this was the precise point—that they preferred the Marx who was not a Marxist—he retorted: "They will evolve towards Marxism." The Soviet existentialists are concerned with problems of freedom and ethics which were banished from the consciousness in the Stalinist era; they are concerned with the quality of individual life rather than with the tactics of ideological class struggle. They enjoy reading such authors as Berdyaev and Solovyov, and take an interest in Freud. They find German existentialist philosophy more interesting than American thought and feel themselves closer in spirit to the Germans than to the Americans. The Germans are said to be deeper, to raise at least the problems of existence though they cannot solve them; the Americans are regarded as proponents of common sense, as relatively superficial.

Both the scientific realists and the existentialists are together in one camp as "anti-dogmatists." "The dogmatists," said a young philosopher, "are the previous people, the immoral ones, who fear that logical methods will unmask their foolish doctrines." "In what way," I asked, "are they immoral?" "They are immoral," he replied, "in their daily practice; they try to suppress their enemies administratively. When a person can prove something, he doesn't need illegal methods." The scientific realists and the existentialists regard each other as "socially progressive" because both oppose the dogmatic Stalinists. This fact of their political unity is perhaps an item of evidence against the historical-materialist theory of ideas, since, on the fact of it, their philosophical differences correspond to no differences in politics, and this indeed may be the beginning of philosophy and the end of ideology in the Soviet Union.

The existentialists and scientific realists do not, of course, exhaust the modes of philosophy found among young Soviet thinkers. A significant group, particularly in the social sciences, is drawn to American pragmatism. The dogmatists continue to insist that pragmatism is a form of subjective idealism, but some younger thinkers are turning to the study of Peirce and Dewey. They are concerned with clarifying such an ambiguous concept as "practice." As Marxists, they hold that the Marxist sociology of revolution is confirmed in "practice," but what does this mean? There is not a large collection of revolutions which would give meaning to probability-frequencies as the verificational basis for their assertions. Confronted by a series of ambiguities in "practice," they propose vague solutions which are remarkably akin to Dewey's logic.

The invasion of revisionism

All the varieties of dialectical materialism in the Soviet Union fasten on different texts of Marx, Engels, and Lenin for their support. The scientific realists make their appeal to Lenin's *Materialism and Empirio-Criticism*, Neo-dialecticians prefer to quote from Lenin's *Philosophical Notebooks*. The positivist-inclined cite from *Anti-Dühring* the passages where Engels speak of the replacement of philosophy by science. The historicists quote the second Preface to Marx's *Capital,* whereas the antihistoricists cite Marx's letter to Mikhailovsky and Engels' letters on historical materialism. The pragmatists like to recite Marx's *Theses on Feuerbach*. The existentialists quote from the *Economic-Philosophical Manuscripts*. When will the revolt against canonical texts begin?

The younger sociologists have as quietly as possible discarded the dialectical methodology. According to Marx, there were no universal laws of social science; each social system had its specific sociological laws, but a law common to diverse social systems was out of the question. The Soviet sociologists, under the pressure of their actual researches, have found themselves obliged to drop this dialectical outlook. Professor Kharchev at Leningrad, for instance, found that one-fourth of the married couples were living under "abnormal housing conditions." This was a situation, he argued, common to all industrial countries; France, for example, with its "hotel families" was in a similar position. I observed that he was engaged in a revisionist enterprise, for according to the dialectical standpoint there should be a capitalist law of population and a socialist law, but not one common to all industrial societies, socialist or capitalist. Professor Kharchev, of course, denied that he was a revisionist; it would be revisionism, he said, to assert that history knows no progress, or to deny that existence determines consciousness, but it was not revisionist to ascertain a general law by means of concrete researches. Thus the dialectical method is being revised out of existence by Soviet methodologists, even as they continue to profess their unswerving loyalty. Similarly, in Moscow, one investigator has found a decline in the average size of the urban family which evidently brings it even lower than the comparable American figure. At any rate, he supports the view that a general pattern with similar birth control practices is emerging in all industrial countries, socialist as well as capitalist. But what then of Marx's attack on the Malthusian notions as arising from specific capitalist conditions? To their great good fortune, the young Soviet demographers have managed to find a canonical text, a letter of Engels to Kautsky in 1881, which acknowledges that even communist society may find itself "obliged to regulate the production of human beings," and "to achieve by planning a result which has already been produced spontaneously, without planning, in France and Lower Austria." [1] They are thus in a position to argue that a universal law and pattern of population common to both socialist and capitalist countries does not contravene their philosophy. Thereby the long paragraph on the dialectical method in Marx's second Preface to *Capital* is rescinded.

The official conception of philosophy as ideology makes it difficult for the ideologists to understand the nature of American philosophy and society. They project the Soviet model on American thought and regard American philosophy as a kind of official ideology akin to their own. I encountered this projection many times. For instance, when I lectured on "Contemporary American Thought," one questioner asked me about the influence of such Catholic philosophical journals as the *American Ecclesiastical Review, New Scholasticism,* and *Thought*. When I replied that their influence was small, he was extremely skeptical, and said that after all President Kennedy was a Catholic, and that consequently, the importance of Catholic ideology must have increased. I assured him that despite President Kennedy's election, I did not know a single colleague who read the periodicals he had named, that the fact that the President was a Catholic had in no way affected philosophical teaching in the United States, and that, if anything, I felt that Kennedy's election had strengthened the liberal rather than the ideological side of Catholicism. The questioner was puzzled. In the Soviet Union, the philosophical views of the head of the government do become those of the universities, and he found it hard to conceive that the religion of the American President was not reflected in the American universities.

The primary task of Soviet philosophers, in the government's eyes, is to serve as officers of ideological warfare against the West and against "ideological coexistence." The Institute of Philosophy should be renamed more accurately the Institute of Ideological Warfare. The Section on Bourgeois Philosophy and Sociology, for instance, instructs each research worker to prepare an authoritative refutation of some bourgeois representative; such "ideologettes" are in preparation against Husserl, Hartmann, Santayana, the German realists, Whitehead, personalism, French positivism, German neo-Thomism, and Reinhold Niebuhr.

This conception of philosophy as idealogical warfare enforces on its practitioners a spirit which we might call *"protivism."* The word "protiv" means "against"; it is the most characteristic word in Soviet philosophical essays. They are "protiv" existentialism, "protiv" pragmatism, "protiv" realism, "protiv" abstractionism, "protiv" whatever emanates from the bourgeois world. Whether it's a biography of Marx, a treatise on Buddhism, or an analysis of American culture, somewhere the Soviet ideologist is called upon by the Institute head, or his section chief, or the party group, or the magazine editors, to sound the keynote of protivism which alone shows that the given work is helping to fulfill the role assigned to philosophy in the seven-year plan.

This protivism ramifies throughout Soviet ideology in manifold ways —choice of titles of books, choice of subjects, choice of arguments. A young scholar told me of the book he is writing on the emergent evolutionists; he would like to call it, he said wistfully, *Man and Movement,* but its title will be *English and American Philosophy in the Epoch of Imperialism.* Another scholar who has turned from contemporary philosophy to ancient Asian thought in order to escape ideological pressures told me he would probably have to compromise by studying the philosophy of Nehru. I encountered an amusing instance of protivism in the person of Professor Sokolov of Moscow State University. He had reviewed my book on Spinoza recently in *Voprosy Filosofii* on the whole favorably, while regretting my lapses into "Freudo-positivism." I mentioned to him that I had sent a copy of my book to Premier Ben-Gurion of Israel who had then responded with a friendly appreciative letter. Professor Sokolov was incredulous: "But how can that be?" he said. "Your book is against (*protiv*) the Judaistical interpretation of Spinoza. How could Ben-Gurion have written you a friendly letter?" I replied that Ben-Gurion was keenly interested in Spinoza's philosophy, and that I believed he would appreciate my study for whatever scholarly merit it might have. But Professor Sokolov remained adamant. The logic of protivism dictated that the Israeli Premier should have taken a stand against my book; my friendly philosophical correspondence with him violated the "laws" of ideological warfare.

The language of protivism, militant, hortatory, embattled, finally becomes a meaningless literary convention. I met a smiling young author who presented me with a passionate pamphlet "protiv" Sidney Hook. I looked at the author and looked at the pages, and decided one was alienated from the other. He was a protivist only when engaged in the ceremonial ritualistic exorcism of some name which was not really a name but an intimation of an unreal bourgeois ghost.

The Soviet bureaucratic ideologists, moreover, evaluate their participation in international philosophical and sociological meetings in strict protivist terms. One day I asked an Institute official which Soviet philosophers were going to attend the forthcoming International Philosophical Congress in Mexico. No Soviet philosopher, of course, can decide simply on his own; he has to be chosen by the Academy of Sciences, and only after having been thus chosen is he allowed to receive the customary invitation and announcement which individual scholars receive, as a matter of course, all over the world. I said I hoped the Academy would send some of the young philosophers who were really interested in discussion with Western and Asian scholars, and whose own thinking was alive. I hoped they would not send a delegation dominated by some of those familiar official figures who had already made their appearance at the International Sociological Congress. The official replied with simple, straightforward bureaucratism, "You are wrong," he said. "Our delegation must be made up of men who can make decisions. Perhaps we can have some young philosophers accompany them, but above all we need experienced men who can make decisions." I said that no decisions were made at an international philosophical conference. The Soviet Academy, however, regards such congresses as international ideological skirmishes in which tactical decisions have to be made on the spot. Theirs is a "delegation," not a group of individual scholars who have decided entirely on their own to attend and who speak for themselves only. The Soviet delegation is organized hierarchically with a chain of command. It holds meetings at which tactics are determined. It is all thoroughly protivist, but the consequence is that the abler Soviet thinkers remain at home while the bureaucrats make jaunts abroad.

Search for intellectual freedom

The restless searching for a new philosophy manifests itself in the purely voluntary students' discussion groups which have come into existence in the universities. There is a tacit understanding within them that their discussions are sincere and private, and not to be repeated to the authorities. I got to know one such group, and found in it a curious mixture of political idealism and technocratic views, and a yearning for more intellectual freedom. The circle was composed of about twelve young instructors and graduate students. We began one evening with a discussion of the theory that the intellectuals were the ruling class in the Soviet Union. "That is not true," said one of them; "if you examine the lists of directorships of big enterprises and leading positions, you will find that most of them are held by uneducated men. The machine-bureaucrats rule, not the intellectuals." Another continued in the same vein: "I think the intellectuals should rule. I believe in technocracy. What is scientific is moral, and what is moral is scientific. Not the voting of the uneducated and ignorant, but the rule of the scientists, that is the best." Another man, however, disagreed. Although a scientist himself, he said he remained a communist, that it was a question of liberalizing the system—allowing foreign papers, journals, and statistics to circulate so they could make meaningful comparisons.

They wanted to know all about the American beatniks, with whose anti-organization and anti-establishment attitudes some of them clearly felt a kinship. They were much interested in hearing also about the all-night vigil in Berkeley after the Soviet resumption of nuclear bomb testing, and about the proliferation of student magazines. Their longing for a single free students' magazine in the Soviet Union was patent. Their ignorance of the details of international political debate was astonishing. What impressed me most was how even in such an intelligent circle the capacity for thinking in terms of political alternatives and concrete reforms has been almost extinguished. The organs of independent political reasoning have atrophied in the Soviet Union from compulsory disuse. It struck me that the most significant practicable reform in the Soviet Union today would be a simple one—to begin the publication in the newspapers of the differences of opinion in the Central Committee, or to start the regular publication of a *Central Committee Record* like our

Congressional Record. Then the habit of political discussion might reawaken among the Soviet people, and they would begin to emerge more fully from their Stalinist torpor.

The younger generation of Soviet thinkers asks above all for a final reckoning with the ethical and sociological problems of the "cult of personality." They do not share the guilt which haunts the older generation, almost universally involved in different degrees in Stalin's guilt. The older men wish to repress the problem; the younger generation observes their evasions; it is around this problem that the future of Soviet thought will be determined. A successful outcome will mean a Renaissance of Soviet Thought, as the burden of guilt is lifted from people's minds. A defeat will mean the repartition of guilt among the younger people, and another Time of Torpor.

The problem of the "cult of personality" virtually haunts Soviet social science and philosophy; the cost of its repression is the destruction of their sincerity. I asked almost all the 150 scholars I interviewed whether he or she was in any way concerned with the sociological and philosophical problems arising from the "cult" phenomena. The most frequent answer I got was "that is not my problem." A young member of the editorial board of *Voprosy Filosofii,* for instance, knows all about alienation in bourgeois society and can discourse at length on how Jaspers and Freud show the bankruptcy of their society, but when I asked him for his explanation of the Stalinist era he took refuge in: "I am not a specialist in this field." A lecturer at the Institute for International Relations pursues his labors by reading the critiques of America by Americans and rewriting them in the clichés of the decline of capitalist society. He too is facile in depicting the common man's alienation in Western society, but when asked about the Stalinist era and present-day alienation he will just pass over the former with an unctuous phrase of how regrettably bad it was, and then go on to a glib mis-description of an all-contented Soviet citizenry.

Next to taking refuge in one's specialty, the most frequent answer I got was that the explanation for the cult of personality was well known, inasmuch as it was based on Stalin's mistakes. How often I heard that self-exonerating phrase about the *oshibki* of Stalin. What is a "mistake," an *oshibka?* A child does an arithmetical problem for homework; it makes a *mistake.* The child wanted to solve the problem, but its skill with numbers was inadequate. Or a child makes a mistake in its spelling. The person who makes a mistake is always credited with motives that are sound; a mistake is a reminder of human fallibility; it does not proceed from vicious motive. Thus, the very use of *oshibka* implies that Stalin was trying to do the right thing. Its use is part of the continuing repression in the Soviet Union of the facts of Stalinism. One Soviet sociologist in Tbilisi said that when something unpleasant has occurred, we prefer to avoid speaking about it; that was why they avoided discussing the causes of Stalinism. I replied that in America the depression was unpleasant, but that we analyzed and discussed its causes. The point, of course, is that a terrible guilt is felt about Stalinism; large numbers were involved in its operations, and that is why the phenomenon is repressed by making Stalin the bearer of all that was rotten in themselves, and mitigating it all with the mild, de-emotionalized word, *oshibki*. No American felt guilty for the advent of the depression; therefore no one feared the analysis of its causes. The continuing use of *oshibki* as an explanation for a whole era's distortions is a sign that the mentality of that era persists. For there is a callousness in equating the millions of destroyed lives with a child's spelling mistakes through the use of the same word.

Soviet philosophers and sociologists are vaguely apprehensive that there are problems whose honest study might shake the foundations of their theoretical structure. For the "cult" confronts Soviet ideology with what we might call its "Great Contradiction." On the one hand, the Soviet ideologist can remain loyal to historical materialism, and explain the Stalinist superstructure in terms of the underlying economic foundation; in that case, he finds himself a critic of the Soviet social system. Or, on the other hand, he can attribute the "cult" phenomena to the effects of Stalin's paranoid personality, his persecution complex, his fears, his irrationality. In that case he would have to have recourse to psychoanalytical concepts; he would find himself becoming a Freudian despite himself, and raising such problems, furthermore, as the factors which made the Communist party so sado-masochist in its psychology that it collaborated in and glorified Stalin's rule during all that time. All sorts of intermediary theoretical positions are possible, but every intermediary position would involve an admixture of an acceptance of the totalitarian potentialities of the Soviet system and the crucial role of unconscious, irrational, "Freudian" factors in history.

Soviet ideologists still shrink from the serious study of Freud. They say the study of "subjective" motives is futile. Once I asked whether the motives of intellectuals in the socialist movement were those ascribed to them by the *Communist Manifesto*. I was told this was an unsound approach "because on this level an antinomy arises between ethical and material motives. The problem has to be dealt with objectively," they said. "One must study the laws of development which determine the shift of intellectuals without reference to their subjective motives which they think determine them." This repression of the "subjective" is probably the most basic reason for the antagonism to Freud in the Soviet Union. Psychoanalytical ideas are suspect because the Soviet regime wants people to accept all its propaganda on the manifest level, and never to enquire into latent meanings. Psychoanalysis threatens the "official face" with the underlying "real face."

A last report—and recommendations

My last talk at the Institute of Philosophy brought forth an outburst of populist bureaucratic denunciation on the part of the Director. I was asked, now that my travels in the Soviet Union were over, to give a last report on my impressions of their philosophy and sociology, and had been reluctant to do so. I explained to the Institute official that were I to speak, much that I would have to say would be unpleasant, and that perhaps it would be better if such a last report were omitted. He said they regarded me as a friend, and that the Institute had had such talks in the past from visiting Americans, whom he named. The names in question, however, were with one exception those of American communists or fellow-travelers, who, I suggested, had probably told their hosts what the latter would like to hear; the exception, a professor of sociology, had been in the country too short a time to have learned very much of what was going on. The official insisted, however, that it would be a worthwhile occasion especially for the audience which, he said, would be made up of the young researchers with whom I had had individual discussions several times. On the day in question, however, although the younger researchers were present, the discussion was monopolized by older ideologists, who had rarely participated in our previous meetings.

So the meeting began. Soviet thought, I said, was at the crossroads; its mood was best described in Turgenev's title, *On the Eve*. I proposed to raise problems to which I did not know the answer, and which I did not know how I would face were I in their place. But I had talked with scholars and students in institutes and universities in a series of "interview-dialogues," the oldest philosophical method in the world. I would compare their sociological studies with work in America.

Soviet social science seemed to me to have failed to confront four important problems: First, there was no research on the conflict of generations. In America we had several studies under way on student movements. In the Soviet Union it was denied that there was any conflict of generations. I had in the course of my travels, however, found ample evidence of such a conflict. At Leningrad University, at an open meeting of the Communist organization of the Philological Faculty, students had challenged and ridiculed the apology which the editor of *Neva* tried to present for the new party line against abstract art. There were recent occurrences at Moscow State University into which I would not enter. No Soviet sociologist, however, had shown any readiness to study the phenomena of conflict.

Second, I had found not a single article or book on anti-Semitism. They denied that there was anti-Semitism in the Soviet Union, but I had visited the synagogues of four Soviet cities, and everywhere had been told that the Jews lived in fear. I could not tell how much anti-Semitism there was; this was a subject for detailed investigation. But questions such as why there had been a recrudescence of anti-Semitism would have to be dealt with scientifically. In America, I added, where I believed there was much less anti-Semitism than in the Soviet Union, the problem was nonetheless studied extensively. At the University of California, several hundred thousand dollars were being spent in such an investigation. (The argument which followed, begun by the chairman calling me "an agent of the cold war," would take too long to tell; and there were several more heated interludes.)

I then spoke of the lack of any sociological article or book analyzing the "cult of personality." I said that in America we devoted much time to the sociology of political leadership. In the Soviet Union, however, although they evidently knew all about racial problems in Birmingham and imperialism in Asia and Africa, they could produce no scientific study of the most important recent phenomenon of political sociology in their own country. I said I didn't mean by a scientific analysis their repeating Khrushchev's phrase about the mistakes (*oshibki*) of Stalin. I could read those speeches too. I meant a sociological analysis: How many victims had there been, year by year? From what social classes had they come? What varieties of accusations had there been? Who were the accusers? How did the accusers profit by the accusations? I said they should study, too, what happened to the children of the people who were sent to Stalin's camps. When millions of people had been killed and tortured, it was not sociological analysis to refer to it as *"oshibki."* I had asked upwards of 150 sociologists and philosophers whether any one of them was studying the cult of personality, and without exception they had all replied: 'That is not my problem." I had been told that historians at the Marxism-Leninism Institute were preparing the publication of the documents on the "cult" period; I had gone to the Institute to confirm this report and spoken with its secretary. He told me emphatically they have no plans whatsoever for such a publication. I said Marx would never have concealed such documents.

I tried next to consider the sociological study of Soviet mass culture.

I said that though they criticized American culture, they did not study their own culture as the Americans did theirs. There was no study extant of the appeal, for instance, of American jazz to their youth. (Someone interrupted and said they have had other things to do.) I continued and said they had not studied the social consequences of tying their moral education to historical models—Lenin's picture as a hunter in a rifle-shop, Lenin playing chess for the chess club, Lenin with children telling them: "study, study, and study"—and present Marx's character as the model for family life. Questioned, I replied that the letters of Eleanor Marx, the daughter who had killed herself, showed there was a deep-seated unhappiness in the family, and that one factor had probably been the birth of an illegitimate son to Marx by the maid of the household, Helene Demuth. I said that on my way to Moscow I had visited the International Institute of Social History to confirm the existence of documentary evidence on this matter, and had been informed the evidence was incontrovertible. The chairman was quite interested, and one of his colleagues then piped up: "That accords with Marx's saying 'Nihil humani a me alienum puto'." The only Marxian joke I ever heard at the Institute.

Many of those present had to leave at this time for a candidate's examination. The chairman proposed another meeting, but I said I was leaving shortly and would summarize briefly what I had to say concerning their philosophical work. I discussed my characterization of their philosophical attitude as "protivism" and the development of "Soviet existentialism." I spoke of the interest in Freud, despite the great difficulty in securing his books. Then I went on to develop my "law of the spectrum," the emergence of diverse philosophies in the Soviet Union, with critical realists in the Russell fashion, positivists, mathematical logicians opposed to the dialecticians, and those who emphasized "practice" indistinguishable from American pragmatists. Heads were shaken in vigorous disagreement. Finally, I said that if I had a "last message" it was that Soviet thought now needed someone who would do for it what John Stuart Mill did for England and Ralph Waldo Emerson for America—to emphasize not "class," not "people," but the importance of the individual.

Notes

1. *Cf. Marx and Engels on Malthus* (London, 1953), pp. 108-109.

The new sociology in the Soviet Union

GEORGE FISCHER

I. Science and politics

Soviet scholarship, or Science in the broad sense, is today extending professional recognition and granting autonomy to a field of learning that until recently hardly existed in the USSR. The field is sociology. Its status as a full-fledged member of the scholarly community, however, is still far from complete. As yet, too, it has not carried out its many stated aspirations and plans. The next few years will tell us more than can be known now about progress in both of these areas. What is already clear, however, is that we are witnessing some significant new beginnings in the field of sociology in the USSR.

Some of the earliest first-hand observations on these new beginnings were made in May 1961. At that time, Robert K. Merton (Columbia University) and Henry W. Riecken (National Science Foundation) took part in an official exchange visit of ten prominent American social scientists. This is how Merton and Riecken concluded their report:

> The degree of detail in analyzing sociological problems appears to be hedged in by official doctrine, value-orientations, and received convictions to a degree which seems scarcely recognized by the research workers themselves. To some extent, this affects their orientation to methods of analyzing empirical data. Multivariate analysis becomes simply irrelevant when practical empiricism calls only for identifying broad aggregates of people who behave in distinctive ways, and when sociological research is conceived as primarily the handmaiden of programmed social action. Yet, once again, and without essaying the dubious role of prophets, we are inclined to believe that as empirical research develops in Soviet sociology, there will occur a growing convergence between at least the methods developed in the USSR and in the United States.[1]

From George Fischer, *Science and Politics: The New Sociology in the Soviet Union* (Ithaca, N.Y.: Center for International Studies, Cornell University, 1964), pp. 1-19, 66.

In the two or three years since the Merton Report, no radical change took place. Very little if anything in this report requires major modification. At the same time, here and there these years did produce crystallization of the field.

Three such areas of crystallization stand out. First, there has been some clarification in the Soviet image of sociology—both the scholarly image and the official image. Secondly, there has been a growth in the number of scholars and institutions more actively involved in the new sociology. Finally, there is now more published research and theory available to suggest and to answer a key question: Why, and in what ways, is sociology in the Soviet Union predominantly a sociology of work?

In Soviet programmatic statements on the new sociology, one particular theme recurs. This is the determination to be scientific—"scientific" not only in the special Soviet sense of Marxism-Leninism as a scientific doctrine of society, but also in the usual sense of rigorous and verifiable methods of seeking knowledge.

In 1962 a major paper on the subject was presented to the Fifth World Congress of Sociology, meeting in Washington, D.C. The statement came from two prominent social scientists, G. V. Osipov and M. T. Yovchuk:

> Concrete social studies provide the foundation for scientific sociology. They are the substance for scientific generalization. . . .
>
> The scientific determination of the methods and the techniques of research is an important part of social study in Soviet society.[2]

A month after the publication of the Osipov Paper, the leading scholars of the country—the senior members of the USSR Academy of Sciences —lent their names to another statement which emphasized the same theme. This statement describes the views and decisions on Soviet social sciences adopted at an annual general meeting of the Academy in October 1962. Echoing recurrent official condemnations of petty, impractical, or overly theoretical scholarship, the academicians' statement stressed:

> The general meeting of the USSR Academy of Sciences considers that an absolute requirement for the success of scientific work in social sciences on actual problems is concrete social investigation . . . .
>
> It is essential to provide wide application to the humanities of precise scientific methods, especially mathematics, cybernetics, statistics, and the like, to broaden field studies, to practice widely scientific experiments . . . .

Acting along these lines, the Academy general meeting decided: "to widen field work significantly, to assure more extensive development of statistical materials and their skillful use, and to apply mathematical and other advanced scientific methods more widely." [3]

Official support for such a policy came at the same general meeting of the Academy. It was voiced in a major policy speech by L. F. Ilichev, CPSU Presidium member and a Secretary of the Central Committee who heads the party's Ideological Commission. In his speech, which preceded the academicians' just-quoted statement, Ilichev insisted that Soviet science as a whole must now pay far greater attention and deference to the social sciences. The high party official pictured the growing output and stature of Soviet social sciences—including sociology—as part of the overall changes of the past few years and the overcoming of the Cult of Personality. In calling for even greater development of the social sciences in the USSR, Ilichev made clear the main reasons for such development, and the proper relationship between science as scholarship, science as doctrine, and politics:

> The Marxist-Leninist science of society forms the scientific basis of the party's domestic as well as its foreign policy .... Now that our homeland has entered the period of full-scale building of communism, many new theoretical questions are coming up before the party ....
>
> This causes a constantly increasing volume of theoretical activity by our party and its headquarters, the party Central Committee.... The specialists and institutions in the social sciences are the party's active helpers in working out scientific principles for directing the development of Soviet society. [4]

How leading social scientists themselves speak of this intimate link of science and politics is illustrated by the Osipov Paper. Referring to "a good many concrete sociological experiments" of recent years, the paper goes so far as to include among them the new program of the Communist party, adopted in 1961. As the Osipov Paper puts it:

> The new program of the CPSU is an example of concrete research conducted by sociologists. The program is based on profound and varied economic, sociological, statistical, and other social research conducted by party, governmental, and scientific organizations, and it directs major social changes for the next twenty years.

Osipov and his co-author, Yovchuk, also spell out the central, underlying purpose of the newer scientific studies. "These studies help us to find ways of influencing social events through public opinion and support." [5]

After dwelling similarly on the internal, domestic tasks of Soviet social scientists, the academicians' statement of October 1962 turns to a second major domain:

> The international obligation of Soviet scholars is to intensify the criticism of bourgeois ideology and first of all the reactionary conceptions of anti-communism. Criticism of bourgeois and reformist ideology must debunk not only the conclusions but also the arguments of anti-communist ideologists fearlessly and on scientific grounds. For this purpose it is essential to study the contemporary economy, politics, culture, and ideology of foreign countries deeply and comprehensively. The direct duty of scholars is to inform the world's public widely about the successes of the Soviet Union in all spheres of life, including the realm of the humanities.[6]

To attack "bourgeois" ideas and foreign criticisms of communism, to acquire significant additional knowledge of the outside world in order to do this all the better, and to continue ceaselessly broadcasting Soviet achievements abroad—these are the clearly formulated international tasks of Soviet social scientists.

If the new sociology is avowedly and unmistakably part and parcel of politics, in the sense of official activities and policy-making, can we speak at all of science—of a new field of scholarship emerging in the USSR? The answer appears to be that both the officials and the scholars involved are now committed to the belief that public policy and the state in general —notably the party and its leaders—can and will gain from encouraging extensive scholarly work and advanced research methods. The framework and goals are to be those of politics, but the methods of fact-gathering, and analysis of the facts, are to conform to the canons of science.

Such an intimate and all-encompassing bond between a dominant state and an emerging field is unique in the annals of modern science. Scholars abroad are bound to wonder whether this intimate bond can produce any scientific harvest whatsoever. No conclusive answer is possible for at least several years. Meanwhile, official statements have offered two different arguments as to why the arrangement is not necessarily detrimental to the new Soviet sociology.

In his major speech to the Academy, Ilichev emphasized the advantages of "the monolithic nature" of Soviet social science:

> Some of our opponents in the West try to present as a shortcoming what is an enormous merit of Marxist-Leninist science—its unity and monolithic nature . . . .
> It seems not to occur to the bourgeois critics that the merits of sociology, and for that matter of any other science, lie not at all in

diversity of points of view. Depth and correctness in reflecting objective reality, foresight as to the ways and laws of its development, and richness in practical results—these are the integral qualities of true science . . . .

The single and unified Marxist-Leninist world view is a source of strength for our sociology.[7]

On a more technical level, the Osipov Paper to the Fifth World Congress of Sociology raises another point that lies at the heart of this singular Soviet link between social science and public policy. According to Osipov and Yovchuk, a social science of the Soviet type can and does permit the use of all-encompassing research methods. The contrast here is to Western or "bourgeois" sociology. In Soviet eyes, sociology in the West is retarded or even crippled by accepting research findings based on only one or two of a great number of possible research methods.

Aided and abetted both by a doctrine or science of society (Marxism-Leninism) and by guidance from the state, Soviet sociology in the view of its spokesmen, benefits greatly by the wide scope of its research methods. These methods, in turn, derive from the field's theoretical and organizational foundations:

> Sociology in the Soviet Union combines the scientific methods of sociological research, [while] in Western sociology they are usually divided into objective and subjective. Sociological research in the USSR includes analysis of statistical reports and official papers, analysis of forms and methods of the activity of workers' organizations, discussions with workers about their sociological problems, social environment, outward and inside observations, written and oral polls, study of personal documents, etc.[8]

Not long ago, a methodological essay by two Leningrad sociologists carried further this distinction between Soviet and Western sociology.

> Bourgeois positivist sociologists usually contrast "theoretical" or "pure" with "applied" sociology. This is a peculiar method of "compensating" for the sterility and complete impotence in the area of general theory by the amount of practical results of empirical research, which is on the whole commissioned directly by capitalist monopolies and government agencies. All of this research is in general aimed at weakening social conflict within the framework of capitalism and finding effective means of "social control" in the interests of the ruling top group. As far as general sociological theory is concerned, it, as R. Merton notes, now stands on the level of medicine in the sixteenth century, and therefore serious demands cannot be made of it.
>
> The situation in Marxist sociology is completely different. Marxist

sociological research, no matter how "theoretical" it is, always retains an applied purpose, and conversely applied research contains within it data for theoretical generalizations. The question is merely one of the degree of practical use, and of the breadth and depth of theoretical conclusions. For a Marxist sociologist, it is mandatory to keep in mind this principle, the unity of theory and practice. Marxist theoretical studies, as the Program of the CPSU emphasizes, must "light the path for practice, to help identify and remove the obstacles and difficulties which impede the successful building of communism." This approach protects the scholar from simple anecdotage [*illiustrativnost*] on the one hand and pure speculation on the other.[9]

A concrete example of this position of the new sociology can be seen in the use made of public opinion polls. A discussion of this example may throw light on the methods and plans of the field, especially since occasional references to recent Soviet work in opinion polling have appeared in the West.

The two authors most closely associated with Soviet opinion polling (B.A. Grushin and V.V. Chikin) are themselves social scientists, and their published work refers to collaboration with sociologists as well as statisticians. However, this opinion polling is not carried out or sponsored by anyone directly associated with the new Soviet sociology. Instead, its initiator and sponsor is the central daily newspaper of the Communist Youth League, *Komsomolskaia Pravda*. For this purpose, the paper organized a Public Opinion Institute of its own, the first known Soviet organization bearing any such name. The youth opinion polls are announced and conducted in the pages of *Komsomolskaia Pravda*. Some of these polls were subsequently described in separate pamphlets, and more recently in a book.[10]

The heart of the "Confessions of a Generation" poll were twelve questions published in *Komsomolskaia Pravda* in January 1961. The book on the poll states that after the twenty-day limit set for mailing replies to the newspaper, the Institute of Public Opinion analyzed the answers with the help of statistics students, researchers of the Philosophy Institute, and the main computing unit of the government's Central Statistical Administration. According to a footnote describing the statistical process, all of the answers received were coded and analyzed with the aid of sorters and computers. This was done by reducing answers to the twelve questions—most of which were open-ended—to 170 possibilities which were then coded. Some of the statistical results are reported with specific breakdowns for occupation, age, size of community, level of education, and the like. Answers to other questions are presented in gross statistical form only.[11]

A lengthy comment on the 1961 youth poll, by a Soviet sociologist—a specialist in public opinion—praised the poll's picture of the younger generation as overwhelmingly devoted to Soviet ways and ideals. But he noted the dearth of Soviet work in public opinion polling, as reflected in part in the "Confessions of a Generation." [12] The general attitude of Soviet sociology appears to go even further than this in contrasting any single research method, like opinion polling, to the catholicity of methods that it regards as one of its main sources of strength and promise. The authoritative Soviet statement at the last World Congress of Sociology leaves little doubt about this:

> Some Western sociologists tend to identify concrete sociological research with the taking of popular polls. In our opinion, this is an erroneous point of view. Public polls can provide valuable results only if scrupulously prepared and conducted in conjunction with other methods of sociological research. Questionnaires are valid instruments of sociological science only if they can be compared with a mass of subjective answers to definite objective data and if they expose the natural link between objective and dependent subjective processes of comprehension. In our opinion, all information gathered from polls should be checked and supplemented with data gathered by other methods.[13]

The new Soviet sociology takes the same view, presumably, of a peculiarly Soviet research method described in the Osipov Paper as "discussions with workers about their sociological problems." The Merton Report refers to these discussions as mass interviews. In Soviet usage they are called "theoretical conferences." "Theoretical conferences" consist of large public gatherings in an enterprise or community being studied. These gatherings are attended by members of the groups under investigation—usually factory workers or peasants on collective farms. They are also attended by leaders and members of research teams, as well as local officials of the party, government, trade unions, and youth organizations. Representatives of these participating groups speak during the "theoretical conferences."

Early in 1963 such a "theoretical conference" took place in Kalinovka, the Russian village which has received attention of late as the birthplace of Khrushchev, and as a spot which he frequently revisits. According to an extensive account in a leading scholarly journal, over 500 local residents participated in this meeting. The topic was "the upbringing of the new man in a collective farm setting." Like the scholarly commentary on the youth polling, the description of the Kalinovka theoretical conference speaks warmly of the attitudes expressed. But it does not mention any specific research techniques employed to quantify or verify the views expressed by various speakers. Nor is any sociologist or sociological center identified with the "theoretical conference." [14]

The new Soviet sociology thus appears to turn its back on any single method such as opinion polling or "theoretical conferences." At the same time, its spokesmen also emphasize that "sociological research in the USSR is much more concerned with actual life situations than with studies under laboratory conditions." This avowal, however, appears together with an equally strong statement in favor of advanced methods of research:

> We believe that the use of mathematical and statistical methods (the law of averages, the law of multitudes, the theory of games, etc.) will be fruitful in concrete social research, for they provide an accurate and objective description of the quantitative aspects of social processes and events. Laboratories for mathematical methods in economics created at the Section of Economics of the Academy of Sciences of the USSR and at the Siberian Section of the Academy are beginning to use mathematics more and more as a means of analysis of concrete economic processes. A large role is reserved for mathematics in modeling social processes and events as well. Economic science has already started work on social modeling, deemed a matter of the utmost importance with a promising future. Sociology is following the same course. By feeding data into an electronic computer it is possible to obtain comparisons between social events and concrete social conditions in the laboratories.[15]

The Soviet image of sociology emerges clearly when we see how the leading scholarly journals reacted to the "Sverdlovsk Study," [16] to which reference was made in the Merton Report and also in the *American Sociological Review*.[17] This volume of 550 pages grew out of extensive local investigation in Sverdlovsk, the industrial center of the Urals region, and unquestionably constituted "a first" for the field. Its topic, too, lay at the heart of the new sociology; this is well reflected in the title of the book, which in English might best be rendered as *The Growth of General Education and Vocational Training of Soviet Industrial Labor*. Despite the important topic and the unprecedented scope of the Sverdlovsk study, fellow sociologists criticized the book sharply in their two main journals, *Voprosy Filosofii* (Questions of Philosophy) and *Filosofskie Nauki* (Philosophical Sciences). To be sure, these and other reviewers hailed the book as a significant step. Their criticisms, however, tell us a good deal about Soviet aspirations in the field.

The *Voprosy Filosofii* reviewers emphasize a point that applies to much present-day Soviet sociology. "This is the first major study of its kind. The team of authors had neither prior experience [in social research] nor some previously worked out methods of research." The reviewers question an approach which includes the workers' political "consciousness" and their overall orientation to society under the heading of "training." They make the point that workers might conceivably be well trained, and work well, while lacking the desired norms and values, and conversely might have these and not perform well. More generally, the review concludes that:

> The book reflects some common shortcomings in the structure of scientific work [in Soviet sociology]. During the first stage of developing concrete sociological investigations in the capital, as well as in outlying areas, the research conducted was quite naturally on the same currently important subjects. This was often done without exchange of experience, without appropriate coordination of activities. Sometimes there was an unwarranted scattering of people and resources, an amateurishness in methods which is the main reason for the slight value of some of the results. [Without rigorous coordination of plans and methods, and also panel-type follow-up], research results will amount to a kind of "fly-by-night" affair, rather like the data of ordinary sporadic surveys.[18]

It is revealing that both of these major reviews of the Sverdlovsk study agree on one shortcoming of the book. As *Voprosy Filosofii* puts it, some chapters lack a theme or thesis, and limit themselves to either established propositions or pure facts. To this comment the review adds that the implied separation here between social theory and social research is wrong—each needs the other.[19] In the words of the *Filosofskie Nauki* review, the book contains too few empirical ("concrete sociological") generalizations.[20]

The significance of these particular comments lies in one question: what kind of theorizing might Soviet sociologists do—above and beyond, that is, the ever reiterated general canons of Marxism-Leninism? In this connection, a 1962 paper by a leading Soviet sociologist—G. M. Andreeva, of Moscow University—specifically brings up Merton's "theories of the middle range." Andreeva's reaction helps to explain why the Sverdlovsk study could limit itself to anecdotage, descriptive statistics, and references to major official statements. As Andreeva puts it:

> . . . a quite definite purpose is assigned [to "theories of the middle range"]—to attain in sociological research a certain level of generalizations. But the suggested "level" is the level of a relatively low order of abstraction, which on principle does not go beyond empirical data.

"Theoretical" knowledge on this level is again in the category of empirical knowledge, for theory itself is in essence reduced to the level of empirical generalizations. . . .[21]

The same explicit opposition to "theories of the middle range" appears in the Osipov Paper to the Fifth World Congress of Sociology:

Merton's view that sociology is not yet ripe for a comprehensive integral theory and that there are only a few theories available at an intermediate level of abstraction whose significance is relative and temporary is well known.

We feel justified in believing that this definition cannot be applied to Marxist scientific sociology. The materialistic comprehension of history, first described by Marx approximately 125 years ago, has been time-tested and has been proved by the entire process of historical development. The materialistic understanding of history is based on the concrete study of social life. The emergence of Marxism in the 1840's and its further development has been organically linked to and supported by research on specific social problems.[22]

Two Leningrad sociologists recently elaborated on this theme:

Thus the [bourgeois] positivist finds himself inside a vicious circle, from which he tries to find a way out through the notorious "theory of the middle range" (R. Merton). This theory is offered as a transitional but quite independent link between empirical data and general sociological theory. The leeway for generalization in it does not go beyond the limits of a relatively narrow circle of observable phenomena. However, this attempt to construct independent "miniature theories" (H. L. Zetterberg) is clearly doomed to failure: not one of the processes we study actually exists in isolation from other processes, and the refusal to consider these interconnections leads merely to distorting the correct understanding of reality. Consequently, what matters is not whether or not "theories of the middle range" have the right to exist, but the fact that they cannot exist in a vacuum, isolated from general theoretical conceptions, and out of touch with a scientific conception of history as a whole.[23]

The authoritative comments on the Sverdlovsk study suggest that rejection of "middle range" theorizing may create a very real problem for the new sociology. All of it could conceivably be as limited in scientific "pay-off" as the Sverdlovsk study was judged to be. It remains to be seen whether the field can fruitfully limit itself to scholarly fact-gathering and reaffirmation of officially molded theory. For the moment, at least, the Soviet image of sociology seems to insist on this particular combination of science and politics.

II. Philosophers, social scientists, sociologists

If in some ways the scientific aspirations of the new sociology currently run ahead of actual performance, there is also still uncertainty as to which scholars, and which scientific organizations, properly belong to the field. Like the Soviet image itself, however, this is an area of ongoing crystallization. It will help us most immediately if we can understand which Soviet scholars are called "sociologists," and why. For at present, there are three possible meanings of the term "sociology" in the USSR and three corresponding groups of scholars who may be referred to as "sociologists."

The Merton Report already pointed to two different Soviet usages of "sociology." In one case it means all of Marxist-Leninist philosophy, and is a synonym for Marxian social and political thought—a synonym which derives from both Marx and Lenin. This first usage enjoys wide currency today. The other meaning is "concrete sociological investigation," [24] that is, social research of an empirical kind. This use of the word is not entirely new—it goes back to the 1920's. But present Soviet statements emphasize that it is this dimension of social science that fell into special disfavor and neglect during the Stalin era, and is now being revived with particular vigor.

Yet it would be wrong to limit the question of Soviet definitions of "sociology" to this dichotomy between theory and research. First of all, "concrete sociological investigation" turns out to be a broadly conceived term, covering empirical research in all of the social sciences. Repeatedly, official and scholarly statements illustrate the fact that "concrete sociological investigation" refers to a wide variety of social research, and not to any one discipline such as sociology. For instance, this is the usage followed most often at the Academy general meeting on the social sciences in October 1962, both by the official keynote speaker, Ilichev, and by the academicians who commented on his speech. The term is used in the same way throughout the Osipov Paper to the Fifth World Congress of Sociology.

Beyond the fact that "concrete sociological investigation" is actually equated with social research rather than with sociology, there is a third Soviet usage that must be considered, and which comes closest to the prevailing meaning of the word "sociology" in the rest of the world. In this sense, "sociology" refers to the work of separate groups of scholars, with a distinctive set of theories and research methods, as well as institutional affiliations. In the Soviet Union this third meaning is the least widely used.

In terms of the actual scholars involved, however, this third usage is important, since it does describe those Soviet scholars who meet the prevailing international conception of the term. These are the "sociologists" in the first sense—philosophers concentrating on the social and political philosophy of Marxism-Leninism—who are at the same time actively engaged in empirical social research. The work of this empirically oriented sub-group of philosophers is at times described as *"sociological* research," in contrast to the *"social* research" carried out by social scientists in general.[25]

Soviet philosophy as a whole deals with three types of general laws: laws of nature, personality, and society. Historical Materialism, the social philosophy of Marxism-Leninism, focuses on the general laws of society alone. "Sociology," in the third sense of the word, is in the USSR today a branch of philosophy that also specializes in the study of the laws of society. However, it studies not only general laws but specific laws as well. This synthesizing of general laws of society with empirical research on related specific phenomena constitutes another key distinction between the new sociology and the rest of philosophy and social science.

One of the dichotomies involved here is between the new sociology and Historical Materialism. For several years, as the Merton Report mentions, a discussion went on in public and elsewhere as to how, if at all, the dichotomy was to be seen. By now the various solutions advanced may number as many as one or two dozen, and the discussion is not yet at an end. But gradually a division of labor appears to be emerging between philosophers in Historical Materialism who deal with general laws and the partly generalizing and partly specializing sociologists.[26]

Meanwhile, however, the actual lines between these three groups of scholars—and the three meanings of "sociology"—are not at all clearly drawn. On the contrary, the same statements are likely to lump them together or to refer to them alternately. This correctly reflects the actual state of affairs. In the past few years, the new active interest in sociology has thrown the three groups together, and most discussions and undertakings relating to the subject are likely to involve spokesmen and participants from all three groups.

A major example of this is the Sverdlovsk study. It was produced by a team of scholars headed by the long-active Soviet social and political philosopher, M. T. Yovchuk, Corresponding (Associate) Member of the Academy. His closest associates were two other philosophers, Professor M. N. Rutkevich and *Docent* (Associate Professor) L. N. Kogan, both of the Philosophy Faculty of Ural University in Sverdlovsk. Unlike Yovchuk, Rutkevich and Kogan are themselves actively engaged in social research. (They head the Ural University's Social Research Laboratory.) Finally, much of the research for the Sverdlovsk study was undertaken by scholars from other social sciences, notably economists, and education specialists.

Another example of the current situation can be seen by looking at the scholars who represent the field at international scientific meetings. In recent years, this group has always included "pure" philosophers, philosophers involved in social research, and other social scientists associated with empirical studies.

Important though this threefold distinction is in clarifying the current Soviet use of the term "sociology," a few additional points ought to be made about the various scholars involved. To begin with, the philosopher-sociologists either themselves direct the organizations now being set up or share this direction with the other philosophers. At the same time, research by other social scientists is being done either under the aegis of the philosophers, or in quite different institutions. Examples of these are research and teaching institutes in economics, education, and psychology. Thus in the realm of institutions, "social research" is apt to be associated with organizations directed by some type of philosopher and not by other social scientists.

A further point is most important. There is something of a generational difference between "pure" social and political philosophers in the Soviet Union, and the philosophers presently immersing themselves in empirical social research. The "pure" philosophers now active and predominant are in their fifties and sixties, while the philosopher-sociologists are in their early forties or (most often) in their twenties and thirties. The older philosophers do not share their involvement in field studies and new research methods. Instead, their domain remains Marxist ideology, and their writings continue to be oriented to current formulations of official doctrine.

This does not mean, however, that the two types of philosophers are altogether different from each other. First of all, the most active scholars in the younger generation are just as deeply involved as their elders in social and political philosophy, in ideology and doctrine, in party membership and party work. And, most immediately, they tend to share their elders' view that philosophy deals not only with the general laws of nature and man but also with the workings of society, and that sociology is properly a branch of philosophy which specializes in both the general and the specific laws of society. This is one reason why the younger generation's writings appear so similar to that of the older generation.

Furthermore, there are a number of prominent younger philosophers who stand closer to "pure" philosophy in the kind of work they do than to the new Soviet sociology. An example is furnished by the learned Secretary of the Philosophy Institute, *Docent* V. V. Mshvenieradze. Another example is Professor I. S. Kon and *Docent* Yu. A. Aseev of the Philosophy Faculty of Leningrad University. While the research of all three includes American sociology, the context is logic or the history of philosophy.

One last point further complicates the picture. Much of the strongest and most decisive support for the new sociology comes from "pure" philosophers and ideologists of both the older and the middle generations. The fact that the Soviet image of sociology now calls for scientific and advanced research methods cannot be ascribed to the research-oriented younger philosophers themselves. They are too few, and their work too recent, to have achieved such a significant shift in official and scholarly views.

In the present paper, the extent and nature of the current older-generation backing has already been brought out through mention of the major social science speech of Ilichev, a top party leader and ideologist. Also notably active in supporting the new sociology are a group of ideologists who currently occupy key positions in Soviet academic life. These backers of the new sociology have held both party and academic posts, and at present seem to stand at the pinnacle of this ideological-academic domain:

(1) Academician P. N. Fedoseev, now one of the vice-presidents of the Soviet Academy and a member of the party's Central Committee. Born in 1908, Fedoseev in the 1940's served as an official in the Central Committee secretariat. From the mid-forties on he was chief editor of the party's main theoretical journal (*Bolshevik,* now *Kommunist*), and in the early 1950's chief editor of its organizational journal, *Partiinaia Zhizn.* Until 1960 Fedoseev directed the Philosophy Institute of the USSR Academy of Sciences.

(2) Academician Yu. P. Frantsev, president of the party's Academy of Social Sciences and also of the new Soviet Sociological Association. In the late 1940's Frantsev worked in the Soviet Ministry of Foreign Affairs, and in the middle fifties as an editor of *Pravda.* Born in 1903.

(3) F. V. Konstantinov, Corresponding Member of the Academy and present director of its Philosophy Institute. Since the 1930's Konstantinov has been in party work. After World War II he joined the

Philosophy Institute. In the mid-fifties he occupied posts in the Central Committee staff as head of the Academy of Social Sciences and then of the *"Agitprop"* department. In the late 1950's Konstantinov became chief editor of *Kommunist*. Born in 1901.

It is from this intermingling and criss-crossing of philosophers, sociologists, and other social scientists that the new sociology is emerging in the Soviet Union. We can now begin to distinguish between these three groups of scholars and the three parallel Soviet usages of "sociology." Yet we can do no more than link the new Soviet sociology with one of these groups: that of the younger social and political philosophers who in their own work stress not only general laws of society but also empirical research on more specific social phenomena related to these general laws ("sociological research"). Beyond that, crystallization has not yet gone.[27]

Conclusion

In all of its theory and research, the new sociology in the USSR represents a singular fusion of science with politics. On the level of theory this means the fusion of academic analysis of society with an official doctrine of society. On the level of research the fusion is between scholarship and all-out service to an omnicompetent state. Within this pattern some Soviet sociologists are starting to ask important specialized questions and to validate their answers empirically.

Scientifically, such first steps and new beginnings are significant no matter what the future may bring. In terms of doctrine and policy, the very closeness in this case of science and politics bestows upon Soviet sociologists a novel role in an intricately changing society. At least in the sense of a barometer or weather vane, it could turn out to be true in the USSR that "as sociology goes, so goes the nation."

Notes

1. Robert K. Merton and Henry W. Riecken, "Notes on Sociology in the USSR," in National Institute of Social and Behavioral Science, Symposia Studies Series no. 10, *Current Problems in Social-Behavioral Research* (Washington, D.C.), March 1962, p. 7. This report is hereafter cited as *Merton Report*.

2. G. Osipov and M. Yovchuk, "Some Principles of Theory, Problems, and Methods of Research in Sociology in the USSR," *American Sociological Review*, vol. 28, no. 4 (August 1963), p. 621, 622. This paper is hereafter cited as *Osipov Paper*.

3. "Zadachi Razvitiia Obshchestvennykh Nauk v Usloviiakh Razvernutogo Stroitelstva Kommunizma, Postanovlenie Obshchego Sobraniia Akademii Nauk SSSR" (The Tasks of Developing the Social Sciences in the Course of Actively Building Communism, A Resolution of the General Meeting of the USSR Acad-

emy of Sciences), *Vestnik Akademii Nauk SSSR,* XXXII. no. 12 (December 1962), 61-62.

4. L. F. Ilichev, "Nauchnaia Osnova Rukovodstva Razvitiem Obschchestva, Nekotorye Problemy Razvitiia Obschchestvennykh Nauk" (The Scientific Basis of Guiding the Development of Society, Some Problems in the Development of the Social Sciences), *Vestnik Akademii Nauk SSSR,* XXXI, no. 11 (November 1962), 11. A *Pravda* summary of the Ilichev speech is translated in *Current Digest of the Soviet Press,* XIV, no. 42 (November 14, 1962).

5. Osipov Paper, p. 622.

6. "Zadachi Razvitiia Obshchestvennykh Nauk v Usloviiakh Razvernutogo Stroitelstva Kommunizma, Postanovlenie Obshchego Sobraniia Akademii Nauk SSSR" (The Tasks of Developing the Social Sciences in the Course of Actively Building Communism, A Resolution of the General Meeting of the USSR Academy of Sciences), *Vestnik Akademii Nauk SSSR,* XXXII, no. 12 (December 1962), 61-62.

7. L. F. Ilichev, "Nauchnaia Osnova Rukovodstva Razvitiem Obshchestva, Nekotorye Problemy Razvitiia Obshchestvennykh Nauk" (The Scientific Basis of Guiding the Development of Society, Some Problems in the Development of the Social Sciences), *Vestnik Akademii Nauk SSSR,* XXXII, no. 11 (November 1962), 30.

8. Osipov Paper, p. 622.

9. A. G. Zdravomyslov and V. A. Yadov, "O Programirovanii Konkretnogo Sotsialnogo Issledovania" (On the Programming of Concrete Social Investigations), *Voprosy Filosofii,* XVII, no. 8 (1963), 74.

10. B. A. Grushin and V. V. Chikin, *Ispoved Pokoleniia* (Confessions of a Generation), (Moscow: Publishing House of the Communist Youth League, 1962).

11. The nature of this and other youth opinion polls may be gathered from the twelve questions around which the 248-page book is built. They were worded as follows:

1. What do you think about your generation—do you like it and are you satisfied with what it is doing?

2. On what do you base your statement?

3. What, from your point of view, are the strongest features of Soviet youth? Where are they revealed most clearly?

4. Are there, in your opinion, negative features in young people that appear widely? If yes, precisely what?

5. Where do you see confirmation of your opinion?

6. What do you think is more typical of your contemporaries, purposefulness or lack of purpose?

7. Do you personally have a purpose in life?

8. What does it consist of?

9. What must you do to achieve it?

10. What have you done already?

11. Do you consider that you will attain your goal?

12. What is your conviction based on?

12. M. Kh. Igitkhanian, "Dukhovnyi Oblik Sovetskoi Molodezhi" (The Spiritual Face of Soviet Youth), *Voprosy Filosofii,* XVII, no. 6 (1963). A translation of Igitkhanian's paper is published in *Current Digest of the Soviet Press,* XV, no. 39 (October 23, 1963), under the title "The Methods and Purposes of Public Opinion Polls."

13. Osipov Paper, p. 622.

14. T. I. Arkhipova and M. V. Belov, "Teoreticheskaia Konferentsiia v Sele Kalinovke" (Theoretical Conference in Kalinovka Village), *Voprosy Filosofii,* XVII, no. 5 (1963).

15. Osipov Paper, p. 622. The extent of potential Soviet interest is reflected

by a paper of a social scientist and statistician published by *Voprosy Filosofii* "for purposes of discussion": P. P. Maslov, "Model Building in Sociological Research," *Soviet Sociology*, I, No. 1 (Summer 1962), translated from *Voprosy Filosofii*, XVI, no. 3 (1962).

16. *Podem Kulturno-Tekhnicheskogo Urovnia Sovetskogo Rabochego Klassa* (The Rise of the Cultural and Technical Level of the Soviet Working Class), edited by M. T. Yovchuk and others, (Moscow: Publishing House of Social and Economic Literature, 1961).

17. A review of the Sverdlovsk study appears in the *American Sociological Review* for June 1963 (vol. 28, no. 3).

18. *Voprosy Filosofii*, XVI, no. 2 (1962), 167.

19. *Voprosy Filosofii*, XVI, no. 2 (1962), 164, 167.

20. *Filosofskie Nauki*, V, no. 2 (1962), 139.

21. G. M. Andreeva, "Burzhuaznaia Empiricheskaia Sotsiologiia v Poiskakh Vykhoda iz Krizisa" (Bourgeois Empirical Sociology Seeks a Way Out of Its Crisis), *Filosofskie Nauki*, V, no. 5 (1962), 39.

22. Osipov Paper, p. 620.

23. A. G. Zdravomyslov and V. A. Yadov, "O Programirovanii Konkretnogo Sotsialnogo Issledovaniia" (On the Programming of Concrete Social Investigations), *Voprosy Filosofii*, XVII, no. 8 (1963), 81.

A more general criticism of the structural-functional theory in contemporary American sociology appears in M. Sh. Bakhitov, "Problema Prichinnosti v Sotsiologii i Kritika Funktsionalizma" (The Problem of Causation in Sociology and the Critque of Functionalism), *Voprosy Filosofii*, XVII, no. 9. (1963). On the other hand, a West German social scientist has argued the "incompatibility" between the new Soviet sociology and Western-type empirical research: René Ahlberg, "Die Sowjetische Gesellschaftwissenschaft und die Empirische Sozialforschung" (Soviet Social Science and Empirical Social Research), *Osteuropa* (Stuttgart), vol. 13, no. 10 (October 1963).

24. *Konkretnoe Sotsiologicheskoe Issledovanie.*

25. An addition to this terminological heterogeneity is a further twofold Soviet usage, which also involves sociology. Soviet scholars and officials often use the terms "social sciences" and "humanities" interchangeably. At other times, Soviet usage designates as "social sciences" only selected areas within the humanities.

"Social science" in the narrower sense covers the areas most directly linked to the Soviet conception of Marxism-Leninism. In philosophy, this means Historical Materialism, Dialectical Materialism, and the most recently established separate area of the Theory of Scientific Communism (the study of the future development of society); in economics, Political Economy (general theory and policy, as against applied economics); in history, the History of the Communist Party in the Soviet Union. All of sociology, it should be noted, falls within this second, more specialized Soviet meaning of the term "social science."

26. A current variant of the Historical Materialism–sociology discussion consists of revising and delineating the standard Soviet university course on Historical Materialism. Professor D. I. Chesnokov, chairman of the Historical Materialism department (*kafedra*) of Moscow University's Philosophy Faculty, contributed to this effort recently in the *Voprosy Filosofii* department headed "Discussions and Comments": D. I. Chesnokov, "O Strukture Isoricheskogo Materializma" (On the Structure of Historical Materialism), *Voprosy Filosofii*, XVIII, no. 7 (1963).

A major earlier statement in the discussion came from Professor P. V. Rozhin, formerly Chesnokov's counterpart as chairman of the Historical Materialism department of Leningrad University, and now the Dean of the entire Philosophy Faculty at Leningrad: V. P. Rozhin, *Vvedenie v Marksistskuiu Sotsiologiiu* (Introduction to Marxist Sociology), (Leningrad University Press, 1962). Rozhin returns to this and related themes in his article, "Marksizm i Konkretnye Sotsiologicheskie Issledovaniia" (Marxism and Concrete Sociological Investigations), *Vestnik Leningradskogo Universiteta,* Seriia Ekonomiki, Filosofii i Prava, 1963, no. 3.

One of the sociologists' published contributions to this discussion is: G. V. Osipov and others, "Marksistskaia Sotsilogiia i Konkretnye Sotsiologicheskie Issledovaniia" (Marxist Sociology and Concrete Sociological Investigations), *Filosofskie Nauki,* V, no. 5 (1962).

27. Only one discipline in the social sciences is even less crystallized in the USSR than sociology, and promises to remain so. This is political science. A first-hand Western account suggests some differences and similarities between the two disciplines: Gordon Skilling, "In Search of Political Science in the USSR," *Canadian Journal of Economics and Political Science,* vol. 29, no. 4 (November 1963).

5 CURRENT RESEARCH AND PROBLEMS

Introduction

Soviet sociology in 1966, in contrast to a decade ago, is now a complex profession which defies any uniform characterization. Soviet sociologists not only come from many different related disciplines, such as philosophy, ethnography, geography, economics, jurisprudence, history, etc., but they are also divided among themselves as to the roles they perform. One can easily distinguish between the statesman-politicians, professional ideologists, administrators, and researchers who in some cases may be identified as administrator-scholars. Unlike his counterpart in the United States, the Soviet sociologist is least of all a teacher of sociology. Although the majority of sociologists are young men, they are not necessarily more liberal than the old guard. The generational conflict between the young and the old, if it exists, does not appear to be very serious. Quite to the contrary, the cleavages among the sociologists seem to run along the student-professor axis.

There was a time when sociological research was conducted in only a few major educational centers of the Soviet Union. Today sociologists are at work in many distant provincial institutions, and some of the most original and daring work has come from these places. In general, it seems, the best empirical research has come from relatively unknown men who were neither statesmen, ideologists, or administrators. Some men who dared to initiate early research programs have been brought to Moscow and rewarded with administrative positions.

The statesmen and the ideologists cannot be surpassed in one area of investigation, however: they are the only ones who can pass ideological judgments and undertake new ideological departures. They also have advantages with respect to the criticism of Western ideas, not only because these touch upon ideologically sensitive issues, but because the statesmen and the ideologists have better access to, and familiarity with, the literature of the West.

The articles in this section attempt a more detailed discussion of the current state of Soviet sociology. G. Osipov and M. Yovchuk, both Branch Directors at the Institute of Philosophy of the Academy of Sciences of the USSR, offer a Soviet view of their sociology. Presented as a paper at the Fifth World Congres of Sociology in 1962, this piece is remarkably up to date, despite the fact that most Soviet material of that period is already dated. It retains its freshness because it was not prepared to be released to a Soviet audience. Yet the content of the article seems to have been written not for international sociologists, but rather for Central Committee members. Much of the article is concerned with justifying empirical social research—an odd argument for Western ears, but a very common and necessary practice within the Soviet Union. One does not want to quibble with inaccuracies, but the statement that "concrete social studies became possible in Russia only after the victory of the October Socialist Revolution in 1917," is entirely false.

Paul Hollander, Assistant Professor of Sociology at Harvard University and Research Fellow at the University's Russian Research Center, provides an examination of Soviet sociology against the background of significant questions as to the nature of sociology as an objective science. Ironically and unintentionally, Professor Hollander's article raises more anxious questions as to the future of American sociology than it does about Soviet sociology. The prospects for the improvement of Soviet sociology seem to be better than those for American sociology, if for no other reason than that they could hardly get much worse. Mr. Hollander identifies two groups of Western social scientists who can be labeled as either skeptics or optimists in their appraisals of Soviet sociology. The skeptics seem to contend that sociology is incompatible with a totalitarian society, while the optimists are hopeful that the need for the services of sociologists in an industrialized society will encourage a more tolerant attitude toward the work of Soviet sociologists. Mr. Hollander is an optimist and offers a valuable discussion of seven specialty areas within Soviet sociology as of the 1960's.

The paper on Soviet criticism of the Western concept of industrial society touches upon a central problem of American writing on Soviet sociology. The heterogeneity of modern Soviet sociology also means that its scholarly products will be uneven in quality. It does not take very great skill, with some knowledge of Russian, to debunk Soviet sociology by ridiculing the worst of its examples. It is more difficult to distinguish worthwhile contributions and original departures. This is a risky venture which involves reading between the lines and hoping that what is still atypical will eventually turn into a trend. Nevertheless, we must face up to the important question whether Western sociologists should follow the Soviet lead and engage in debunking or "protivism," as it is called by Feuer in an earlier selection. The author's answer is an emphatic "no." Soviet sociologists have little choice in the manner of their political and ideological involvements. Western scholars, on the other hand, do have a choice, and there is no excuse for anyone who abandons his scholarly role for that of a propagandist.

The short selection by George Fischer emphasizes that the major efforts of Soviet sociologists have so far been centered on problems which affect man's work activities. Fischer offers a thoughtful explanation of why research in these areas is considered important to the state. Four major reasons favoring sociology of work studies are isolated by Professor Fischer: (1) rapid industrialization; (2) the ideal of educating men; (3) demographic dislocation; and (4) greater flexibility in political manipulation. All these factors certainly played an important part in re-establishing Soviet sociology as a whole.

The last two selections are offered as examples of Soviet empirical research, one in sociology of work and the other in sociology of religion. They come from a quarterly journal of translations entitled *Soviet Sociology,* under the editorship of Stephen P. Dunn, which offers many more valuable studies in both theory and empirical research. The studies provide valuable data, the reliability of which, unfortunately, cannot be ascertained. Granted that Soviet empirical research covers only limited areas of Soviet experience, it nevertheless provides us with significant new information about the life of the Soviet people and some of the consequences of socialist and industrial reconstruction.

Some principles of theory, problems and methods of research in sociology in the USSR: a Soviet view

G. OSIPOV and M. YOVCHUK

Institute of Philosophy and the Academy of Sciences of the USSR

EDITED BY THEODORE F. ABEL

Today hardly anyone doubts the need for sociological theory to ensure success and effectiveness in sociological research. The main characteristic of sociological research in the USSR is that it is based upon historical materialism which is the universal sociological theory.

The subject of scientific sociology, in our opinion, is the perception of social life in its entirety, in its internal integrity and the reciprocity of its phases, relations, and processes. Marxist sociology, being a synthesized science, bases itself upon the aggregate of findings of other social sciences, studies universal laws of social development as well as the concrete forms of the way they manifest themselves under varying conditions. Marxist sociology employs the theory and method of scientific sociology, i.e., historical materialism, in specific sociological research in order to understand the inner mechanism of social events and the laws of their development, and to analyze specific social situations that arise in the process of social life.

The materialistic interpretation of history, introduced by Marx and developed further by Lenin and his followers, leads sociology from the restrictions of risky constructions into a spacious scientific social perception that aids the process of reformation of social reality. Lack of a general theory of social development turns the task of sociologists into

Paper read at the Fifth World Congress of Sociology in Washington, D.C., 1962, later published in *American Sociological Review*, XXVIII, No. 4 (August 1963), 620-623.

a perplexing undertaking. This statement is supported by many Western sociologists.

Robert Merton writes in his *Social Theory and Social Structure* that since war, exploitation, poverty, discrimination, and psychological insecurity are plagues of mankind in contemporary societies, social science is obliged to furnish a solution to these problems if it does not wish to be totally useless. He suggests that it is quite possible that sociological scholars are about as prepared to solve these pressing dilemmas at the present time as Harvey or Siddengham were to recognize, study, and cure coronary thrombosis. Referring principally to west European and American sociology, Merton describes it as being on the same level as natural science was in the seventeenth century and that it is quite possible that sociology is not yet ready for an Einstein of its own since it has not yet even found a Kepler. Merton's view that sociology is not yet ripe for a comprehensive integral theory and that there are only a few theories available at an intermediate level of abstraction whose significance is relative and temporary is well known.

We feel justified in believing that this definition cannot be applied to Marxist scientific sociology. The materialistic comprehension of history, first described by Marx approximately 125 years ago, has been time-tested and has been proved by the entire process of historical development. The materialistic understanding of history is based on the concrete study of social life. The emergence of Marxism in the 1840's and its further development has been organically linked to and supported by research on specific social problems.

Engels' work on the "Condition of the Working Class in England" (Russian edition of the works of Marx and Engels, Volume 2, page 231) was substantiated by his personal observations and authentic reports. For his work on the *Capital* Marx analyzed stacks of "blue books," in which he found positive statistical material and documentation on the staggering state of capitalist exploitation. Lenin, for his book *The Development of Capitalism in Russia,* studied statistical records of state, district, and county matters as well as the budgets of individual peasants' households. The scientific basis of these and numerous other social studies, which have achieved acclaim for their world-wide historical significance, is the theory of historical materialism and the method of materialistic dialectics constituting the living soul of Marxism.

Concrete social study became possible in Russia only after the victory of the October Socialist Revolution in 1917. During the first 20 years methods were also developed during this period, represented by the works more than 300 books and pamphlets were published which threw light upon the results of specific new social processes. New approaches and of S. G. Stroumilyn on the influence of culture and education upon the productive capacity of common labor in the USSR, a book by A. I. Todorovskiy, *With a Rifle and Plow,* and a monograph by S. M. Vasileyskiy, *Methods and Technique of Social Studies.*

Social research may be directed toward the study of various facets of public life, but in our opinion, not every empirical study can be called sociological. Only when specific observations are related to the process of social-historical development and to their interdependence with all aspects of a society can a sociological regularity be established. Concrete social studies provide the foundation for scientific sociology. They are the substance for scientific generalization.

The personality cult of Joseph Stalin slowed down the progressive advancement of concrete social research in some measure. Nevertheless Marxist sociology in the USSR through its research has aided in the discovery of daring theoretical and practical solutions to most important problems that arise in building new societies. The development of economically and culturally underdeveloped nations has been directed immediately towards socialism, even though they had not yet experienced the capitalist stage of their development at the time of the Socialist Revolution in Russia. This was done in conformity with the scientific principles of Marxist sociology further developed by Lenin and his followers. Following the principles of sociology of Marx and Lenin, Soviet scientists in collaboration with representatives of the public education system have evolved, experimentally tested, and carried out the general, specialized, and industrial education and training of both the younger generation and the adult population. The information obtained furnished valuable material for the solution of a most difficult problem, namely, the eradication of differences between physical labor and intellectual work.

At present the science of sociology in the USSR contributes to the solution of social problems which mankind has not faced before. These problems arise in the course of creating a class-free Communist society, and they fall into three inter-connected categories. First, it is necessary to create the material and technical basis for Communism and to deal with the changing character and significance of labor that results from progress in scientific and technical fields. Second, problems arise in the evolution of Communist social relations and the liquidation of the last vestiges of inequality between social categories and groups, between men and women, and so forth. Third, the formation of a new kind of man, the development of his scientific outlook and new moral standards based upon the elimination of substantial differences between intellectual and manual work and between urban and rural life, and the direction of his efforts to attain a higher cultural level, present scientists and administration with a variety of new problems.

Numerous new processes and events, such as the rapid growth of forces of production, advances in Socialist democracy, an upsurge of culture, the formation of new morale, and the elimination of the negative inheritance of the old regime, are in continuous development in the USSR. This evolution demands new solutions and experimentation. Both provide a vast accumulation of new experience requiring generalization, intelligent comprehension, and propagation. This rich and varied social experience opens wide possibilities for concrete sociological research offering the opportunity to study general regularities in the development of society in the forms they manifest in the economic, social, political, and spiritual life of the Socialist society.

Since the general sociological theory of Marxism embraces the entire social-historic process and the general laws of its development, these can be applied to concrete social research into aspects of the social process manifest in a particular time, place, and historical situation. This effective use of theory in practice is illustrated by works like the *Eighteenth Brumaire* and *The Civil War in France* by Marx, and the *April Theses* by Lenin. These are brilliant examples of the scientific analysis of particular historic situations from the point of view of the scientific sociology of Marxism. They reveal revolutionary situations in one or another country at a definite period. Similar works are the *Housing Problem* by Engels, *Immediate Tasks of the Soviets* and the *Great Start* by Lenin, in which exactness and scrupulousness in research match the genius of theoretical deductions and inferences.

The term "historical situation" has a definite scientific meaning that makes it possible to better understand the particular and general traits of a concrete individual event. The term implies that social development involves the cooperation of various facets of social life in which economic drives sooner or later find their way through an endless series of changes, influenced by different sub-structures. The sub-structures constitute the political forms of class struggle and its results, and include political, juridical, philosophical, religious, and other theories. Social cooperation is not automatic. It is always an outcome of the industrious activity of people. During the transition period from Capitalism to Socialism in the creation of a classless society, spontaneous social development makes way for planned and deliberate development. New social factors such as public ownership appear, and the new objective laws of socialism, which permit the planning of social development, begin to function in the economic life of the society. On this objective planning new shoots of what may be called the general will appear.

The concept "historical situation" has vital methodical significance for concrete sociological research in the USSR. It insures that the whole aggregate of acting forces relevant to a given situation is considered. Social phenomena are analyzed as complex and varied facts subject to numerous influences. It directs attention to the elements that determine intelligence, will, and the actions of people which, in this final analysis, determine the relations in the economic life of a society and the laws of its development. Finally, it takes into consideration such a new social factor as general will acting according to a single general plan. The general will is the social, political, and spiritual unity of the new Socialist society, and it is a powerful lever in the transformation of social reality. Such a systematic development of social reconstruction has not been and could not have been known to any preceding social-economic formation. The Soviet sociologist is part of this force, part of the united Socialist body. When he is certain of the support of the general will he can conduct social research and experiments, and he can make practical recommendations which, if scientifically supported and practically sound, may be approved and carried out by the society.

The scientific determination of the methods and the techniques of research is an important part of social study in Soviet society. Sociology in the Soviet Union combines the scientific methods of sociological research; in Western sociology they are usually divided into objective and subjective. Sociological research in the USSR includes analysis of statistical reports and official papers, analysis of forms and methods of the activity of workers' organizations, discussions with workers about their sociological problems, social environment, outward and inside observation, written and oral polls, study of personal documents, etc.

Some Western sociologists tend to identify concrete sociological research with the taking of popular polls. In our opinion, this is an erroneous point of view. Public polls can provide valuable results only if scrupulously prepared and conducted in conjunction with other methods of sociological research. Questionnaires are valid instruments of sociological science only if they can be compared with a mass of subjective answers to definite objective data and if they expose the natural link between objective and dependent subjective processes of comprehension. In our opinion, all information gathered from polls should be checked and supplemented with data gathered by other methods.

We believe that the use of mathematical and statistical methods (the law of averages, the law of multitudes, the theory of games, etc.) will be fruitful in concrete social research, for they provide an accurate and objective description of the quantative aspects of social processes and events. Laboratories for mathematical methods in economics created at the Section of Economics of the Academy of Science of the USSR and at the Siberian Section of the Academy are beginning to use mathematics more and more as a means of analysis of concrete economic processes. A large role is reserved for mathematics in modeling social processes and events as well. Economic science has already started work on social modeling, deemed a matter of the utmost importance with a promising future. Sociology is following the same course. By feeding data into an electronic computer it is possible to obtain comparisons between social events and concrete social conditions in the laboratories. These studies help us to find ways of influencing social events through public opinion and support.

However, sociological research in the USSR is much more concerned with actual life situations than with studies under laboratory conditions. Furthermore, it is based upon the cooperation of scientists and practical staff in government, economic, trade-union, cooperative, and other organizations, as well as with the staffs of statistical bureaus. In our opinion, sociological research demands the closest cooperation between scientists from various branches of learning. It will be fruitful only if it is the joint effort of philosophers, sociologists, economists, lawyers, statisticians, ethnographers, demographers, psychologists, and other representatives of social sciences, and specialists from other fields such as mathematics, electronic computation, city planning, physiology, medicine, education, and many other branches of learning.

The last few years have witnessed a good many concrete sociological experiments based on a newly created network of scientific centers and an able staff. The new program of the CPSU is an example of concrete research conducted by sociologists. The program is based on profound and varied economic, sociological, statistical, and other social research conducted by party, governmental, and scientific organizations, and it directs major social changes for the next twenty years. Social planning in the USSR is based upon systematic preliminary exploratory studies. New social forms are investigated. Particular problems are studied in different places and times to provide comparative information. These studies are called the lighthouses of Soviet society. The following examples are only a few among such studies.

In the Sverdlovsk economic region scientists and staff studied the standards of workers in industrial plants and the results were published in *The Rise in Cultural and Professional Levels of the Soviet Working Class*. The scientists and teaching staff of Voronezh reported their sociological research in *The Common and the Personal*. Leningrad had published a series of works under the general title *Aspects of Marxist Sociology*.

There are many sociological research programs going on throughout the USSR. At the Institute of Economics of the Siberian Section of the Academy of Science of the USSR, extensive mathematics research on the problem of free time is in progress. (G. A. Frudenskiy and others). The sociological research division of the Institute of Physiology of the same Academy (A. A. Zvorykin, I. I. Changley, C. V. Osipov, and others) is studying problems in developing new principles of work and conditions at plants in the Moscow, Gorky, Moldavian Republic, and other regions. The sociological research sector of Moscow University is at work on social problems of automation at the first ball-bearing plant and other works (G. M. Andreiyeva and others). Problems of the general development of personality and the change in the social structure in Soviet society are being studied at sociological research sectors of the Ural University and the University of Kiev (M. N. Rotkevich, L. N. Kogan, and others). A similar sector of the Leningrad University (V. P. Rozhin, V. A. Yadov, and others) is studying processes of transforming work into the primary life requirement and the development of social consciousness. Their work is being conducted at Leningrad plants. Problems of family relations in a Socialist society are being examined at the Leningrad philosophical section of the Academy of Science of the USSR (A. G. Kharchov and others). The distribution of information gathered by various scientific establishments and universities is being carried out through the Soviet Sociological Association under President Y. P. Frantsev.

The program of concrete sociological research conducted in the USSR envisages scientific analysis of the following problems in the near future.

(1) *The alteration of the social structure of society in the process of building Communism.* Problems under study include the eradication of class distinctions between the working class, peasants, and intellectuals, and the difficulties involved in bringing physical and mental workers closer together. Other problems include the equalization of the economic and cultural conditions of urban and rural districts, the development of outlying districts of the country, especially the formerly backward districts, and the narrowing of differences in the standard of living in various sections of society that are related to the rise of income and a sizable increase in the distribution of public funds.

(2) *Modifications in the character of work.* Changes in the professional structure of the working class and of farmers that have resulted from mechanization and automation and the development of material resources are being studied, as well as changes in the meaning of labor and the diversification of the functions of workers. These changes have made it imperative to study ways and means for raising the cultural and

professional level of workers and farmers, and to give special attention to the methods of general polytechnical and professional education of the growing generation and of the working population.

(3) *The transfer of Socialist State functions to public self-governing organizations.* This idea is being studied and tried at different levels in many social areas, such as the management of public affairs, management at industrial plants, the organization of public education and cultural work, the improvement of living conditions and health, and the maintenance of public order.

(4) *Soviet family life and functions in relation to living space and material and social conditions.* These studies include the problem of the participation of women in productive work, the development of public relations and public services, the augmentation of powers for consumption of the public, and the use of free time by workers and employees.

(5) *The spiritual life of people and the maximum development of personality.* These problems touch upon the influence that an increase in public work and the development of culture, education, public opinion, a scientific outlook, etc., has upon the spiritual life of various categories of the population of the Soviet society, as well as the need to overcome the effects of old mores and morality on the consciousness and behavior of people.

This list of problems in sociology could be greatly extended. Soviet Marxist sociologists have every opportunity to carry out large programs of research and thus to contribute to the solution of significant problems of contemporary life.

The dilemmas of Soviet sociology

PAUL HOLLANDER

In discussing the problems and defects of American sociology, Soviet sociologists sometimes refer to a book written by the eminent American sociologist, Robert Lynd. In this book, *Knowledge for What?* (Princeton, 1939), Lynd castigated American sociology for failing to engage itself effectively in the solution of prominent social problems. Today, the same question—knowledge for what?—acquires new dimensions and significance when applied to the recent and current work of Soviet sociologists. What is the nature of the knowledge *they* are seeking? What use are they, or other groups in their society, going to make of that knowledge? Is it intended to supplement existing mechanisms of social control, or could it become a point of departure for social change unanticipated at present? Could it become a solvent of restraints and rigidities which, despite destalinization, continue to characterize the Soviet social order?

It is more than likely that official spokesmen of Soviet sociology would contend that the alternatives implied by the above questions are false ones. In their view, Soviet sociology can be, and is, both a tool of social control and an agent of controlled social change in a dynamic and at the same time planned society.[1] In the Western perspective, by contrast, the utilization of social-scientific information is inseparably tied to the issue of the autonomy of the social sciences; there has been a traditionally strong awareness of the impact of the relationship between science and society upon the results of social inquiry. Soviet observers have themselves shown a lively interest in the interaction between Western, particularly American, sociology and its social-political environment. Thus, perhaps, it is only fair for this survey of Soviet sociology to start with the same concern.

In Western societies, sociology is frequently evaluated in two simplified ways: either as a potentially dangerous instrument of social

From *Problems of Communism*, November-December 1965, pp. 34-46.

manipulation (an imagery deriving from such partial applications as advertising and political propaganda), or as a fine fruit of Western rationalism and an expression of the frank examination of the societal self. The latter positive conception of sociology credits the discipline with power to combat prejudice, falsehood, and obscurantism. Some note, however, that this potential of sociology can be realized only when it is free from external, and particularly political, interference.[2]

To be sure, there are other conceptions of sociology which differ from those just mentioned. In the United States in particular, critical and skeptical voices are sometimes raised, both within and outside the profession, cautioning against taking sociology too seriously, as a force either for good or for evil. The most common criticism is that sociology all too often indulges in ponderously stating the obvious. The more radical critics, carrying the argument further, claim that American sociology refuses to come to grips with the truly important problems of society, either when it soars to the heights of abstract theorizing, or when it is free from external, and particularly political, interference.[2]

The questions raised regarding the overall character of American sociology also have a ready applicability to its Soviet counterpart, particularly in view of the strikingly close interdependence between Soviet sociology and Soviet society. This interdependence is freely admitted by Soviet sociologists and is likely to constitute one of the few points of agreement in East-West social-scientific discourse. Many of them, in fact, acknowledge that the relationship between political objectives and institutions and the pursuit of scientific goals can be suffocating. No secret is made of the fact that the social sciences, and sociology in particular, atrophied in the period of the "cult of personality," [4] during which there was a total lack of objective inquiry into the fabric of Soviet society. It is for such reasons that Western observers of Soviet sociology feel compelled to look first of all at the official Soviet attitudes toward sociology, secondly at its proclaimed goals, and lastly at its substantive findings.

Contrary to the implications of Soviet statements about the ideological bias of Western sociologists and the hostile attention paid by them to developments in Soviet sociology, very little has in fact been written in the West on this subject.[5] This is by no means surprising. The paucity of comments on and studies of Soviet sociology in the West generally, and in the United States in particular, corresponds to the small number of sociologists focusing their attention on Soviet society. This seemingly paradoxical phenomenon of widespread indifference toward Soviet society, even under conditions of competitive coexistence, can be explained by a number of factors. American sociologists have been traditionally preoccupied with their own society; they face linguistic barriers; and, most importantly, they are disinclined to become students of a society which they cannot themselves investigate empirically.

Among the attitudes of the minority concerned with Soviet sociology, two basic positions can be discerned. On the one hand, there is much justified suspicion, stemming in part from the time when even the word "sociology" was banned from Soviet scholarly discourse, except to be applied in a pejorative sense to Western studies.[6] It is easy, after all, to be skeptical of the accomplishments of a discipline which was extinct for decades and never had well-established traditions; and it is correspondingly difficult to see how political-administrative decisions and sudden legitimation can have imparted scholarly maturity to Soviet sociology in a short space of time.

The nature of Soviet society itself lends further support to such skepticism. Sociology and the social sciences in general represent a most sensitive area of inquiry in a society whose leaders adhere to firm ideological preconceptions and insist that a body of social thought conceived more than a century ago—namely, Marxism—remains largely applicable and relevant to the present. The continued penetration of Soviet sociology by philosophy, and the acknowledged Soviet desire to saddle sociological investigation with the task of providing empirical support for the official system of values, make for uneasiness among those who see sociology as a means of expanding knowledge about society, regardless of the preferences of those who rule it. The lack of institutional autonomy for Soviet sociologists is yet another reason for misgivings, because it is seen as impinging upon the questions they can ask, the methods they can use, and the conclusions they can reach. In the view of the skeptical group of Western observers (among them are Feuer, Inkeles, and Labedz), the prospects of sociology in the USSR will remain dim as long as Soviet society as a whole remains totalitarian and hence hostile toward findings which could call into question its officially-proclaimed value premises.

Last but not least among the factors that make it difficult for most American sociologists to take a favorable approach to Soviet sociology is the very antagonism which Soviet sociologists show toward their American counterparts. Their compulsion to dismiss American sociology as unscientific, fraudulent, and degraded by subservience to the "monopoly capitalists" does little to invite a sympathetic response and at the same time hinders truly fruitful exchanges of social-scientific opinion and experience. Soviet claims to the contrary notwithstanding, not even the most critical American statements regarding Soviet sociology can match the shrill hostility and venom of the abuse which Soviet sociologists feel obliged to heap on their American colleagues as their contribution to the ideological struggle.

On the other hand, in spite of the psychological obstacles created by Soviet sociologists themselves, there is nevertheless a group of several American sociologists who take a more optimistic and positive approach to the present state and prospects of the Soviet social sciences. Such American observers as Fischer, Kassof, Merton, and Parsons are united in their desire to give more than the benefit of the doubt to Soviet sociology. They recognize the difficulties (partly admitted, partly denied on the Soviet side) which restrict the scope and depth of sociological inquiry in the USSR. One can also discern on the part of some of them a lurking expectation and hope that current trends in Soviet sociology may have a liberalizing and rationalizing impact upon Soviet society. Such hopes are generated by the linking of the development of Soviet sociology to the fruits of industrialization, and by the attribution to sociology of indispensability in an increasingly complex modern society. Among them one also finds an effort to separate what is viewed as a ritualistic ideological element from the substantive findings of Soviet sociologists. It is unlikely that the latter would themselves approve of this effort.

The survey of Soviet sociology that follows will address itself to seven topics: 1) Soviet criticisms of "bourgeois" sociology; 2) the impact of ideology on Soviet sociology; 3) time-budget and leisure studies; 4) the sociology of work; 5) studies on marriage and the family; 6) public opinion polls; and 7) studies of crime and delinquency.

On "bourgeois sociology"

> Even honest bourgeois sociologists arrive at false conclusions, inasmuch as they are far from a scientific understanding of the laws of social development.
> —M. KH. IGITKHANIAN, in *Voprosy filosofii*, June 1963.

> Against bourgeois falsification of the history of social thought of Babylon
> > —Chapter heading in G. F. ALEKSANDROV,
> > *Istoriia sotsiologicheskikh
> > uchenii, drevnii vostok* (Moscow, 1959).

As already indicated, a considerable proportion of the resources and intellectual energies of Soviet sociologists is expended in criticisms of Western and particularly American sociology. To get a complete picture of Soviet sociology itself, therefore, it is necessary to review briefly the scope and nature of these criticisms. Ironically, many of them appear to be projections of criticisms which could be directed at Soviet sociologists themselves. This is especially true of the Soviet charge that American sociologists are totally subservient to the ruling classes or cliques of their society, being dependent upon them for facilities and financial support ("The majority of American sociologists, particularly the 'industrial sociologists,' are in the service of the most powerful monopolies" [7]). From this alleged dependence of American sociologists, it is asserted, stems their active support of the social-institutional order of their society. This support is said to take two forms: diverting attention from genuine problems by trivial investigations; and formulating false theories about the sources of these problems and their remedies.

Soviet critics also like to stress the fatally handicapped character of American sociology resulting from its rejection of the only genuine scientific theory of society, Marxism, and its attendant disregard of structural-economic factors. In particular, it is frequently charged that American sociologists treat problems in a fragmented manner, failing to grasp the broader interconnections between them.

The alleged effort to reduce everything to psychological explanations and structural-functional theory—with a consequent neglect of social conflict and an overemphasis on the role of values in society—is singled out as one of the major causes of the undesirable state of affairs in American sociology. "Bourgeois sociologists" are criticized for stressing the role of the irrational in social life. For example:

> Bourgeois social psychologists strive to present matters as if ideology had an extremely limited part in the formation of public opinion. They maintain that the major role in the formation of public opinion is played by irrational and emotional factors.[8]

Apparently, the Soviet critics are unwilling to entertain the possibility that ideological positions themselves can be rooted in irrational and emotional factors.[9]

More recently, the so-called "convergence" theory (or the concept of a single type of industrial society) has come under unusually heavy fire from Soviet sources, which have assailed it as one of the most insidious ideological weapons devised by American sociologists. Zamoshkin, for example, ascribes to this theory "a leading position in the ideological struggle conducted by imperialism against communism." [10] Persistent Soviet concern with convergence is further illustrated by the following passage in a *Kommunist* editorial:

> Of late, anti-Sovietism has often been presented under the guise of the theory of the "growing together" of capitalism and socialism, as a

result of capitalism's "modernization" and some "internal degenera-tion" in socialism. Capitalism and socialism are portrayed as different variations of a "single industrial society." . . . Two purposes are thus pursued at once: first, to explain the defects of capitalism . . . , and second, to ascribe the same defects to socialism. Anti-Sovietism thus acquires the appearance of an "objective," scientific analysis of the path of development of the two systems.[11]

Even those Soviet studies of Western society and social thought which seem less polemical at first sight take every opportunity to attack the "bourgeois" social sciences.[12] Yet, notwithstanding all this criticism, Soviet sociologists and their ideological advisers—presumably in the spirit of "catch up and overtake"—never tire of stressing the need to make use of the advanced *techniques* of Western sociological investiga-tion.[13] The same ambivalent fascination with Western techniques and technology that has manifested itself in other spheres of Soviet activity is also apparent in the field of sociology.

Ideological limits

> The Soviet sociologist is . . . part of the united socialist body. When he is certain of the support of the general will, he can conduct social research . . .
>> —G. Osipov and M. Yovchuk, "Some Prin-ciples of Theory, Problems, and Methods of Research in Sociology in the USSR," *American Sociological Review,* No. 4, 1963, p. 622.

> Properly organized scientific investigation of social phe-nomena is the foe of voluntarism and arbitrariness, for any opinion, even the most authoritative, is considered no more than a hypothesis unless tested by experiment and practice. The development of social research is closely bound up with the democratic nature of our social system; it is inconceivable without it.
>> —V. Shubkin, in *Kommunist,* No. 3, February 1965.

Sentiments such as those expressed in these quotations indicate that there is some room for tension between the authoritative conception of the sociologist's role in Soviet society and the assumed results of socio-logical investigations. Hence, it may be worthwhile to see what Soviet sociologists consider to be their tasks, what guidance they receive from the appropriate authorities, and how they view the relationship between ideology and sociology, Marxism-Leninism and field studies. While the necessity of "concrete sociological investigation" (i.e., gathering factual data) is recognized, there remains a certain ambivalence toward ascer-taining facts of social life which might prove incongruous with established theoretical premises and the desired results of investigation. ("It goes without saying that the practical orientation of concrete social research in party work has nothing in common with creeping empiricism, with the blind worship of facts." [14])

Appropriately enough, in the realm of sociology as in other spheres, one also finds both the claim and a genuine effort on the part of the Soviets to "unite theory and practice." Marxism-Leninism is viewed as providing the ultimate inspiration and vindication of all sociological activities, yet at the same time it is being admitted that the "complexities" of the period of transition from socialism to communism raise problems which cannot be solved merely by the application of a relevant citation from Marx or Lenin. Reliance upon ideological authority for inspiration in sociological research raises additional problems in view of the inseparability of ideological authority and political power. The predicament of Soviet sociologists in search of secure ideological vindication of their work is illustrated by the fact that footnote references to the works of N. S. Khrushchev, which were formerly abundant in Soviet sociological writings, have now disappeared from the more recent publications.[15]

Soviet authors are fond of saying that much of their research is geared to problems whose solution is demanded by "life itself." Exactly how the requirements of this elusive entity are conveyed to Soviet sociologists is not always clear to the outside observer, nor is it known by what devices they make their selection among the problems with which "life" confronts them.

In view of all this, what explains the emergence and recent growth of sociology in the USSR? The upsurge is certainly part of the drive for greater efficiency proclaimed by Soviet spokesmen and observed by Westerners. This drive is focused primarily on production, but also extends to the realm of non-economic administrative activities. Soviet sociologists are expected to contribute to the better functioning of party, Komsomol, and trade union organizations. Even more ambitiously, they are called upon to assist the regime in achieving its ultimate goal: that is, by inculcating the appropriate attitudes and personality traits, they are to help create the "new Soviet man," fit to live under communism.

In retrospect, destalinization appears to have been the necessary precondition for the emergence of sociology. To the extent that Stalinist totalitarianism implied a pathological indifference toward many aspects of social reality, to the extent that it reflected a total disregard for the wishes and attitudes of the population, and to the extent that it relied upon massive coercion, it was deeply suspicious of any effort, activity, or inquiry which had the slightest potential for calling into question the wisdom of the supreme leadership and its value premises. As long as coercion was used as the major, if not single, cement of social organization and instrument of social change, and as long as ideological claims provided the *only* rationale for whatever policies the regime initiated, there seemed to be little need or room for sociological investigations.

Conversely, the resurrection of sociology seems to reflect an effort on the part of the post-Stalin leaders to diminish their isolation from the masses and from social realities, and to understand better their own society, which their predecessors had managed in such a high-handed as well as inefficient fashion. The peculiarly problem-solving character of actual Soviet sociological research (as distinct from the ideological discussions frequently called "sociological") is also indicative of the regime's desire to fill in the gaps left by decreasing reliance upon coercion. Yet it would be going too far to suggest that there is an *inherent* incompatibility between sociological research and a totalitarian society. To think so would be to overestimate the potency of sociological inquiry and to ignore the possibility of conducting it on a limited scale, within the bounds of the dominant, officially enforced value prescriptions. Sociology need not be a subversive force or a force irresistibly gnawing at official restraints on personal freedom as long as it exists in a narrowly prescribed institutional and conceptual framework, and as long as the political institutions of society are intent upon and capable of exercising control over it.

To be sure, sociological research and its findings can lead to consequences unintended and unforeseen, but even in societies where sociology is unrestricted by political pressures, we have yet to see any major social upheaval or dramatic transformation that can be ascribed directly to the work of sociologists. At the same time, the very effort to keep research within the bounds of ideological respectability can lead to conflict between the legitimate curiosity generated in the course of "concrete investigations" and the possibility that satisfaction of this curiosity may produce findings that do not accord with the basic official assumptions about the nature of Soviet society. Such conflicts can, however, be avoided or minimized by 1) restricting the scope of sociological investigations; 2) using methods that increase the likelihood of obtaining the desired, ideologically correct results; 3) finding some appropriate quotation in the "classics" or reinterpreting these so as to create an illusion of harmony between their propositions and the results of specific investigations; and 4) by a more broadminded and tolerant attitude toward the revealed deficiencies of popular attitudes and Soviet institutions. Each of these mechanisms is used to a certain degree.

Leisure with a purpose

> Our society cannot reconcile itself to the fact that there
> are still people who fritter away their free time.
> —L. BIBIK AND M. MARKOVICH, *Politicheskoe
> samoobrazovanie,* No. 7, 1962.

> The process of molding the new man and his Communist
> consciousness takes place not only while he is working but
> also in his non-working time.
> —G. S. PETROSIAN, *Vnerabochee vremia tru-
> diashchikhsia v SSSR,* Moscow, 1965.

A major substantive area of Soviet sociological investigation is the study
of time budgets and the utilization of non-working time. Such studies
were among the first actual research activities undertaken with the post-
Stalin rebirth of sociology.[16] Several underlying elements, both practical
and ideological, unite the numerous studies which have been undertaken
in this field, for instance those by Prudenski, Petrosian, and their numerous associates and followers. In the first place, these studies have been
prompted by the realization that not only the quantity of time spent
outside work but also the manner in which it is used is relevant to work
itself, or, in other words, that the productivity of labor depends to a
large degree on the ways in which non-working time is spent. This is
particularly so in view of the actual and anticipated reduction in hours
of work.

The concern with non-working time has two further components. One
is the ideological abhorrence of idleness, the veneration of activity for
its own sake, which has been an enduring part of the Soviet system of
values. The second is the impulse to be in control: those in command
of Soviet society want to know in detail how the citizen spends his time
outside the most tangible institutional frameworks (such as the work-
place); they want to regulate and influence systematically his non-working hours. In the last analysis, concern with non-working time amounts
to concern with privacy. While the welfare of the citizen is part of the
motivation for the studies in this field (as evidenced by the desire to
reduce the amount of time spent on housework by women, by recommendations to improve cultural-recreational facilities, etc.), non-working
time and leisure are seen as essentially collective rather than private
concerns, as resources over which ultimate control rests with society
rather than with the individual. The definitions of the categories used
in these studies illustrate the official preoccupation with the socially useful aspects of time spent away from work:

Non-working time (*vnerabochee vremia*) . . . [that which] is not directly absorbed by participation in socially productive activities. Non-working time includes the routine activities of daily life and free time. The rational organization . . . of non-working time is one of the most important objective indicators of harmonious personality development and hence a necessary element of social planning. Free time (*svobodnoe vremia*) is the part of non-working time which includes study, . . . voluntary public activities, leisure, hobbies, creative activities, etc. Leisure is one of the parts of free time, connected with the restoration of the psychic and physical energies of man.[17]

As the last of these definitions suggests, the Soviet conception of leisure and its acceptable uses differs markedly from that prevailing in the pluralistic societies of the West. The Western concept allows for a variety of legitimate interpretations, ranging from the opportunity for self-development and spiritual enrichment to recreation, relaxation, and simply "having a good time," and is thus closely tied to the values of individualism, privacy, and freedom of choice. On the other hand, the Soviet concept is narrower and more functionalized, heavily stressing the "rational" and socially beneficial uses of leisure. Thus, Petrosian observes:

Free time does not amount to idleness. . . . This is the time devoted to study, to the raising of [occupational] qualifications, self-education, and self-development (attending lectures, cultural groups, and museums; the reading of fiction, journals, newspapers, etc.); to sports and hobbies (hunting, fishing photography, etc.); to active rest and rational leisure (visiting places of entertainment, walks and excursions, travel, open-air festivals, creative disputes, bringing up children, etc.); and also to participation in the life of society.[18]

The actual findings of Soviet time-budget studies contain the usual admixture of positive and negative elements. The positive ones focus mainly on the decline in working hours and the increasingly rational and creative uses being made of non-working time, as in the pursuits enumerated above by Petrosian. (To these should be added the watching of television, which in the USSR is considered a useful rather than a wasted expenditure of time.) Other positive findings stress the progressive reduction of distinctions between urban and rural uses of free time because of the general closing of the gap between town and country. In conjunction with this latter question, there have also been many studies concerning the diminishing differentiation between manual and mental labor, which is seen at once as a precondition and essential feature of a fully Communist society. (In fact, most of the discussions on the nature of Communist society convey the impression that the achievement of communism requires little more than the elimination of these distinctions.)

On the negative side, there have been studies pointing up the persisting inadequacy of cultural and recreational facilities in certain areas, the insufficient use made of those available, the indifference of some party, Komsomol, and trade union officials toward the utilization of free time, and the continuing disadvantages of women, who are not yet freed completely from the double burden of work and household chores.

Time-budget studies frequently include recommendations as to the best utilization of free time, stress the need for its rational organization, and exhort party, Komsomol and trade union organizations to concern themselves more actively with the matter. Most typically, these studies emphasize the need to utilize free time for the improvement of the citizen's occupational qualifications, technical skills, and level of education. Chapter headings such as "Free Time and the Raising of the Cultural-Technical Level of the Workers" abound in the pioneering time-budget study edited by Prudenski, which contains many other evidences of interest in improving and shaping the free-time activities of workers.[19] Petrosian's previously cited study reflects a similar concern:

> Workers sometimes do not know how to use their free time. It is therefore necessary for the leaderships of the relevant social organizations [to concern themselves with] the most rational utilization of the workers' free time . . . . In some plants the organization of collective cultural activities is particularly unsatisfactory—[such as] collective attendance at theaters, movies, museums and recreational evenings, [the organization of] excursions, picnics, meetings with eminent individuals, etc. . . . Raising the level of the work of party, Komsomol and trade union organizations in the sphere of cultural and other services . . . is the precondition for the greatest rational utilization of the free time of workers.[20]

Workers and their attitudes

> The establishment of socialist production relations signifies an objective change in the position of workers in society, which in turn leads to a substantial change in the attitude toward labor. However, this latter process proceeds in an extremely complex way.
>
> —A. G. ZDRAVOMYSLOV AND V. A. YADOV,
> *Voprosy filosofii*, No. 4, April 1964.

A second major area of investigation is what Western sociologists would call the sociology of work. Here again the main emphasis is on problems of productivity and efficiency. More specifically, Soviet sociologists are studying such questions as: What factors make for work satisfaction? How can the turnover of labor be reduced? What is the impact of social relationships at the plant on workers' participation and initiative? In studying work satisfaction, the sociologists are making painstaking efforts to devise a proper balance of material and spiritual motives and incentives. The legitimacy of material incentives is increasingly, if vaguely, admitted, but at the same time the concept of the Soviet worker as motivated in large part by a sense of civic duty is also retained. Thus, e.g.:

Moral and material motives operate in unison in any form of labor activity. The basis for this interaction lies in the fact that labor fulfills a dual function under socialism: it is a means of satisfying a person's vital needs and also a means of expressing and enriching the personality. It is therefore incorrect to consider motives of a material nature "inferior" to those of a moral nature. At the same time, the precise correlation of these motives . . . is far from a matter of indifference.[21]

Questions relating to the worker's attitude toward his job have been receiving particular attention, partly as a result of the familiar problems arising from mass production, mechanization and automation, such as monotony. Not all the findings support the claim that the attitudes of Soviet workers differ sharply from those of workers in capitalist countries. The study just quoted showed, for instance, that 54.4 percent of the workers questioned were dissatisfied with or indifferent toward their jobs. Not surprisingly, some of the findings also indicate that, just as among capitalist workers the more highly skilled Soviet workers tend to derive greater satisfaction from their jobs. Thus far, Soviet studies on work satisfaction seem to have focused disproportionate attention on industrial as compared to agricultural workers.

Marriage and family

. . . scientific research on the family and the dissemination of sociological information about the family have not only intellectual but also an enormous moral-educational significance, serving as one of the instruments of the formation of the Communist personality and Communist social relations.

—A. G. KHARCHEV, *Brak i semia*, Moscow, 1964, p. 5.

Sociological studies of the family and marriage were most severely retarded by Stalinism. In reviewing Soviet writings in this field, Kharchev, the most prominent Russian scholar of the subject today, mentions not a single work produced between 1937 and 1958.[22] From a quantitative point of view, progress in the field still remains slight, but the emergence in recent years of a thoroughly changed approach can be gauged from a comparison of the bibliographical references contained in the last major work of the Stalinist period, S. Ya. Volfson's *Semia i brak v ikh istoricheskom razvitii* (Moscow, 1937) and those given in Kharchev's most recent book, *Brak i semia v SSSR: opyt sotsiologicheskovo issledovaniia* (Moscow, 1964). While Volfson relied almost exclusively on the works of Marx, Engels, Lenin, and Stalin, plus party and Komintern resolutions, Kharchev's makes use of both Soviet field studies and some of the relevant Western literature.

The still underdeveloped state of this important sociological field of inquiry is not hard to explain. For one thing, despite increasing interest in the subject and recognition that sociology could be of significant help in solving problems of family life,[23] Soviet society still has not shed certain inhibitions which derive from the basically puritanical official system of values, and which restrain inquiry into the more intimate aspects of personal relations. Concern with sex remains suspect and is regarded as not far removed from immorality.[24] Family and marital relations continue to be treated largely as if sex played no part as an area of conflict or compatibility.

The predilection to avoid the more subtle psychological issues involved is yet another obstacle to the development of this field of study. It cannot be ruled out, either, that the subject receives low official priority in terms of resource allocations for research because it is less relevant to the more tangible areas of societal efficiency. Work satisfaction is, after all, more directly related to per capita production than are the motives for marriage and divorce. Research may also be inhibited by the possibility that certain findings about marriage and interpersonal attraction might confront the investigator with evidence of all too many "survivals," including the persistence of desires for privacy and personal autonomy conflicting with the official preference for a more politicized and collectivized personal life.

In spite of the somewhat less doctrinaire approach taken in recent years, Soviet studies in this field continue to resemble those of the past in that they still start invariably with an attempt to demonstrate the decay and inferiority of the bourgeois family. Correspondingly, their set goal is to prove that Soviet marriages are motivated by love and high moral principles rather than material-economic considerations. Although

Kharchev has presented a sampling showing that the majority of respondents professed to have given priority to love, the claimed irrelevance of economic motives is nevertheless open to serious doubt in a society where housing is a major problem and income differentials remain great.

There is, in fact, some evidence that the Soviet family faces more problems than official pronouncements would care to admit. Some of these problems are peculiar to Soviet society; others can be found in most modern societies. For example, a 1964 survey of newlyweds in Leningrad revealed that only about 10 percent of them expected to live in their own apartments.[25] In the absence of further inquiry into the subject, one can only speculate on the effects of semi-communal housing on marital relations and the stability of the Soviet family. Other problems have been reflected in published criticisms of Kharchev's book. One critic observed that unregistered marriages are widespread, and that the number of unwed mothers in the USSR increased from 282,000 in 1945 to 2,700,000 in 1960.[26] The same article further noted that 28 percent of divorces in the Leningrad area were caused by marital infidelity, 21 percent by loss of love or incompatibility of character, and 17 percent by inability to have children or sexual separation. Another reviewer criticized Kharchev for failing to give due attention to the sexual aspects of marriage, which he said had been "treated with embarrassment." [27]

In view of the present backwardness of Soviet sociological studies of the family and growing official concern with the pathological aspects of family relationships, it is reasonable to expect an upsurge of work in this field. The practical relevance of these studies to the solution of such problems as juvenile delinquency is becoming increasingly clear to the more farsighted Soviet social scientists and policy-makers.

Public opinion

> . . . there are real grounds for the opinion of many bourgeois sociologists that the results of a newspaper poll cannot be representative, for this is precisely the case in capitalist countries, where every bourgeois press organ expresses the viewpoint of definite privileged social groups. . . . The principle is different in a socialist society, where the press represents the entire people and reflects the *basically unanimous* world outlook . . . of all classes and social groups.
> —M. KH. IGITKHANIAN, *Voprosy filosofii*, No. 6, June 1963. (Emphasis added.)

The introduction of public opinion polls in the Soviet Union represents one of the most striking departures from the climate of Stalinism. The total absence prior to destalinization of any inquiry into popular attitudes rested on the manifest premise that public opinion was completely unanimous on all issues of importance and revealed itself through the chosen instrument of history and the embodiment of the general will of Soviet society—the party and its leaders. This assumption of complete congruence between official pronouncements and popular attitudes made it superfluous to ascertain the exact nature of public opinion on specific issues. From what we know about Stalinist totalitarianism in general, moreover, it is clear that the regime's disregard of public opinion represented a mixture of indifference and perverse paternalism deriving from the belief of the leadership in its boundless omnipotence and omniscience.

Against this background, the current sanctioning of public opinion polls in the USSR ranks as one of the foremost evidences in Soviet sociology of a desire on the part of the post-Stalin leaders to understand their society better and thereby reduce their need to rely upon coercion. As in the case of other sociological studies, the official explanation of public opinion polls invokes the "increasing complexity" of the tasks confronting Soviet society in the current transition to communism and the multitudinous problems of everyday life requiring careful attention and concrete solutions not to be found in the ready-made ideological prescriptions of the regime.

Yet this new Soviet concern with public opinion has a paradoxical quality. For one thing, assertions of a fundamental and essential unanimity persists. For another, public opinion is not seen as an autonomous force relatively independent of the institutions of society, but rather as an integral part of them, as a resource to be manipulated even while it is being gauged and assessed. The following illustrates this view:

> The role of public opinion in the establishment of a single norm of Communist social intercourse is determined by the thorough transformations taking place in the life of our society. . . .
>
> Public opinion supporting the patriotic initiative of Soviet citizens, particularly in the development of new forms of socialist competition, strengthens spiritual motivation in the field of work.[28]

Nevertheless, the emergence of opinion polls seems to reflect implicit official recognition that differences of opinion are legitimate in certain areas of life as long as they do not call into question basic ideological propositions. It may conceivably also reflect an increased confidence on the part of the leadership in the masses under the conditions of destalinization. To be sure, the long exposure of the Soviet people to totalitarian terror, coupled with the use of certain dubious polling practices,[29] substantially reduces the chances of uncovering too much unorthodoxy or deviant opinions. Older Soviet citizens in particular are not used to revealing their views freely to investigators or institutions inevitably identified with the state.

Soviet opinion polls cover a fairly broad range, from the aspirations and values of youth to the preferences of theatergoers, from attitudes toward military service to favorite leisure-time activities, from observations about conditions of work to opinions on the adequacy of cultural amenities in rural areas—and even to the choices of Soviet youth as to what objects might be dispatched to Mars to represent earthly achievement in our time.[30] Few of the findings are likely to cause much official apprehension, although some do occasionally reveal disquieting trends, such as the spread of apolitical attitudes, cynicism, frivolousness, and dissatisfaction with available opportunities. The short- and long-range purposes of the polls may be summarized as follows:

1) To gather information needed in order to achieve greater efficiency, or for the purpose of gauging the mood of various strata of the population, youth in particular. (Significantly, the Public Opinion Institute of *Komsomolskaia pravda* is the major agency which conducts such investigations.)

2) To combat apathy and instill a greater sense of participation. Eliciting popular opinions implies an interest on the part of the regime in acting upon them and hence can be seen as a first step toward taking popular wishes into account in the formulation of policies.

3) To "educate" the public in a special way, by using polls to illustrate correct and improper attitudes. The assumption seems to be that the bulk of the opinions gathered will be correct and that giving wide publicity to actual examples of proper opinions and attitudes—together with a careful dosage of negative examples—will serve to enliven propaganda and enrich indoctrination. The effect of the polls is thus to support the overall *agitprop* effort.

Communism and crime

> It is rather easy to differentiate two groups of crime in socialist society: 1) crimes whose basic cause is the existence of capitalist countries in the world; and 2) crimes deriving from the vestiges of capitalism in men's minds.
> —M. D. SHARGORODSKI, "The Causes and Prevention of Crime," trans. in *Soviet Sociology*, Summer 1964, p. 24.

A sociology of crime based on actual investigations barely exists in the Soviet Union. There are, however, numerous discussions of the problem

—legal, ideological and journalistic—and if not systematic studies, at least theories and explanations of crime in a socialist society are being offered.

It is one of the irrational, yet ideologically explainable facets of Soviet society that considerations of societal efficiency and the desire to combat a major problem have not so far led to serious sociological study of crime in the USSR. This is all the more surprising since the existence of crime in Soviet society is admitted and official explanations of its persistence have been put forward. The dubious nature of these explanations, however, is measured by the fact that they have inspired hardly any actual studies or "concrete investigations," while on the other hand social scientists are rarely called upon to render assistance in solving problems of crime. Practical recommendations regarding crime are generally limited to calling upon party, Komsomol, trade union and other public organizations, local collectives, parents and teachers, and legal authorities to take a more active part in meeting the challenge.[31]

What sort of social-theoretical explanations, then, are being offered for the persistence of crime in Soviet society? Briefly summarized, the following major propositions emerge: 1) Crime is caused by "survivals" or vestiges of pre-Soviet values and attitudes which cannot be eradicated rapidly because social consciousness lags behind social existence. 2) Outside capitalist influences contribute to antisocial behavior among Soviet citizens through ideological warfare, propaganda, and corrupting examples. 3) Parents, teachers, and collective organizations occasionally fail to instill the proper attitudes in the young and to take care of the faltering. 4) World War II accounts for some criminal behavior, especially among those age groups directly affected by it. 5) Heavy drinking is another cause of crime (but despite the perceived correlation between drinking and anti-social behavior, no explanation is offered for the prevalence of excessive drinking in the USSR).

Problems and "unproblems"

The current limitations and peculiarities of Soviet sociology can perhaps best be illustrated by a comparison with socialist realist literature, with which it has many features in common. These similarities may be enumerated as follows: emphasis on the future, on the emergent patterns of social life, particularly those which herald the advent of a fully Communist society; the search for the "typical" (or, as two Soviet sociologists put it, "the process of concrete sociological research includes . . . [the] determination of the characteristic social situation" [32]); the desire to present models of behavior, to distinguish between appropriate and inappropriate forms of conduct, between positive achievements and negative "survivals"; avoidance of portraying fundamental social conflicts; reliance on the premises of Marxism-Leninism and their prevailing interpretation by the party; and emphasis on a practical approach ("The practical orientation . . . is common to all the intellectual disciplines in the Soviet Union—the natural sciences, economics, psychology, and, indeed, the arts under the formula of socialist realism" [33]). Finally, it should be noted that Soviet sociology and socialist realism have their distant yet unmistakable ancestry in nineteenth-century Western sociology and nineteenth-century Western critical realism, respectively. In each case, however, the Soviet adaptation represents a crucial departure from the Western original in that it disavows the questioning attitude toward society which was fundamental to both Western sociology and Western literary realism.

Perhaps because of the youthful nature of the discipline, a spurious sense of discovery permeates much of Soviet sociological writing. For example, it is pointed out with pride that "Soviet sociologists regard social life not as a chaos, not as a tangled conglomerate of accidental events, but as a natural connection of these phenomena in which there is mutual conditionality." [34] Or again: "The subject of scientific sociology, in our opinion, is the perception of social life in its entirety . . ." [35] Not infrequently, propositions which Western social scientists now regard as axiomatic are presented as fresh insights peculiar to Marxist sociology:

> In our opinion, all information gathered from polls should be checked and supplemented with data gathered by other methods. . . . In our opinion, sociological research demands the closest cooperation between scientists from various branches of learning.[36]

On other occasions, Soviet sociologists claim, as if it were peculiar to their approach, that they rely upon all forms of data-gathering: e.g., questionnaires, interviews, statistical sources, documents, personal diaries, etc.

Another source of pride among Soviet sociologists, namely the close cooperation that exists in the USSR between sociological investigators and party and government officials at the level of data-gathering and field studies, seems a dubious advantage from the Western social scientist's viewpoint. For the very association of the sociologist with the government raises the crucial problem of eliciting candid responses and trustworthy information from the Soviet citizen. This problem can be dismissed only on the premise that the Soviet people identify with the political institutions and leaders of their society to the degree claimed by the authorities. In the outsider's view, however, neither general historical experience nor contemporary social-scientific evidence support the likelihood of such a complete identification. The reliability of Soviet sociological research is further impaired by methodological weaknesses, notably by poor sampling techniques and the use of the distinctively Soviet device of the "mass" or "group interview."

The current state of Soviet sociology is also marked by neglect of many important areas of inquiry. Besides the scant sociological attention devoted to crime in general, and particularly to crimes against public property, the following topics remain virtually ignored and constitute—to borrow Feuer's term—"unproblems": the processes leading to the concentration of power and its abuse, both at the top and at local levels, and resulting in such evils as the "cult of personality" and "harebrained schemes"; the recruitment and selection of personnel for high political and managerial positions; the social backgrounds of various elite groups; the reintegration into Soviet society of the surviving victims of Stalinist repression who have been rehabilitated and released from concentration camps; attitudes toward various ethnic groups, including the Jews, colored foreign students, etc.; problems of old age; participation in and effectiveness of criticism and self-criticism; and the causes of capitalistic "survivals" in Soviet society. (A genuine sociological study of this last phenomenon would have to include a precise definition of the concept of "survivals," an inquiry into the conditions of transmission, the degree of susceptibility of various age and social groups, the determinants of persistence, and the specific ways in which Western influences can reactivate "survivals.").

To speculate on the future prospects of Soviet sociology requires no less courage than to try to predict the future of Soviet society as a whole. In this writer's view, however, it appears improbable that the trends in Soviet sociology will diverge from those prevailing in other realms of Soviet life. For better or for worse, the state of Soviet sociology is likely to remain a striking illustration of the interdependence between the political institutions and economic needs of a society on the one hand and its capacity to examine and understand itself on the other.

Notes

1. *Cf.* A. M. Kulkin and N. I. Kondakov (eds.), *Stroitelstvo kommunizma i obschchestvennye nauki*, Materialy Sessii Obshchevo Sobraniia Akademii Nauk SSSR October 19-20, 1962, Moscow, 1962; and L. F. Ilichev, *Obshchestvennye nauki i kommunizm*, Moscow, 1963.

2. "Sociology can thrive only under freedom. Indeed, the extent to which sociologists may pursue their interests, fully publish their results, and freely state their conclusions, is one important index of the degree to which a nation qualifies as a free and open society. A nation cannot have quality in sociology by fiat. It

can, if it chooses, write a kind of "contract" for that kind of sociology which guarantees, in advance, to produce results which affirm the established order and confirm received doctrine. It may then get what it orders, as it does in the Soviet Union, but it will not get good sociology. Only a nation which provides the conditions for free inquiry may with reason hope for development of social-science knowledge which permits an ever deeper understanding of man in society." Alex Inkeles, *What Is Sociology?* Englewood Cliffs, N. J., Prentice-Hall, 1964, p. 117.

3. A good example of such criticism is M. Stein and A. Vidich (eds.), *Sociology on Trial,* Englewood Cliffs, N. J., Prentice-Hall, 1963.

4. For admissions to this affect, see, e.g., V. Fokin (ed.) *Sotsiologiia v SSSR,* Vol. 1, Moscow, 1965, pp. 4-5; L. F. Ilichev, *op. cit.,* pp. 9-46; G. K. Ashin *et al.* (eds.), *Voprosy organizatsii i metodiki konkretno-sotsiologicheskikh issledovanii,* Petrozavodsk, Rosvuzizdat, 1963, p. 7; G. Osipov and M. Yovchuk, "Some Principles of Theory, Problems, and Methods of Research in Sociology in the USSR," *American Sociological Review,* No. 4, 1963, p. 621.

5. For Western observations on Soviet sociology, see: Joseph Roucek, "Russian Sociology and 'Sociology' Under Communism," in J. Roucek (ed.), *Contemporary Sociology,* New York, Philosophical Library, 1958, pp. 892-921; Robert K. Merton and Henry W. Riecken, "Notes on Sociology in the USSR," in National Institute of Social and Behavioral Science Symposia Series, No. 10, *Current Problems in Social-Behavioral Research,* March 1962; Lewis S. Feuer, "Problems and Unproblems in Soviet Social Theory," *Slavic Review,* March 1964, and "Meeting the Philosophers," *Survey,* April 1964; George Fischer, *Science and Politics; The New Sociology in the Soviet Union,* Cornell University Center for International Studies Monograph, 1964; Elizabeth A. Weinberg, *Soviet Sociology, 1960-1963,* Massachusetts Institute of Technology Center for International Studies, 1964; and Talcott Parsons, "An American Impression of Sociology in the Soviet Union," *American Sociological Review,* February 1965.

6. See, e.g., G. Aleksandrov, "Bankrotstvo burzhuaznoi sotsiologii," Moscow, 1948.

7. V. P. Rozhin, *Vvedeniie v marksistskuiu sotsiologiiu,* Leningrad, 1962, pp. 63-64.

8. A. K. Uledov, *Obshchestvennoe mnenie sovetskovo obshchestva,* Moscow, 1963, p. 194.

9. A similar point has been made by Feuer in discussing Soviet hostility to Freudian psychology. See *Slavic Review,* March 1964, p. 122.

10. Yu. A. Zamoshkin, "Teoriia Edinovo industrialnovo obshchestva na sluzhbe antikommunizma," in *Marksistskaia i burzhuaznaia sotsiologiia sevodnia,* Moscow, Izd. "Nauka," 1964, p. 94.

11. *Kommunist* (Moscow), No. 10, July 1965 (trans. in *Current Digest of the Soviet Press,* August 4, 1965, p. 4.)

12. See, e.g., M. A. Dynnik, V. V. Mshvenieradze, *et al.* (eds.), *Sovremennaia filosofiia i sotsiologiia v stranakh zapadnoi Evropy i Ameriki,* Moscow, Izd. "Nauka," 1964; A. G. Zdravomyslov, "Problema Interesa v sotsiologicheskoi teorii," Izd. Leningradskovo Universiteta, 1964; A. A. Arzumanian *et al.* (eds.), *Gorodskie srednie sloi sovremennovo kapitalisticheskovo obshchestva,* Moscow, 1963; B. A. Denisov, "Kritika sovremennykh burzuaznykh teorii o budushchem obshchestve," *Vysshaya shкola* (Moscow), 1961; M. A. Kirillova, "Amerikanskie sotsiologi o Seme," *Sov. Pedagogika,* No. 11, 1964; and Yu. A. Zamoshkin, "Problema amoralizma i prestupnosti v sovremennoi Amerikanskoi sotsiologii," *Voprosy filosofii* (Moscow), No. 7, 1963. For a more general criticism of Western sociology, see: G. V. Osipov, *Sovremennaia burzhuaznaia sotsiologia* (kriticheskii ocherk), Moscow, 1964.

13. E.g., see "On Two Neglected Fields of Sociological Research," in *Kommunist,* No. 17, November 1963 (trans. in *Current Digest of the Soviet Press,* February 26, 1964).

14. "Apply Social Research to Party Work," *Pravda,* May 11, 1965 (trans. in *Current Digest of the Soviet Press,* June 2, 1965, p. 11).

15. E.g., see G. V. Osipov, *op. cit.* (f.n. 12); and *Sotsiologiia v SSSR, op. cit.* (f.n. 4).

16. It is perhaps significant that time-budget studies have a tradition in Soviet sociology going back to the 1920's. Early investigators of this subject included Strumilin (1922), Mikheev (1932), and Lebedev-Patreiko (1933).

17. *Sotsiologiia v SSSR, op. cit.,* II, 485, 487, 495.

18. Petrosian, *Vnerabochee vremia trudiashchikhsia v SSSR,* Moscow, Ekonomika, 1965, p. 16.

19. G. A. Prudenskii, *Vnerabochee vremia trudiaschikhsia,* Novosibirsk, 1961, pp. 53, 99, 119, 121, 125, 181.

20. Petrosian, *op. cit.,* pp. 179-170.

21. A. G. Zdravomyslov and V. A. Yadov, "An Experiment in Concrete Research On Attitudes Toward Labor," *Voprosy filosofii,* No. 4, April 1964 (trans. in *Current Digest of the Soviet Press,* July 8, 1964, p. 12).

22. A. G. Kharchev, "On Some Results of a Study of the Motives for Marriage," *Filosofskie nauki,* 1963, No. 4 (trans. in *Soviet Sociology,* Spring 1964, p. 43).

23. "Literature About Communist Morality," *Pravda,* June 9, 1965, p. 4 (trans. in *Current Digest of the Soviet Press,* June 30, 1965, p. 32).

24. *Cf.* " 'Delicate' Topic," in *Sovetskaia pechat,* No. 4, April 1964, pp. 19-20 (trans. in *Current Digest of the Soviet Press,* June 17, 1964, p. 19); also *Gigiena polovoi zhizni,* Moscow, 1964, p. 19.

25. See *USSR Today,* March 1964, p. 56.

26. *Novyi mir* (Moscow), December 1964, pp. 260-262 (trans. in *Current Digest of the Soviet Press,* March 17, 1965, p. 9).

27. I. S. Kon, in *Nauchnye doklady vysshei shkoly—filosofskiie nauki,* No. 1, 1965 (trans. in *Current Digest of the Soviet Press,* June 2, 1965, p. 14).

28. A. K. Uledov, *Obschestvennoe mnenie sovetskovo obschestva,* Moscow, 1963, pp. 324, 356.

29. There is, for example, a pronounced ambivalence with regard to preserving the anonymity of poll respondents. For instance, a soldier who had made unfavorable comments about army life in answering a questionnaire was described in a published report as "not brave enough to give his last name and come forth openly against the collective." (*Krasnaia zvezda,* July 7, 1964: trans. in *Current Digest of the Soviet Press,* December 9, 1964, p. 11.) It is also questionable whether the sampling procedures used are such as to yield truly representative results. In a recent major poll conducted by *Komsomolskaia pravda,* for example, the newspaper questioned a self-selected sample of 17,000 out of its total four million readers, with only 601 collective farmers included in the sample.

30. G. Oganov and V. Chikin, "Seven Thousand Rockets Take Off for Mars," *Komsomolskaia pravda,* October 20 and 24, 1963 (trans. in *Current Digest of the Soviet Press,* December 4, 1963, p. 7).

31. Characteristically, the relatively few studies of crime undertaken in the USSR have not been made by sociologists, nor have the results been published in social science journals. *Cf.* O. L. Morozov *et al.,* "Opyt kompleksnovo obsledovaniia prichin i uslovii, sposobstvuiushchikh soversheniiu prestuplenii podrostkami," *Sovetskoe gosudarstvo i pravo,* No. 9, 1963.

32. V. V. Mshvenieradze and G. V. Osipov, "Sociology in the USSR," *Social Science Information Bulletin,* October 1962, p. 57.

33. Parsons, *op. cit.,* p. 122.

34. Mshvenieradze and Osipov, *op. cit.,* p. 64.

35. Osipov and Yuvchuk, *op. cit.,* p. 620.

36. *Ibid.,* p. 622.

The concept of industrial society under criticism by Soviet sociologists

ALEX SIMIRENKO

Social scientists generally agree with Max Weber that it is proper to be subjective about the value of one's own science. Having committed our lives to the study of social phenomena, we like to think that the conditions of society which make an objective social science possible are of the highest value not only for the scientists but also for mankind. It is natural for us to interpret the development and expansion of sociology in various countries and our own as a hopeful sign, and its stifling and demise as a bad omen. It is not surprising, therefore, that since 1956 many of us have been hopefully following the revival of sociology in the Soviet Union as a distinct discipline. Even today the future of sociology in the USSR is uncertain, and new political developments in the nation and the world may well disrupt or dwarf its future growth as it was disrupted in the 1920's. What Alexander Herzen said of Russia a hundred years ago is applicable today to Soviet sociology: ". . . One must not put blind faith in the future; every foetus has the right to develop, but for all that not every foetus does develop. The future of Russia does not depend on herself alone: it is bound up with the future of Europe as a whole." [1]

Whatever the future holds for Soviet sociology, today it has already produced empirical works worthy of admiration by Western sociologists. It is becoming generally accepted to present research reports in a simple, straightforward review of data without undue ideological commentary. These studies cover such varied topics as the budgets and expenditures of Soviet families, social relations in religious sects, work relations in industry, leisure practices of Soviet man, ecology of a Caucasian town, changing structure of professions in the Soviet Union, cultural tastes of Soviet workers, and the realization of vocational plans of Soviet youth. Publication of empirical studies in the Soviet Union is still a relatively rare phenomenon due to the infancy of Soviet sociology and the small number of its practitioners, estimated by Merton and Riecken to "be counted, at the most in the hundreds rather than the thousands." [2] George Fischer writes that "we should probably put the figure in the dozens." Consequently, much of the writing of Soviet sociologists has been in the nature of theoretical and methodological discussion in which a debunking of American and generally Western ideas is most prominent. The writings of Soviet sociologists in the first half-decade of their development have consisted primarily of criticism of the bourgeois sociology conceived to be in the service of capitalist society. In the last few years, however, criticism of Western sociology has diminished, accompanied by improvement of the quality of such criticism.

Soviet critique of sociology in the West

There is nothing startling in these frequently sharp attacks on American and Western sociology. One of the striking features of Soviet society as it emerged from its world isolation during the post-Stalin era was its superior technical and industrial position coupled with predominantly nineteenth-century Russian and European culture. Intelligentsia who came in contact with foreigners, including foreign Communists, attested to this situation by their embarrassment.[3] With Stalin gone and Stalinism on the defensive, there still remained a problem of channeling the information about the outside world to Soviet society in a fashion that would not disturb the foundations of the Soviet system. There was only one traditional solution to this problem—an ideological critique of Western ideas which provided an opportunity for summarizing these ideas, because they were usually unknown to the Soviet reader. It would be quite appropriate to refer to such criticism as a strategy of "creative debunking." The post-Stalin era has seen a flood of such creative debunking on all conceivable subjects designed to satisfy Soviet curiosity about the outside world. It is not surprising, then, that similar strategies were used to acquaint Soviet readers with sociological ideas as well.

It would be an exaggeration to say, however, that all Soviet criticism of Western ideas is designed to inform Soviet readers about the world outside. Some of these writings still follow a pattern of old-fashioned propaganda designed to uphold the authority of the party in all spheres of thought.[4] Other work, representing a more recent development, is designed to offer a serious, and therefore more constructive, scholarly appraisal of Western ideas. Such criticism is not always easily distinguishable from other kinds of Soviet debunking. A superficial examination of such writing couched in the traditional Soviet form may not reveal significant departures in Soviet social thought. But a serious critique differs from a run-of-the-mill ideological attack in its range and depth of knowledge of non-Soviet literature, its ability to recognize significant and influential Western scholars, and its successful separation of important scholarly works from obscure ones. In addition, serious criticism contains a plea for a dialogue and a debate between Soviet and non-Soviet scholars on particular issues.

Some Soviet criticism of American sociology was reported in a recent article by Allen Kassof, entitled "American Sociology Through Soviet Eyes." [5] It is regrettable that the author fails to rise above the level of an ideological debater who is eager to score points for his side. Mr. Kassof makes it appear that American sociologists have little to learn from their Soviet colleagues, and that whatever accomplishments the Soviet side can boast about have been accomplished with the aid of techniques borrowed from the United States and the West in general. Although the author acknowledges that "Soviet criticism . . . raises some potentially worthwhile questions about the practice of sociology in the West," he fails to tell us what these "worthwhile questions" are. Instead, Mr. Kassof concludes that Soviet sociologists do not possess an "intellectual discipline" for a "reasoned and responsible" debate; that they are "closed-minded" and unable "to appreciate genuinely free discussion and exchange."

If it was Mr. Kassof's intention to persuade American sociologists to continue ignoring Soviet sociological criticism of Western ideas, he succeeded admirably. Yet in many ways, Mr. Kassof's description of contemporary Soviet criticism is a caricature of Soviet sociology which fails to present the best critique that our Soviet colleagues have to offer. In part, this caricature is achieved simply by quoting primarily from Soviet writing published in 1961 and 1962, while implying that a similar picture of Soviet sociology persists in 1965. This disregards the enormously rapid advancement and change of Soviet sociology since 1963.

The purpose here is to correct some of the impressions of Soviet sociology formed on the basis of Kassof's article, and to bring up to date the latest developments in Soviet criticism of American sociology. In order to permit a fuller exposition of such criticism, only one major theme in the current Soviet sociological criticism has been selected. It is the criticism of the concept of industrial society which was touched upon briefly by Mr. Kassof.

The concept of industrial society

Perhaps the best and most balanced Soviet presentation of the concept of industrial society and its criticism, so far, has been the work of two well-known scholars, Mark Borisovich Mitin and Vadim Sergeevich Semenov.[6] Mr. Mitin is a philosopher and academician who is now chief editor of the journal *Problems of Philosophy*. Born in 1901, he joined the Communist party in 1919. He served as an editor of the journal *Problems of History,* was a Stalin prize winner in 1943, and is a member of the Central Committee of the Communist party. Mr. Semenov is a prolific young writer who is a specialist in the field of social stratification. With a degree of Doctor of Philosophic Sciences, he is a senior scientist at the Institute of Philosophy in the Academy of Sciences of the USSR.

Mitin and Semenov, with other Soviet scholars, regard the sociological concept of industrial society as the major weapon in the ideological arsenal of the United States and its allies. They see the concept as functioning in the interest of the ruling classes and justifying their internal and external policies. According to Soviet sociologists, Western supporters of the concept claim that it represents an "objective" and "scientific" explanation for the development of capitalism and the whole of the contemporary world; that it underlines the character of the world's social problems and draws perspectives for the future of mankind. The concept of industrial society, in short, competes with the main thesis of communism for the explanation of the world's social forces and its future.

According to Mitin and Semenov, the general idea of industrial society has found its characteristic expression in the work of Raymond Aron, in his lectures on the development of industrial society and social stratification.[7] Aron is said to ignore the differences between socialism and capitalism, and instead to use the concept of industrial society to discuss the social consequences of large-scale industrialism in general, without regard to the socio-political structures of various countries. Aron would maintain that the difference between property arrangements in capitalist and socialist countries is an insignificant problem. Socialism and capitalism are only two versions of an industrial society in which the problems of capital accumulation, industrial growth, and attitudes toward work are of greater importance than property arrangements. According to Aron, both Western and Soviet society represent the same type of a "progressive industrial society."

Needless to say, Mitin and Semenov object to Aron's formulations. In their words:

No one can deny that on a general technological level of economy it is possible to find considerable similarity in the development of capitalist and socialist countries. This is understandable, since some of these similar features are determined by the regularity of technological development rather than being directly determined by the social relations of production. . . . For example, it is characteristic of all industrial countries to accelerate the development of heavy industry, especially the construction of machinery; industrialism is accompanied by the centralization of the economy and other spheres of life, and the increasing role and significance of science in society, etc. All this is true. At the same time it is impossible not to notice the basic difference in the nature of these processes in the socialist and capitalist countries, which are determined by the different forms of property and contrasting productive relations. But such processes as growth of heavy industry, production of machinery, a growing laboring class, transformation of the peasantry, an increasing importance of science, and the centralization of the economy proceed in a qualitatively diverse fashion in socialist and capitalist countries.

Thus, growth of the laboring class under conditions of capitalism is invariably accompanied by unemployment, while the decline of the peasantry takes place at the cost of mass destruction of peasant households caused by the private property owners' dominance of the means of production. The proletariat is in the position of an exploited class of society. In the conditions of socialism, these necessary changes connected with the process of industrialization carry a qualitatively different character.[8]

Concluding their discussion of Aron's ideas, Mitin and Semenov state that certain superficial similarities in the development of industrial countries under socialism and capitalism have permitted bourgeois sociologists to generate their concept of industrial society. It is accomplished, however, only by the "metaphysical separation of the productive forces (or, more exactly, technological indices of the economic development of society) from the productive relations and forms of property." [9]

According to Mitin and Semenov, a much more complete theory of industrial society than Aron's has been given by W. W. Rostow in his work entitled *The Stages of Economic Growth*,[10] in which he formulates a contemporary analysis of industrial societies in a historical perspective of five stages.

Mitin and Semenov state that Rostow's theory denies the necessity of socialism and the inevitable replacement of capitalism by socialism:

If R. Aron preferred to avoid the concept of socialism and capitalism and suggested instead an artificial idea of a "single industrial society," W. Rostow has gone much further: he attempts to erase the whole of the Marxist historical conception explaining the inevitable destruction of capitalism and victory of socialism by substituting for it the theory of "growth stages," which reduces the whole history of mankind to a preparation, rise, and later development of the "industrial society." [11]

Rostow's claim that there are broad similarities between his conception and that of Marx, and that "they are both views of how whole societies evolve, seen from an economic perspective, . . . [that] both accept the fact that economic change has social, political, and cultural consequences," [12] is seriously questioned by Mitin and Semenov:

> What do authors of the theory of "industrial society" have in mind when they talk about an "economic perspective"? This is nothing else but a generalization derived from technological indicators of economy: the degree of industrial development, of technology, of the economy as a whole, development of science, and especially the rate of capital accumulation, that is, that portion of the national profit which is reinvested in the economy. At the same time, supporters of the concept of "industrial society" as a rule fail to note such an extremely important element of the productive forces as producers and workers." [13]

Rostow's claim for studying society as a developing whole is challenged on the basis of his refusal to analyze the forces of production. Rostow is accused of subjective idealism and voluntarism, for he claims that economic factors do not play a significant role in the development of post-traditional societies; his idea of economic stages, therefore, is considered deceptive, a maneuver to give the theory of industrial society a superficial scientific credence.

Ideological roots of the concept of industrial society

The most original part of Mitin and Semenov's criticisms of the concept of industrial society lies in their analysis of its ideological uses in the United States and the West in general. To preserve the essence of the argument, these portions of their criticism are translated in full:

> In the past five years, the theory of the development of a "single industrial society" has become extremely popular in the capitalist world. It is being defended and propagandized by such American sociologists as S. Lipset, W. Moore, A. Feldman, D. Bell, E. Shils, A. Inkeles; by such American economists as S. Kuznets and B. Hoselitz; and many sociologists and economists of England, West Germany, and other capitalist countries. The bourgeois sociologists have forcefully advocated this theory at the Fifth International Congress of Sociology held in Washington in September 1962. In recent years the doctrine of the "industrial society" has given birth to

several related theories, in particular the theories of "mass society" (Daniel Bell), "modernization," etc.

Today the concept of a "single industrial society" is the principal weapon in the ideological war against communism and is part of the official doctrine of the United States and other imperialist states. It is being used to justify the most important domestic and foreign actions of the imperialist countries.

It is possible to isolate a number of causes for the wide popularity of this conception and its emergence as an integral part of official imperial ideology.

1) W. Rostow suggested a relatively complete picture of the world historical process which resembled a general theoretical explanation of societal development. This created quite a stir in bourgeois social science circles, whose theoretical generalizations are ridden with poverty and who dabble in details of secondary or tertiary problems.

2) Of considerable importance was the fact that the theories of a "single industrial society" and "stages of growth" raised significant questions about the direction and trend of social progress, the inter-relation and competition between systems of socialism and capitalism, the paths of development of underdeveloped countries, etc. Concern for these themes of vital contemporary importance is a rather rare occurrence in modern bourgeois science.

3) The theory of "industrial society" appeals to the bourgeois ideologists with its technologically economic approach to social proc-esses. It would be difficult today to expect even temporary popularity for an idea that rejected at the outset the economic side of social development. Therefore, the bourgeois sociologists, eager to underline the "scientific" nature of the "theory of stages," point out its "eco-nomic" and almost "materialistic" character.

4) The theory of a "single industrial society" concentrates attention on the productive growth of consumer products in industrial countries. Formulating this as its own index of progress, the theory emphasizes not the rationality of man but his prejudices and habits, as well as his indifference toward the fundamental processes determining con-temporary development.

5) Most important, the theory of "industrial society" and "stages of growth" is frankly directed against Marxism and is part of the ideological struggle against communism. While hypocritically an-nouncing that his conception of "stages of growth" is similar to that of Marx, W. Rostow reveals its actual class nature when he says that his "theory of development represents an alternative to the Marxist interpretation of modern history." . . .

The theory of "industrial society" fulfills at the present time a number of social functions. With different degrees of effectiveness it is being utilized in these three ways:

—as a theory which attempts to deny that the modern world is split into two parts (the world of socialism and the world of capitalism), but asserts the existence of a "single industrial society";

—as a conception advocating the unity of capitalist countries;

—as a theory asserting a uniformity of social arrangements in capitalist countries.

In all these aspects, the concept of "industrial society" fulfills class functions: it conceals contradictions and antagonisms growing out of the bourgeois structure, while it defends the system of exploitation and perpetuates capitalism.

In recent years, bourgeois politicians and ideologists have been increasingly voicing the idea that the "industrial society" inevitably creates an internal homogeneity and "social uniformity" in capitalist countries. Antiquated theories of bourgeois reformists, appealing for "class peace" and "cooperation," now appear in the guise of conceptions of "uniform" and "single" Western society.

The theory of a "single industrial society" is actively used to substantiate and advertise the "socially united Europe." This concept had a direct influence on the development of doctrines substantiating such forms of imperialist integration as the "Common Market," "Euratom," and the "European Coal and Steel Community."

But the most far-reaching aims of the proponents of the "industrial society" theory are revealed when it is used to justify the doctrine of a "single world" and to deny differences between socialism and capitalism.

At first glance it may seem that when the proponents of the concept of "industrial society" talk of the unity of socialism and capitalism and the "growing similarity" between them, they assert views quite contradictory to those expressed by the militant, frankly slanderous, and adulterated conjectures of anti-communists. But this is not true. The theory of a "single industrial society" and of a "growing similarity" between capitalism and socialism is, by its very nature, a frank anti-communist, anti-Marxist conception.

Slurring over the basic contrasts between capitalism and socialism, and analyzing specific differences in terms of technical performance of the economy, is one of the strategies used to deny the objective inevitability of the replacement of capitalism by socialism.

While discussing the "unity" of capitalism and socialism the theorists of the "industrial society" arbitrarily transfer the social ills of the capitalist society to the socialist world. This is done, for example, by the American bourgeois sociologists and anti-communists, Z. Brzezinsky and S. Huntington, the authors of *Political Systems: USA and USSR* (1964).

The theorists of "industrial society" make wide use of the technological indicators of the economy and speculate on the idea that capitalist countries retain definite advantages in the development of economy and technology, while the United States still holds first place in the world in the production of consumer goods. According to W. Rostow's "theory of stages," the USSR and other socialist countries are still in the fourth stage, the stage of "maturity," while the United States has already entered the fifth stage—the higher and last stage of development, a stage of "mass consumption." Other Western capitalist countries are supposedly now entering this fifth stage.

Thus, when in reality the new world is represented by the Soviet Union and all the socialist countries, while the backward countries a step behind are represented by the imperialist states, in the interpretation of the "industrial society" theorists of this new world are represented by the United States and other developed capitalist countries, while the industrialized socialist countries are backward by one whole stage of development.

Advertising "industrial society" as the mainstream of human history, bourgeois ideologists are emphatically denying the fact that socialism and communism represent a higher form of socio-economic organization. Proclaiming "industrial society" as the stage of "mature development," and "mass consumption" as the crowning point of human history, they "concede" socialism and communism only as a "possible variation" of development through stages of "transitional society," the "take-off," and "maturity." At the same time, it is a variation conceived as a "worse" and a "more damaging one."

The rise and development of "industrial society" is, according to W. Rostow, the general law of history. As far as socialism and Marxism are concerned, the most favorable condition for their development exists at the beginning stages of the industrialization process. Communism, asserts Rostow, represents itself as a "disease of the transitional period."

The main class conclusion of the bourgeois theory of a "single industrial society" can be reduced to the idea that in the resulting development of such a society and the increasing similarity between socialism and capitalism, capitalism will be victorious, while communism will die out and disappear.[14]

Discussion

The above summary of Soviet criticism portrays both the strong points and the continued weaknesses of Soviet sociologists. The dogmatic tone of Mitin's and Semenov's article is not entirely admirable, but it does represent a great improvement compared with past writings by the same authors and with the works of many other Soviet sociologists today. It should be noted, however, that Mitin's and Semenov's article compares quite favorably with the dogmatism of Allen Kassof and his criticism of Soviet sociology. Never once do Mitin and Semenov accuse Aron or Rostow of being "closed-minded."

Furthermore, even the best of Soviet sociologists suffer from inadequate knowledge of America and the West due to the isolation of Soviet society. They continuously identify all social scientists both as ideologists and scholars, while men like W. W. Rostow are thought to represent the views of most Western social scientists. Contrary to the assumptions of Mitin and Semenov, the scholarship of W. W. Rostow is not very highly thought of by many Western social scientists.[15]

But no matter how eagerly American sociologists, including the proponents of the industrial society theory, may want to dissociate themselves from Rostow's ideas, it must be acknowledged that these ideas represent one logical extension of the general concept of industrial society. Soviet sociologists, who are constantly attuned to political and ideological overtones in scholarly works, have quite correctly noticed the similarities in the assumptions buried in such divergent works as Aron's and Rostow's.

We have yet to hear from our American proponents of the concept of industrial society about the validity of these Soviet criticisms. In view of developments in Soviet sociology since 1963, and granting no major political upheavals, it could be said that whosoever may wish to answer the various charges hurled by Mitin and Semenov will probably find Soviet sociologists worthy of their match and eager for debate.

Irrespective of the correctness of specific points made by Mitin and Semenov, their general argument is well taken. They agree that industrial societies as presented by both socialist and capitalist countries reveal many significant similarities which distingush them markedly from the countries of the underdeveloped world. They insist, however, that we also look at the crucial differences which exist between the various industrial countries. Such an examination would lead us into the development of a typology of industrial societies which is still in an embryonic stage. By calling for a typology of industrial societies, Soviet sociologists are performing a useful service for sociology in general. They are wrong, however, to think that Western scholars are not concerned with this problem. Such concern, for example, is well illustrated in the latest work by Herbert Marcuse, who perceptively differentiates between the socialist and capitalist types of industrial societies:

But while these prospects for the containment of qualitative change in the Soviet sytsem seem to be parallel to those in advanced capitalist society, the socialist base of production introduces a decisive difference. In the Soviet system the organization of the productive process certainly separates the "immediate producers" (the laborers) from control over the means of production and thus makes for mass distinctions at the very base of the system. This separation was established by political decision and power after the brief "heroic period" of the Bolshevik Revolution, and has been perpetuated ever since. And yet it is not the motor of the productive process itself; it is not built into this process as is the division between capital and labor, derived from private ownership of the means of production. Consequently, the ruling strata are themselves separable from the productive process —that is, they are replaceable without exploding the basic institutions of society.[16]

The development of a sound typology of industrial societies will necessarily involve the cooperation of sociologists from many countries, including the Soviet Union. Comparative empirical research must be undertaken if such a typology is to take shape. Granted the many obstacles for genuine cooperation between Soviet and American sociologists, there is no reason why an exchange of views and a debate on such issues as those raised in this paper cannot take place. Such a debate is the first requirement for any joint scientific action in the future.

Unfortunately, most Soviet criticisms of American sociologists are never answered; we leave the impression that either we are not interested in what they are saying, or we are afraid to scrutinize our own ideas too closly in the light of Soviet criticism.

Having followed the rise and development of the new Soviet sociology since 1956, I would venture a guess that we could probably go considerably further in our relations with our Soviet colleagues beyond the mere exchange of ideas. Recent developments in Soviet sociology seem to indicate the possibility of cooperation between Soviet and American social scientists. A limited cooperation of such nature is already under way between sociologists in the Leningrad University, headed by Vladimir Yadov, and Professor Frederick Herzberg at Western Reserve University. Writing in the January issue of *Soviet Life,* Vladimir Yadov states that "during his stay in Leningrad, Professor Herzberg told us about his job-attitude investigation of engineers and suggested that we do a similar study in Leningrad. We agreed. For our part, we suggested that Professor Herzberg do an occupation-motivation study of American workers by our method. Professor Herzberg agreed." [17]

The major obstacle to joint American-Soviet comparative empirical research may well be the Communist party's lack of tolerance of objective studies of what might be interpreted as "social ills" of Soviet society. Quite understandably, many of the ideologically sensitive areas of Soviet life have generally been avoided by Soviet sociologists in their past research. Nevertheless, their recent empirical work has acquired considerable boldness which probes even the supposedly seamy sides of Soviet life. The rising level of objectivity of Soviet sociology is well exemplified in one study which established a disparity between the vocational plans of secondary school graduates and their subsequent execution after graduation. Although only 8 percent of the young people planned to enter a full time job, while 80 percent had hoped to continue their education, as many as 32 percent had actually taken on full-time jobs and only 44 percent went on to continue their studies. What is more startling is the frankness with which it was revealed that the fulfillment of educational goals of the young people was related to the social positions of their families. Of the 93 percent of children of urban intelligentsia (professionals) who wished to continue their studies, as many as 82 percent fulfilled their aspirations. On the other hand, in the least successful group, children of agricultural laborers, 76 percent wanted to continue their studies but only 10 percent succeeded in doing so.

The release of these findings is a hopeful sign that Soviet sociology has reached a new level of sophistication and stronger support as an objective science within the party. The day may well be approaching when Soviet sociologists are able to agree to test some crucial sociological ideas with us.

Notes

1. Alexander Herzen, "An Open Letter to Jules Michelet," in *From the Other Shore and the Russian People and Socialism* (London: Weidenfeld and Nicolson, 1956), p. 201.

2. Robert K. Merton and Henry W. Riecken, "Notes on Sociology in the USSR," in *Current Problems in Social-Behavioral Research,* Symposia Studies Series No. 10 (Washington, D. C.: National Institute of Social and Behavioral Science, March 1962), p. 10.

3. The much criticized essay by Victor Nekrasov, entitled "On Both Sides of the Ocean," contains one of the best records available of the Soviet embarrassment

at their ignorance of twentieth-century developments outside of Russia. Translated in *The Current Digest of the Soviet Press*, XV, Nos. 9 and 10 (March 27 and April 3, 1963).

4. A good illustration of the point are two Soviet books with similar titles, printed only eight months apart: I. Iskhakov, *Sovremennaia burzhuaznaia sotsiologiia: oruzhie antikommunizma* (Contemporary Bourgeois Sociology: Weapon of Anti-Communism), (Tashkent: Uzbekistan, August 1964), which represents an old-fashioned ideological debunking, and an edited volume by the Academy of the Social Sciences entitled *Sovremenny kapitalizm i burzhuaznaia sotsiologiia* (Contemporary Capitalism and Bourgeois Sociology), (Moscow: Mysl', April 1965), which represents a serious discussion and criticism of the ideas of Parsons, Rostow, Aron, and Dilthey.

5. See *American Sociological Review* XXX, No. 1 (February 1965), 114-121.

6. M. B. Mitin and V. S. Semenov, "Dyizhenie chelovechestva k kommunizmu i burzhuaznaia koncepciia 'edinogo industrialnogo obshchestva,'" (The Movement of Mankind Toward Communism and the Bourgeois Conception of a "Single Industrial Society"), *Voprosy filosofii* (Problems of Philosophy), XIX, No. 5 (May 1965), 35-46.

7. R. Aron, *Le Dévelopment de la Société industrielle et la Stratification sociale,* I, Paris, 1957.

8. Mitin and Semenov, *op. cit.,* pp. 37-38.

9. *Ibid.,* p. 38.

10. W. W. Rostow, *The Stages of Economic Growth: A Non-Communist Manifesto* (Cambridge: Cambridge University Press, 1960).

11. Mitin and Semenov, *op. cit.,* pp. 38-39.

12. Quoted from Rostow, *op. cit.,* p. 148.

13. Mitin and Semenov, *op. cit.,* p. 39.

14. Mitin and Semenov, *op. cit.,* pp. 40-43, translated by Alex Simirenko.

15. This is especially true among sociologists, who generally are not familiar with Rostow's ideas. Gladys Meyer, reviewing his book for the *American Sociological Review,* states that "Mr. Rostow confuses Marx and vulgar Marxism. . . . It is only defensible as seriously wrought sociology of knowledge, but Mr. Rostow's treatment is journalistic, patronizing pathos." Recognizing what this work really is, Miss Meyer concludes her review by predicting that "probably, however, it will win friends and influence people." (*American Sociological Review*, XXVI, I [February 1961], 159). Similar response had come from the quarters of political scientists in a review of Rostow's work by Andrew Gyorgy in the *American Political Science Review.* He says: "A reviewer's principal critical comment must be directed against the essential narrowness of the Rostow concept. Indeed, it is not a theory but a series of cleverly connected observations on certain phases in the nineteenth- and twentieth-century growth of selected nations. . . . This book is not so much a 'Non-Communist Manifesto' as an 'Affluent Society Manifesto' viewed from a distinctly Western-American perspective." (*American Political Science Review*, LIV [Deceber 1960], 1058). Other reviewers of *The Stages of Economic Growth* were less charitable. Robert Marris, writing in the *Spectator,* said: "The book is in essence propaganda, and the author seems unable to escape the influence of long association with his government." (*Spectator*, May 6, 1960, p. 672).

16. Herbert Marcuse, *One Dimensional Man* (Boston: Beacon Press, 1964), p. 43.

17. Vladimir Yadov, "The Soviet and American Worker: Job Attitudes," *Soviet Life,* January 1966, no. 1, p. 37.

Empirical research of Soviet sociologists

GEORGE FISCHER

Though international topics are emphasized in the programs and writings of the new Soviet sociology, they do not loom large in its scholarly work. On this level, social phenomena abroad command a distinctly lower priority than do the same phenomena within the country. The ongoing research of Soviet sociologists is deeply ethnocentric; it is wholly immersed in Soviet life. Systematically selected and officially approved, these ethnocentric areas are summarized in the Osipov Paper. In this paper, the key areas fall under the following headings:

1. The alteration of the social structure of society in the process of building Communism.

2. Modifications in the character of work.

3. The transfer of Socialist state functions to public self-governing organizations.

4. Soviet family life and functions in relation to living space and [to] material and social conditions.

5. The spiritual life of people and the maximum development of personality.

However, some important qualifications must be made here. This list speaks of social research in the USSR and not specifically of sociology. As far as the field of sociology goes, the key areas today are fewer in number. To begin with, the sociology of the family (area 4) is currently by and large the subject of research by Soviet psychologists and educators, rather than sociologists. Similarly, the area of values and personality (area 5) is beginning to produce social research by philosophers in the area of ethics, as well as in the currently reviving field of social psychology. The traditionally physically oriented Soviet field of ethnography is also moving in the direction of social research related to both family life and values. Aside from a marginal involvement in connection with its central pursuits, sociology has not emphasized such research. A final qualification concerns area 3. In this area—which

From George Fischer, *Science and Politics: The New Sociology in the Soviet Union* (Ithaca, N.Y.: Center for International Studies, Cornell University, 1964), pp. 32-38.

Soviet usage equates with political sociology—there is some active re-research by sociologists. But of the major centers only Moscow University appears to be engaged in this research, and even here work is just beginning.

A recent *Voprosy Filosofii* editorial leaves no doubt at all that the field does indeed single out industrial and occupational sociology at the expense of these other areas:

> However, the sphere of empirical sociological research remains rather narrow. Studied most intensively are problems connected with the growth of the scientific and technical level of workers and employees, the increase in leisure time, and the merging of mental and physical labor. Yet philosophers continue to speak only in general terms, operating with randomly chosen facts, about such all-important social processes in our life as the transformation of the CPSU into the party of the whole people and the growth of its leadership role, as well as the increasing role of civic organizations and subjective factors in building communism.[1]

Why is the officially blessed new sociology today in fact a sociology of work? The answers to this question are deeply rooted in the nature of Soviet society and Soviet politics. At least four reasons of basic importance can be mentioned:

1. The Soviet Union is the first major society in man's history which is catapulting into advanced industrialization from a social and cultural foundation which quite recently was largely non-modern. Inevitably, therefore, Soviet society even today contains a large number and variety of what Soviet usage calls "vestiges of capitalism"—values and behavior patterns incompatible either with modern industrial society in general or with its singular Soviet variant in particular. Nowhere are such incompletely modern patterns of behavior likely to matter so much in a rapidly industrializing society as in the area of work, and particularly factory work in a relatively novel urban and technological setting. Since the Soviet Union has consistently placed industrial output and labor productivity above popular involvement in either private life or public life, the area of work becomes all the more important. By the same token, this area becomes all the more logical as the focus of the Soviet type of policy-oriented, problem-solving science.

2. Closely related to this is the Soviet conception of how to socialize or re-socialize a population that was in part unprepared for the grandiose tasks and rigorous procedures of the Soviet system, and in part resistant to them. Soviet theory and practice has approached this problem in large measure through the area of work. The novel, collective, and

demanding nature of work in a revolutionary and modernizing society, and especially in industry, in the Soviet conception became the ideal means by which to transform the population, by which to create the New Soviet Man.

Socialist Competition and similar publicized ventures are only part of this Soviet conception. From the outset, policy-makers and social scientists in the Soviet Union thought of all aspects of work as a unique and invaluable "school for communism." Much of the new sociology is aimed at a systematic analysis of which policies and practices contribute most to making a maximally effective "school for communism" out of work.

3. Demography plays a notable role in the Soviet preoccupation with industrial and occupational sociology. Because of the rigors of forced industrialization and collectivization, and the unrivalled population losses of World War II, Soviet population increase ever since the 1930's has been slower than it was in the 1920's. At the same time, an unevenly modernizing agriculture continues to retain a significant share of the country's manpower, while another sizable portion of the labor force consists of unskilled rather than skilled factory workers. Together with the ever-growing complexity of advanced technology and industrial life in general, all this puts a special premium in the Soviet Union on work and in particular on the recruitment, training, utilization, and productivity of skilled industrial labor. Each of these aspects of labor policy can and does have a close link to an industrial sociology like the Soviet one.

4. Only after considering these basic social, economic, and demographic factors is it proper for us to turn to recent political developments in seeking explanations for the focus of the new Soviet sociology. Within this broader context, the transformation of the "absolute totalitarianism" of Stalin into the "enlightened" rule of Khrushchev has played a decisive role. Most specifically, the past decade has involved a twofold change. On the one hand, there has been a definite nation-wide shift from heavily coercive policies to policies emphasizing material and moral appeals. On the other hand, the post-Stalin leadership has sought to soften the popular impact of its continuingly rigorous policies by a variety of new, more flexible, and more gentle mechanisms.

For post-Stalin leadership, as for its predecessors, unceasing industrial expansion remains the keystone—both to create the good society of the future and for present-day success at home and abroad. For this reason, much of the policy-making of the past decade has concentrated on questions directly related to industrial manpower and labor productivity. And much of the search for less harsh, more popular policies has perforce also focused on industry and on factory workers. In this all-important grouping toward more subtle, more sophisticated policies, the new social science has been regarded as necessary and helpful. For no matter how slowly or unevenly official theories and practices might change, these leaders were clearly conscious of the aridity and inutility of the Stalin-era social sciences; this point is brought out in the already-cited Ilichev speech to the Soviet academicians, and in numerous other official statements. What was wanted in the place of the former situation was a group of scholars every bit as loyal and disciplined, but at the same time more sophisticated, original, and enterprising in their policy recommendations.

The youthful and often able pioneers of present-day Soviet sociology closely fit the needs of present policy. All of them are dedicated party members and active policy advisors on one level or another. All of them appear to share their leaders' impatience with pure Stalinism in policy and scholarship, as they do their urgent search for adaptations of the system to an ever more complex society and a rapidly changing world. And it is in the area of work—of how to assure increased labor productivity—that the new Soviet sociology seems to be called upon to make its central contribution to post-Stalin policies.

These, then, are some of the fundamental reasons why Soviet sociologists are devoting themselves today so largely to the sociology of work. They explain, too, the particular ways in which the subject is approached.

During its first few years the new Soviet sociology showed some definite structural similarities with American research in occupational and industrial sociology. In both countries, early research focused on a limited number of problems and methods. In both countries, labor economics played a major role at the outset—the Institutional School of Thorstein Veblen, John R. Commons, Selig Perlman, and others in the United States; the now venerable Academician S. G. Strumilin and the labor studies of the 1920's in the Soviet Union.[2] In both countries the study of leisure can be seen as a contemporary approach to work in a changing setting. Finally, in both countries there is at present a preoccupation with the revolutionary impact of the latest technological changes, notably automation. And if Marxist theory and empirical research are conceived of as an organic whole in the Soviet Union, in the United States occupational and industrial sociology moved over the years toward synthesizing the European tradition of theoretical and historical breadth with the American tradition of specialization and comprehensive field studies.

Along with these similarities, a host of differences persists. Among these, few are more important than that of orientation toward research. In their report, Merton and Riecken conclude:

The Soviet orientation toward empirical social research might be described as "practical empiricism": As an effort to obtain just enough systematic information on which to base recommendations for policy and action, with little interest in pursuing, through empirical research, the more theoretical implications of what has been observed. In spirit and outcome, it is most like market-research in the United States: on a low level of abstraction and largely confined to ferreting out facts that can be taken into account in making practical decisions.

At present, the rage of practical problems attacked by sociological investigation is mostly limited to problems connected with industrial work and education. The many specific examples of research under way or just completed can almost all be encompassed under the single heading: the engineering of social change.[3]

Beyond this research orientation toward "practical empiricism" and "the engineering of social change," another difference looms large between Soviet and American research on the sociology of work. Increasingly, American research attempts to embrace three different levels of the work situation: the individual, the group of which he is a part, and the organization in which he works. On each of these levels, there is a further emphasis on two components, labor and management. Moreover, attention is often paid to the role of mediating agencies like unions and government on the one hand and the individual personality on the other.

In the past few years, the research of Soviet sociologists has covered only a few of these topics. The Merton Report noted the limited emphasis on the group. The exceptions to this limitation lie in the area of officially sponsored collective endeavors, notably Socialist Competition and in recent years also the Brigades of Communist Labor. But even these exceptions so far have received only partial attention from the new sociology. Even less subject to systematic study is the whole organizational level, be it economic management, the unions, or party and government organizations per se. These organizations enter into the picture only as generalized sources of policies, plans, and decisions, but not as an element to be studied alone or in terms of its interaction with individual workers or groups of workers.

Still another aspect of this Soviet-American difference pertains to personality studies of workers. In 1963 a major collection of essays on this subject was published by the Psychology Division of the Soviet Academy's Philosophy Institute. Part of the research included grew out of the comprehensive Gorky study of Osipov's Social Research Division in the same institute. This suggests that the Gorky study itself and other forthcoming publications in this area may well include personality studies.

To date, however, they have not been among the major ingredients of Soviet sociological research on work. Nor do these essays go as far in depth analysis or documentation as comparable American studies.[4]

A leading sociologist, A. A. Zvorykin of the Philosophy Institute, describes the shortcomings of the initial Soviet research on work, as he sees them:

> Unfortunately, the generalization of practical experience accumulated on the job and the scientific elaboration of labor problems generally lag as yet and constitute a backward area of theoretical work.
>
> . . . . The opinion is still common that sociological studies have no direct relationship to research into labor problems . . . . Studies of the psycho-physiological aspects of the labor process cannot be effective if they do not take into consideration the influence of the individual upon the labor processes and do not investigate social problems of [work].
>
> . . . . Whereas numerous large research institutions are engaged in studying long-range prospects for the development of technics and technology, problems of labor . . . are the concern of a small number of organizations, and their activity is virtually uncoordinated.

In the same paper, Zvorykin also enumerates specific aspects of work that preoccupy him and his colleagues in the field:

> Work and equipment; work and the organization of production; work and the cultural-technical level of workers; eliminating the differences between mental and physical work; the conversion of agricultural work into a variety of industrial work; work as the basis of upbringing the younger generation; the transformation of socialist work into communist work and the role of the most advanced ideology in the process—these are by no means a complete list of the problems involved in the development of work and the influence of changes in its nature upon the shaping of the man of communist society.[5]

In terms of its initial research, what the new sociology explores is above all the individual worker. The focus has been the worker's desire and ability to adapt himself to rapidly changing technology. Part of the analysis is on the level of short-run needs, and part of it reaches out toward things to come. Within this duality, the sociology of work commands the center of the stage. The main themes of this Soviet sociology of work are: the impact of technological change, the education and training of industrial labor, and attitudes toward work. Beyond that, the social theory of Soviet sociologists concentrates on a closely related subject, class structure.

Notes

1. Editorial, "KPSS—Partiia Vsego Naroda" (The CPSU is the Party of the Whole People), *Voprosy Filosofii,* XVII, no. 8 (1963), 11.

One of the fields in which Soviet sociologists are beginning to do empirical research is esthetics: A. K. Melekhova, "Opyt Sotsiologicheskogo Issledovaniia Esteticheskikh Vzgliadov i Vkusov Rabochikh Promyshlennykh Predpriiatii Urala" (An Essay in Sociological Investigation of the Esthetic Views and Tastes of Workers in Industrial Enterprises in the Urals), *Filosofskie Nauki,* vol. 6, no. 5 (1963).

2. A perceptive appreciation of Strumilin appears in R. W. Davies, "Some Soviet Economic Controllers-I," *Soviet Studies* (Oxford), XI, no. 3 (January 1960), 286-296. According to the author, Strumilin manifested the same absorption with regulating overall social change—as against studying or evaluating it—that characterizes at least some of the leading sociologists in the USSR today.

3. Merton Report, p. 4.

4. *O Chertakh Lichnosti Novogo Rabochego* (On the Personality Characteristics of the New Worker), edited by K. K. Platonov (Moscow: Publishing House of the USSR Academy of Sciences, 1963). Two essays in the volume refer specifically to the Gorky study: V. I. Bashilov, on the stimulation of inventions by workers, and N. G. Valentinova, on the role of personality in overcoming the monotony of assembly-line work.

5. A. Zvorykin, "Approaches to Work under Communism," *Soviet Sociology,* I, no. 2 (Fall 1962), 33-35, 29 (translated from *Voprosy Ekonomiki,* 1962, no. 7).

Soviet workers' attitude toward work: an empirical study

A. G. ZDRAVOMYSLOV and V. A. IADOV
Translated by William Mandel

Concrete investigation of the transformation of work into the felt first necessity of life, in the course of the building of communism, poses a series of theoretical problems to investigators. What is attitude toward work in general? What is a communist attitude toward work? What are the major factors furthering (or, on the other hand, inhibiting) the process of establishment of a communist attitude toward work? Is it possible to guide this process, and what must be done to accelerate it? The search for answers to such questions requires, aside from everything else, an investigation of the shaping of the communist attitude toward work as it relates to technological progress and to the change, on that basis, of the content and nature of what one does at work. It must be emphasized from the outset that contrary to the assertions of the theoreticians of the "single industrial society," the interrelation between technological progress and change in attitude toward work is fundamentally different under the socialist and capitalist systems. Under capitalism, technological progress is now proceeding in the interests of large-scale monopoly capital. Under socialism this progress serves the interests of the working people. The establishment of socialist relationships of production signifies an objective change in the position of working people in society, and this in turn leads to a significant change in attitude toward work. However, this latter process proceeds in highly

"An Attempt at a Concrete Study of Attitude Toward Work," from *Soviet Sociology*, III, No. 4 (1965), pp. 3-14. (The article appeared originally in *Voprosy filosofii*, 1964, No. 4.)

This study was carried out by the personnel of the Sociological Research Laboratory of Leningrad State University, consisting of V. V. Vodzinskaia, M. M. Grigorian, A. A. Kissel', G. I. Saganenko, and A. S. Shaev (with the participation of E. V. Beliaev, S. I. Golod, and B. V. Ornatskii) under the guidance of the authors.

complex fashion. It is related not only to changes in the economy, but to changes in the consciousness of the masses of the working people, and to recognition by them of their own historical role. In this connection, the job of the researcher is to bring to light those new conditions and factors specific to socialist society which influence attitude toward labor, to discover resources that have not yet been utilized in developing a communist attitude toward work, and to develop practical recommendations on this basis.

Without claiming to develop this problem in all its complexity and diversity, we shall consider primarily certain aspects of the conversion of work into a felt necessity of life, as this is occurring in our society. We shall examine this transformation, in particular, from the standpoint of social psychology and in connection with the establishment of the foundations of a new morality, a new understanding of the social significance of work. Moreover, the discussion will not be of the attitude toward work of the individual in the abstract, but that of a particular portion of the Leningrad working class—the working youth.

In order to have a basis for judging the attitude of working youth in Leningrad toward work, it was necessary to take into consideration the variety of conditions under which they work. Therefore we began by selecting enterprises representing the most typical branches of Leningrad industry. At these enterprises we chose 2,665 workers, aged 30 and under, by the technique of random selection of district sampling, with consideration of the nature of the work performed.

Next, our goal was to obtain information on the attitude toward work of the working youth in our sample. The means employed to gather material were:

a) a questionnaire directed at the worker. This questionnaire was employed to determine the degree to which the worker was satisfied with his work and with his trade, his understanding of the social significance of labor, and of the motivations determining his choice of skill, and his satisfaction or dissatisfaction with his work;

b) an individual card for the worker, in which the results of his work were recorded with respect to indicators for degree of conscientiousness, discipline, and initiative.

Both documents were essential to obtaining the necessary information, inasmuch as it is impossible to judge attitude toward work without obtaining knowledge of the subjective aspect of the matter. However, the questionnaire made it possible to discover not so much the attitude as such, as the workers' opinion about it. Therefore the use of the card to establish the objective forms of behavior in which attitude toward work is revealed makes it possible to determine with greater accuracy the real situation in the field in which we are interested.

Without pausing to describe all stages in the collecting and processing of the material, let us examine the general picture of the attitude toward work of the young people studied and the interrelations among various elements in this picture. Then let us proceed to clarify the influence and character of work upon change in the attitude toward it. Finally, let us analyze the motives determining satisfaction or dissatisfaction with work, in connection with work activity.

Analysis of the data on the individual cards has made it possible to identify the following five groups of working youth, distinguished by level of consciousness and initiative:

1. The best workers: active in rationalization of work processes, systematically offer suggestions on improvement of the organization of production, overfulfill output standards, do good quality work, and perform the key jobs in their areas—292 persons (11.2 percent of the total number of workers surveyed).

2. Workers who overfulfill or greatly overfulfill their output quotas, do good quality work, perform key jobs, but display only average initiative (do not regularly advance proposals for rationalization)—413 persons (15.9 percent). Together, the first and second groups constitute more than a quarter of all workers surveyed.

3. Workers who fulfill and overfulfill their output quotas but differ from the prior group either by producing work of lower quality or by a somewhat lower level of initiative—829 persons (31.9 percent).

4. Workers who fulfill their output quotas and do work of average quality, but manifest no initiative—956 persons (36.8 percent).

5. Workers who do not meet their output quotas and do work of average quality, or meet their quotas but do work of poor quality—107 (4.1 percent).[1]

This distribution permits certain conclusions to be drawn with respect to those qualities in a worker that place him among the leaders, and also makes it possible to introduce greater precision into the concept of communist attitude toward labor, and to outline a policy for educating people in this direction. Thus, the initiative of the worker, expressed in active participation in rationalization of production, special undertakings on the job, etc., is apparently one of the most significant features of the new attitude toward work. Initiative is a means, characteristic of socialism, for the worker to affirm his individuality. It is associated with the development of a sense of ownership of the socialist enterprise, a feeling inconceivable ur.der capitalism. As a rule, this feeling is usually associated with a sense of responsibility for the work performed.

As a consequence of the fact that the basic purposes of production under socialism and capitalism are opposite, the two systems give rise, through the system of organization of labor, to different types of personalities among working people. The organization of labor at a capitalist enterprise demands of the worker conformity of thought and behavior, loyalty to the entrepreneur. Under capitalism, the advancement of the worker is largely dependent upon these qualities. At the same time, the basic interests of the working class are opposed to these tendencies and guide the mind and activity of the working people along opposite paths. The very position of the worker in the system of capitalist production, as well as the fact that the long-term and short-term interests of proletarians do not coincide, make for a duality in the attitude of the worker of the capitalist enterprise toward his job.

A different situation obtains at a socialist enterprise. Here, evaluation of personnel is based on fundamentally different considerations. The management of an enterprise and public opinion hold in high esteem the worker who speaks out against routine in the technological equipment and organization of labor. It is not accidental that in our country the most honorable appellation is that of innovator. Initiative is rewarded not only by the entire moral atmosphere of socialist production, but by material stimuli. At the same time, the initiative of the employee of the socialist enterprise has nothing in common with individualism under capitalism. It is directed not to opposing the individual to the group but to solving a joint problem of the group as a whole, to the fulfillment and overfulfillment of a production program as the basic task, to the strengthening of attitudes of collectivism in work crews, departments, etc.

Initiative and collectivism are two important traits characteristic of the personality of the new type. To further them is *one of the essential prerequisites* for shaping the all-round man. It is the objectively distinctive features of socialist production that cause these characteristics to take root. At the same time, *their establishment appears to us to be one of the most important components of the program for the cultivation of the Soviet worker in general and the young worker in particular at each industrial enterprise and at every point of production.*

Let us now consider in greater detail the subjective indices of attitude toward work.

Let us begin *with the level of satisfaction with one's particular job* as the most concrete factor in attitude toward work in its subjective aspect. To shed light upon this aspect of the matter, every worker was asked: "Does your present job suit you?" Inasmuch as what interested us in the given instance was not the individual motivation of the attitude toward work, but the mass-scale picture of satisfaction with the job, the persons surveyed were offered a specific choice of answers on a comparative scale of evaluation:

1. Fully satisfied with my job.
2. More satisfied than unsatisfied.
3. It makes no difference what job I have.
4. More unsatisfied than satisfied.
5. Entirely unsatisfied with the job.
6. Can't say.

The answers were cheked with the help of two further questions, which, in the questionnaire, were widely separated from the basic question: 1. Would you wish to switch to another job? 2. Let us assume that, for some reasons, you are not working for the time being. Would you return to your previous job?

Analysis of the answers to all three questions demonstrated the following distribution of young workers in terms of degree of satisfaction with their particular jobs:

1. Entirely satisfied with their jobs: 427 persons (16.0 percent).
2. Satisfied with jobs: 664 persons (24.9 percent).
3. Indefinite opinion: 1,153 persons (43.3 percent).
4. Dissatisfied with jobs: 297 persons (11.1 percent).
5. Entirely dissatisfied with jobs: 124 persons (4.6 percent).

The same means was employed to determine distribution with respect to *satisfaction with one's skill:*

1. Maximally satisfied: 391 persons (14.7 percent).
2. Satisfied: 774 persons (29.0 percent).
3. Indefinite opinion: 1,161 persons (43.6 percent).
4. Not satisfied: 216 persons (8.1 percent).
5. Entirely dissatisfied: 123 persons (4.6 percent).

Finally, *understanding of the social significance* of work was established as follows: the worker was asked to choose one of the following four judgments with respect to the value of his work (we present at the same time the number choosing each value-judgment):

1. That job is good where you do the greatest good, where you are needed: 617 persons (23.2 percent).

2. One cannot ignore earnings, but the most important thing is the meaning of the work, its usefulness to society: 830 persons (31.1 percent).

3. The main thing is your earnings, but it is also necessary to think of the meaning of the work: 819 persons (30.7 percent).

4. Any work is good if it is well paid: 399 persons (15.0 percent).

The elucidation of the connection among these subjective aspects of attitude toward work, on the one hand, and the object results of one's work (among people of approximately the same level of skill) on the other, demonstrates that such a connection is present in all cases and that it becomes stronger as one proceeds from understanding of the social usefulness of work to satisfaction with one's skill and, further, to satisfaction with the job itself.

It must be emphasized that the influence of the worker's state of mind on man-hour output, the connection between certain experiences and emotions stimulated by specific types of work and the results of the work, are all relationships that have also been discovered by psychologists. The Soviet investigator T. N. Pavlov, in an experiment on performance of a metered task, has found that when the subject has a good attitude toward the operation being carried out, 1.5 to 2.6 seconds were needed for an operation, while 2.5 to 3.3 seconds were needed if the attitude was bad.

A good mood and a feeling of satisfaction with the job constitute an important element in an individual's overall morale. Its significance goes far beyond the confines of interests having to do purely with production. It would be excessively utilitarian to see in this only supplemental opportunities for increasing the worker's productivity on the job. Stable satisfaction with one's work, a good mood, optimism—these constitute the general emotional background creating highly favorable conditions for successful efforts at developing the individual in general. On the contrary, a depressed mood induced by particular circumstances of one's activity at work disseminates into the individual's perception of other aspects of life not directly associated with production. A negative emotional background is created. The pessimism created by these factors constitutes a favorable soil for the acquisition of backward and unhealthy views, habits, and value judgments.

Naturally, one's morale and mood are determined by the full totality of one's conditions of life, including the attitude toward the family, the state of consumer services, and so forth. But it would hardly be an exaggeration to say that one of the most important and, perhaps, the primary factor influencing morale is one's activity at work, successes and failures in one's work. Every basis exists for the assertion that our society is capable of governing the emotional set of the individual under conditions of social production, and of eliminating all negative influences upon his morale. Careful and systematic studies in this direction, followed by the introduction of optimal working conditions (in terms of social psychology as it is being discussed here), could play a major role in solving problems of this order. At the same time, all this will help achieve new solutions of a number of problems associated purely with production and with the maximum utilization of opportunities for improvement of man-hour output, including psychological resources.

However, if we are not to fall into subjectivism, it is necessary to clarify the role of objective factors in shaping a communist attitude toward work. This makes it necessary to trace the manner in which the distributions found and presented above change under the influence of these factors. In analyzing our data it is convenient (and appropriate) to operate with generalized distribution indices, which may be obtained by the use of a convention of evaluation of each group in a range from +1 to −1, and calculation of weighted mean estimates in each distribution.[2]

Let us assemble the distributions we have found into a single table (Table 1 on the next page).

Now let us trace the degree of influence of the nature and content of work upon attitudes toward it. To do so we must compare the picture obtained to that of the picture of the attitude toward work in occupational groups associated with diverse levels of technological progress. Six such control groups were chosen, constituting about 50 percent of the sample population.

Group I. Occupations consisting of unskilled manual labor not employing machines or mechanisms and typified by substantial and constant physical effort. In our sample this included loaders, stokers, woodchoppers, knock-out men, ash-men, timbermen, carriers, etc. The workers in this group totalled 146.

Group II. Skilled manual work requiring special knowledge: metalworkers of all types, equipment-adjusters, electricians, and loom-setters in the textile industry. In our sample, workers of these trades totalled 285 persons.

Group III. Mechanized work not subject to an externally dictated pace: lathe-hands, milling-machine, boring-machine, slotting-machine and drill operators, and other machinists (411 persons).

Group IV. Jobs serving a conveyor, at regulated pace: workers in the footwear industry doing machine operations requiring comparatively high skill—women operating sewing machines, milling machines, tighteners, and workers in other specialized operations (307 persons).

Group V. Workers operating automatic equipment from control panels but lacking the skills of set-up men (54 persons).

Group VI. Workers engaged in both controlling and adjusting automatic equipment (46 persons).

Now let us consider Table 2.

Analysis of the table shows that the most pronounced differences between the objective and subjective indices are found in occupational groups at opposite ends of the ladder of technological progress (I and

TABLE 1. DISTRIBUTION OF SAMPLE POPULATION IN TERMS OF OBJECTIVE
AND SUBJECTIVE CRITERIA OF ATTITUDE TOWARD WORK

Criterion of attitude toward labor	Group no. and conventionalized evaluation of group					Index of attitude toward work in sample population
	1	2	3	4	5	
	+1	+0.5	0	−0.5	−1	
Attitude toward work shown by objective indicators	292	413	829	956	107	−0.03
Satisfaction with job	427	664	1,153	297	124	+0.16
Satisfaction with trade	391	774	1,161	216	123	+0.21
Understanding of social significance of work	617	830	....	819	399	+0.08

TABLE 2. INDICES OF ATTITUDE TOWARD LABOR IN CONTROL GROUPS BY OCCUPATION, AS COMPARED TO THOSE OF THE SAMPLE POPULATION

Criteria of attitude toward work	Index of work attitude in sample population	Control groups by occupation					
		I	II	III	IV	V	VI
Attitude toward work in accordance with objective indices	−0.03	−0.17	+0.11	−0.03	+0.08	+0.07	+0.45
Satisfaction with job	+0.16	−0.12	+0.68	+0.18	+0.15	+0.26	+0.22
Satisfaction with trade	+0.21	−0.14	+0.43	+0.24	+0.15	+0.27	+0.35
Understanding of social significance of work	+0.08	−0.31	+0.19	+0.05	+0.15	+0.18	+0.26

V, VI). The subjective indices diverge most sharply in the groups engaging in manual labor (I and II). The heavy unskilled-labor group (I) shows the maximal downward deviation for the entire set of indices.

What is the cause of these differences? It might be guessed that the difference in earnings or the different levels of living of these groups of working youth constitute the reason. However, appropriate comparisons show that workers doing unskilled heavy labor earn more than any of the others (except for those both controlling and adjusting automatic equipment). Consequently, differences in earnings alone are apparently not the reason for differences in attitude toward work. The same picture may be seen in per capita income. Thus we may assume that neither wages nor per capita income are factors independently influencing attitude toward work.

It would be erroneous to interpret the foregoing in the sense that these factors do not influence attitude toward work in general. It may be assumed that each of them (wages in particular) exercise an influence primarily within the confines of the given occupational group, inasmuch as all the other differences, including those in workers' skills and earnings, are determined by differences in the nature, the quantity and the quality of the work. In other words, wages are not the basic, but a secondary, dependent factor. The principal factor exercising a determining influence upon attitude toward labor is the content and nature of work itself. This relationship of the factors under consideration is typical specifically of socialist society and is in accordance with the principle of socialism: distribution by quantity and quality of work.

The relationship established between the content of a job and the attitude toward it calls forth a need for a more concrete approach to the motivations of workers' performance at work. These motivations should be examined not in general, but within the confines of the most typical occupational groups. At the same time, consideration of the problem of motivation of activity at work requires more precise definition of certain initial concepts.

By the motivations for work we mean the individual's own stimulus to work, which is more or less stable and, in varying degrees, conscious. These stimuli might be subdivided into factors of a material and moral order, although both pass through the human consciousness and acquire a certain moral coloration, being subject to moral judgment in the eyes of public opinion.

Material motivations are those stimuli to work which are aimed not directly at the work process as such, but at that which follows from the work process for the given individual in the light of the economic laws of distribution operative under socialism.

Motivations of a moral order also involve the social significance of the work and its content.

In the first place, this is awareness of the social significance of labor (including the role of work in creating the foundation for communism in material products and technology and in the further progress of the common weal) and the associated effort to work for the common good, a sense of duty and responsibility to society.

In the second place, this is a stimulus which is provided by the content of the very work process: the sense of satisfaction from the creative concentration of one's intellectual and physical powers, satisfaction from things well made, etc.

In the third place, this includes stimuli associated with the sense of collectivism and comradeship and of mutual assistance on the job.

Interest in the content of the work and social evaluation of work constitute the basis for such a group of motivations as professional pride, striving for public recognition within the confines of the group and in society as a whole, a desire to master one's skill even better and to acquire a higher rating.

Moral and material motivations function together in any form of work activity. The bases of this interaction lie in the fact that, under socialism, labor fulfills a dual function. It is the means of satisfying the vital needs of man and the means of fulfilling and enriching the personality. Therefore it is incorrect to regard motivations of a material order as something "worse" than moral ones. At the same time, it is by no means material what the relationship between these motivations is, what the trend in their mutually dependent development is, and what changes toward motivations of a moral order are occurring in the existing relationship. It is also important to know to what degree the given relationship depends upon the content of the work, how effective particular motivations for work in various jobs are, etc.

To reveal the picture of the motivations determining satisfaction or dissatisfaction with the job, the questionnaire contained a question about the aspects of his job which were attractive or unattractive for the worker.

Comparison of evaluations of various aspects of job activity such as variety in the work, opportunities for upgrading, organization of the work force and so forth (which we shall refer to, in the future, as "elements of the job situation") by workers satisfied and dissatisfied with their jobs, makes it possible to determine the significance of these aspects for the persons surveyed and thus to obtain a sequence of motivations in accordance with their influence upon satisfaction or dissatisfaction. The evaluation of a particular element of the situation was determined by the formula:

$$V = \frac{(+1)a + (0)b + (-1)c}{n} = \frac{a-c}{n},$$

where a is the number of workers offering a positive evaluation of the given element of the job situation,

b—the number holding a neutral attitude toward it,

c—the number offering a negative evaluation of it, and

n—the total number offering an evaluation.

In Table 3 we present two series of evaluations: V_1 is the evaluation of various aspects of the work by workers satisfied with their jobs, and V_2, evaluation of the same aspects by workers dissatisfied with their jobs. The bottom line presents the difference between the evaluations, which is the indicator of the significance of the evaluated element of the work situation to satisfaction or dissatisfaction with the job.

This table demonstrates primarily that all elements of the job situation have a certain motivational value for satisfaction or dissatisfaction with the job, for in all cases the evaluation of the elements by the dissatisfied workers was lower than that of the satisfied workers. At the same time, the table shows differences both in the degree of influence of the motive (the difference in the evaluation ranges from 0.72 to 0.10) and in the nature of that influence. Certain elements of the job situation (relations with fellow workers on the job, and the significance of the product) are regarded positively by all workers *(coincident positive evaluation)* and consequently are not causes of dissatisfaction with the work. On the contrary, the nature of the evaluation of flow of work *(coincident or nearly coincident negative evaluation)* testifies that, under the existing circumstances, that element of the job situation is not a cause of satisfaction with the work. The fact that the evaluation, on the part of workers satisfied with their jobs, of uniformity of flow of work approached zero indicated that even among them the number of those who reported uniformity in flow was quite insignificantly higher than those who noted non-uniformity. This is a warning of the seriousness of the problem of organization of work rhythm, which can and must become an important means of developing a communist attitude toward work on the part of the entire mass of our youth.

Evaluation of the remaining elements of the job situation demonstrates that satisfaction or dissatisfaction with them corresponds with satisfaction and dissatisfaction with the work as a whole *(divergent evaluation)*. Consequently, this group of motives jointly has a most significant influence upon satisfaction or dissatisfaction with the job. Dissatisfaction with these particular elements of the job situation emerges as a decisive cause of dissatisfaction with the job as a whole, while satisfaction with them is a cause of satisfaction with the work.

TABLE 3. COMPARISON OF EVALUATIONS OF VARIOUS ELEMENTS OF THE JOB SITUATION BY WORKERS SATISFIED AND DISSATISFIED WITH THEIR JOBS

Groups of workers, relative to satisfaction with work \ Evaluated elements of work situation	Variety or monotony of work	Job requires initiative or does not make one think	Offers chance to raise classification, or does not	Does not induce physical fatigue, or is physically hard	Earnings good or poor	Good or poor organization of labor process	Uniform or non-uniform supply of work	Attentive or inattentive attitude on part of management	Good or poor relations with fellow-workers	Significance of product manufactured is or is not meaningful to worker
Satisfied with work, V_1	+0.33	+0.40	+0.25	+0.13	+0.31	+0.16	+0.01	+0.24	+0.70	+0.42
Not satisfied with work, V_2	−0.15	−0.32	−0.33	−0.19	−0.30	−0.22	−0.20	−0.11	+0.60	+0.07
Difference between evaluations ($V_1 - V_2$)	+0.48	+0.72	+0.58	+0.32	+0.61	+0.38	+0.21	+0.35	+0.10	+0.35

If we arrange the motivations analyzed according to their influence upon satisfaction or dissatisfaction with the work, we obtain the following sequence:

1. Content of job (requires initiative or not) $V_1 - V_2 = 0.72$
2. Earnings   "   0.61
3. Chance of upgrading   "   0.58
4. Variety in work   "   0.48
5. Organization of labor process   "   0.38
6. Consideration of workers by management   "   0.35
7. Physical demands of job   "   0.32

Thus, the content of the work comes first in the scale of motives of worker satisfaction.

Most significant for the workers is the inclusion or non-inclusion of mental functions in the labor process. Earnings are second to this motive, although they still occupy a rather high place on the scale. The foregoing indicates change in the content of material incentive of the worker in socialist society. His interests lie not only in the sphere of consumption but in that of production.

Therefore it is natural that differences in occupation have a decisive influence upon the structure of motivations for satisfaction with the work. Analysis of these motives within the occupational control groups (in accordance with the method described above) yielded the following results.

I. *Unskilled Manual Laborers.* As we know from Table 2, this group yields the maximum negative deviation from the mean, despite comparatively high earnings. This is the least stable occupational category and has the largest number dissatisfied with their job and trade. What motivations underlie this attitude?

The most unattractive features both for those satisfied and those dissatisfied with the work lie in the fact that the work is physically difficult and the chances of improving one's classification are very slight. First among these negative features in the given group of workers are various aspects of the content of the work and the conditions of labor (evaluation of physical difficulty of work by satisfied workers was −0.64, and the chances of upgrading were evaluated at −0.18). Change in these two factors and, above all, the elimination of physical fatigue, is most important for the group as a whole in terms of transforming work into a felt necessity of life. Lack of prospects is second in importance. This circumstance is also related to the content of the work, which in the given instance does not require significant knowledge or special training.

With respect to earnings, Group I is the only one in which the number of workers expressing dissatisfaction with their earnings is greater than the number expressing satisfaction with them. Thus, earnings have a powerful stimulating influence upon the group as a whole. It is precisely the level of earnings that keeps workers in this group. Evaluation of all other factors does not show this group to advantage relative to the others.

Here the divergent evaluations point to specific factors in the shaping of a communist attitude toward work, capable of being utilized within the confines of the occupational group under consideration. First among these motivations is the organization of the work process ($V_1 - V_2 = 0.87$), which could be organized in such a way that the worker would be provided, at an even pace, with work having a certain variety.

II. *Skilled Manual Labor Group.* From the viewpoint of subjective satisfaction with both job and skill, and also in understanding of the social significance of the work (Table 2), this group constitutes the diametrical opposite of the former, despite the fact that the workers here are also engaged in manual labor and earn comparatively less.

Analysis of the significance of motives reveals the following features of Group II. To begin with, evaluation of the need for initiative in the work is found to be positive and quite significant not only among those satisfied ($+0.59$) but also among those dissatisfied with their work ($+0.42$). This element in the work situation is a constant within the group. Also very pronounced (although negative) is the evaluation of their earnings by those not satisfied with their jobs (-0.05) as compared to an average estimate by all the dissatisfied of -0.30). The evaluation of the uniformity of work supply and organization of the labor process are close to the mean (see Table 3). The chance of upgrading proves to be the most powerful differentiating element in terms of satisfaction or dissatisfaction with the work ($V_1 - V_2 = 0.86$). Variety in the work and the attitudes of management are second and third in the series of divergent evaluations (0.69 and 0.37, respectively).

III. *Machine-Tool Operators.* The lower indices of attitude toward work in this group, as compared with Group II (see Table 2) are explained by the following circumstances. The work of a machine-tool operator calls for less use of mental functions, and more in the way of automatic motions, than that of the skilled manual worker. Therefore the evaluations of variety in the work and of need for initiative change places between groups II and III. On the other hand, in this case earnings have a considerably greater differentiating influence upon satisfaction or dissatisfaction with the work ($V_1 - V_2 = 0.64$), thanks to more vigorous quota-setting, which results in a somewhat lower wage level. These conditions lead to comparatively lower stability in the group.

IV. *Skilled Machine-Operators Working on Conveyors.* The subjective indicators show this group to resemble most nearly that of unskilled manual workers. However, evaluation of the content of the work is lower here: the work is not found to be attractive because it is monotonous and does not require one to think (evaluation of variety by the satisfied workers is −0.06, that of the content of the work is +0.05). At the same time, conditions of labor receive a higher evaluation. As distinct from groups II and III, it is not the chances of upgrading, but earnings, that constitute the most important basis for differentiation ($V_1 - V_2 = 0.97$).

V. *Control-Panel Operators.* This group is distinguished for the fact that no element of the job situation yields a coincident negative evaluation. No aspect of the work is regarded negatively by the satisfied workers, while a number of highly important characteristics (evenness of work load, physical burden of work), which received differential evaluations in the prior groups, are given positive evaluation by both the satisfied and dissatisfied workers. The divergent evaluations are arranged in the following order by significance: earnings ($V_1 - V_2 = 1.30$), diversity in work (+1.16), management attitudes (+0.86), prospects for upgrading (+0.58), and organization of work process (+0.38).

VI. *Control-Panel Operators with Set-Up Skills.* Evaluations in this group are in many ways similar to those in the preceding one. The monotony of the work receives a uniform coincident negative evaluation. In fact, when an automatic system is properly adjusted and everything is going normally, all that remains for the worker is visual monitoring of his instruments and regulation of the production process by means of the control panel. It would seem that the problems arising here may be resolved by cybernetic replacement of the monitoring functions performed by human beings.

In Group VI the physical difficulty of the work in general ceases to be significant in relation to satisfaction or dissatisfaction with the job. The role of relations with one's fellows on the job also diminishes in these two latter groups in the same manner. This testifies to the important changes occurring in the structure of the personnel unit under conditions of automated production. The worker's relation to the group becomes more complicated and indirect.

The importance of the products manufactured acquires greater motivational significance; this is evidence of a rise in the sense of responsibility felt by the worker toward society as a whole. This is also testified to by the higher level of understanding of the social significance of work in groups V and VI (see Table 2).

Thus, analysis of motivation in occupational groups confirms once again the conclusion drawn with respect to the fact that *the attitude toward work is governed by its content and nature.* The structure of motivations, their significance, and their influence vary in each group.

This analysis permits, further, the conclusion, found in our literature, that the division of motivations into material and moral is quite general and needs to be rendered more concrete so as to make possible a deeper penetration into the essence of the motivation of the labor activity of the worker. Reduction of the problem of material incentive to wages alone appears to be entirely false. The facts demonstrate that the worker is no less interested in improvement in his conditions of labor, the chances of improving his skill, i.e., the development of his individuality at work, and not outside it. Here we encounter a new content of material concern. The Soviet worker is ever more deeply aware of the fact that the prospects for his development lie not in the sphere of consumption but in that of work. This is a new attitude toward work, inconceivable under capitalism. Work activity becomes the principal content of the interests of working people in a socialist society.

To make a further verification of this idea, let us compare the findings with certain studies by American sociologists and psychologists devoted to determining the motivations of American workers in their work.

A survey of 6,000 workers conducted by the National Industrial Conference Board in 1947 showed three major factors to be most important in terms of influence upon the attitude toward the job and the firm:

1) job security (guarantee against unemployment);

2) opportunity for advancement; and

3) earnings (see R. Bellows, *Psychology of Personnel in Business and Industry,* New York, 1961, pp. 134–135).

A survey conducted by K. Wolff shows that men regard as most important: 1) steadiness of employment; 2) chances of advancement; 3) type of work; 4) wages; 5) working conditions. Analogous data were obtained by Jurgensen (see M. Viteles, *Motivation and Morale,* New York, 1953, p. 303). The findings of these surveys show that American workers regard as secondary all aspects of the work pertaining to its content. Comparison of these data with our own speaks for itself.

When the Soviet worker evaluates his job, the very question as to whether it is steady or not does not arise. He is not afraid of not finding employment for his abilities and remaining without means of subsistence. Under these conditions the worker does not hang onto any job, but is in a position to choose his type of occupation in accordance with his interests and inclinations. Motives of a material order naturally still retain their significance but, as already noted, their content changes seriously. The situation is different in the capitalist world. In explaining what the American worker regards as material incentive, the American investigators Strauss and Soiles write: "In our society money is significant not only as a means of satisfying the needs for food, clothing, and housing, but also because it becomes a condition for achievement in life, success and social status. To be successful means to have a high income, and a 'good job' means one that is well paid and offers the chance of advancement, which means to make more money" (see J. Strauss and L. Soiles, *Personnel, the Human Problem of Management,* 1960, p. 28). However, in socialist society money loses its significance as the symbol of wealth and, what is most important, wealth itself is not the basic form of personal achievement.

Let us draw some conclusions.

The establishment of a communist attitude toward labor is most closely associated with the building of the foundation for communism in material goods and technology and with change, on that basis, in the nature and content of activity at work. At the same time, it would be inaccurate to present this process merely as a direct consequence of technical progress in socialist society.

Changes in the content and nature of work activity due to technological progress have a dual influence upon the conversion of work into the felt first necessity of life. Directly, this is a consequence of changes in the conditions of work, which itself becomes interesting for the worker. Indirectly, it occurs through change in the structure of occupational groups and personnel units at work, improvement in the qualifications of each worker, elevation of the level of his education, and expansion of his general horizon. The decisive task in transforming work into a felt first necessity of life consists, after the triumph of the socialist revolution, in eliminating heavy physical work on the basis of all-round mechanization and automation of production. Then the work process will, by its very nature and content, offer a man the opportunity for all-round development. However, in unskilled manual labor expansion of the worker's horizon and improvement of his education do not improve but, rather, impair his attitude toward the given type of work activity, and impel the worker to change jobs. Even an appeal to the social usefulness of the work very often fails to help, because another type of job will be not less but more useful to society, due to its greater productivity. It is no accident that in our study this occupational group proved to be the least stable.

The work we have done confirms the need for a concrete approach to problems of education for communism. It is possible to render this general proposition more precise in two respects. A concrete approach assumes consideration of occupational differences and, above all, of differences between unskilled and skilled labor employing complex equipment inasmuch as, for the reasons demonstrated above, each step in the ladder of technological progress has its unique interaction of factors defining the attitude toward work and a corresponding structure of motives for work activity. Moreover, given a concrete approach, it is necessary to take into consideration the peculiarities of each group of working youth in its attitude toward work. For example, one must not give workers who display initiative and participate actively in the organization of the work process the same assignments as those who barely turn out their quotas. Clearly, it is desirable to set up evaluation of attitude toward work without confining oneself merely to consideration of quota fulfillment.

Our study also permits certain conclusions with respect to the major emphasis desirable in developing the working youth. Clearly, advancement of the worker's initiative would seem to be the answer. For it is precisely initiative that moves a worker forward and carries with it the other significant characteristics of the new attitude toward work—conscientiousness, discipline, and so forth.

Analysis of the motives for satisfaction in one's work helps to determine the means for developing in the young worker (with consideration of the specific qualities of occupational groups) the sense of being owner of the socialist enterprise. At the same time, regardless of occupational differences, the most important stimulus for the elements of working youth we surveyed is found to be the need to put mental functions to work in one's job. One of the important means for shaping a communist attitude toward work proves, further, to be uniformity in the flow of work to the individual.

Comparison of the significance of various motives indicates that the meaning of material incentive changes under the conditions of the building of communism. In considering material interests it is necessary to consider not only earnings but conditions of labor in the broader sense, as well as the nature and content of work activity. Of no small importance (particularly to the young worker) are the prospects for improving skills, depending both upon the nature of the work and upon its organization.

Moral motives are distinctive in that they are considerably less dependent upon the content of the work. The level of awareness of the workers, expressed in their evaluation of their relations with fellow workers and the significance of what they produce, is rather high even among workers dissatisfied with their jobs. This indicates that a merely verbal approach to the development of a communist attitude toward labor is out of the question. The entire complex of problems listed above may be resolved only by carrying out the principal task formulated by the June (1963) Plenum of the Central Committee of the CPSU—strengthening of the connection between ideological and organizational work.

Notes

1. The remaining 68 persons showed contradictory combinations of the criteria we had chosen and are therefore not included in the distribution.

2. In computing the index, the following procedure is employed: groups are arranged in declining order of the characteristic of interest to us (for example, from highest degree of satisfaction with the job to greatest dissatisfaction; see second row in table). Then each group is given a conventional point score: the first is +1, the second +0.5, the third 0, the fourth −0.5, and the fifth −1. Then the mean weighted estimate of the entire distribution is computed in accordance with the formula:

$$J = \frac{(+1)a + (+0.5)b + (0)c + (-0.5)d + (-1)e}{N} = \frac{a + \dfrac{b - d}{2} - e}{N}$$

where a, b, c, d, and e are the numbers of individuals in the first, second, etc., groups, and N is the total sample.

The vitality of the baptismal ceremony under modern Soviet conditions: an empirical study

D. M. APTEKMAN

Translated by William Mandel

During 1963 the Institute of Sociological Research, operating on a volunteer basis, made a study, in the Vyborg Raion of Leningrad, of the causes of the vitality of the ceremony of baptism among various population groups. The data are to a certain degree reflective of the specific nature of the *raion,* which is one of the largest industrial *raions* of Leningrad, and also has the suburbs of Pargolovo and Levashovo under its administration.

The religious ceremonies associated with turning points in the life of the individual (birth of a child, death of near and dear ones and, less frequently, marriage) are still comparatively widespread. We know that religiosity is most actively manifested in everyday life.

In the Orthodox Church, religious rituals play the dominant role. This is stated by churchmen themselves: "Strict observance of the ritual —this is what everyone visiting Russian cathedrals today witnesses" (*Zhurnal Moskovskoi patriarkhii,* 1957, No. 7, p. 23). The clergy seek, by means of the rituals, to create and confirm religious feelings and to influence people's minds.

The choice of the baptismal ritual as the object of study was determined by a number of circumstances.

The "mystery" of baptism is one of the most widespread religious rituals practiced. In previous years, as many as 25 percent of the total

"Causes of the Vitality of the Ceremony of Baptism Under Modern Conditions," from *Soviet Sociology,* IV, No. 2 (1965), pp. 10-16. (The article appeared originally in *Voprosy filosofii,* 1965, No. 3.)

number of children born were baptized, and it was only in 1962-1963 that a downward trend in the number of baptisms was to be observed.

A substantial group of young people (the parents and often, with them, godfather and godmother) participate in this ritual. We cannot omit from consideration the circumstance that the sacrament of baptism has a negative psychological influence upon the child itself. Some of the children subjected to baptism are three and older, and a few are already in school. The very fact of being in church creates a psychological split in the child. What the child sees in church contradicts what he has learned from books and children's radio programs and, in the case of schoolchildren, the knowledge obtained at their lessons.

In this investigation, consideration was given to occupation, party or Komsomol status, education, family status, degree of participation in public life, in competitions for communist labor; attitude toward duties on the job were determined on the basis of evaluations provided by civic organizations. Reasons for the performance of the ceremony were clarified by interviews, usually with each parent separately, with subsequent comparison of the two. If there were discrepancies in explaining the motivations, the members of the family were interviewed again.

All told, 472 persons were studied on the basis of objective data, and 352 of them were interviewed on the reasons for performance of the ceremony. The quantitative difference is largely due to the fact that about 100 parents, chiefly young mothers, quit their jobs after the birth of the child.

Study of the dissemination of this religious ritual among various occupational groups showed that the percentage of baptisms was highest among construction workers (37 percent of the children born in 1963). Dominant in this category of workers are those whose residence in Leningrad is brief, who are of low skill, and are inadequately educated.

Workers in the light industries rank second; here the practice of the religious ceremony is most common among workers of small, poorly mechanized enterprises, former industrial cooperatives recently nationalized.

Performance of the religious ritual is least widespread among skilled workers in heavy and metalworking industry. Improvement in the level of mechanization and automation of the labor processes, change in the character of labor leading to overcoming the significant differences between mental and physical labor, make for a rise in awareness, help in shaping a scientific world view, and consequently in overcoming religious prejudices. There can be no doubt about the influence exercised by a large collective, which systematically develops a sense of organization, a feeling of responsibility for the common cause, stimulating a rise in education and level of culture. Also of certain significance is the fact that workers in this category are by a considerable majority native-born Leningraders, in whose lives atheist traditions are strong.

The religious ceremonies are least common among non-manual personnel. Only 1 percent of children born into families of medical personnel were christened, and the parents of children christened did not include a single physician. Among non-manual personnel, a higher percentage of baptisms is found among engineers and technicians (7 percent); here, too, the majority of parents baptizing their children have had secondary technical, and not higher, education.

The results of the investigation revealed a direct correlation between the influence of religious ritual and level of education. The total number of parents who baptized their children divided as follows in terms of education: higher, 0.6 percent; incomplete higher, 1.7 percent; specialized secondary, 9 percent; general secondary, 14 percent; seven-year school, 51.4 percent, and four-year school, 23.3 percent. Thus, nearly three-fourths of the persons covered by the survey had had seven years of schooling or less. From this, one may draw with confidence the conclusion that the teaching of atheism to children in the seven-year schools is unsatisfactory. The curriculums and textbooks used in these schools usually do not take the needs for cultivation of atheism into consideration, and are hardly capable of aiding significantly in shaping firm materialist convictions. Whereas the introduction of the course in social studies has resulted in systematic cultivation of atheism in the higher grades, in the seven-year school the pupils are given a limited number of unconnected facts that chiefly describe the reactionary role of the church in times gone by.

It is necessary immediately to intensify the atheist emphasis in instruction in the seven-year school [now eight years, but seven when these parents attended—TRANS.], particularly in the courses in natural science, and the appropriate changes have to be made in course outlines and textbooks.

It is also essential immediately to raise the level of general education of those young people already employed in the economy, while special attention has to be given to the problem of developing a scientific materialist world view among these young people.

Individuals detached from the social interests of the group are most often apt to be influenced by vestiges of religion. Civic organizations usually comment on such persons as follows: "Satisfactory worker. No gross violations of labor discipline. Doesn't participate in civic affairs." Only 11 percent of the parents who baptize their children take systematic part in civic activity. Less than a quarter of those surveyed participate in the competition for communist labor (as part of brigades, teams, and departments); those who have taken on individual obligations in this respect are few and far between.

In the course of the survey, serious shortcomings were found in the organization of character-building work in certain work groups. Civic organizations often pay attention only to advanced workers and "black sheep." When this is the case, a substantial portion of the personnel is disregarded, although it is precisely among such "unnoticed ones" that the level of religiosity is usually higher.

The party, Komsomol, and trade-union organizations in a number of enterprises have a poor knowledge of the family composition of their workers and white-collar staffs, and take no interest in their lives off the job. This is why it was a complete surprise to some leaders when a leading worker—in individual cases even an active Komsomol member or shock-worker of communist labor—would be found to be strongly influenced by religious people.

Identification of the reasons and motivations for performance of the sacrament was a most important goal of the study.

It must be admitted that the survey technique was not such as to permit the investigation entirely to rule out elements of subjectivism in the responses of the persons queried, but it did, in practice, reduce error to a minimum (by the device of dual interviews). In our opinion, possible deviations from the truth are so insignificant as not to change the basic percentages (in control surveys, variations in motives stated were within 5 percent). The statements of the persons surveyed are highly instructive and interesting both for students of social psychology and for propagandists of atheism.

The chief conclusion that may be drawn from the data obtained is that the reason for baptizing children in the majority of cases is not religiosity on the part of the parents, but their indifference, their conciliatory attitude toward religion, combined with the influence of incidental factors.

Only 8 percent of the number queried stated that they were religious and baptized their children as an expression of their convictions. Watchman N., born in 1923, with six years of schooling, said in her interview: "I believe in God and keep an ikon. That's why I baptized." "We're all religious, baptizing is not forbidden, and so we baptize," was the explanation given by K., a working woman in a clothing and knitwear factory.

The majority of the people in this group are over 35. A considerable proportion of them are unmarried mothers.

It should be noted that even the individuals who regard themselves as religious lack, to a considerable degree, self-conscious, firm religious convictions. Their relationship to religion is confined chiefly to intermittent churchgoing on religious holidays and to the performance of religious rituals. The religiosity of many of the convinced believers is the result of unfortunate developments in personal life: experiences of an intimate character, moral difficulties associated with personal misfortunes, and the influence of religious persons in their environment. For example, K. (born in 1941, has incomplete secondary education) stated in the interview: "I don't usually go to church, but I arranged the baptism myself, because my baby has no father and people I know said that not to baptize is a sin."

About one-third of the parents whose children were baptized had performed this sacrament at the demand of relatives. Religious elderly people bring much pressure to bear upon young parents, and speculate to a considerable degree upon the difficulties in everyday life that still exist. For one thing, they take advantage of the difficulties many parents encounter in seeking to place their children in day-nurseries. Despite the enormous scale of construction of housing and cultural and service facilities, the number of preschool institutions for children is not yet capable of fully satisfying the needs of the working population, particularly in areas of large-scale housing construction. This makes possible situations in which grandmothers present a peculiar sort of "ultimatum" to parents. Often, these "ultimatums," plus the fact that the parents themselves do not maintain their principles on philosophical matters, transform a demand made by relatives into a deciding argument. S., a worker in the "Svetlana" Plant, born in 1941, a secondary-school graduate, said in her interview: "My husband and I knew of the baptism and agreed to it, because we were in no position to say anything in opposition to my mother. Mama said: if you don't baptize her, I won't take care of her. We don't yell at her for this, because nothing happened to the baby as a result of its being baptized, while mama looks after her, and we both work." A typical explanation of the reason for performing the ceremony is that given by D., a technician of a design office and member of the Komsomol, who said: "Great-grandma presented an ultimatum: if you don't baptize your son, I won't baby-sit with him. At first I wouldn't agree but then I did. Grandma and great-grandma are religious; they believe not only in God but in the devil. My son took sick, and grandma paid three rubles to another lady in the apartment to do magic."

In the course of the survey, a number of factors were revealed testifying to the particular activity manifested by religious people who, speculating on the personal sufferings of people, persuade them that they have to perform a religious sacrament. The Sh. family is an example. Some time ago their seven-year-old daughter died tragically. When a son was born to the family in 1963, religious people close to the family insisted to the young mother that her first child had died because she was not baptized. Having suffered deeply as a consequence of their loss, Sh. and his wife yielded to the influence of the religious.

Religious relatives are particularly persistent in demanding baptism in families where children are ill for a long period. Thus, B., born in 1923, who has had seven-year schooling, explained the baptism by the fact that "the infant is always sick. Grandma wrote from the village, and so did my sister in Leningrad; they said I ought to baptize him, saying maybe he is sick because he isn't baptized." As a rule, parents lacking a firm materialist world view, and hoping that "maybe it'll help," go through with baptism, without realizing that they are thus doing even greater damage to the child.

More than 36 percent of parents who baptized their children gave motives that indicated an indifferent attitude toward religion. Here again the strength of conservative tradition makes itself felt. N., born in 1930, who has only a four-year-school education, said he baptized his child "by tradition." An assembler at the "Svetlana" Plant, G., said: "We're all baptized; everybody does it." T., a Komsomol member, and an assembler at the OKB, explained the baptizing of her child by the fact that this is a "deep-rooted custom, and there's nothing bad in it."

Many parents have baptism performed without any purpose whatever, "just in case," having fallen under the influence not only of relatives but of strangers. Not being convinced atheists, they are sometimes willing to behave in accordance with the advice of acquaintances, neighbors in the apartment, etc. A design technician at the "Russkii dizel" Plant, M., born in 1934, who had a seven-year schooling, had her son baptized on the advice of a friend who had her own daughter baptized at the same time. D., born in 1930, a worker at the "Svetlana" Plant, with a seven-year schooling, said: "It makes no difference, baptized or not baptized," but immediately added: "But if the child is baptized, you feel more comfortable." A machinist at the same plant, I., born in 1935, with seven years of education, holds that "it does no harm to me or to anybody else, although this ceremony doesn't produce anything." The same view is held by milling-machine operator I., born in 1939, with seven years of education, and by a brazer at the Svetlana Works, V., born in 1928, with five years of schooling, as well as by others.

In a number of cases, the performance of religious ceremonies is associated with peculiarities in the mode of life of the individuals concerned, making for retention of vestiges of the past.

Survivals of private-property psychology, petty-bourgeois individualism, nationalism, xenophobia, and shortsightedness exercise significant influence in preserving religious ritual. In the suburbs of Pargolovo, Levashovo, and Kolomiagi, where most people own their own homes, the percentage of baptisms in church is over three times as high as the average for the *raion*.

Survivals of individualistic psychology are expressed above all in the absence of high ideals in life and self-isolation in the narrow circle of personal interests. An individual incapable of rising to an understanding of social problems and infected by the bacilli of the psychology of the complacent looks at life from the subjectivist standpoint of his own ego. A convincing illustration of this is the evaluation of carpenter N.: "On the job he is an average worker. Is fond of money, and approaches everything in terms of personal gain. Withdrawn, and always dissatisfied with everything and everybody."

People under the influence of individualist moods do not consider religious prejudices from a social point of view even if they themselves are not religious. This is the judgment one can make of the views of truck-driver M., woman bricklayer R., railway maintenance-of-way man P., and others. Technician M., born in 1936, with a secondary-school education, a Komsomol member, stated that he ascribed no serious significance to the religious ritual. The same answer was given by welder N., born in 1938, who has a fifth-grade education, and was recently expelled from the Komsomol for gross violations of labor and Komsomol discipline.

It is not uncommon to find the performance of the religious ceremony to be associated in the minds of certain Soviet citizens with their nationality. A mechanic in a radio repair shop, R., born in 1928, with a secondary-school education, and inspector Z., born in 1925, with fifth-grade education, hold that baptism "is not a religious but an old Russian custom." Such views are particularly typical of persons of Jewish and Tatar nationality, in whose families the performance of a religious ritual associated with the birth of a child is quite widespread.

As already noted, the emotional element, which is played upon particularly by churchmen, plays a major role in the retention of this sacrament. The clergy, with centuries of experience, have developed a ceremonial "technique" that has a direct influence upon the feelings of individuals who are not even religious in the full meaning of that word. Here, aesthetic influences emerge as one of the means of winning the individual to religious concepts. "There can be no doubt," said Gorky, "that there are many who turn back to religion for aesthetic reasons, because there is fine singing in church" (M. Gorky, *On Religion* [O religii], Moscow, 1941, p. 186). The survey showed that 10.3 percent of those who baptize do so specifically because of the emotional impact of that ceremony.

The development of new solemn rituals based upon the best folk traditions and customs, and permeated with elements of the new, socialist culture, will be of the greatest importance in overcoming the emotional influence of the religious ceremony.

This is evidenced by the fact that, with the introduction of a cere-monial registration of birth in Leningrad in the fourth quarter of 1963, the number of baptisms in church diminished sharply.

It should be borne in mind that the development of new rituals helps not only to overcome religious psychology but to affirm the communist world view. "A given world view," N. K. Krupskaia wrote in this regard, "only becomes part of one's flesh and blood when it becomes associated with emotional experiences. Only then is it firmly established" (N. K. Krupskaia, *Anti-Religious Propaganda* [Antireligioznaia propaganda], a collection of articles, Moscow, GIZ, 1929, p. 45).

Analysis of the reasons for the performance of religious ceremonies in the *raion* made it possible for the Ideological Commission of the Raion Committee of the CPSU to develop a number of concrete recommenda-tions. A set of measures was outlined to promote improvement of the work of developing a scientific materialist world view, development of atheist persuasions, and irreconcilability to survivals of the past, and to make possible a broader involvement of the entire working population in the life of society.

"Days of Atheism" are conducted regularly in the *raion*. Members of the faculties of higher educational institutions, scientific personnel of the Central Geophysical Observatory, and of the Institute of Evolutionary Physiology deliver lectures at the enterprises on topics in the realm of atheism and natural science. Evenings built around special topics and the showing of movies on atheism are conducted at all houses of culture and clubs. The libraries of the Vyborg Palace of Culture and the Pargolovo and Udel'nensk libraries do much to publicize books of an atheist nature.

The Raion Committee of the CPSU, and the party organizations, are giving considerable attention to training propagandists of atheism. Circles and seminars on scientific atheism, attended by worker agitators, are held successfully at the largest enterprises. For the past five years, the Raion Committee of the CPSU has operated a school of propagandists and organizers of atheist activity.

Councils on atheism, which include representatives of party, Kom-somol, and trade-union organizations, have been established under the party committees. Recently, these councils have done much to explain the harmfulness of religious ritual and to drive it out of the lives of men. It is planned to intensify this work. It has been proposed to civic organizations that they interest themselves more deeply in the lives of the working people, giving special attention to families in which children are expected, and assisting in placing children in preschool institutions. The Ideological Commission has demanded of medical personnel at children's clinics that they intensify their work of explaining to mothers the harm of the religious ceremony of baptism to the health of the child.*

We know how irreconcilable Lenin was to those who strove to combine membership in the Communist party with a disinterested attitude toward religion. In a note to the Organization Bureau of the Central Committee with respect to Em. Iaroslavskii's letter, "A Tribute Paid to Prejudice" [*Dan' predrassudkam*], Lenin said: "I am in favor of expelling from the party individuals who participate in rituals" (*Leninskii sbornik* XXIV, p. 290).

However, until recently, individual Communists and Komsomol members continue to show a conciliatory attitude toward cases of performance of religious rituals in their families, thus yielding their own convictions, ideals, and philosophical principles. Only thus may we explain the fact that 2.5 percent of the families in which baptisms occurred were those of members and candidates for membership in the Party, and 12 percent are families of Komsomol members. A Communist and a Komsomol member have no right to maintain any connection with religion. Moreover, they are required to engage in active propaganda of the scientific world view among the people with whom they have constant contact in home life, and not to permit deviations from their principles of party loyalty with respect to world view.

Study of the reasons for the survival of the ceremony of church baptism has shown that clergy still commit the illegal act of "receiving" the children of non-religious parents to the Christian religion without the parents' agreement. The ceremony is performed in secret, at the request of religious grandmothers or other relatives, when the parents of the infant are at work. In such instances, violence is done to the freedom of conscience of people who are atheists. Recently the number of such occurrences has diminished. However, due to the imperfection of forms for monitoring the observance of Soviet legislation on religions and to the limited participation of the public in this work, such instances have not been done away with entirely.

The work done by party and civic organizations has already yielded

---

* Aptekman is presumably referring to the fact that in the Orthodox Church, baptism is by total immersion in the baptismal font.—EDITOR, *Soviet Sociology*.

its first results. In 1964 the number of religious baptisms diminished by more than 35 percent from the 1963 figure.

Our society contains all the objective prerequisites for completely overcoming the influence of religious ceremonies. What is most important now is systematic, purposeful work on the part of the party and civic organizations in the atheist education of every Soviet person.

Index